Adobe® Photoshop® for Fashion Design

Susan M. Lazear

San Diego Mesa College

Prentice Hall
Upper Saddle River, New Jersey
Columbus, Ohio

Library of Congress Cataloging-in-Publication Data

Lazear, Susan.
   Adobe Photoshop for fashion design / Susan Lazear.
     p. cm.
   Includes bibliographical references and index.
   ISBN 978-0-13-119193-8 (alk. paper)
  1. Fashion design—Computer aided design. 2. Fashion drawing—Computer aided design. 3. Adobe Photoshop. I. Title.
   TT518.L393 2008
   746.9'20285—dc22

2008048423

Editor in Chief: Vernon Anthony
Acquisitions Editor: Jill Jones-Renger
Editorial Assistant: Doug Greive
Production Coordination: DeAnn Montoya, S4Carlisle Publishing Services
Project Manager: Kris Roach
Operations Specialist: Deidra Schwartz
Creative Director: Jayne Conte
Art Director Cover: Bruce Kenselaar
Cover Designer: Osbaldo Ahumada
Director of Marketing: David Gesell
Marketing Manager: Leigh Ann Sims
Marketing Coordinator: Alicia Wozniak
Copyeditor: Bret Workman

Pearson Education Ltd., London
Pearson Education Singapore Pte. Ltd.
Pearson Education Canada, Inc.
Pearson Education—Japan

Pearson Education Australia Pty. Limited
Pearson Education North Asia Ltd., Hong Kong
Pearson Educación de Mexico, S.A. de C.V.
Pearson Education Malaysia Pte. Ltd.

Prentice Hall
is an imprint of

www.pearsonhighered.com

10 9 8 7 6 5 4 3 2 1
ISBN-13: 978-0-13-119193-8
ISBN-10:   0-13-119193-4

Preface

This book is my second contribution to educating people interested in combining technology with fashion. As with my book *Adobe Illustrator for Fashion Design,* this endeavor has been a labor of love. It is the culmination of many years of teaching design techniques to fashion students at the college level. I have worked with computers since the mid-1980s, and thus have witnessed the growth and development of art tools in software over time. I came into computer design early on, and at that time I naïvely thought that a computer could do the designing for me. I didn't "draw" well, and I just believed that a computer somehow could do that for me…like magic! I was successful, however, at learning how to design, and I taught myself how to manipulate basic paint programs to perform my task. Then one day, I realized it was indeed I who was pushing the mouse and making the design decisions: I, and not the computer, was doing the designing. So, for those of you embarking on this path with apprehension, fear not: The computer will make your life easier. It will help you tear down your barriers and eliminate your fear of drawing.

My career path has been a varied one. I have taught at the college level since 1980. A move to San Francisco led me to employment in the fashion industry where I worked for Zoo-Ink, a textile printing company, and then for American Design Intelligence Group, a fashion computer graphics service bureau that blazed the trail to merchandising apparel using computer graphics. My freelance work led me to knitwear design work with Esprit, Levi Strauss, and other San Francisco-based companies. While doing this work I developed a link between a knitting machine and a personal computer. With this discovery Cochenille Design Studio (www.cochenille.com) was born, a business that develops software for the textile arts. It was through Cochenille that all my skills came together: I could teach, write, create, and develop tools for others to use. My business and skills allowed me to travel the world extensively and to share my love and passion for computer design. My enjoyment of teaching pulled me back to education, and in the year 2000, I began to teach full-time at Mesa College in San Diego. I feel that my role as an educator is manifold. Not only do I teach students how to use tools such as Adobe Photoshop and Illustrator to design, I also teach them how to think, and how to see as a designer sees. My students inspire me, and I hope that I do the same for them.

I trust you will benefit from the materials presented in this book. I have made every effort to make the instructions clear and easy-to-follow. Samples of my students' work are given to inspire you. Many students come into class with absolutely no drawing skills and with great fear of what lies ahead. By the end of the semester, however, they have gained the knowledge and confidence to proceed forward on their own. I wish the same results for everyone. We should not be afraid of technology: we should embrace it and let it make our lives simpler.

Susan Lazear

Acknowledgements

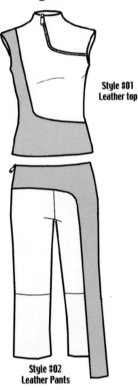

Cherry Blossom

Style #01
Leather top

Style #02
Leather Pants

Mia Omatsuzawa

Photoshop is such a great tool! I have enjoyed the process of getting to know the software over the past fifteen years or so and watching it evolve into the major force it is. My path in developing the exercises in this book has been a pleasant one. As I sorted through the thousands of images created by my students over the past several years, I was amazed at what one can do in the digital realm. You think I would know this, but reviewing the students' artwork brings it all into perspective.

I have traveled a wonderful path in the development, conceptual planning, and writing of this book, and many people have aided me along the way. Thank you to my students and the Fashion Program at Mesa College. A special thanks goes to the Honors program on campus, as it is through this program that I have been able to test new ideas in fashion design and bring technology into our curriculum in a major way. Currently, we are developing and submitting paperwork to offer a new degree at our college: Computer Fashion Technology. It will be a proud day when the first students are awarded this degree, as I have played a major role in the development and testing of various courses related to fashion technology.

Thank you to Sonia Barton, who attends to the day-to-day operation of my business, Cochenille Design Studio. Her abilities and support for the cause allow me to embark on projects as major as this book. Thank you to all my technical readers and testers around the world, who meticulously scoured through my chapters and provided additional insight on how information is received and processed. Special thanks to Leah Taggert, a new Australian friend and my best technical reader, who found ways to simplify the written word.

Thank you also to Adobe, for giving us Photoshop, and to the staff at Pearson, who waited patiently for me to finish this second writing project, which, just like the Illustrator book, grew threefold.

I want to acknowledge and thank my family. My parents gave me encouragement to seek knowledge. My sons, Blake and Danny, put up with their mother as she hunkered down in front of a computer to conquer new software, and forgave me for being a geekette, often to their embarassment when they were little. Last of all, thanks to my network of colleagues and friends. Your patience with my absence from social events has been appreciated over the past few years. I am now ready to play.

Hippie Chick
Cotton Capri Pants
Style # : S-05

Beach Baby
Knit & Mesh Shirts
Style # : S-03

TROPICAL
BEACH

Rie Sawada

Adobe Creative Suite CS4

As this book was ready to go to press, Adobe was about to release Photoshop CS4. Although it was too late to present the new features of CS4 throughout the entire book, the following discussion should provide an overview of what has changed in this version of the software.

The CS4 User Interface

Photoshop's interface has changed slightly, as shown below.

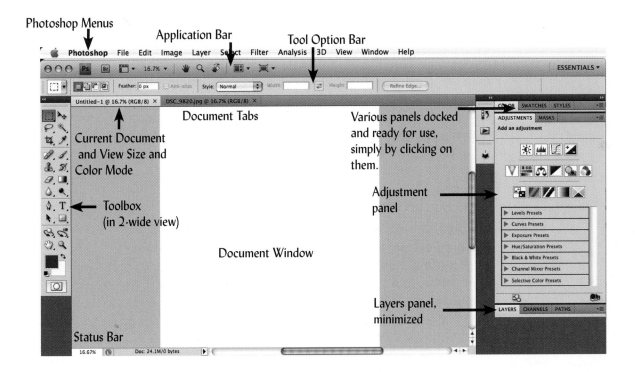

Application Bar

You will see a new row of tools at the top of the screen. This is called the **Application Bar**. Through this bar, you have quick, one-click access to commonly used functions such as *Zoom* levels, *Panning*, *Viewing Extras* (grids, rulers, guides), *Rotating the Canvas* (which will be loved by tablet users), and *Arrange* documents. In addition you can launch *Adobe's Bridge* with a simple click of the mouse. The Workspace pop-up has been moved to this bar.

The Application Bar

Document Tabs

If you open multiple documents, you can now see all their titles at the top of the current document, displayed as tabs. Using the new features in the *Application Bar* or the *Window>Arrange* menu, you can choose to consolidate all your documents to tabs, or to float the documents, as in the past.

Three documents are open, and tabs are used to display the current and open files.

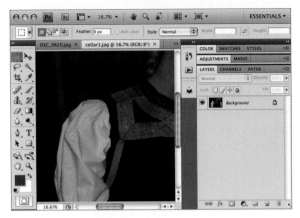

The Application Frame groups all parts of Photoshop into one movable and resizable window.

Application Frame

Adobe has added the ability to turn on an *Application Frame* (**Window** menu). This allows all panels (palettes), documents, the Toolbox, and so on, to become a single, resizable window. What a great feature! It allows you to manage window clutter and clean up your working environment if you want to work wtih other programs simultaneously. As you downsize the application frame, panels begin to compress into a minimized state, as necessary.

New Panels

Adobe now uses the term **panels** to refer to what used to be called *palettes*. Illustrator, Acrobat, and InDesign all use this term, and now Photoshop has followed suit. This book will use the term *palettes*, as it was written before CS4 was released, and thus the term palette was relevant. Long-time users of Photoshop will understand, and new users of CS4 will simply need of translate the term in their mind.

Adjustments Panel

The *Adjustments* panel is a great new addition that should save users a tremendous amount of time. It eliminates steps in choosing adjustment commands, and then working through the dialog to select your options. Now, you can simply go to the panel and, with minimal effort, click, choose, and create your nondestructive adjustment. You will see that Adobe has provided you with new modifiable *presets*. Clicking on the arrowhead will open and display your preset options for a specific adjustment.

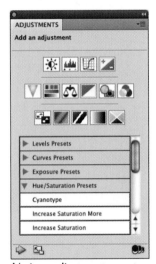

Various adjustment presets can be seen in the lower portion of the panel.

Panels, as they appear on the right side of the Workspace

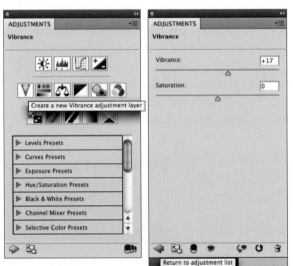

The process of using the Vibrance adjustment

A new adjustment, *Vibrance,* has been added. Using this as the example, simply click on the icon for the adjustment, and the panel changes to open the adjustment sliders. Make your changes, observing the image, and then click on the arrow in the lower-left corner of the panel to complete the adjustment.

You now have "on-image" adjustments for *Curves*, *Black & White*, and *Hue/Saturation* adjustment layers. This means that you can apply your adjustment to a specific tonal range.

Masks Panel

The new *Masks* panel facilitates the process of creating and editing pixel and vector masks. Once you have begun the process of creating a mask (e.g., creating a selection or drawing with a vector tool), you can activate the mask directly from the *Masks* panel and then use the functions the panel provides. Apply effects such as feathering and control the density (opacity) of the mask, so that you can see through it to the layer below. The *Refine Mask* options let you adjust the edges, work with a color range, and invert your mask easily. Buttons across the bottom of the panel allow you to apply, or enable/disable the mask. You may also load the mask as a selection.

The new Masks panel facilitates the creating and editing of masks.

Tools Panel

CS4 has restructured the Toolbox (Tools palette) slightly and it is now called a *Tools panel*. The **Crop** and **Slice** tools are now stacked in one slot and the **Measuring** tools have moved to the upper area. In Photoshop Extended, there are two new tool sets: **3D Rotate** and **3D Orbit**.

Photoshop CS4's Tools panel in single- and double-width mode

Photoshop Menus

The following changes have been made to Photoshop's menus:

File Menu

A new menu command called *Share My Screen* allows you to share your screen with others in *Adobe's ConnectNow* community. All you need is an Adobe ID, which is free.

Edit Menu

The new *Content-Aware Scale* menu command allows you to resize an image and retain important visual content. Whereas normal scaling resizes each pixel equally, *Content-Aware Scale* assesses the importance of the content in the image and affects primarily pixels that it judges not to have important visual content.

Note that *Content-Aware Scale* works on layers and selections, but not on backgrounds, layer masks, adjustment layers, and other adjusted art.Experiment!

Original Art prior to scaling operations

Regular Scaling   Content-Aware Scaling

Image Menu

- o The *Rotate Canvas* command is now called *Image Rotation*.
- o CS3's *Pixel Aspect Ratio* **Image** menu command was removed and placed in the **View** menu of CS4.
- o *Auto Levels*, *Auto Contrast*, and *Auto Color* were moved to the main **Image** menu in CS4 (as opposed to the *Adjustment* submenu) and *Auto Levels* is now called *Auto Tones*.
- o *Vibrance* is a new image adjustment (taken from RAW).
- o The *Adjustments* submenu commands have been rearranged.

Layers Menu

The *Change Layer Content* and *3D Layers* commands are no longer in the **Layers** menu. These have been moved, or incorporated into other functions in the new **3D** menu command.

Select Menu

CS4 adds *Edit in Quick Mask Mode* as a menu command (in addition to the button in the Toolbox).

Filters Menu

The *Patternmaker* filter has been removed, which is unfortunate, as it was a fun tool to use in quick pattern development (see Textile Design Exercise #3). CS4 adds a *Browse Filters Online…* command so that you can search for additional Plug-In filters.

View Menu

Pixel Aspect Ratio has been placed in this menu in CS4 (as opposed to the **Image** menu of CS3 and earlier versions).

Window Menu

There are several new commands in the **Window** menu that allow you to open new panels or go online. *The Extensions* command allows you to go online and explore **Kuler**, an Adobe online community, for colors and inspirations. You may also connect to Adobe using the *Connections* command.

New panels accessed through the Window menu include:
- o 3D
- o Masks
- o Notes
- o Application Frame
- o Application Bar

3D Painting and Compositing

These are various functions relating to painting and compositing 3D models. You no longer need to navigate the typical dialog boxes and special layer content. This book does not cover 3D.

Other new functions exist in CS4, but they will not be covered in this section.

Photoshop CS4's Window menu commands

Table of Contents

Illustration by Osbaldo Ahumada

Illustration by Nania Pongpitakkul

Illustration by Melisa
Farnsworth

Chapter 2: Focus on Selections and Layers   pages 25–60

Composite and rendered
fabric by Jodi Smart, Interior
Design student

Self Portraits à la Warhol

Julie Velasquez

Karol Topete

Jeanne Reith

Chapter 5: Menus   pages 117–154

Ksenia
Galyga

Peggy Liu

Coloring an Original
Hand-drawn Sketch
by Keith Antonio

ORIGINAL

MOTIFS

Motif Development by
Theresa Mays

Fashion illustration by
Banu Tavlasoglu

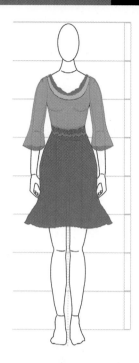

Flats drawn on croquis by
Jeanne Reith

Trend Colors by Mariel
Diaz-Mendoza

Knit Illustration and Flats
Kristine Delosreyes

Back

Front

Textile Design Exercises pages 355–440

Motif development
for textile design Julie
Velasquez

Composite, illustration, flats and
color prediction for knitwear,
Fall/Winter 08–09
Denise Schutte

Student Gallery

Various Work
Mesa Fashion Students

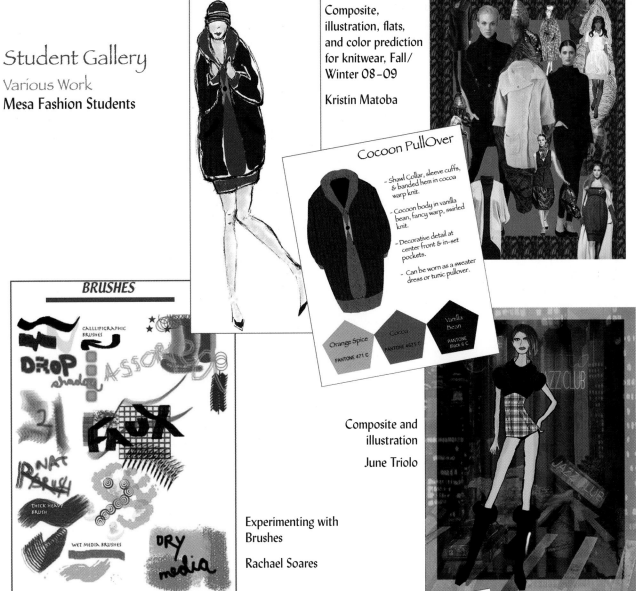

Composite,
illustration, flats,
and color prediction
for knitwear, Fall/
Winter 08–09

Kristin Matoba

Cocoon PullOver

- Shawl Collar, sleeve cuffs, & banded hem in cocoa warp knit.

- Cocoon body in vanilla bean, fancy warp, swirled knit.

- Decorative detail at center front & in-set pockets.

- Can be worn as a sweater dress or tunic pullover.

Orange Spice
PANTONE 471 C

Cocoa
PANTONE 4625 C

Vanilla Bean
PANTONE Black 6 C

BRUSHES

CALLLIFIGRAPHIC BRUSHES

DROP shadow

ASSORTED

FAUX

NAT BRUSH

THICK HEAVY BRUSH

WET MEDIA BRUSHES

DRY media

Experimenting with
Brushes

Rachael Soares

Composite and
illustration

June Triolo

EGYPTIAN CHEST
PAINTED WOOD WITH
IVORY & BONE INLAY
1400-1300 B.C.

ANCIENT
EGYPTIAN
CHAIR
PAINTED WOOD
1400-1300 B.C.

KING TUT'S
GOLDEN THRONE
(REPLICA)
PAINTED WOOD WITH GOLD LEAFING
INLAY OF STONE, BONE & IVORY

Egyptian Composite, and
textile renderings in furniture

Susan Fefferman

Introduction

Welcome to the design world of Photoshop! Together we will travel on a creative digital journey and explore the abilities of one of the most powerful software programs in the world, Adobe Photoshop. Through a series of exercises you will explore the basics of designing fashion and related drawings.

Painterly Effects with Photoshop by Genevieve Aguilar

Intended Audience

This book is written to assist Adobe Photoshop users, both new and old, in developing skills relevant to designing fashion apparel and textiles. You will use many of the tools and functions in the same manner that you use them for other types of artwork. At the same time, however, you will learn how to "think" and prepare drawings of clothing, fashion poses, textile prints, and more. Instructions are written with the assumption that you know very little about Photoshop. Experienced users should be able to skim sections at times; but it is recommended that you do read all that is written, in case you can pick up a new trick.

Layout of the Book

The early chapters of this book provide you with an overview of Photoshop. Chapter 1 introduces you to the Photoshop environment and basic operations of maneuvering through the program. Chapter 2 introduces Photoshop's two primary functions: selections and layers. Chapter 3 allows you to get your feet wet with a fun self-portrait lesson. Chapters 4 through 6 take you on a tour of Photoshop, as you explore the Toolbox, menus, and palettes.

Illustration with Photoshop by Kristin Matoba

Once you have built a foundation with Photoshop, you can move on to the *Basic Exercises* section of the book. Each exercise is designed to teach you something about a basic skill that is commonly used in Photoshop design or will be utilized more fully in a fashion sense in the next section of the book. The exercises will teach you about working with selections, improving scanned images, plus some basics on Filters. The *Fashion Exercises* section of this book has specific exercises that teach you how to utilize the tools and skills you are building with Photoshop to draw flats, fashion poses, and other fashion-related techniques. The exercises in textile design and presentation techniques at the end of the book will further enhance your abilities with the program.

Sample Note
Notes will be presented in the sidebar to reinforce a point or to make a comment.

Files on the DVD

The DVD that accompanies this book includes files utilized in the exercises as well as additional files for your viewing. These are organized in folders with labels indicating their content or correlation to specific chapters in this book. Portfolios of student work are also included.

Tips
Check the sidebar for tips, which typically are designed to save you time in working in Photoshop.

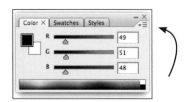

The palette menu is accessed through the arrowhead that appears in the upper-right corner of the palette.

Artwork Used in the Book

The artwork used throughout this book and on the DVD was created either by me or by my students in the Fashion Program at San Diego Mesa College. I have taught at Mesa since 1989 and oversee all the computer fashion classes.

Version of Photoshop?

Software versions can roll out quickly, which makes programs and texts outdated before they've barely been used. The information presented in this book attempts to discuss Photoshop in a manner that is generic to multiple versions of the software. Instructions are specific to the Creative Suite versions of Photoshop (CS1 through CS4), but owners of earlier versions will be able to utilize the vast majority of the techniques discussed. As this book was about to go to press, CS4 was about to be released. Please see pages v–viii in the Preface to learn what is new in CS4.

How to Approach Your Studies with This Book

To get the most out of this book, you should be comfortable with your Macintosh or Windows computer. Be familiar with mouse and menu operations as well as loading/saving files and working with dialog boxes/ windows. If you are a new user, you may want to take the time to practice these basic operations. Refer to your operating system's manual or Help files for assistance.

This text is written in a format that, once understood, will make your learning easier. The main text of the manual appears in this column of each page. Additional comments, tips, notes, and illustrations will generally appear in the margins.

Working with Menu Operations

Various types of menus exist in Photoshop. The most common menus are found in the Menu Bar at the top of the screen. In addition to these menus, you have palette menus and context menus.

Menu Bar Menu Commands

Text in bold italic type refers to a Menu Bar command item, as the following example demonstrates:
* On the *File* menu, click....

Text in regular italic type means that an action occurs through the selection of a menu and commands, as the following examples illustrate:
* On the *File* menu, click on the *Save As* command. To do this, single-click on the *Save As* command from the *File* menu. OR

* Choose the *File>Save As* menu function. To do this, single-click on the *Save As* command from the *File* menu.

Palette Menus

Most of the palettes in Photoshop have menus that are accessed by clicking on the arrowhead that appears on the upper-right corner of the palette. When you click with your mouse on this arrow, a menu with function options specific to the palette appears. You can slide down to the appropriate command. Typically, several of the functions can also be accessed through the icon bar at the bottom of the palette.

Context Menus

Context menus appear when you *Ctrl+click* (Mac) or *right mouse+click* (Windows) as you are using a tool. The context menus present various options available to the selected object and/or tool currently being used.

Working with Tools, Dialogs, and Palettes

Text in bold nonitalic type signifies that an action occurs through the use of a tool, dialog box field, button, or other nonmenu function, as the following examples show:

- Click on the **OK** button in the window.

- Choose the **Rectangular Marquee** tool.

The use of keyboard shortcuts allows you to speed up the design process, so you will often be given keyboard shortcuts to certain menu commands, tools, and operations. In general, on the Macintosh, the *Command (Cmd)* key is used in conjunction with another key. The Windows equivalent is the *Control (Ctrl)* key. These keys as well as others (such as the *Shift* and *Option/Alt* keys) are known as *modifier* keys. In this book, these shortcuts will be presented as follows:

Cmd/Ctrl+C	This keystroke combination copies an object or selected text to the clipboard.
Spacebar+Cmd/Ctrl	Press these keys and click with the mouse to zoom in.
Opt/Alt+Drag	Use this key operation to copy a selected object.

In all cases, the Macintosh key will precede the Windows key. In the first two examples above, the Mac *Command* key (Cmd) is followed by the Windows *Control* key (Ctrl) and then the appropriate keyboard letter is given. In the third example above, the Mac *Option* key (Opt) is followed by the Windows equivalent, the *Alt* key.

Various shortcuts for tools in the Toolbox and functions in Photoshop do not use modifier keys. Reference to these tools will be made as follows:

Select the **Lasso** tool (L).

Layer Properties...
Blending Options...

Duplicate Layer...
Delete Layer

Convert to Smart Object

Rasterize Layer

Free Transform

Color Range...
Load Selection...
Reselect

Sample context menu, which appears when you Ctrl+click (Mac) or right mouse+click (Windows) on the document

Note: Palettes vs. Panels in CS3
In Creative Suite 3, all programs but Photoshop refer to the traditional "palette" as panels. Only Photoshop has retained the old name.

Candy Land

- Brilliant colors
- Innovative Knits
- Frilly Details
- Baby Doll Silouettes

Presentation for Knitwear
Trends, Fall/Winter
2008/2009
by Melisa Farnsworth

Overview of Adobe Photoshop

Adobe Photoshop is the leading image editing program for graphic artists. Its uses are multiple, ranging from Web design to catalogue work to photographic work and beyond. The depth of the program is mind boggling, and many artists master only parts of the software. This book will focus on various tools and operations that assist in the production of fashion drawings and illustrations, and textile design. In this chapter, we will take a quick look at what Photoshop is all about and introduce you to several basic concepts critical to a sound foundation in working with a raster-based program.

Creative Art with Photoshop by author

The Photoshop Approach to Design

Adobe Photoshop is a raster or pixel-based design program. Images are represented by small dots (pixels) of color on the screen and thus Photoshop becomes the perfect medium for continuous tone images such as photographs or digital paintings, both of which are generally portrayed through subtle shadings and gradations. Raster images are also known as bitmap images, in which each pixel or bit (the smallest unit of design) is *mapped* to a position in the color palette (and thus a color). Therefore, Photoshop remembers each and every pixel in the drawing according to its color and location in the palette.

If asked to choose three or four words to describe Photoshop, one would most likely come up with the following:

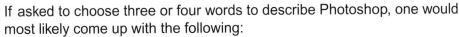

- o Pixels
- o Selections
- o Color
- o Layers

Thus, as you can imagine and will learn through the study of this book, one tends to work in Photoshop by drawing or editing *colored pixels* through the use of *selections* and *layers*. Selections, defined by *shape* (outlining a given area of the image) or by *color,* are integral to working in Photoshop, and the designer is constantly defining and manipulating selections of pixels. Layers (stacked one above the other) allow you to work with greater freedom in that you can easily isolate portions of a drawing to be edited independent of other areas of the drawing. This may not make sense yet, but it will shortly, as you begin the various exercises in this book.

In order to better appreciate Photoshop and its use in the design world, it will help to have an understanding of the approaches to design of the two basic types of design software: pixel (raster) and object (vector). Photoshop is an example of a pixel-based program and Adobe Illustrator is an example of an object-based program. It should be noted, however, that Photoshop does contain vector tools for your use. The number of tools and their depth do not approach those found in Illustrator, but they are still handy for use. This book will cover the vector side of Photoshop briefly in a drawing flats exercise and a clipping mask exercise.

Painterly Effects with Photoshop by Peggy Liu

A circle drawn in Photoshop (above) and Illustrator (below). The close-up snapshot above shows you the pixelating that occurs in raster art.

Pixel-Based Documents

- Tend to have larger file sizes
- Are created through painting, scanning, digital cameras, and so on
- Freehand drawings are generally more difficult to edit as one must deal with individual pixels.
- Scanned or photographic images are easy to edit using a multitude of tools and functions.

Object-Based Documents

- Files store the basic information of each object in the image.
- Tend to be smaller in file size.
- Individual objects are remembered as "objects" and thus may be easily edited and resized.
- Photographic or scanned images may not be edited pixel-by-pixel, and must be 'placed' or imported for use.

Pixel-Based Design

If you draw a diagonal line in a pixel-style program, you choose the tool and color, then move to the screen/document. Click your mouse to set the starting point of the line and then hold and drag the mouse diagonally to define the angle and length of the line. Release the mouse. As you perform these actions, pixels (tiny dots) of color are laid in place on the document and thus define the line. The program draws a series of pixels to form the line at the angle and length you specified. The predetermined color and pen thickness are utilized in the drawing of the pixels. Once the image is set in place, each pixel or dot becomes a fixed point on the document and if you want to edit the line, you must erase part or all of it, and redraw the pixels in the area. When the line prints, each pixel or dot is sent to the printer. If you used a low document resolution, as would be suitable for the Web (72 dpi), you will see the jagged edge of the pixels. If you used a higher document resolution, suitable for commercial printing (300 dpi), the shape will appear smoother, although you can still see the slightly jagged edge upon close examination. Anti-aliasing (discussed below) aids in reducing the apparent jagged edge.

Object-Based Design

If you draw a line in a vector-style program, you choose the appropriate tool, click your mouse to set the starting point and then hold and drag the mouse to define the width and height of the line. Releasing the mouse ends the object. As you define the line, the program notes the coordinates of the endpoints of the line, and it also notes the color and line thickness. When it prints the line, it sends this same data information to the printer. It tells the printer to print a line by giving the coordinate positions, and the thickness and color of the line. The line will print perfectly smooth. Object-based imagery can be scaled up or down without losing clarity, whereas pixel-based imagery cannot always be scaled up successfully.

Photoshop Concepts and Terminology

Although the process of drawing pixels in itself is simple, there are many subtleties to working efficiently in Photoshop. The following list of concepts and terminology will assist in your understanding.

Concept 1: Painting vs. Drawing in Photoshop

Although Photoshop is primarily used as a raster program, it also contains tools for drawing vector art. The term *painting* will generally be used to refer to artwork creating using pixels and tools such as **Brush**, **Pencil**, **Gradient**, **Eraser**, **Paint Bucket**, **Smudge**, **Blur**, and so on. These are the tools you want to use with photographic images, scans of artwork, or when you want to create in a manner that simulates hand drawing. The term *drawing* will generally be used to refer to artwork created using vectors. The tools in Photoshop that allow you to create vector images are the **Pen** tool and various **Shape** tools. Note that the **Line** and other **Shape** tools offer you both a raster and object option, so you must be careful when choosing the mode you want when drawing these shapes. Things can become a little confusing, as we want to think of the creation of any artwork as drawing. Try to shift your mind to differentiating between painting and drawing for the purpose of this book. Although Photoshop is capable of creating both raster and vector art, the primary focus of this book is on raster imagery.

Concept 2: Pixels Need to Be Understood

When you paint original art in Photoshop or load a digital image you must deal with pixels. The term pixel is short for picture element and it represents the smallest entity of a raster image. Pixels are like dots, and each pixel in an image is linked to a color in the palette (thus the term bit-mapped); this information is saved when the file is saved.

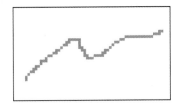

Pixels can be seen in the above illustration. Pixels are dots drawn on the document in a raster program.

Concept 3: Understanding Resolution

The higher the resolution of your document or image, the more pixels you will have and the finer the detail. As an example, a 5 × 7 inch file set at a resolution of 72 will be 360 pixels by 504 pixels. The same 5 × 7 inch file set at a resolution of 300 will be 1500 pixels by 2100 pixels. The amount of detail you can show in a resolution of 300 is much greater that what can be seen in a resolution of 72. Of course, file size will differ between the two resolutions. The 72 resolution file will initially be 532 kB and the 300 resolution file will be 9.01 MB. Monitor resolution

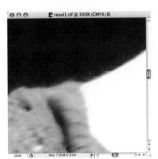
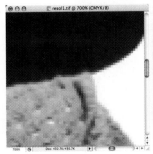

The original image (right) at 300 dpi.
A closeup at 300 dpi (left) and a closeup at 72 dpi (center).

and printer resolution are two other types of resolution to consider. See page 19 for a description of these.

Concept 4: The Role of Anti-Aliasing

Aliasing exists when pixels of sharp edges appear jagged. Anti-aliasing is when edges are smoothed out through the averaging of the pixels. The jagged edges are smoothed by adding pixels that are averaged in color between the sharp edge and the color next to it (typically, but not always, the background color). If you zoom in close to look at the edge of an anti-aliased image, it will appear slightly blurred. However, the edge will appear smoother in zoomed out modes and in printing. Several tools in Photoshop provide you with the option to turn anti-aliasing on or off. Although anti-aliasing allows raster images to look smooth, it can sometimes present problems in creating quick color changes, as the user must deal with the multiple colored pixels.

Anti-Aliasing Example:
The upper image was drawn with the Pencil tool (which does not anti-alias). The lower stroke was drawn with the Brush tool (which does anti-alias). Both tools used a tip of 5 pixels.

Concept 5: Using Foreground vs. Background Palette Colors

The *foreground* and *background* colors, located at the bottom end of the Toolbox, assist you in working with color. Typically you use the foreground color to paint, fill, and stroke selections. The background color is used to fill in erased areas (as the **Eraser** paints to the background color) and as the color at one end of a gradient spectrum. The default foreground color is black and the default background color is white. Foreground and background colors are designated by using the *Color* palette, the **Eyedropper** tool, the *Swatches* palette, or the *Color Picker*.

The foreground and background colors in the Toolbox.

Concept 6: Selections are Created by Shape or Color

When you want to edit or manipulate an image you need to choose or select the pixels you want to alter. This process is called *making a selection.* Selections can be made through defining the pixels you want by outlining them with a shape (using the various **Selection** tools such as the **Lasso**, **Polygon**, **Rectangle**, etc.), painting the selection (using the **Quick Selection** tool or **Quick Mask** function), or by choosing the pixels by color (using the **Magic Wand** tool). When you create a selection by color, you can experiment with setting the *Tolerance* level to increase or decrease the number of shades of color of the pixels (to either side of the selected color) you want to include in the selection.

A selection made with the Rectangular Marquee (left), by painting the selection with the Quick Selection tool (center), and using the Magic Wand tool to select by color with a tolerance of 32 (right). The selection is outlined by a marquee or "marching ants."

The selection on the image on the left was edited using the Hue/Saturation Adjustment and the selection on the image on the right was transformed using the Edit>Transform>Rotate menu command.

Concept 7: Editing and Transforming Selections

Once you have created an active selection (as indicated by the marching ants of the marquee), you may alter only this area. This is generally what you want, but occasionally, you will forget to deselect a selection, and you will not understand why the operation you think you are performing to the entire document is not working. Remember to *deselect* (*Cmd/Ctrl+D* keyboard shortcut) a selection when you no longer need it. Editing techniques such as altering the contrast, colors, blurring, sharpening, and so on can be performed to selections. Transformations such as scale, skew, and rotations can easily be performed using the various transformation commands in the **Edit** menu or the options bar.

Concept 8: Use of Layers

Layers are integral to working efficiently in Photoshop. They allow you to separate portions of your art so that editing and future work is simplified. When you use the clipboard and paste in art, it always enters on its own layer. Layers may be named, reordered, merged, linked, and combined, among other operations. *Adjustment* layers, created using the button at the bottom of the *Layers* palette, or with the new Adjustment Panel of CS4, are temporary layers that affect the image (and the layers below them), but are not permanent unless you want them to be. They are often used to experiment with image processing techniques without worry of permanent results. *Fill* layers, also created using the **Adjust/Fill** button at the bottom of the *Layers* palette, allow you to fill a layer with a solid fill, gradient or pattern. Fill layers do not affect the layers beneath them. Chapter 2 explains in detail the use of layers.

Concept 9: Use of History Palette (History States and Snapshots)

The *History* palette keeps a running history or log of your steps of operation as you work, and it allows you to back up to any point of time in the development of your image. This is particularly freeing and encourages you to experiment without concern. Each operation you perform is called a *state*. You may back up to a prior state, but once you start to work on the image again, you lose all steps that were performed after that state in time and a new set of states is generated as you work. A *snapshot* is a function of the *History* palette that allows you to make a temporary copy of your image at any point of its development. Snapshots can be named and stored at the top of the *History* palette and you can easily move in and out of a snapshot to compare techniques. Snapshots are not saved with the image and are lost when your session if over. Read more on the use of the *History* palette on page 22 and in Chapter 6.

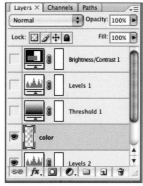

The Layers palette for the image on the right. Note that both regular layers and Adjustment Layers are used. The name of the layer indicates which adjustment was used.

The History palette showing the process of work (or states) on the fashion drawing above. Note the snapshot that is taken at a given point in time.

Terminology Refresher

The following is a summary of the different terms discussed in this chapter. See if you understand each one and review the concepts as necessary to firm up your knowledge.

> **Painting**—the laying down of colored pixels in a raster paint-style program.

> **Drawing**—the use of vector images through specialized vector tools in Photoshop (such as the Pen tool).

> **Raster/Bitmap**—a type of software in which each pixel in the document is mapped to the color palette and recorded in memory when the file is saved. Painting and editing are achieved through altering pixels.

> **Vector**—a type of program where objects are recorded. An object-based program. Photoshop has tools and the ability to work with vector objects (but not to the depth of Illustrator).

> **Pixel**—short for picture element, the smaller unit or dot of design in a raster paint program.

Resolution—the number of pixels or dots in a given area, usually expressed as pixels per inch. Higher resolution images have more pixels, allow for more detail, and have a larger file size. There are three different types of resolution: image, monitor, and printer. See page 19 for more information.

Anti-aliasing—the process in which edges of a bitmapped image are smoothed by averaging the edge color of the image with the color it is next to.

Foreground vs. Background Color—defined colors in the Toolbox of Photoshop that allow you to control which colors you paint, draw, or erase with.

Selections—defined or targeted groups of pixels, chosen either by shape or by color. Selections are made so that edits or modifications may be performed only on those pixels.

Editing—the process of altering selected pixels through a multitude of means including color and contrast adjustments.

Transformation—the process of manipulating selected pixels through techniques such as scaling, rotations, skewing, and so on.

Layers—a method used to separate art into workable entities. Layers are like sheets of transparent film, each one sitting above the other. They contain artwork sitting on a transparent background. One looks down at the image from the uppermost layer to the lowest layer. See Chapter 2 for a full discussion on layers.

History State—the moment in time during which an operation was performed. History states are recorded in the *History* palette and you may move back to any state of time as you work. Realize that once you commence work again, you lose all states after that point in time, as new states are now being recorded. The *History* palette (and therefore states) are not saved in a file.

Snapshots—a function of the *History* palette that allows you to record a specific moment in time so that you may return to it, and go back out of it. Snapshots are not saved with the file. Snapshots differ from states in that you can always return to a snapshot during your working session, whereas some states can be lost once you commence working again.

The General Approach to Design

There are various approaches to designing fashion and textile images using Photoshop. *These include:*

Painting and Drawing Freehand

This utilizes the basic drawing tools such as the **Pen**, **Brush**, **Line,** and **Shape** tools. The most recent versions of Photoshop offer the user a variety of **Brush** tools that replicate the various art mediums such as watercolor, charcoal, and so on. Some tools allow you to choose between raster or vector options. Make sure you know which type of tool you need for a project.

Traced fashion pose by Kathy White

Utilizing a Digital Image

In this approach you begin by loading a raster image from a scanner, digital camera, or other source and you use this image as a starting point for creating new art. *You might choose this approach for the following reasons:*

- o To trace the art to build a pose or garment shape
- o To use a scanned fabric or art as a starting point for fabric design, which includes tracing a component of the image to use as a motif in textile design
- o To create a *Clipping Mask* around the edge of a digital image of a garment (layouts for catalogues)
- o To build a composite/collage

Editing a Digital Image

Photoshop is often used to improve a digital image. This is true image processing and parallels the processes one would use in a darkroom. Other editing functions are used to develop fabric or recolor artworks. *You might choose this approach:*

- o To touch up or improve the image
- o To color correct the image
- o To recolor an image (e.g., fabric and multiple colorways)

Creative effects with layers

The General Process of Design

The process of creating art in Photoshop typically involves a routine combination of steps. *These are:*

1. Set up the Document or Load a Digital Image

If you are creating new art, this involves choosing the document size, orientation, resolution, color mode, and background contents to open a document on the screen. You then need to choose which palettes you want available for use while you work on the project. These are opened using the *Window* menu or accessed from the Palette dock.

If you are going to work with an existing digital image you need to load it using the *File>Open* or *File>Browse* menu command. You will then adjust the color mode if necessary (using the *Image>Mode* menu command).

Editing a digital image by changing its color

The New dialog for setting up a file

2. Draw, Edit, and/or Manipulate the Pixels

At this point, you are ready to paint, draw, or image process. There are many operations you can perform, depending on the project and the need. *Typical editing functions involve the following:*

- o *Adjusting* the image using various *Image>Adjustment* commands such as Levels, Color Balance, Hue/Saturation, and so on.
- o Using *Filters* to alter the image (using various **Filter** menu commands such as Sharpen, Blur, Noise, etc.)
- o *Touching up* the image to correct flaws such as dust, removing an unwanted art using a variety of tools and functions
- o Moving a selection of pixels
- o Resizing a selection of pixels
- o Utilizing layers to assist in the design process

User Interface and the Working Environment

The first step to mastering any software program is to become familiar with its working environment. Photoshop gives you more power than you will most likely ever use, yet its environment or user interface can be quite manageable. You have some control over the initial tools you see in the Toolbox and you have complete control over which palettes are displayed and ready for use. Photoshop allows you to set up personal workspaces (*Window>Workspace>Save Workspace*) so that you can customize the environment for given tasks.

Upon opening Photoshop, you will see the Toolbox, palettes, the options bar, and the Menu Bar, but a document does not automatically appear. It is up to you as the user to either create a new document or open an existing file. This is achieved via the *File>Open* or the *File>New* menu commands. Once a document is open, you will see the following on your screen:

- o Document window
- o Toolbox
- o Various docked palettes (panels in CS4)
- o Menus
- o Options bar

The Macintosh Environment, CS4

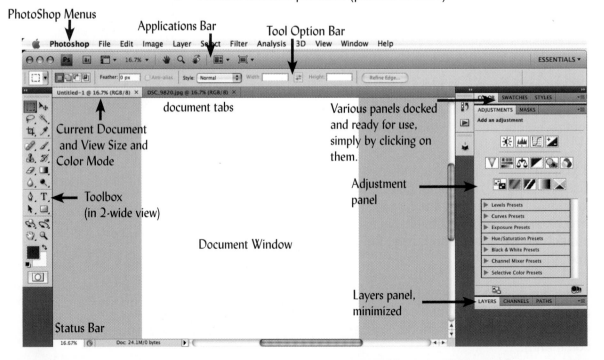

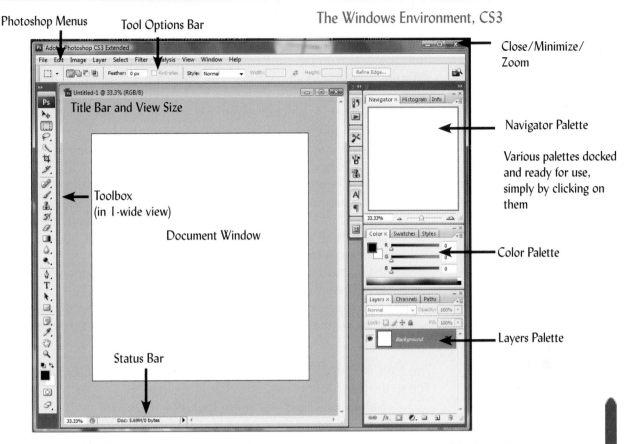

Photoshop Menus

Tool Options Bar

The Windows Environment, CS3

Close/Minimize/
Zoom

Navigator Palette

Various palettes docked
and ready for use,
simply by clicking on
them

Title Bar and View Size

Toolbox
(in 1-wide view)

Document Window

Color Palette

Status Bar

Layers Palette

The Document Window

Your current artwork is displayed in a document window. Across the top of the document you will see the **Title Bar,** which includes the current display size/zoom level of the document and the color mode (e.g., RGB, CYMK). Close/minimize and zoom controls are located in the upper-left corner (Mac) or the upper-right corner (Windows) of the document. Scroll bars will appear if the image is larger than what will fit in the current document window. A **Status Bar** appears in the lower-left corner of the window. Here you can see various things according to the setting you choose to display. Click and hold on the arrow on the right side of the **Status Bar** to see the display options. **Note:** In CS4, when the Application Frame is turned on, all open documents are stacked and individually accessed by clicking on the appropriate tab at the top of the document area.

Window Control

Macintosh

Red—close
Yellow—minimize
Green—zoom

Windows

Dash—minimize
Box—maximize
X—close

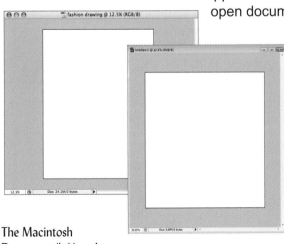

The Macintosh
Document (left) and
the Windows Document (right)

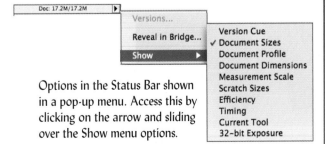

Options in the Status Bar shown
in a pop-up menu. Access this by
clicking on the arrow and sliding
over the Show menu options.

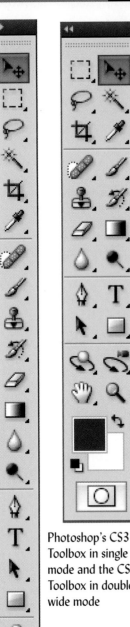

Photoshop's CS3's Toolbox in single mode and the CS4 Toolbox in double-wide mode

Note:

CS4 Toolbox
See page v for a discussion what is new in CS4's Toolbox.

The Toolbox (Tools Palette) (Tools Panel in CS4)

The **Toolbox** or *Tools* palette is a floating window that contains various tools that allow you to perform specific tasks. The tools vary slightly in different versions of Photoshop. *The following are some of the Toolbox's useful features:*

o To select or activate a tool, you simply click on it and the tool will darken to show you that it is the active tool.

o Tools are organized in groups according to function (e.g., Selection tools, Retouching tools, etc.).

o Some tools are stacked under other tools and can be accessed by clicking and holding on the top tool, and then sliding over to the desired tool when the palette of tools opens. If you see a small black diamond in the lower-right corner of a tool, you know that additional tools are hidden beneath.

o If you hide the Toolbox, you can reopen it by choosing *Tools* in the **Window** menu.

o The Toolbox may be displayed as a single or double row of tools. Click on the arrowhead above the Toolbox palette to choose your view.

The tools in Photoshop CS3 are organized into groups according to function. *These are as follows:*

Selection Tools—(the top four tools plus hidden tools) These allow you to create selections, either by shape, by painting, or by color. Tools in this group include the Rectangular, Elliptical, Single Column and Single Row Marquee tools, the Lasso, Polygonal Lasso and Magnetic Lasso tools, Quick Selection, Magic Wand, and the Move tool.

Crop and Slice—(the next two tools plus hidden tools) These functions allow you to crop an image or slice it for Web pages. Tools in this group include the Crop, Slice, and Slice Select tools.

Retouching—(the next five tools plus hidden tools) These functions allow you to touch up images, as if working in a darkroom. These are considered editing tools. A large number of tools exist in this group. They are: Spot Healing Brush, Healing Brush, Patch, Red Eye, Clone Stamp, Pattern Stamp, Eraser, Background Eraser, Magic Eraser, Blur, Sharpen, Smudge, Dodge, Burn, and Sponge.

Painting—(three tools plus hidden tools) These tools are used to paint with pixels and include the Brush, Pencil, Color Replacement, History Brush, Art History Brush, Gradient, and Paint Bucket.

Drawing and Type—(four tools plus hidden tools) This group of tools serve to draw and edit vector images, and create type. They include

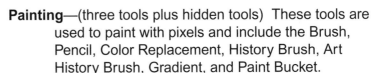

the Pen (and its variants, Add, Delete, and Convert Anchor Point tools, Horizontal and Vertical Type tools and type Masks, Path and Direct Selection tools, and various Shape tools). Note that the Shape tools may be drawn as raster images by simply choosing the mode in the options bar before you begin drawing.

Annotation, Measuring, and Navigation—(four tools plus hidden tools) The Note and Audio Annotation tools allow you to create annotations as you work. The Eyedropper and Color Sampler allow you to sample colors, and the Ruler and Count allow you to measure. The lower two tools allow you to maneuver around your document by zooming in or out (Zoom tool) and panning around the document (Hand tool).

Foreground and Background Color—These icons are positioned beneath the tool groups. You use them to set the current *foreground* or *background* color simply by clicking on the chosen option and picking a color from the *Swatch* or *Color* palette or the *Color Picker.*

Standard Mode vs. Quick Mask Mode—This icon is a toggle in that it changes according to whether you are in Standard mode or Quick Mask mode. Quick Mask assists you in paint selections. See Chapter 2, pages 37–40 for further discussion.

Screen Modes—The lower icon in the Toolbox allows you to choose which screen display you want. In CS3, when you click and hold on the icon, you may choose between Standard Screen Mode, Maximized Screen Mode, Full Screen Mode with Menu Bar, and Full Screen Mode. *Clicking+holding* on the current mode will open a pop-up menu and allow you to change modes. In CS4, Screen Modes has been moved to the Application Bar at the top of the screen.

CS4 Changes
In CS4, tools have been reshuffled slightly. See page vii of the Preface for details.

Foreground and Background colors

Standard mode

Quick Mask mode

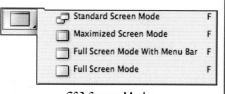

CS3 Screen Modes

The Options Bar

The **options bar** allows you to view all options for the tool currently selected in the Toolbox. Thus, when you switch tools, the options in the options bar change to reflect those available for the tool.

Gripper bar →

The options bar for the Magnifier tool

The following is true of the options bar:

o   You can *move* and *reposition* the options bar by clicking and holding on the gripper bar and moving it to a new location. Return the options bar to its position under the menus by dragging the gripper bar to just under the Menu Bar. It will snap in place.

o   Double-clicking on the gripper bar on the left side of the tool options bar allows it to *collapse* in size.

o If you close the options bar, you can reopen it by choosing *Options* in the **Window** menu.
o Once you *change settings* for a certain tool, those settings will remain for future use until you change the settings again.
o You can *reset* any tool (to its original defaults) by pressing the *Ctrl* key as you click (Mac) or *right click* (Windows) on the tool icon in the upper-left corner of the screen.
o In CS1 and CS2, an area known as the *palette well* exists on the right side of the tool options bar (if you are using a screen resolution greater than 800 x 600). You may store palettes here for easy access.

Palettes (Panels in CS4)

A *palette* is a floating window that contains functions according to theme. Palettes allow you to modify images or to monitor your status. They are accessed through the **Window** menu. If a palette is open, a check mark appears beside the palette name in the **Window** menu. The choice of which palettes to open varies from user to user and from project to project. Any given palette window may contain multiple functions, each organized like a manila folder with a tab.

The following is true of palettes:
o Palettes are *docked* to the right side of the screen. They can be collapsed to icon view by clicking on the double-arrows on the right side of the palette dock. Once in icon view, you can expand the palettes by clicking on the double-arrows once again. When in icon view, you can click on a palette name to open the palette.
o Each palette has a *tab* to indicate the name of the palette.
o Palettes can be *grouped* so that several appear in a window together. Clicking on a palette tab brings the selected palette to the front.
o You can *tear a palette away* from the group by clicking on its tab and dragging the palette away from the others. Likewise, you can group palettes by dragging independent palettes into a window that contains a group.
o Many palettes have *menus* accessed by clicking on the arrowhead that appears on the upper-right side of the palette. These menus contain commands pertinent to the function of the palette.
   o In CS1 and CS2, palettes can be *collapsed* to the *palette title* only (by double-clicking on a tab). Double-clicking a second time returns the title to the full palette.
   o The layout and position of palettes are remembered when you close the program so that the next time you open it, all will appear as you last left it. Custom workspaces can also be used.

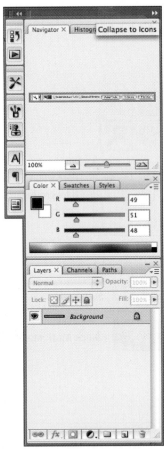

Above: The default view of palettes in CS3. Several palettes are expanded and several appear in icon view. All palettes can be collapsed to icon view.

Below: Palettes collapsed to icons (left) and the color palette name clicked to expand only this palette (right)

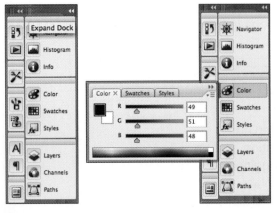

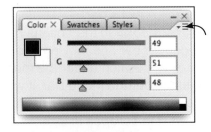

Palette Options menu. Click on this to access additional options.

Menus

The menus are organized according to function. Each menu has numerous commands, some of which open a dialog (those ending with ...) and others have additional submenus (those ending with a black arrowhead). When you examine the menus, you will see that various commands have keyboard shortcuts that are shown the right of the command name. These usually begin with the *Cmd* key on the Mac, and with the *Ctrl* key on Windows.

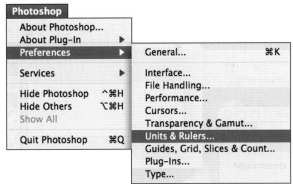

Choosing the RGB Color option from the Mode submenu of the Image menu

Basic Maintenance Operations

Preferences

Preferences define the settings you choose to use as you work and design in the program. You have control over various Preference settings and can access these through the *Photoshop>Preferences* menu (Macintosh) or *Edit>Preferences* (Windows). People most commonly change the units, display, grids, and guideline preferences to suit their needs.

Default settings are those settings determined by Adobe for general use. You may alter these to suit your purpose, but if you wish, you may return all your settings to the original default. *To do this:*

o   Press and hold *Opt+Cmd+Shift* (Mac) or *Alt+Ctrl+Shift* (Windows) as you launch Photoshop. You will be prompted to delete the current settings.

o   Mac users can open the *Preferences* folder in the *Library* folder, and drag the *Adobe Photoshop CS Settings* folder to the Trash.

As you work with the various tools in the Toolbox of Photoshop, you will learn to change their settings to better suit your purpose. If you want to reset a tool to its original setting, *Ctrl+click* (Macintosh) or *right+click* (Windows) on the tool in the options bar to reset the tool.

Note:

**Tab Key
Hides the Palettes**
Pressing the tab key hides all the Photoshop palettes. Pressing it a second time brings them back into display.

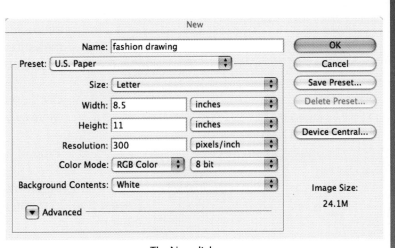

Photoshop's Preferences

Setting up a Document

To create a new document, choose the *File>New* menu command. A dialog will open and present you with several options. *These are as follows:*

o   You may choose to name the document at the moment of creating it or later. Type the file name you want to use into the blank *Name* field. Note that the file is not actually saved with this name until you perform the *File>Save* command.

The New dialog

Tip: A Quick Reset

When you are in a dialog, pressing and holding the Opt/Alt key and clicking on the Cancel button will reset all changes you made back to the beginning, which is essentially cancelling without closing the dialog. A handy tip!

o   You may choose the *document size* in one of two ways. You may either select a *preset* size from the pop-up menu, or you may type in your desired size, width and height, in pixels, inches, centimeters, millimeters, points, or picas. Use the measurement mode pop-up menu to select your choice of measurement.

o   Choose a *Resolution* for your document in pixels per inch or pixels per centimeter. The higher the resolution, the smoother your image will print, but the larger the file. A common low resolution is 72 pixels per inch. Using higher resolutions such as 150 or 300 dots per inch will create significantly larger files, but more polished results. To experiment with this, create the same basic drawing in each of these resolutions on the same size page, and print out the results. You will see the visual difference.

o   The *Color Mode* allows you to choose between Bitmap (black and white only), Grayscale, RGB, CMYK, or Lab Color. Most people use RGB or CMYK. If you are going to print your job commercially, you must use CMYK, as this matches the inks used for printing.

o   The *Background Contents* option allows you to choose the background color of your document. If you choose "White", you will have the traditional white screen, representative of a sheet of paper. If you choose "Background Color", your document will open in the background color of the palette. If you choose "Transparent", you will initially see a light gray checkerboard on the screen (which is representative of a transparent background). When the background is transparent you can move objects around with a transparent negative space to the outside of the object itself. This can be very handy.

o   *Advanced Settings* may be set. These include Color Profile and Pixel Aspect Ratio.

o   You may choose your personal settings and then click on the *Save Preset...* button to name and save your settings for future use. See below.

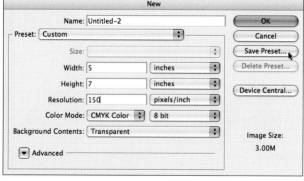

Creating a Preset using the File>New dialog (above) and entering the Preset Name (below)

Creating a Preset

Photoshop allows you to create and save *Presets,* which are preferred settings for your documents. *To do this:*

1. Set up the various options in the *New* file dialog according to your liking (e.g., width, height, measurement mode, resolution, color mode, and background contents).

2. Click on the **Save Preset** button. A dialog window will open.

3. Type in a name for your preset and click **OK**.

Now, when you create a new document, you can click on the *Preset* pop-up menu in the *File>New* dialog and choose your custom setup.

What Is Resolution?

There are three types of resolution used in computer graphics. These are image resolution, monitor resolution, and printer or output resolution.

Image resolution is measured by the number of pixels per inch (ppi) in the image. Images with a high resolution (e.g., 300 ppi) will have more pixels and thus the file size will be larger. Imagery will print smoother, but will take longer to save and print. Photoshop varies from 72 ppi to 300 or more ppi. If you are preparing images for the Web, use 72 ppi. If you are preparing images for printing, use higher resolutions (like 300 ppi).

Accessing the preset from the Preset pop-up menu

Monitor resolution is measured in dots per inch (dpi). Typical monitor resolutions display 800 x 600, 1024 x 768, and so on. The translation of image resolution to monitor resolution is one to one, so if you have an image with 100 ppi image resolution displayed on a monitor with 72 dpi display, the image will be approximately 30 percent larger on the screen when displayed at 100 percent.

Output or printer resolution is the number of dots per inch printed by the printer. Higher resolution printers will print higher resolution images with smoother results.

The File Save As... menu command (above) and file format options (below)

Saving Files

When you save a file you have various options. *The most commonly used menu commands are:*

File>Save	Saves changes made to the current file.
File>Save As...	Saves changes to a different file.
File>Save a Copy	Saves an identical copy of the file you are working on and leaves the original file active.
File>Save for Web	Assists you in saving files with smaller file size, suitable for Web graphics.

File Formats

A file format is the language in which a file is saved. Traditionally, various graphic software developers created their own unique file language to save files. As years passed, greater standardization of file formats occurred.

By default, Photoshop saves files in its own native language, which saves not only the artwork itself but various other functions such as layers, adjustment layers, text objects, and so on. *The following file formats are a few of the options:*

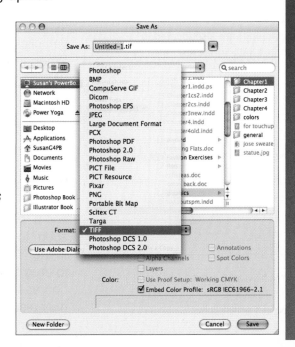

> PSD – Adobe Photoshop's native file format
> JPEG – a format used for photos requiring small size
> PDF – Portable Document Format, a file format developed by Adobe that allows files to be read and viewed using Adobe

Acrobat Reader. Users can download the Reader at no charge from Adobe's website and view files without owning the software that the files were created in. Editing the files is typically not possible. The PDF format is fully cross-platform compatible, and thus serves as a means for Macs and PCs to see the same thing.

Accessing Photoshop's Help files

Using Built-in and Online Help

Online help can be found in the **Help** menu. Choosing *Help>Photoshop Help* will load the built-in Help. Choosing *Help>Photoshop Online...* will take you to Adobe's website where various help documents can be found in the Support area.

Maneuvering Your Way around a Document

As you work on project documents, you will need to move around a document either by zooming in or out, or by panning.

Zooming in and out

If you look at the title bar of a document you can see the zoom level of the image you are working on. There are several ways to zoom in and out of your artwork. *These include:*

The Zoom tool (above) and the zoom-in and zoom-out cursors

o Choose the **Zoom** tool in the Toolbox, then move to the area of the image you want to magnify. Note how the cursor has changed to a magnifier with a *plus* symbol. If you click, you will zoom into the image, at that point of the image. You can also drag a box around the area you want to zoom. If you want to zoom out, press the *Option* key (Mac) or *Alt* key (Windows) and note how the magnifier cursor now displays a *minus* symbol. When you click, you will zoom out.

o When the **Zoom** tool is selected, you can use the various options in the options bar.

Zoom tools plus (+) and minus (−).

Note: **CS4 Zoom and Panning**
In CS4, zoom functions and the Hand tool (for panning) are also located in the Applications Bar.

Zoom level indicated in the lower-left corner of the document

In the Navigator palette, drag the slider to change magnification or type in a new number.

o The zoom level is displayed in the lower-left corner of the document. You can double click, or *click+drag* over the numbers in the zoom level and type in a new number to zoom to that level.

o In the *Navigator* palette you have the option to drag the magnification slider left or right to decrease or increase the magnification. You may also double-click on the magnification number and type in a new number.

o   You may use the keyboard shortcuts to zoom in and out. See the sidebar to the right for the various options. Try to adopt the power three-finger shortcut suggested at the end of this chapter. This will allow you to pick up speed as you work.

o   With the **Zoom** tool active, *Ctrl+click* (Mac) or *right+click* (Windows) to open the *Zoom Context* menu.

Panning

Panning allows you move the document up or down, or left or right without changing the zoom level. You can pan only when the document is larger than the area currently viewed on screen (and thus you should see scroll bars on your document). *There are several ways to pan an image:*

o   Choose the **Hand** tool, and move over to the document, and *click+hold* your mouse down. Now, drag the mouse, left or right, up or down, to pan in the desired direction.

o   In the *Navigator* palette you have the option to drag the proxy preview window (the red rectangle) around the work area in the palette.

o   You can use the scroll bars on the document window to move up and down, or left or right in the document.

o   With the **Panning** tool active, *Ctrl+click* (Mac) or *right+click* (Windows) to open the *Panning Context* menu.

o   No matter what tool is selected, press and hold the *Spacebar* on the keyboard, and then *click+drag* the mouse to pan the image.

Power Three-Finger Shortcut

If you can train yourself to do the following, you will pick up great speed in working with Photoshop (and Illustrator for that matter, as the shortcuts used are the same).

1. Place your index finger on the spacebar, your third finger on the *Cmd/Alt* key to the left, and your fourth or fifth finger on the *Option/ Ctrl* key.

2. Keep your hand positioned here at all times while working in the software and use the various combinations of these three keys to pan around the document, zoom in, or zoom out.

The advantage of using these shortcut keys is that you do not need to swing your mouse/cursor over to the Toolbox to select the appropriate tool. Rather, you keep the cursor where you are as you work. As long as the keys are depressed you remain in the zoom or panning mode. As soon as you let go of the keys you return to your working mode.

Keyboard Shortcuts for Zooming (without the use of the Zoom tool)

Zoom In
Cmd+ (plus key)   (Mac)
Ctrl+ (plus key)   (Windows)
or
space bar+Cmd+click (Mac)
space bar+Ctrl+click (Windows)

Zoom Out
Cmd– (minus key) (Mac)
Ctrl– (minus key) (Windows)
        or
space bar+Cmd+option+ click (Mac)
space bar+Ctrl+Alt+click (Windows)

Continuing to click with the mouse continues the zooming in/out process.

Using the Hand tool (above) and the proxy preview (right) to pan an image

The red rectangle is the proxy preview window. Move this around to pan what you see on the document.

Fit on Screen
Actual Pixels
Print Size

The Panning Context menu

Going back in Time

During the editing process, you may wish to return to a previous point in time and undo some or all of the operations you have just performed. Fortunately, Photoshop provides you with various ways to go back in time, either to a prior version or a prior state of the file.

The File>Revert menu command returns you to the last saved version of the file.

File>Revert

Choosing the *File>Revert* menu command loads the document you are working on, in its last saved mode. Thus if you are working and become unhappy with various changes you have just made but not saved, you can revert to the last saved version.

Adjustment Layers

An *Adjustment Layer* allows you to experiment with the various adjustment options without permanently changing or modifying the pixels in the image. The "changes" appear in the adjustment layer and do not become part of the image until you make them permanent. An adjustment layer affects all layers beneath it. You may turn the view of the adjustment layer on and off by clicking on the eye in the Edit column of the *Layers* palette. This allows you to experiment.

To create an adjustment layer:

The Adjustment Layer button at the bottom of the Layers palette, and the options you have to choose from

1. Click the **New Adjustment Layer** button at the bottom of the *Layers* palette. A pop-up menu with options will appear.

2. Choose the adjustment type you want to create. The adjustment layer will appear above the layer you were on when you chose the option and it will affect all layers beneath it.

CS4 adds the new Adjustment panel. See page vi in the Preface for an introduction to this.

History States (History Palette)

The *History* palette tracks the various edits you are performing on a document, with the bottommost item being the most current. If you want to return to a prior history *state*, you simply click on that item in the palette and the image will be restored to that state. Program-wide changes such as changing a color in the palette, changing a preference setting, and so on are not recorded as history.

The History palette records each step you perform as a state.

By default, the *History* palette works in linear mode, which means that when you back up to a prior state and commence to paint or edit, you lose the option of returning to any of the subsequent, more recent states. If you choose to work in nonlinear mode, and back up to a chosen point in history or delete an earlier state, subsequent states won't be deleted. As you resume your editing, new edits will show up as the latest states. To toggle between the two modes, choose *History Options* from the palette menu, and check the *Allow Non-Linear History* option.

Note: Although nonlinear mode sounds great, it can get a little confusing, so many users prefer to work in linear mode.

Snapshots

A snapshot is similar to a history state, but with one significant difference. Once created, a snapshot will stay on the palette even if the history state at which it was created is deleted. The snapshot will remain until you close the document. It is a good idea to create a snapshot just prior to performing a series of questionable operations.

To create a snapshot:

1. In the *History* palette, click on the state where you want a snapshot to be created.

2. Click on the **Create a new snapshot** button at the bottom of the *History* palette (or *Ctrl+click/right+click* on the history state). A snapshot called *Snapshot 1* will appear in the upper palette. You can rename this, if you like, by clicking on the name to select the text, and change the text.

3. If instead, you choose to use the palette menu to take the snapshot (New snapshot...), a dialog will open and you can type in the name for your snapshot at this time. You may choose where the snapshot is to be taken; from the Full Document, with Merged Layers, or the current layer.

Clicking on the Create new snapshot button to take a snapshot (above), and the resulting snapshot (below)

Snapshots appear at the top of the *History* palette. They may be deleted by clicking on the snapshot thumbnail and then clicking on the **Delete current state** button at the bottom of the *History* palette (the Trashcan).

Saving Your Workspace

What you see on the screen of Photoshop is a combination of palettes, bars, and windows. The arrangement of these elements is called a *Workspace*, and you have the option to customize or create your own workspace. You may indeed create several workspaces to suit the needs of different types of projects, or to reflect how you choose to view a project at different points in time.

To create a custom workspace:

1. Open the palettes you want to use and position them where you like for best efficiency in your work.

2. If you want to change the font size of text displayed in the options bar, palettes, and tool tips, change this in the *General Preferences*.

3. Choose the *Menu* and *Keyboard* set you want to work with (in the **Edit** menu).

Choosing the menu command to create a Workspace (above) and naming the workspace (below)

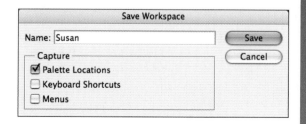

4. Choose the *Window>Workspace>Save Workspace* menu command. A *Save Workspace* dialog will open.

5. Choose the options you want to include and type in a name for the workspace. Click **OK**.

The workspace will be saved. You can recall this at any time by choosing the *Window>Workspace* menu and locating your workspace at the bottom of the menu. You can revert back to the default workspace by choosing the *Window>Workspace>Default Workspace* menu command.

This completes the quick overview of Adobe Photoshop. Chapter 2 will fast forward to a detailed discussion of working with selections and layers. Chapter 3 will walk you through a quick exercise to get you going. Chapters 4 through 6 will cover the various functions of Illustrator's Toolbox, menus, and key palettes. Basic Exercises, Fashion Drawing Exercises, Textile Design Exercises, and Presentation Exercises will follow, teaching you skills necessary for fashion design.

Collage, flats, and illustration of garments inspired by a trip to Africa

Kinsey Wilton

Focus on Selections and Layers

If one was asked to choose two terms that describe the nature of Photoshop, they would have to be *pixels* and *image processing*. Then, if asked to choose two terms that describe the manner in which you successfully work with pixels and image editing in Photoshop, it would be through the use of *selections* and *layers*. Thus, much of what is achieved in Photoshop can be summed up in four concepts: *pixels, image processing, selections,* and *layers.*

This chapter jumps right into a discussion of techniques and skills involving the creation of *selections* and the use of *layers*. You will be introduced to a variety of approaches for making selections and the tools and menu commands that are used to achieve the task. The use of layers as a means of organizing and controlling your work will be discussed as well, and you will learn how to utilize the many layer options available to you. These are considered to be the primary skills of using Photoshop, so let's get to it.

Terminology Refresher

Pixel—short for Picture Element. The smallest drawing element, a single dot on the screen.

Image Processing—the name given to the type of functions that allow you to control various aspects of your imagery. These include changes in the lightness/darkness, contrast, color, sharpness, and transparency of your image, among numerous other functions.

Selection—a targeted group of pixels that are isolated from the rest of the image. These become the pixels that changes will affect. Selections can be made in numerous ways, to be discussed in this chapter.

Layers—are similar to sheets of acetate film and are stacked one above the other in Photoshop. You can use them to separate your art in a manner that makes it easier to work. For example, text may be placed on one layer, the fashion figure on a layer, clothing on another, and so on.

Comparisons to Fashion Design

The four concepts introduced above have parallels in fashion design. In any form of design, one works with the *elements and principles of design.* It is through the employment of these that pleasing clothing, art, and buildings are created. Possibly the best way to distinguish between an element and a principle of design, is to use an analogy with cooking recipes. When you prepare a dish by using a recipe, you are given a list of ingredients and a methodology to prepare the food. The ingredients equate to the elements of design, which are the basic components from which all art is created. In clothing design, these are

Fashion Composite by June Triolo
There are nine layers in this image, one for the fashion figure and eight for the composite background.

Fast Forward

Even if you read nothing else of the explanatory material in this book, READ THIS chapter.

It covers essential skills that will speed your work in Photoshop, including the following:

• Selection tools
• Quick Mask
• Selection menu commands
• The Layers palette

silhouette, details and trims, color, and texture. The methodology portion of your recipe, or how you put the ingredients together (e.g., whipping, mixing, folding), equates to the *principles of design*, which are proportion, scale, rhythm, emphasis, and so on. Thus, you take your elements of design and combine them using the principles of design to create your own original piece.

Photoshop has similar parallels. You are given your elements, *pixels* and *image-editing tools*, and you can work with these in many ways. The use of *selections* and *layers* is the primary way in which you control the pixels and image editing. Once you achieve some level of mastery in these two techniques, you will be able to do amazing things. Therefore it is important to achieve a sound understanding of how each of these techniques can be handled in Photoshop. And believe me, there is more than one way to achieve just about anything. The key is to learn your tools and find the best and most effective way to perform the task at hand.

Selections

Most of your work will involve creating a selection and manipulating it in some form or manner. *Selections can be made in several ways:*

1. **By Shape**—achieved through outlining or surrounding the pixels you want using an assortment of drawing tools and techniques. For the most part, these tools are found in the upper portion of the Toolbox.

2. **By Color**—achieved by using the **Magic Wand** tool and *tolerances*, or by using the *Select>Extract* menu command.

3. **By Painting**—achieved through the use of the new **Quick Selection** tool or the **Quick Mask** in all versions of Photoshop.

Selections are defined so that you may alter them, move them, manipulate them, and so on. Basically, when you want to change something, you first select it and then perform an operation on it. Selections can be manipulated using a variety of tools in Photoshop. This allows you to edit targeted areas of the image only. For example, you may lighten a model's face by selecting it, and using the *Levels* command to edit the lightness/darkness and contrast.

The following are features of selections:
- o A selection may encompass an *entire layer* (achieved by clicking on the layer name), or a *targeted group* of pixels (defined by various methods to be discussed).
- o A defined selection is indicated by a marquee, or a dotted line, also known as *marching ants*.
- o Once made, selections become the *editable pixels* on the document. This sometimes gets you into trouble if you forget that you have a selection made and you are trying to alter the entire layer.
- o Each selection-related tool in the Toolbox has options that appear in the *options bar*. Once a tool is chosen, you may control the use of the tool further by adjusting the various options.

A marquee (marching ants) surrounds the crown of the hat in the image above.

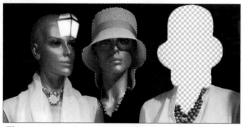

Selection options for the
Polygonal Lasso tool

o   Selections can be *moved* (to reposition the selection)
    using the **Move** tool or the *arrow keys* on the keyboard.
    If you hold the *Opt/Alt* key as you move a selection, you
    will create a copy of it on the same layer.
o   Selections may be *copied* to a new layer while leaving
    the selection on the original layer by using the *Layer
    Via Copy* command (accessed by *Ctrl+clicking* (Mac) or
    right+clicking (Windows). In a similar manner, selections
    may be *cut* to a new layer while leaving the selection on
    the original layer by using the *Layer Via Cut* command
    (accessed by *Ctrl/right+clicking).*

The process of moving a selection using the
Move tool. This was performed on a layer (as
opposed to Background), as indicated by the
transparent void.

o   When you move a selection on the *Background* (using
    the **Move** tool), the pixels beneath the moved area become the
    background color in the palette.
o   When you move a selection on a *Layer* (using the **Move** tool), the
    pixels beneath the moved area are transparent.
o   Selections may be *deleted, copied, and pasted* to another position
    on the same layer or a different layer, or even moved to another
    document.
o   Once you create a selection, various *menu commands* can alter
    the selection.
o   If you want to redefine the selection *inside the current selection*,
    you need to end the selection either by "clicking away" outside the
    selection, or by using the *Select>Deselect* menu. Then re-create
    the selection.
o   Selections can be *saved* using the *Select>Save* menu.
o   There are various additional selection-related functions found in
    the **Select** menu. These will be discussed later in this chapter.
o   Selections can be *stroked* (outlined) using the *Edit>Stroke...*
    menu.
o   Selections can be *converted to a Path* (for precise shaping using
    vector tools) and then converted back into a selection. Use the
    Paths palette to assist.
o   Selections can be *painted* using the **Quick Selection** tool CS3
    and CS4 or *Quick Mask*.
o   To *Select All* opaque and partially opaque pixels on a layer (not
    background), *Cmd/Ctrl+click* on the layer in the *Layers* palette.
o   To *Expand* or *Contract* a selection by a specific number of pixels,
    use the *Select>Modify* menu command.
o   To *Add* or *Subtract* from a selection as you are creating it, use the
    various *Selection* buttons in the *options bar* or keyboard shortcuts.
o   A technique called *Feathering* softens the edges of a selection
    once the selection is moved or copied and pasted. This is turned
    on by typing a number in the feathering field in the *options bar*
    prior to creating the selection. Or, if you have already made the
    selection, you can click on the **Refine Edge** button in the *options
    bar* (or choose the *Select>Refine Edges* menu and add the
    feathering function at that point in time.

Note: Background vs.
Layer
    The Background is
not the same as a layer. It does
not erase to a transparency,
but rather to the current
background color in the
palette. A background can
be converted to a layer
and vice versa.

A feathered selection, pasted
into a new document

Tip: Feathering Tips
    To feather a
selection after it has
been created, choose
the Select>Refine Edge
command and alter the
feathering option.
Remember to turn the
feathering function off (by
deleting any number in the
field) when you no longer
need it.

Quick Deselect

The fastest way to end a selection is to use the keyboard shortcut for Deselect. This is Cmd/Ctrl+D on the keyboard.

o   If you are in the process of creating a selection and want to end it, double-clicking will cause the outlining shape to jump to the beginning of the selection.
o   Selections can be used as a technique for erasing imagery.

Creating Selections by Shape

To define a selection by shape, you can use an assortment of **Selection** tools found in the Toolbox. These are located in the upper portion of the toolbox. After you choose a tool, you will see that various options appear in the options bar.

Move Tool

Jump ahead to page 33 to read about the Move tool, an essential component of the selection process.

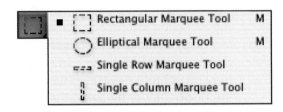

The Marquee Selection tools, stacked beneath the Rectangular Marquee

The following tools allow you to create selections by shape:

Nudging a Selection

Once a selection is created, you can use the arrow keys on the keyboard to nudge the position of the selection itself (not the imagery).

Marquee Tools *(M)*

There are four selection tools under the initial rectangular Marquee tool. Each allows you to select a portion of your document by shape.
To use any of these tools:

1.   Position your cursor on the image where you want to begin a selection.

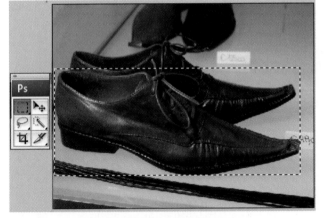

2.   *Click+hold+drag* the mouse to define the opposite edge of the selection. Release the mouse.

Once you have used one of the **Marquee** tools to define a shape, marching ants will outline the shape for your review.

Rectangular Marquee

The **Rectangular Marquee** allows you to select a square or rectangular shape (hold the *Shift* key while you make the selection to create a square selection). This tool is probably the most commonly used marquee tool. It is the **only** selection tool to use when "defining a pattern" for repeat textile design.

The Rectangular Marquee in use (above) and the Elliptical Marquee in use (below)

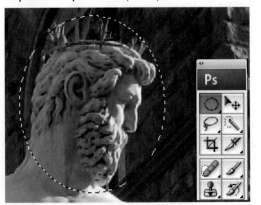

Elliptical Marquee

The **Elliptical Marquee** allows you to select an elliptical, oval, or circular shape. Hold the *Shift* key while you make the selection to create a true circle.

Single Row or Single Column Marquees

Both of these tools allow you to select a single-pixel horizontal row or vertical column of imagery. This is particularly useful for cleaning up at the edge of an image.

The *selection-by-shape* tools are stacked under the **Rectangular Marquee** tool. *Click+hold* on the **Rectangular** tool to open the pop-up menu, then slide over to the tool of your choice.

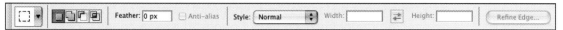

The options bar that appears when you choose a Marquee Selection tool

Marquee Selection Options
The following are settings available in the options bar:

Feathering (**Rectangular** and **Ellipse** tools only)
This is an option that, when set prior to making your selection, allows you to soften the edge of the selection, once copied and pasted into a new layer or document. Feathering does not work with single row/column marquee. If you forget to set feathering, you can turn it on after the selection is made using the **Refine Edges** button. (CS3 and CS4 only)
Feathering is utilized in the Composite/Collage exercises.

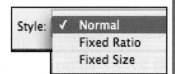

No feathering (upper left) and 3 pixels feathering (lower right)

Anti-Alias (Elliptical Marquee only)
This selection option may be turned on or off. The check mark indicates that it is turned on. When used, the selection of an edge of an image is smoothed by averaging colors between the imagery edge and the background color.

Anti-alias turned on (left) and off (right) in the options bar

Feathering Tip
To feather a selection after it has been created, click on the Refine Edges button and set feathering.

Style Options (Rectangular and Elliptical Marquees)
The **Rectangular** and **Elliptical Marquee** tools provide you with three style options. *These are:*

Normal—This mode allows you to select a rectangle of any size and shape. Opening the *Info* palette (from the **Window** menu) allows you to view the size of your selection in pixels, inches, and so on (depending on how you have set up your preferences).

Fixed Ratio—This option allows you to control the proportions (aspect ratio) of your selection. Once you have selected this style option and set your desired width and height, all selections you make will be in the proportion you set. This is a handy aid for cropping images that must be in certain proportions (e.g., standard photo frame proportions, 5 × 7, 8 × 10, etc.).

Style:	✓ Normal
	Fixed Ratio
	Fixed Size

Three options for the Style of the Rectangular and Elliptical Marquees

Fixed Size—This option allows you to create a selection of a predetermined size. Once you have selected the option and set the size, one click on the screen results in a selection of the specified size. This is handy for creating "snapshot" images of garments to be used on merchandising layout pages. It is also handy for defining the thumbnail view of an Internet graphic to be utilized in Web page design.

Lasso Selection Tools (L)

These tools offer another method of defining a selection in your document. They allow you to surround an irregular nongeometric shape through a series of clicks as you outline the desired art. You must close your selections to complete them. This means you must return to the starting point. This happens in various ways according to which of the three lasso tools you use.

Lasso Tool (L)

Use this tool in a freehand manner to surround the shape you want to select. The **Lasso** requires a steady hand to accurately select what you want, and thus is often used to quickly define the starting shape of a selection. *To use the tool:*

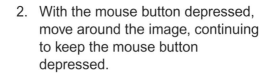

1. Position your mouse, then *click+hold* the mouse to start the selection.

2. With the mouse button depressed, move around the image, continuing to keep the mouse button depressed.

3. Release the mouse. The selection will automatically move from whatever point you were at to the beginning point, and thus close the selection.

The **Lasso** tool is handy to use when you want to erase a portion of the screen. Make a quick sweep of your hand to surround/select an area, and then press the *Delete* key (which will erase to the background color or transparency, depending on whether you are on the *background* or a *layer*, respectively).

Polygonal Lasso (L)

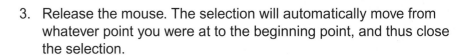

This lasso tool allows you to move around the desired area, setting points known as fastening points each time you click. It is a good tool to use if you do not have a steady hand. Your polygon will be composed of a series of straight segments. Each click of the mouse sets a point between segments. *To use the tool:*

1. Position your cursor and *click+release* with the mouse to set the first point. You will see a small circle appear by your cursor.

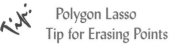

Quick Escape

Press the Escape key to abort the creation of a selection that is in process.

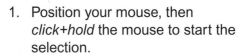

Polygon Lasso Tip for Erasing Points

As you create the polygon selection, if you want to back up and remove the most recently created points, press the Delete/Backspace key to remove the last-created point. If you continue to press the Delete/Backspace key, corner points will continue to be deleted. If you created a curve using the Opt/Alt+Drag function, there will be a lot of points to erase, but it is possible.

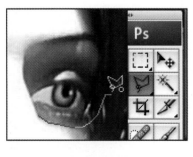

2. Move the mouse to position the next point and *click+release*. A straight segment will now exist between the two points.

3. Continue to set points by clicking and releasing the mouse as you move around the area you want to select. You will create a polygon composed of a series of straight segments.

As you finish the polygon, place your cursor over the position of the first point. Again, you should see the small circle appear. This communicates to you that you are "on top" of the initial point and the polygon can be completed with precision simply by clicking the mouse one last time. You can complete the polygon at any point in time simply by double-clicking the mouse; however, you may not have the precision you need. This tool works well for outlining a fashion garment or pose.

Although a polygon is composed of a series of straight segments, you can achieve curves fairly easily by creating a series of short straight segments (since after all, a curve is technically created by a series of straight lines). You may also create a curve by pressing the *Opt/Alt* key on the keyboard and moving the mouse to draw a freehand curve. Release the *Opt/Alt* key to resume drawing the selection with straight segments.

Magnetic Lasso (L)

This selection tool is unique in that it looks for a contrasting edge, defined by color contrast, and then snaps to this edge. Thus, the **Magnetic Lasso** tool works best on images that have a definite color contrast in the areas where you want to place a selection.

To use the tool:

1. Begin a selection by clicking with the mouse and releasing.

2. Move your cursor around the edge of the image and watch how it snaps to the edge (you do not need to click the mouse). Fastening points will appear as you move the mouse.

Tips:

o If you want to have greater control over the edge of the selection, you can click the mouse to set a fastening point where you want one.

o If you want to erase the last-drawn point to back up in the selection, press the *Delete/Backspace* key. You can continue to back up by pressing the key multiple times.

o Press the *Esc* key to cancel the selection you are currently building.

As with the **Polygon Lasso** tool, you can complete a selection by returning to the originating point, or by double-clicking your mouse (in which case, the selection will travel along its found edge and close the

---

ズマ **Magnetic Lasso Selection Aid**
You can use a temporary adjustment layer to create a greater contrast on the edge between the image you are selecting and its background. Choose Brightness/Contrast from the new Fill/Adjustment layer pop-up menu (located at the bottom of the Layers palette). Move the Contrast and/or Brightness slider to the right to achieve a great contrast. Make your selection, and then remove the adjustment layer.

ズマ **Magnetic Lasso Erasing Tip**
As you use the tool, you can press the Delete/Backspace key (Mac/Windows) to back up in the drawing of the lasso. Each time you press the key, you will back up one step.

Options for the Lasso selection tool

shape). This tool works best for making selections where there is a definite contrast between the foreground and background of the area you want to select.

Lasso Selection Options

The *Feather* and *Anti-alias* options (as discussed above) are available for all the lasso tools. *Additional controls include the following:*

Width *(Magnetic Lasso tool only)*
The *Width* option allows you to specify the detection width of the cursor of the tool as you click around an image. The higher the number, the greater width of the detection area.

Edge Contrast
The *Edge Contrast* setting lets you increase or decrease the lasso's sensitivity to detect the edge of the image. Higher values detect only edges with sharp contrasts. Lower values can allow you to detect the edge on lower-contrast images.

Frequency
The *Frequency* setting allows you to set how many '"fastening" points will be laid in place as you surround an image. The higher the value, the quicker the selection border is set in place.

Shift+Select and Opt/Alt+Select
You can use the Shift key to assist in the process of adding to a selection (in lieu of the Add to Selection button). The Opt/Alt key can be used to subtract from a selection. These are handy shortcuts to know as you do not have to go to the options bar to select the function.

Adding to and Subtracting from Selections

Although these functions exist for all selection tools, they will be introduced now. You will be referred back to them in later discussions. You may easily create, add, or remove areas from a selection as you are building it by choosing the appropriate button in the options bar. *The options are:*

New Selection—When the new selection option is active, each time you click on the document with your mouse, you start a new selection, as long as it is outside the current selection.

Add to selection—This option allows you to continue to add selections to your document. You can either add a new selection in a different area of the screen or expand your existing selection.

Subtract from selection—This option allows you to remove areas of selections from the existing selection.

Intersect selection—This allows you to create a selection based on the overlapping of the existing selection on the image and the new selection you create with any selection tool.

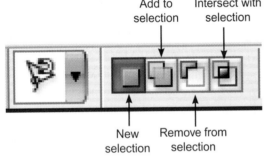

Add to selection   Intersect with selection

New selection   Remove from selection

Refine Edge (CS3 and CS4)

This is another options bar function that works with all the selection tools. It is an amazing new addition to the selection process. Once you have created a selection, you can fine-tune it using the *Refine Edge* options.

Refine Edge...

To use this option:

1. Create a selection using the tool of your choice.

2. Click on the **Refine Edge** button in the options bar. A *Refine Edge* dialog window will open.

3. Turn on the *Preview* by clicking on the check box. This will allow you to see how changes affect the selection.

4. Experiment with the various settings (Radius, Contrast, Smooth, Feather, Contract/Expand) by moving the sliders.

At the bottom of the dialog you will see different *Preview* modes. These are *Standard, Quick Mask, On Black, On White,* and *Mask.*

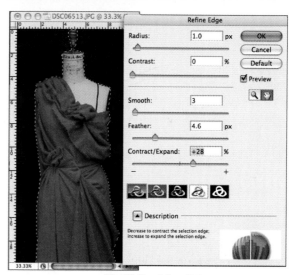

The Refine Edge dialog

o Press **F** to cycle through the *Preview* modes.
o Press **X** on the keyboard to temporarily view the image. Press **X** again to return to the *Preview* mode, or press **F**.

5. Experiment to your heart's content, and click **OK** to finalize your decisions and view the selection on your document.

Remember, this great new function can be used with all selection tools!

Note: **Refine Edge/ Refine Mask**
The new Refine Mask function in the Masks panel of CS4 has the same functionality as the Refine Edge dialog.

Move Tool   (V)

The **Move** tool is considered a selection tool as it is integral to the selection work flow. Once you have created a selection, you use this tool to move the selection around on your document. Once the tool is active, the cursor changes to an arrowhead. Position the cursor on the screen (it really doesn't matter where), and *click+hold+drag* the mouse. As you move the mouse, the selection will move on the screen. The selection is lifted away from its original position and moved to your desired position. If you are on the *background*, the background color (as defined in the Toolbox) will remain in the original position of the selection, once it is moved. If you are on a *layer*, transparent pixels will remain in the original position of the selection.

Tip: **Remember to Deselect**
If you are attempting to do something and are not getting results, check to see if you have a selection active. Deselect the selection and try again.

Creating Selections by Color or Color Range

There are times when you want to select a color or color range for editing. Photoshop provides functions to facilitate what might be considered a difficult process. These are the **Magic Wand** tool and the *Color Range* command found in the **Select** menu.

Fashion Use:
o Selecting multiple colors of a similar shade to turn them into one color (as would be necessary with textile design and printing)
o Selecting areas to delete, such as the background color around a pose
o Selecting colors in fabrics to change for new colorways

Magic Wand Tool   (W)

This is a selection tool that allows you to make selections based on *similarity in color, shade or transparency level* as opposed to shape. For this reason, odd-shaped selections based on color may be created. The **Magic Wand** tool works hand-in-hand with the various setting in the options bar. See the discussion on the *Select* menu, pages 40–43, for numerous commands in the menu that work in conjunction with this tool.

To use the Magic Wand:

1. Choose the layer you want to select pixels from by clicking on it.

2. Set the *Tolerance* setting in the options bar (see below). Determine whether you want *Anti-alias, Contiguous,* and *Sample All Layers* on or off.

3. Move your cursor to the image and click on a color or shade in the image. You will see marching ants surround the selected pixels. Note how this selection differs from a "shaped" selection.

4. If you want to add to the selection, you can press and hold the *Shift* key and continue to click with the **Magic Wand.** You can also use various commands found in the options bar or in the *Select* menu (discussed on pages 40–43).

Varying the tolerance setting while selecting the red fabric. The image above uses a setting of 32 and the image below uses a setting of 70. Note the difference in the amount of pixels selected.

Magic Wand Tool Options

In addition to the *Add to, Subtract from,* and *Intersect with selection* buttons, there are various other options that you can set to assist in improved selections. *These are:*

Tolerance

The *Tolerance* option in the options bar allows you to set the range of colors to be selected. For example, when you choose the **Magic Wand** tool, set the tolerance to 15, and then click on your image, you will select the color and 15 shades to either side of the color. The selection will be contiguous (if contiguous is checked), meaning that the tool selects until it hits a boundary that doesn't match the color criteria it was given.

Anti-Alias

When the *Anti-alias* function in the options bar is checked, the selection you are making will smooth out its edge.

Contiguous

When the *Contiguous* function in the options bar is checked, only the pixels in the color range adjacent to where you click will be selected. Otherwise, all pixels in the image (or layer of the image) of the same color range will be selected.

Sample All Layers

The *Sample All Layers* option allows all colors within the range on all layers to be selected.

Refine Edge...
See discussion on page 32.

Color Range Command   (Select Menu)

The *Color Range* command, located in the **Select** menu, allows you to select areas of an image based on colors, luminosity, or hue range. *To use this function:*

1. Click on the layer you want the selection to occur on. The *Color Range* command will sample from all layers, but the selection will appear on the current layer.

2. Choose the *Select>Color Range* menu command. A dialog will open.

3. Examine and experiment with the various pop-up menu items (explained below). You can preview the selection you are creating in the preview window of the dialog.

4. Click **OK** when you are happy with the selection. The marching ants will show you the selected pixels.

At this point, if you need to alter the selection you can do so with any of the selection tools.

The Color Range menu command, found in the Select menu

The following are controls available in the Color Range dialog:

o The *Select* pop-up allows you to choose between *Sampled Colors* (chosen by you with the Color Range Eyedropper), *color* (Reds, Yellows, Greens, etc.), or a *luminosity range* (Highlights, Midtones, Shadows).

o The *Fuzziness* slider lets you alter the range of selected colors. Moving the slider to the left reduces the range and moving it to the right increases the range of selected colors.

o The *Selection vs. Image* radio buttons allow you to view either the selection or the original image. You can hold down the *Cmd/Ctrl* key with either option set to view the alternate mode (while the key is depressed).

o The *Selection Preview* pop-up allows you to choose the method for previewing the selection while in the dialog.

o The *Invert* button lets you invert what is selected.

o The various *Color Range Eyedropper* tools work in conjunction with the *Sampled Colors* option of the Select pop-up. Choose the **Selection** radio button option of viewing the image and use the *Eyedropper* to click on an area of the image where you want to sample colors. Observe the selection preview window to see what is selected. You may add to the selection using

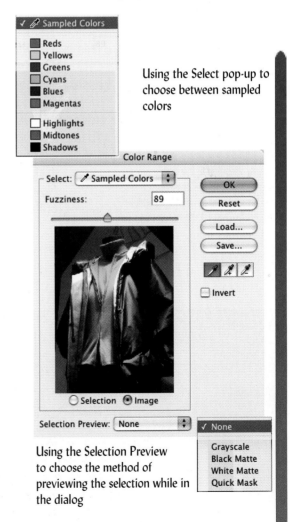

Using the Select pop-up to choose between sampled colors

Using the Selection Preview to choose the method of previewing the selection while in the dialog

Color Range Eyedropper tools: Sample Eyedroppper, Add to Sample Eyedropper, Subtract from Sample Eyedropper

the *Add to Sample Eyedropper* (the dropper with the plus sign). Conversely, you may subtract from the selection by using the *Subtract from Sample Eyedropper* tool.

Experimenting with Fuzziness settings to create the selection. Compare the results of using a Fuzziness of 57 versus 124.

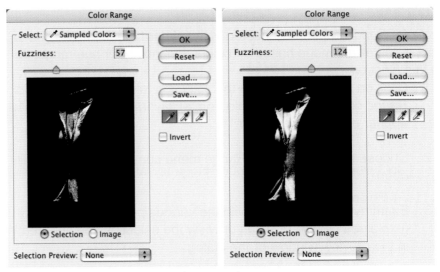

Creating Selections through Painting

Quick Selection Tool (CS3 and CS4) (W)

This is a new and wonderful selection tool, first introduced in Photoshop CS3. The **Quick Selection** tool allows you to create selections by essentially *painting them* with a brush tip that is adjustable. As you drag the mouse to paint, the selection will expand outwards and find the defined edges of the artwork.

To use the tool:

The three modes of the Quick Selection tool: (L-R) New, Add to, and Subtract from

1. Select the **Quick Selection** tool in the Toolbox. Note that there are three selection options in the options bar, *New*, *Add to*, and *Subtract from*. Choose either the **New** button or **Add to** button as the starting option.

2. Adjust the tip of the brush in the options bar by clicking in the *Brush* pop-up menu and either move the dimension slider or type in a new pixel size. If you have a pressure-sensitive tablet, you can choose this option at the bottom of the window.

3. Start painting with the mouse. Once you commence painting the selection, note how Photoshop automatically moved you into *Add to* mode, as it assumes you want to continue adding to the selection. If you want to adjust the tip of your brush "on the fly" as you paint, press the right bracket (]) on the keyboard to increase the tip size, and press the left bracket ([) to decrease the tip size.

Painting the selection using the Quick Selection tool

4. Continue painting, adjusting the brush tip as necessary to get into small areas or sweep over large areas.

5. If you want to remove some of the selection, click on the **Subtract from** button and paint over the area you want to remove. You can flip back and forth between the *Add to* and *Subtract from* modes using the keyboard. Press and hold down the *Opt/Alt* key to toggle into the opposite mode as you paint. Release the key to return to the selected mode.

Quick Selection Tool Options

Various options exist to assist in improving your selections. *These are:*

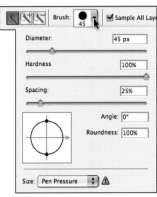

Selection Mode
Choose between *New*, *Add to*, and *Subtract from*, as discussed above, to continue building the selection. As you make selections, you can use keyboard shortcuts for adding to a selection (*Shift* key) or subtracting from a selection (*Ctrl/Alt* key) while in *New* mode.

Brush Size
This allows you to adjust the brush tip size (as discussed above).

Sample All Layers
When checked, this mode allows you to create the selection on all layers instead of just the current layer.

Auto-Enhance
This assists you in finding the contrast edges of the image as you paint. This is similar to the settings you have at your control in the *Refine Edge* dialog.

Refine Edge
As discussed earlier, this option allows you to control the selection by adjusting the *Smooth*, *Contrast*, *Radius*, and other options.

Quick Mask   (Q)
Quick Mask is another method of painting a selection. This is a mode you can move into, whereby nonselected areas are represented by color, and you can paint to add more color or remove color. This method can be a little confusing at first to new Photoshop users. So, read slowly, and carefully. Better still, experiment as you read.

What Is a Mask?
It is a device, be it a stencil, silk-screen, or other instrument, that allows you to protect part of the surface you are working on. In Photoshop, masks created through the process of painting allow you to define areas of your artwork to be protected. A mask is a form of a selection, as the nonmasked areas actually become the active selection and can be edited.

Quick Mask Mode vs. Standard Mode
Typically, when you work in Photoshop, you are working in *Standard mode*. The *Quick Mask* mode allows you to take artwork

Adjusting the brush tip size using the pop-up brush menu

Note: **Mask Mode Confusion**
People are often confused by Quick Mask instructions, with reference to the Mask Mode button in the Toolbox. This is because the mode you are actually in (Standard vs. Quick Mask) and the name of the button (Edit in Quick Mask Mode vs. Edit in Standard Mode) seem to be at odds with each other. Keep in mind that the name of the button refers to the mode you will move into, if you activate the button.

Standard mode (left) and Quick Mask mode (right)

Quick Mask

Remember, by default...

Color in Quick Mask = nonselected areas in Standard Mode.

Clear areas in Quick Mask = selected areas in Standard Mode.

with or without a selection, convert it to nonmasked and masked areas, and add or remove more masking to the image by painting with the **Brush** tool. To move into *Quick Mask mode,* click on the *Standard mode* button at the bottom of the Toolbox. The icon becomes grayed and the foreground and background colors in the Toolbox change to white and black (respectively). Once in *Quick Mask mode,* nonselected areas of the image are converted to a temporary mask, represented by a color of your choosing (the default is red). The mask appears as an overlay and its opacity is adjustable, so that you can see the artwork underneath (the default is 50%). You can edit the mask by painting with paint tools, or through the use of a filter. Once you exit *Quick Mask mode,* the non-masked areas are converted to a selection. This selection can be saved and it will become an alpha channel (which stores the mask as an editable grayscale image). It will be saved with the file, and can be recalled back into this or another file at any future time. You can view it in the *Channels* palette.

To use Quick Mask:

1. Load an image and begin the process of making a selection using any of the selection tools. *Note:* It is not necessary to have a selection, as the entire process can be achieved in *Quick Mask mode.* Typically, starting with a selection created with the selection tools saves time.

 Edit in Quick Mask Mode button

 Edit in Standard Mode button

2. Click on the *Edit in Quick Mask Mode* button near the bottom of the Toolbox. This will move you into *Quick Mask mode.* CS1 and CS2 users should click on the *Quick Mask mode* button. Typically red is the color used to indicate the nonselected areas, and the opacity setting of this is at 50%. This appears as an overlay. You may change this color or its opacity, as would be necessary if your image had a lot of red in it. (See the tips at the end of this section for instructions on how to change color and opacity.)

3. Choose a painting tool (such as the **Brush** tool). Note that the foreground/background colors are now white (foreground) and black (background). Painting with white will erase the mask and increase the selection. Painting with black will add to the red mask and decrease the selection.

4. With white as your active color, paint in the areas where you want to erase the mask (and increase the selection). Switch to black (press *X* on the keyboard to toggle black to the foreground color), and paint in the areas where you want to remove the mask, and thus increase the selection. In the case of the image on the next page, you will be painting with black to decrease the selected areas of the image. Let the chart below be your guide. Remember that you can change the size of your brush tip by changing the number in the options bar, or by pressing the left and right bracket keys, *[* and *],* on the keyboard.

5. Click on the *Edit in Standard Mode* button to toggle out of *Quick Mask* and into *Standard mode,* and see what the selection looks like. CS1 and CS2 users, click on the *Standard mode* button.

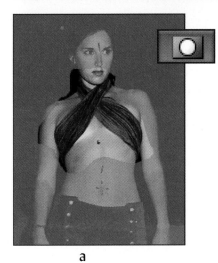
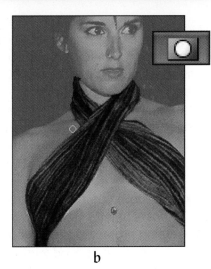

a   b   c

Working with Quick Mask:

a. The initial selection and moving to Quick Mask mode. Red represents the nonselected area.
b. After some painting in Quick Mask, using primarily black to paint away the red mask and decrease the selected area
c. Returning to Standard mode and viewing the selection

6. Move in and out of *Quick Mask* as you work, painting with black or white as necessary to create the selection you want.

Selection

in Mask mode	= clear
in Standard mode	= surrounded by marquee

Nonselection

in Mask mode	= color (e.g., red)
in Standard mode	= nonselected area

Painting Colors in Toolbox

White	erases the mask	and	increases the selection
Black	adds to the mask	and	decreases the selection

To save the selection:

1. In Standard mode, while viewing your active selection, choose the *Select>Save Selection...* menu command (from the Menu Bar). A dialog will open.

2. Name the selection. Note that the file name appears in the dialog. Click **OK**.

Your selection now appears in the *Channels* palette as an alpha channel. White represents the selected area. The selection will be saved with the file, and can be recalled into the same or different files at any point in time.

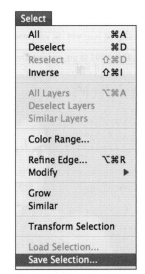

Step 1: Saving the selection using the Select>Save Selection menu.

Step 2: The Save Selection dialog.

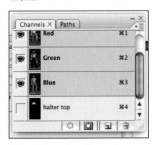

The Channels palette showing the halter top channel

A Few Extra Bits... on Quick Mask

To edit the masking color or opacity, or to change what the color represents (masked area vs. selected area), double-click on the either **mask mode** button to open the *Quick Mask Options* dialog.

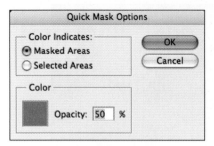

The Quick Mask Options dialog

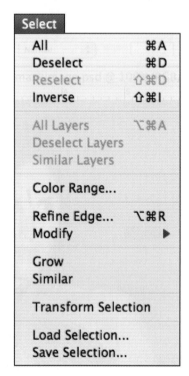

The Select menu and its various menu commands

o   To change the *color*, click on the color box, and when the *Color Picker* opens, choose a new color. This is sometimes necessary, as the masking color is too similar to your artwork and it is difficult to discern what to paint or erase.

o   To change the *opacity* of the mask, simply type in a new number.

o   Choose what the *Color Indicates* (Masked vs. Selected Areas) by clicking on the appropriate button, but bear in mind that the instructions above are for the default mode.

Lastly...

o   Masks are stored as alpha channels and can be viewed in the *Channels* palette. They are grayscale images, with black representing protected areas and white representing the editable areas.

o   Masks may be opaque or semitransparent, which allows for creative effects.

The Select Menu

Various menu commands exist in the ***Select*** menu to assist you in the process of creating a selection. These will be discussed in this chapter and not Chapter 5, the chapter on Photoshop's menus.

All   *Cmd/Ctrl+A*

The *All* command allows you to select everything in the document. Selecting *All* and pressing the *Delete/Backspace* (Mac/Windows) key is a quick way to erase the entire layer you are on.

Deselect   *Cmd/Ctrl+D*

Deselect allows you to turn the current selection off. It is wise to learn the keyboard shortcut for this, *Cmd/Ctrl+D*. Often you may attempt to do something and it doesn't work. Chances are, you still have a selection on the document, and forgot it was there. Thus what you are attempting to do to the entire layer/document isn't working as expected. Try pressing *Cmd/Ctrl+D,* or go to the ***Select*** menu and see if *Deselect* is black (not dimmed), as this will communicate to you that you have a selection.

Reselect   *Shift+Cmd/Ctrl+D*

Reselect is a command used to return to a selection if it was just deselected.

Inverse   *Shift+Cmd/Ctrl+I*

The *Inverse* command is handy to use when it is simpler to select the part of the image you don't want (e.g., due to consistency of color and therefore a simpler task for the **Magic Wand**), and then invert the selection. An example would be the selection of a fashion model who stands against a simple backdrop. Select the background area (using the **Magic Wand** tool and color tolerance), then *Inverse* the selection to have the model selected. See the example on the next page.

Two Questions

When we are working in class and students call me over as they are frustrated that things are not working, I always ask two questions, and I tell my students to make these two questions part of their mantra:
1. Am I on the right layer?
2. Do I have a selection active?

a　　　　　　　　　　　b　　　　　　　　　　　c

Select>Inverse Example:
a. The background is selected using primarily the Magic Wand tool.
b. Then, the selection is inversed using the Select>Inverse menu command.
   A small amount of feathering is turned on in the Refine Edge dialog. A setting of 2.5 was chosen.
c. Finally, the selection is copied to the clipboard and pasted into a blank document.

All Layers　　Opt/Alt+Cmd/Ctrl+A

The *All Layers* command allows Photoshop to create selections on all layers not just the active layer. This does not include the Background.

Deselect Layers

The *Deselect Layers* command allows you to deselect layers that are selected.

Similar Layers

Once you have a particular type of layer active (e.g., text, layer, adjustment layer, etc.), the *Similar Layers* command selects all layers of the same type.

Color Range...

The *Color Range* command was discussed on pages 35–36.

Refine Edge... (CS3 and CS4)　　Opt/Alt+Cmd/Ctrl+R
The *Refine Edge* command opens the *Refine Edge* dialog, which allows you to change several things, all in one place (as opposed to multiple places in prior versions). You may preview the results in several ways, as dictated by your choice of active icon in the lower window.

The Refine Edge dialog

Radius—allows you to control the size of the region around the selection boundary in which edge refinement occurs. The higher the number, the more precise the boundary in images with subtle transitions or fine detail. This works well in areas with hair.

Contrast—allows you to experiment with sharpening the selection's edges. Increasing the percent of contrast removes "noise" at the edge.

a   b

Smooth—softens the edge.

Feather—allows you to soften the edge of a selection prior to cutting it out or adding a filter effect. You can set the width (in pixels) of the feathering you want. This is similar to the feather command in the options bar of the selection shape tools, yet it differs in that you can set the feathering amount *after* you create the selection and you can feather selections that were created with any selection tool. Values can range from 0 to 250.

Contrast Example:
a. This image has no contrast setting.
b. This image uses a Contrast level of 37%.

Contract/Expand—allows you to shrink or enlarge the selection boundary. Values range from 0 to 100%.

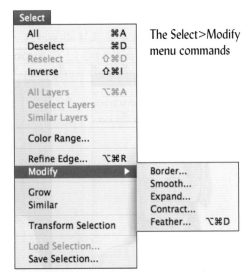

The Select>Modify menu commands

Preview Modes within the Refine Edge dialog

You may choose to preview your selection in different modes. Click on the appropriate icon at the bottom of the dialog. These are, left to right: *Standard, Quick Mask, On Black, On White*, and *Mask*. Pressing *F* on the keyboard will cycle you through the modes, and pressing *X* on the keyboard will allow you to see the original image. Press *X* again to return to the preview mode.

Modify

The *Modify* menu command has several submenu options, each of which serves an interesting purpose. The *Border* option allows you to create a border selection (of a specified number of pixels) around the original selection. Essentially you are framing an existing selection with a new selection. The *Smooth* option allows you to clean up stray pixels left inside or outside a color-based selection. *Expand* and *Contract* allow you to grow and shrink (respectively) your selection by a specified number of pixels. *Feather* softens the edge. These commands are similar to those found in the *Refine Edge* dialog. There are subtle differences, however, so do experiment.

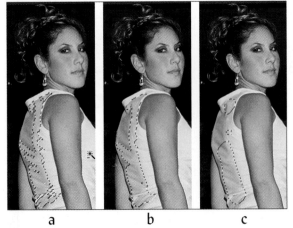

a   b   c

Experimentation: Comparing Refine Edge... and Modify commands
a. A selection is made with the Magic Wand tool using a tolerance of 15.
b. In the Refine Edge... dialog, Smoothness is set to 15.
c. Using Select>Modify>Smooth, the radius is set to 15.
Note how there are slight differences in the selected areas.

Grow

The *Grow* command allows you to expand your selection to include all adjacent pixels falling within the tolerance range specified in the Magic Wand options.

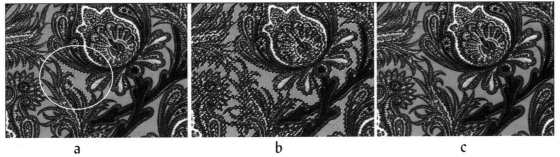

a   b   c

Using the Select>Similar Menu Command

a. A selection is made with the Magic Wand tool, using a tolerance of 25 (see inside white circle).

b. The Select>Select Similar command is chosen, and all pixels of similar color are selected.

c. Using Image>Adjustment>Hue/Saturation, the pink color changes to blue.

Similar

The *Similar* command allows you to select pixels of the same colors as those currently selected, throughout the entire image. This is extremely handy when you want to alter all pixels of the same color (or color range) of an image.

Fashion Use:
- o Selecting all incidents of a selected range of colors to turn them into one color (as would be necessary with textile design and printing)
- o Selecting all incidents of a selected range of colors to delete, such as the background color around a pose
- o Selecting all incidents of a selected range of colors in fabrics to change in the development of new colorways

Transform Selection

The *Transform* command allows you to resize or rotate an existing selection. The familiar bounding box will appear when you choose this command, and you must confirm your transformation when you are through by clicking on the check mark in the options bar. Bear in mind that it is the *selection* you are modifying, not the artwork beneath. This is how this *Transform* command differs from the one in the **Edit** menu (which transforms the image under the selection).

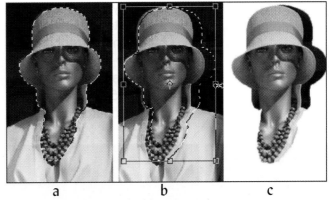

a   b   c

Transform Selection Example:

a. Selection is made of head and hat.

b. The Select>Transform Selection command is used to select the selection only and move it to stretch it to the right. The selection was widened to extend beyond the head and into the background area.

c. The result is a unique drop shadow effect created when the selection was copied and pasted into a new document.

Load Selection and Save Selection

The *Load Selection* and *Save Selection* commands allow you to first save a selection once it has been created and then load it for use at a later time. This is particularly handy if the selection was complicated to create. One needs to build the selection only once. The selection will be saved as a channel. You can load the selection back into the same document or into a different document.

Choose white for your layer. You can now see the outline against a white background.

This function is handy for creating a quick outline of a fashion pose. Exercise 9 in the Fashion Exercises walks you through the process.

Converting a Selection to a Path

If you are comfortable working with vector paths, you can convert a selection to a path and tweak it as a vector object, using traditional vector editing processes.

To convert a selection to a path:

1. Create the selection using whatever selection tools work best for the given artwork.

2. Open the *Paths* palette using the *Window>Paths* menu command.

3. With the selection active, click on the **Make Work Path** button at the bottom of the palette. The selection will be converted into vector paths, with anchor points and direction lines for curves.

4. If you want to edit the path, use the **Pen** and **Selection** tools in the Toolbox. See pages 101–112 for a discussion on how to use these tools.

When you are through editing, you can leave the path and work with it as a vector object, or you may convert the path back to a selection. This procedure allows you to easily tweak paths (if you are familiar with the vector world and tools).

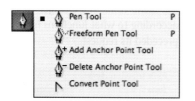
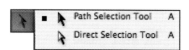
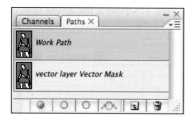

Pen and Selection drawing tools used to create and work with vector objects in Photoshop

The Paths palette with a Work Path layer and a Vector Mask layer

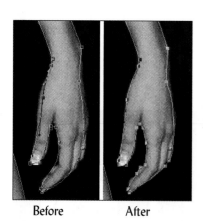

Before　　　After

Closeup of vector paths before and after minor editing with the Pen and Selection tools

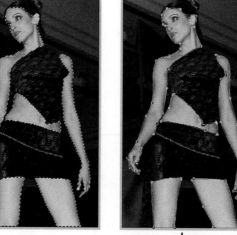

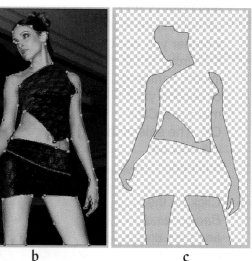

a　　　　　b　　　　　c

Converting a Selection to a Path:
a. The selection is created using the Quick Selection tool.
b. The selection is converted to a path, using the Make Work Path button in the Paths palette. This creates a work path in the Paths palette.
c. Editing is done with the Pen and Path tools, and a solid fill is applied to the vector path.

Layers and the Layers Palette (Panel in CS4)

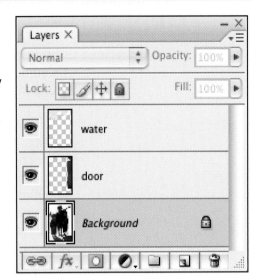

The Layers palette

Layers are one of the most powerful features of Photoshop. They are used to isolate imagery and allow you to work with various elements of your artwork more independently. When a document is created, you begin with a Background (which may be white, black, or transparent, as specified in the *File>New* dialog), which is initially locked. This is not a layer. Using the *Layers* palette you can add layers, each one acting like a sheet of acetate transparency film. Each layer can hold imagery that sits on the see-through layer. You view your design by looking through all the layers (holding imagery) to the background. Typically, you only work on one layer at a time, and it is necessary to click on the layer name to make it the active layer. The name of this active layer appears in the title bar of the document.

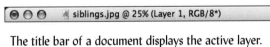

The title bar of a document displays the active layer.

Layers only exist in PSD, TIF, and more recently, Photoshop PDF files, so if you wish to conserve the layers, be careful not to save an image in a mode that does not support them. As you add layers, you increase the size of your document and use more RAM. If you choose *Show>Document Sizes* to be displayed in the *Status Bar* (in the lower-left corner of the document), you will see two numbers if you are using layers. The number to the right shows you the amount of RAM the layered unflattened document is using. The number on the left shows you what size the image would be if flattened (and therefore one layer).

Viewing the document size (in megs) in the Status Bar of your document

Background vs. Layers

Every new file opens with a *Background*. This is not a layer.

The Background

o   The Background is not considered to be a layer. It always sits at the bottom of the stack, under all layers.

o   Several functions of the Background are "locked." You cannot change the blending mode, opacity, fill, or lock mode unless you turn the Background into a layer (thus, these options at the top of the palette will be dimmed).

o   To convert the Background into a layer, either double-click on the layer name (which opens a dialog showing the current layer name as Layer 0) or choose the *Layer>New>Layer from Background* menu command.

o   When you erase on a Background, you erase to the current background color as set in the Toolbox.

A Background versus a layer in the Layers palette. Note that the Background has a lock by default, and layers do not.

Layers

o   Layers sit above the Background.

o   Layers are not locked unless your request them to be, and you can change their blending mode, opacity, fill, or lock mode.

o   To convert the layer into a Background, choose the *Layer>New>Background from Layer* menu command.

o   When you erase on a layer, you erase to transparency.

Overview of the Layers Palette (Panel in CS4)

The following illustrations show you the various components of the *Layers* palette. Many of the functions available through the palette can also be found in the **Layers** menu.

The *Layers* palette shows you all layers, layer types (e.g., text), layer groups, effects, and other information that is important to know as you work on a project. The *Layers* palette menu, accessed through the arrowhead in the upper-right corner of the palette, provides further commands to achieve tasks. A *button task bar* at the bottom of the palette contains icons that allow you to perform functions such as create a new layer, delete a layer, and so on.

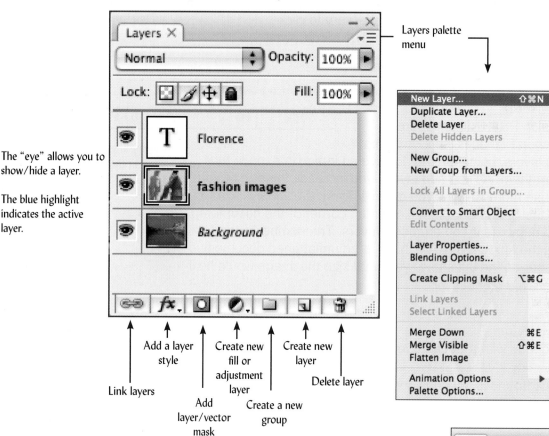

Layers palette menu

The "eye" allows you to show/hide a layer.

The blue highlight indicates the active layer.

Link layers

Add a layer style

Add layer/vector mask

Create new fill or adjustment layer

Create a new group

Create new layer

Delete layer

Blending mode

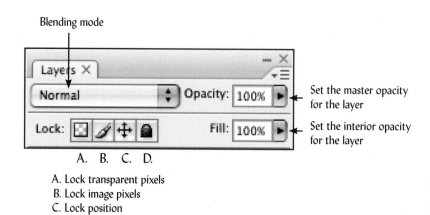

Set the master opacity for the layer

Set the interior opacity for the layer

A. B. C. D.

A. Lock transparent pixels
B. Lock image pixels
C. Lock position
D. Lock all

Example of various types of layers and layer effects, including text, grouped layers, layer effects (fx), and a layer mask

Layer Options

At the top of the *Layers* palette several functions are available when working with a layer. These will be dimmed and unavailable when working on the Background.

Blending Modes—This is a pop-up menu that allows you to choose how the pixels from one layer (or layer group) blend with the pixels on layers beneath them. The default mode is *Normal*, which is no blending. Experiment with the different modes and layers to see the effects, or consult Adobe's Help files for samples and further explanation.

Note: Different types of files (e.g., 32-bit, Lab Color, etc.) have differing Blending modes available to them.

A layer set that contains the fashion sweater and the statue layers

Opacity—This controls how opaque or transparent the layer is. Your choice of opacity affects all pixels, effects, and blending modes you have set on a layer. You may choose from 100 percent opaque (which has no transparency) to 0 percent, which is practically completely transparent. Using *Opacity* allows for creative effects in your work.

Fill—*Fill* is similar to *Opacity*, but different. Here you set the opacity level for the pixels on the layer only. It will not affect any special effects (such as a drop shadow) or blending modes. Again, you can choose from a scale of 0 (transparent) to 100 (opaque).

Locks—You have four different lock options. You can lock *transparent pixels*, *image pixels*, *position of art*, or *lock all*. These can be turned off or on as you work.

Layer Palette Button Bar

Across the bottom of the *Layers* palette is a row of buttons that allow you to quickly perform various functions. *These are:*

Add layer style—By clicking on this button, you will access a pop-up menu, which will allow you to choose a special effect to add to your layer. Once you have selected a style from the list, a dialog opens, allowing you to control the settings of the effect. If you check the *Preview* box, you can see how your image will be affected. The *Drop Shadow* is the most commonly used style. You may use more than one effect at a time. Once a layer effect is created, you will see an **fx** symbol appear in the

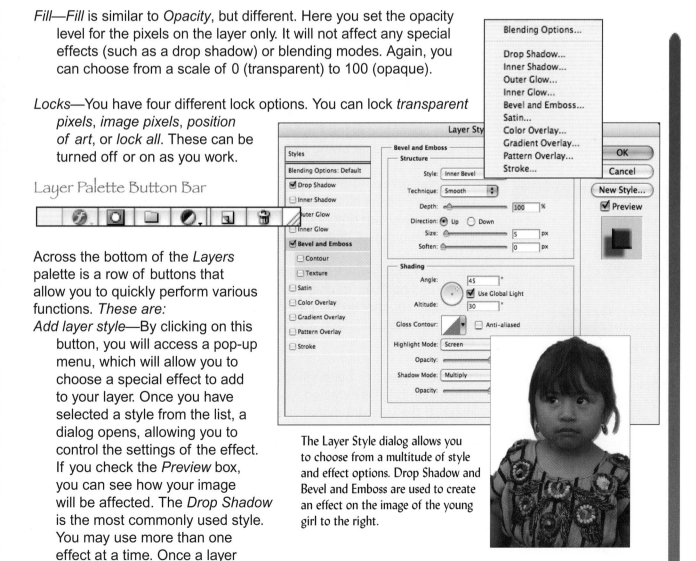

The Layer Style dialog allows you to choose from a multitude of style and effect options. Drop Shadow and Bevel and Emboss are used to create an effect on the image of the young girl to the right.

The Layers palette showing a layer mask and a vector mask, as indicated by the two thumbnails on the layer.

palette on the right side of the layer it is on. The effect itself appears just beneath the layer, indented inwards. If you want to remove an effect, click on the name of the effect and drag it over the **Delete** button in the lower-right corner of the palette.

Add layer/vector mask—This option allows you to create a layer or vector mask. You need to have a layer in order to have access to the button. Masks allow you to hide portions of the current layer so you can see through to the layers below. A detailed discussion of layer and vector masks will follow on pages 57–58.

Create a new fill or adjustment layer—Clicking on this button opens a pop-up menu with options for *fill* layers or *adjustment* layers. Fill layers include *Solid*, *Gradient*, or *Pattern* layers. The advantage of a fill layer is the flexibility one has to change it. *Adjustment* layers allow you to experiment with various adjustment options without permanently changing or modifying the pixels in the image. The changes appear in the adjustment layer only and do not become part of the image until you ask. An adjustment layer affects all layers beneath it. You may turn the view of the adjustment layer on and off by clicking on the eye. *Note*: If you make adjustments using the *Image>Adjustments* menu command, these change the image and cannot be turned on or off (although you can go back in the *History* palette). Thus many people prefer to use adjustment layers over permanent adjustments until they are sure of the results. When you are ready to commit to an adjustment layer, you can merge it down onto the layer you were altering, thus combining it. This is often achieved with the *Merge Visible* command in the *Layers* palette menu, so that you can control which layers are receiving the adjustment.

Fill and adjustment layer options

Create a new group—This button allows you to group layers. You can either *shift+select* all the layers you want to group and click on the button, or you can drag the multiple selected layers over the button to create the group. A dialog will open, prompting you for a group name.

Create a new layer—Click on this to add a layer. It will be given a layer name and number. To change the name, double-click on the name and edit it, or choose the *Layer Properties...* option in the *Layer* palette menu. A dialog will open and you can rename the layer and assign a color to it.

Delete layer—Use this button if you want to delete a layer or mask. If the mask thumbnail is selected, you will be asked if you want to delete the mask. If the layer thumbnail is selected, you will be asked if you want to delete the layer.

The Layers palette menu, accessed by clicking on the arrowhead in the upper-right side of the palette

Layers Palette Menu

You can access the *Layers palette menu* by clicking on the arrowhead to the upper-right side of the *Layers* palette. Several of the menu commands duplicate functions found in the layer options area, the button bar, or the ***Layer*** menu at the top of your document in the Menu Bar. Through the palette menu, you have additional options. *The most important and* *commonly used ones are:*

> *Duplicate Layer*—creates an exact duplicate of the active layer and names it with the same name, plus the word *"copy"*.

> *Delete Hidden Layers*—allows you to quickly delete hidden layers. You will be asked to confirm that this is what you want to do.

> *Layer Properties*—allows you to name and assign a layer color to the layer.

> *Blending Options*—opens the *Layer Style* dialog where *Blending* options are available.

> *Create a Clipping Mask*—allows you to create a clipping mask so that the base layer exposes imagery from the layers above. See page 58 for further instructions.

> *Link Layers*—allows you to link layers so that you do not need to keep selecting the multiple layers you want to perform operations on at the same time. This operation can also be performed using the **Link** button.

> *Merge Down*—causes the active layer to merge down one level with the layer beneath it.

> *Merge Visible*—merges all visible layers into one, and leaves invisible layers alone. The eye icon indicates visible layers.

> *Flatten Image*—merges all layers into one layer. You will be asked if you want to discard hidden layers. If you cancel, the image will not flatten. Flattening an image reduces file size dramatically.

Layer Basics

Now that you have toured the *Layers* palette and its various buttons, menus, and functions, read through the following list of layer basics. Understanding this list will assure you greater productivity. Some of the information is redundant with what has already been discussed, but the mastery of layers is vitally important to productive work, so a little repetition is not a bad thing.

o *Layers sit above the Background* and are *transparent* in areas where there is no image. Thus the image is opaque (unless a transparency level has been set) and the nonimage area is transparent. Transparency is indicated by the familiar gray and white checkerboard pattern.

o Typically, only *one layer is edited at a time.* Click on a layer to make it the active layer. You can select *multiple layers* to work on (pressing the *Shift* key on the keyboard as you select the layers), or you can *link* layers (using the **Link** button on the palette), so that your work affects all active layers.

o Each layer can have its own *opacity* and *blending mode* (with the layers beneath it) to control how the layer behaves with those below it.

When to Flatten?

A good time to flatten an image is when you need to send a file via the Internet, as the file size is dramatically reduced. You may also want to flatten images when you are creating published works, as the file size of the published document will be smaller as well. Always make a backup copy of the file prior to flattening, so you have access to the version of the file with layers.

o You may use the various *Lock settings* to control which part of a layer (image or nonimage area) is locked and thus cannot be changed. These locks appear at the top of the palette.

o When an image is introduced to the document from the *clipboard* (*Edit>Paste*), it appears above the active layer on its *own unique layer.*

o Text is placed on its own unique Type layer.

In summary, layers may be:

o **created** (*New Layer* from the **Layers** menu, the *Layers* palette menu, or click on the **Create a new layer** button at the bottom of the palette).

o **named** by naming the layer in the *New Layer* dialog that opens from steps discussed in the above point, or double-clicking on a layer name to edit the name.

o **deleted** by choosing *Delete* from the palette pop-up menu or by clicking on the **Delete layer** button at the bottom right of the palette.

o **stacked** (this happens naturally, with the most current layer on top).

o **reordered** by clicking and dragging layers to new positions in the *Layers* palette.

o made **visible** or **invisible**. Click on the *eye* icon in the *Edit* well to the left of the layer's thumbnail and name. The eye is a toggle; it toggles on and off.

o made **active** for drawing or editing by clicking on the layer, which then highlights to a light blue color to let you know it is the active layer.

o **duplicated** by choosing the *Duplicate Layer* option from the *Layer* palette menu.

o **unlocked/locked**, therefore made editable or not editable (by clicking on the lock in the palette or setting the lock in the *Layer Properties* dialog).

o **edited and transformed** by clicking on the layer and then using options from the *Edit>Transform* menu in the Menu Bar.

o **converted to a Background** by choosing the *Layer>New>Background from Layer* menu command. *Note*: If a background already exists, you will not see this option.

o **merged** by choosing the various merge options found in the *Layers* palette menu (e.g., *Merge Down, Merge Visible*).

o **flattened** by choosing the *Flatten Image* option found in the *Layers* palette menu. This greatly reduces file size; however, design flexibility is sacrificed.

o **grouped** through the creation of *layer sets*. Click on the **Create a new group** button at the bottom of the *Layers* palette. Type a name for the set in the dialog that opens, then drag the layers you want to group as a set on top of the *Layer Group* folder layer.

o **linked** by *Shift+clicking* on the appropriate layers and clicking on the **Link** button at the bottom of the palette.

o **created in specific modes**, such as *fill* or *adjustment* layers, allowing greater flexibility in the design process. Use the **Create a new fill or adjustment layer** button at the bottom of the palette.

Flattening Layers

Always save a version of your file with layers, then save another version and flatten that version, then resave it. You never know when you will want to get back and edit a file. Many tears have been shed (my own tears included) when layers are lost upon flattening and no backup layered version of the file was saved. Hopefully, you will never have to learn this lesson.

- o given an **effect** or **layer style** that can be applied in a flexible manner and easily removed. Use the **Add a layer style** button.
- o given a l**ayer mask,** added so that you can see through the mask you create to the layers below. Use the **Add layer mask** button at the bottom of the palette.

New layer button

Layer Operations
To create a new layer:
Why? *To allow greater flexibility in working by isolating artwork.*
1. Choose *New Layer* from the *Layers* palette menu and name the layer in the dialog that opens, OR,
Click on the **Create new layer** button at the bottom of the *Layer* palette. You will need to double-click on the layer name to rename it, OR,
Paste an image from the clipboard and note that a new layer is created automatically.

Delete layer button

To delete a layer:
Why? *To clean up your work, remove unnecessary layers.*
1. Click on the layer, and then click on the **Delete layer** button at the bottom of the *Layer* palette, OR,
If the layer is hidden, choose the *Delete Hidden Layers* option from the *Layers* palette menu.

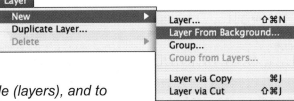

New>Layer From Background menu command

To change the Background to a layer and vice versa:
Why? *To control if the layer has a transparency mode (layers), and to control if the layer sits at the bottom of the stack (background).*
- o To convert the background into a layer, either double-click on the *Background* (which opens a dialog window showing a layer named Layer 0) or choose the *Layer>New>Layer from Background* menu command.
- o To convert a layer into a background, choose the *Layer>New>Background from Layer* menu command (which will exist in the menu once no Background exists in the *Layers* palette).

To reorganize the stacking of layers:
Why? *To control what images lay in front of, and behind other images.*
- o Layers order as follows: top to bottom in the list = front to back in the illustration.
1. Click on a layer to select it, then *hold+drag* the layer to its new position. Observe the little triangle on the left side.

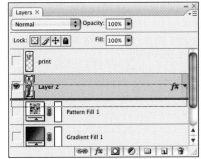

Moving a layer from one position to another

To create a layer group when layers already exist:
Why? *To save time when you want operations to affect multiple layers at the same time. To create the group and put the layers in it, in one operation.*
1. *Shift+click* on all the layers you want to add to the group.
2. Choose the *New Group from Layers...* menu item in the *Layers* palette menu. A dialog will open. Type in the group name, and click **OK**.

Creating a layer group from selected layers using the palette menu

Create a new group button

Four lock modes (left to right):
lock transparent pixels, imagery
pixels, position, or complete layer

Dragging the slider to experiment
with the opacity setting of a layer

Opacity and Fill pop-ups in the
Layers palette. These allow you
to control the transparency of
the entire layer (Opacity) or the
artwork only (Fill).

Merging and flattening options in
the Layers palette menu

To set up a layer group (without adding layers):

Why? *To save time when you want operations to affect multiple layers at the same time. To create the group and add layers to it manually.*

1. Click on the **Create a new group** button at the bottom of the *Layers* palette or choose the *New Group* option from the *Layers* palette menu. If you chose the menu approach, enter a name for the group, and click **OK**.
2. Drag and drop the layers you want in the group over the *Layer Group* icon in the *Layers* palette.

To lock a layer or portion of the layer (imagery vs. background):

Why? *To control what is editable on a given layer.*

1. Click on a layer to select it.
2. Click on the appropriate lock at the top of the *Layers* palette. You can lock transparent pixels, imagery, the position, or the entire layer.

Two images: the left image layer is set to 50% opacity, and the image on the right is 100% opacity.

To set the transparency level of a layer:

Why? *For creative control, so that you can see through one layer to the next.*

1. Click on a layer to select it.
2. Either type a new number in the *Opacity* or *Fill* field, or click on the pop-up arrow and drag the slider to the level of opacity you want. Settings range from 0 (fully transparent) to 100 (opaque).
   o If you use the *Opacity* slider, you are setting opacity for everything on the layer (effects, etc.). If you use the *Fill* slider, you are only setting opacity for the pixels on the artwork, and no effects.

To drag and drop layers from one document to another:

Why? *To speed up the work flow, and avoid extra file saving, editing, and so on.*

1. Open two files. Position them on your screen so you can see both windows.
2. Select a layer in one document, and drag it into the second document. A new layer will appear in the *Layers* palette of the second document.

To merge layers:

Why? *To simplify your layers, and retain a level or organization. There are two approaches:*

1. Hide all layers you don't want to merge.
2. Choose the *Merge Visible* option from the *Layers* palette menu.

OR

1. Click on a single layer that you want to merge with the layer below.
2. Choose the *Merge Down* option from the *Layers* palette menu.

To flatten an image:

Why? *To reduce file size. To merge all layers into one background.*

1. Choose the *Merge Down* option from the *Layers* palette menu.

To link layers:

Why? *To eliminate the need to continually select multiple layers you want to perform operations on.*

1. *Shift+click* on the layers you want to link.
2. Choose the *Link Layers* command in the *Layers* palette menu or click on the **Link** button at the bottom of the palette.
3. Choose the *Select Linked Layers* option in the palette menu when you want to work with linked layers.

The Link Layers option in the Layers palette menu. The Select Linked Layers option beneath it allows you to quickly select all the linked layers so that you may use them or unlink them.

To set the blending mode of a layer:

Why? *For creative control, so that you can control how the current layer blends with the layers below it.*

1. Click on a layer to select it.
2. Choose the blending mode of your choice from the pop-up list that appears in the blend pop-up menu.

a. Original art   b. Pattern on layer above   c. Color Burn   d. Soft Light

The Blending mode pop-up menu and menu options

Blending Modes in Action:

a. A selection is made of the top in the original image.
b. The selection is moved to a new layer and filled with pattern, no blending mode.
c. The Color Burn blending mode is used on the pattern layer.
d. The Soft Light blending mode is used on the pattern layer.
Note how the choice of blending modes allowed for the shadows of the top to continue to show.

Add a layer style button

To add a layer style or effect:

Why? *For creative control: to add dimension.*

1. Click on a layer to make it active.
2. Choose the **Add a layer style** button in the *Layers* palette and choose a style from the pop-up menu.

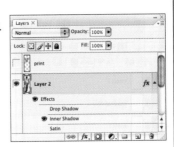

The Layers palette showing layer styles/effects associated with the art to the left

precedence over layers beneath it. The opacity and blending mode attributes are assigned according to those set on the base layer.

4. To release a clipping mask, choose the *Release Clipping Mask* menu option in the *Layers* palette menu.

This completes the discussion of *Selections* and *Layers*.

Quick Start: Self-Portrait à la Warhol

This chapter walks you through a quick overview of the design process in Photoshop. This will be followed by an art lesson that allows you to get your feet wet without a lot of experience. In the first part of the lesson, you will take a digital image of yourself and create multiple copies of it. In the second part of the lesson, you will experiment with a variety of techniques incorporating adjustments, filters, painting, layers, and other techniques. Treat this portion of the exercise as "play" and explore techniques without worrying about the final product. Then, in the last part of the exercise, you will create a self-portrait piece of art simulating the style of well-known American artist, Andy Warhol. Your Photoshop techniques will simulate his approach to art through outlining, painting, overlays, and other creative effects. Read through Chapters 2, 4, and 5 to see the type of creative tools you have at your fingertips. The lesson in this chapter will guide you, but explore the tools as there are more approaches you can take with your art. If you are new to Photoshop, you may need to first practice some of the Basic Exercises before proceeding with this chapter

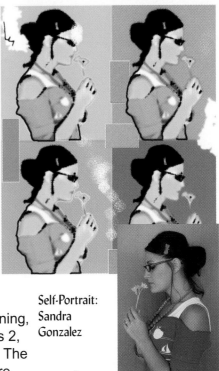

Self-Portrait: Sandra Gonzalez

Research Tip
Prior to starting your own artwork, use the Internet to research Warhol and get a sense for his style.

Self-Portraits of Jose Clark (above) and Alicya Astudillo (below)

The General Process of Design
Creating art in Photoshop typically involves a routine combination of steps. *These are:*

1. Set up the Document or Load a Digital Image
If you are creating new art, this involves choosing the document size, resolution, color mode, and background contents to open a document on the screen. You then need to choose which palettes you want while you work on the project. Many of these are open by default and docked on the right side of the windows. If a palette you want to view is not displayed, open it by clicking on its icon in the docking palette or by using the *Window* menu. If you are going to work with an existing digital image you need to load it using the *File>Open* or *File>Browse* menu command. You will then adjust the color mode if necessary (using the *Image>Mode* menu command).

2. Draw, Edit, and Manipulate the Pixels
At this point, you are ready to paint, draw, or image process the file. There are many operations you can perform, depending on the project and the need. *Typical editing functions involve the following:*
- Adjusting the image using various *Image>Adjustment* commands
- Using filters to alter the image (using various *Filter* menu commands such as Sharpen, Blur, Noise, etc.)
- Touching up the image to correct flaws such as dust, or removing unwanted art using a variety of tools
- Moving and/or transforming a selection of pixels
- Utilizing layers to assist in the design process

Ksenia Galyga

Crystal Ferris

Melissa Luna

Elizabeth Celaya

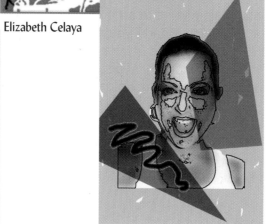

Misty Frank

Thais Pacci Barreto

Student Gallery
Self-Portraits
Mesa College Students

Pontus Wickbom Burevall

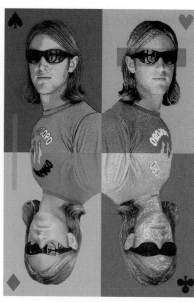

Mary Drobnis

Genevieve Aguilar

Quick Exercise, Part 1: Setting up and Preparing Multiple Copies of Your Photo

Goal

To load an image of a person (yourself or other) and prepare it for experimentation by creating multiple copies of it.

Photoshop Tools and Functions

◆ Fixed Ratio Rectangular Marquee
◆ Resizing an image
◆ Adding canvas
◆ **Selection** tools
◆ Copy and Paste functions
◆ Layers (*Layers* palette) and layer transparency

Quick Overview of the Process

In this exercise you will begin with a photograph of yourself and build a self-portrait using a variety of Photoshop tools and skills.
The steps are as follows:

1. Crop and resize the image to approximately 3.5 x 5 inches in size.
2. Increase the canvas size to have some play room.
3. *Copy* and *Paste* the cropped photo so you have several copies to work with. Each "paste" will paste into a new layer. You can hide the copies until you are ready to use them for each specific function.

This exercise will utilize a photo of me, the author. It was taken in the mirror of a bathroom, with no flash, using fluorescent lighting, and after a week of nonstop writing. (Yes, I still had a sense of humor.) Thank goodness it's à la Warhol! My students and I were fortunate enough to have visited the traveling Warhol art exhibit in San Diego just prior to commencing this exercise. As you can guess, that was the inspiration for this exercise and my students LOVED it.

Step-by-Step

Loading and Prepping Your Image

When you first open Photoshop, it does not open with a document window. Get used to this, as it is how things work. Since you are loading existing artwork (a digital image), you will not create a new document; rather, you will load an existing one.

1. Choose *File>Open* and direct the dialog to the folder where your art is stored. If you are looking for sample photos, portraits exist on the DVD in a folder called **Self-Portraits,** which sits inside the **Exercises** folder. This exercise uses a photo called **Susancamera.jpg**. We are not concerned with proper color corrections, as this is an art project, and it's going to get crazy, so we will not worry about levels, color corrections, and so on. At this point, we want to crop the image and then reduce it to 3.5 x 5 inches. This will be done in two operations.

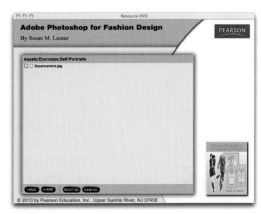

Step 1: Opening the portrait image from the DVD.

2. Select the **Rectangular** marquee tool and then, in the options bar, choose the *Fixed Ratio* style and set the ratio to 3.5 inches wide and 5 inches high. Now, go to the document, and envision where you want to crop it. Start in one corner, and *click+drag* the mouse. You will see that the marquee is forcing itself to a

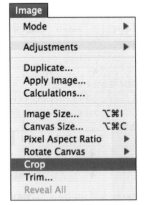

Step 2: The Rectangular Marquee tool (left) and the Fixed Ratio option (right).

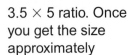

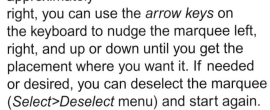

Style: Fixed Ratio   Width: 3.5   Height: 5

3.5 × 5 ratio. Once you get the size approximately right, you can use the *arrow keys* on the keyboard to nudge the marquee left, right, and up or down until you get the placement where you want it. If needed or desired, you can deselect the marquee (*Select>Deselect* menu) and start again.

3. Once you have the marquee where you want it, choose the *Image>Crop* menu. The image will crop to the selected size.

Image

Mode ▶

Adjustments ▶

Duplicate...
Apply Image...
Calculations...

Image Size... ⌥⌘I
Canvas Size... ⌥⌘C
Pixel Aspect Ratio ▶
Rotate Canvas ▶

Crop
Trim...
Reveal All

Step 3: Using the Crop function to removed unwanted parts of the artwork.

Step 2: Creating the selection using a fixed ratio of 3.5 wide and 5 high.

4. Choose the *Image>Image Size* menu and resize the image so that it is approximately 3.5 × 5 inches using a resolution of your choice. The higher the resolution, the larger the file, but the finer the detail. Click **OK**. Note that step 3 simply got the file into the right proportions. Step 4 resizes it to the actual dimensions wanted.

5. Save the file with a new name (e.g., **selfportrait**) and in a Photoshop (.psd) format. Choose the *File>Save As* menu and when the dialog opens, direct it to the folder where you want to save your file, then change the format to Photoshop (which will have a .psd extension, Photoshop's native format). Then, name the file and save it by clicking **Save**.

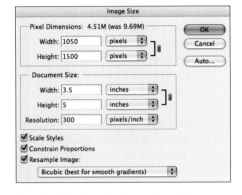

Image Size

Pixel Dimensions: 4.51M (was 9.69M)
Width: 1050 pixels
Height: 1500 pixels

OK
Cancel
Auto...

Document Size:
Width: 3.5 inches
Height: 5 inches
Resolution: 300 pixels/inch

☑ Scale Styles
☑ Constrain Proportions
☑ Resample Image:
Bicubic (best for smooth gradients)

Step 4: Adjusting the image size of the artwork.

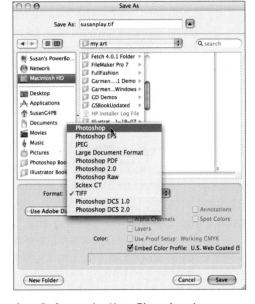

Save As

Save As: susanplay.tif

my art   Q search

Susan's PowerBo...
Network
Macintosh HD
Desktop
Applications
SusanG4PB
Documents
Movies
Music
Pictures
Photoshop Boo
Illustrator Book

Fetch 4.0.1 Folder
FileMaker Pro 7
FullFashion
Carmen....1 Demo
Carmen...Windows
GD Demos
CS8ookUpdated
HP Installer Log File
Illustrat 1-19-07

Photoshop
Photoshop EPS
JPEG
Large Document Format
Photoshop PDF
Photoshop 2.0
Photoshop Raw
Scitex CT
✓ TIFF
Photoshop DCS 1.0
Photoshop DCS 2.0

Format:

Use Adobe Di

☐ Annotations
☐ Spot Colors
☐ Alpha Channels
☐ Layers
Color: ☐ Use Proof Setup: Working CMYK
☑ Embed Color Profile: U.S. Web Coated (S

New Folder   Cancel   Save

Step 5: Saving the file in Photoshop format.

Adding More Canvas and Erasing Background Imagery

We now want to add some canvas to our document so we have some room to make multiple copies for experimentation. We will make the document a full 8 × 10 inches.

1. Ensure that you have the default colors of black and white set as the foreground and background colors in the Toolbox.

2. Choose the *Image>Canvas Size...* menu command. A dialog will open. Type 8 and 10 in the canvas size section, and set the anchor to the upper-left corner. Click **OK**. The original image will now be in the upper-left corner and you will have plenty of space to work and experiment.

Step 1: Setting the foreground and background colors in the Toolbox.

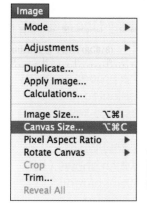

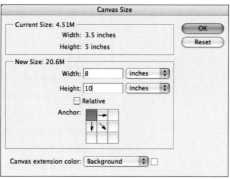

Step 2: Adding more canvas to the artwork using the Image>Canvas Size menu command and the Canvas Size dialog.

At this point, you have the option to remove the background imagery. This is purely an art decision. You may want to consider removing some, but not all, of the background. In this exercise, we will remove the yellow portion of the imagery.

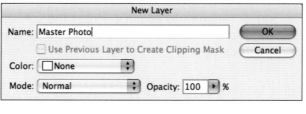

Step 3: Turning the Background into a layer and renaming it Master Photo.

3. Double-click on the *Background* in the *Layers* palette to open a dialog and rename it *Master Photo.* Click **OK**. This will turn the background into a layer and now anything that you erase or delete will become transparent. This will allow more freedom later in that you can overlap your imagery, should you choose. Hopefully, your artwork has a somewhat neutral background.

4. Choose an appropriate *selection* tool such as the **Magic Wand** or the **Quick Selection** tool. Review the discussion of Selection tools if you are not sure which to use. If your background is rather similar in tone/value, both the *Magic Wand* and *Quick Selection* tools will work well. Select the area outside of the face.

- If you are using the **Magic Wand**, set an appropriate tolerance, and press down and hold the *Shift* key to keep adding to the selection of background imagery as needed. Experiment with the tolerance setting in the options bar.

Magic Wand

Quick Selection (CS3 or CS4)

Step 4: Selecting the yellow background of the image and deleting it.

- If you are using the **Quick Selection** tool, work with the Brush tip size, and the

Subtract from and *Add to* options in the options bar to aid the building of your selection.

When you get the proper amount of background selected, press the *Delete/Backspace* key on the keyboard. The deleted area will display as a gray/white checkerboard, which shows you that the area is transparent.

Step 5: Deleting the white background of the image.

Click on the white area with your Magic Wand tool and press the Delete/Backspace key.

The Magic Wand tool

The Move tool

The Rectangular Marquee tool

5. Choose the **Magic Wand** tool, and click on the white background area in the remainder of the document that surrounds your photo on the artwork to select it. Press the *Delete/Backspace* key on the keyboard to delete the white and create a transparent background on the layer.

Creating Multiple Copies of the Portrait

1. Choose the **Move** tool and click on the portrait, then *hold+drag* it to move it away from the edge slightly.

2. Choose the **Rectangular Marquee** tool and frame off the remaining portrait.

3. Choose the *Edit>Copy* menu command to copy the portrait to the clipboard.

4. Choose the *Edit>Paste* menu command to paste in a copy of the portrait. Note that a new layer is created as you do this. The new image will be almost directly on top of the old image, so choose the **Move** tool and move the new portrait to a different place on the document.

5. Repeat pasting in the portrait and positioning it until you have four portraits (and four layers).

6. Name each layer. Click on the *Layer* name, and type in a new name. The layers in the example here were named *Master Photo*, *portrait2*, *portrait3*, and *portrait4*. You will find that if you turn off the eye of a layer, it disappears from view. This will be helpful in upcoming steps.

Step 6: Creating layers.

7. Save the file.

2. Click on the *Master Photo* layer to ensure it is the active layer. By default, all artwork on the layer is selected and ready for alteration; therefore, unless you only want to change part of the portrait, you are ready to experiment.

3. Choose one of the following functions to alter the image and create a high-contrast version:
   o *Image>Adjustments>Brightness/Contrasts*
   o *Image>Adjustments>Posterize*
   o *Image>Adjustments>Threshold*
   o *Filter>Sketch>Torn Edges*
   o *Filter>Sketch>Graphic Pen*
   o *Filter>Sketch>Stamp*

4. When the dialog opens, experiment with sliders and settings to achieve the effect you want. The illustrations that follow show you the settings that were used for each adjustment and the results.

5. Use your *History* palette to back up or undo an experiment. Feel free to explore other adjustments and filters to create a high contrast image. Choose your favorite result to finalize this layer.

Adjustment Layers
If you like, you can use adjustment layers instead of Adjustments from the Image menu. This will allow you to combine adjustments. Review adjustment layers on pages 56–57. CS4 users can use the Adjustment panel to facilitate their work.

Do Experiment
The techniques suggested in this exercise are only a starting point. Do feel free to experiment with other adjustments or filters.

Brightness/Contrast   Posterize   Threshold

Adjustments used to create high-contrast images (with settings used)

Torn Edges   Graphic Pen   Stamp

Sketch filters (using default settings)

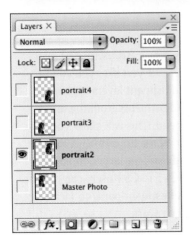

Steps 1–2: Setting up to
experiment on the portrait2 layer.

Inverted Color and Duotone

1. Turn the view of the *Master Portrait* layer off, and turn the view of the *portrait2* layer on. Again, use the eye icon in the *Layers* palette to achieve this.

2. Click on the *portrait2* layer to ensure it is the active layer.

3. Choose the following function to alter the image and create an inverted color version:
   o *Image>Adjustments>Invert*

   Choose the following function to alter the image and create a duotone version:
   o *Filter>Pixelate>Color Halftone*
   o *Filter>Sketch>Halftone Pattern*
   o Experiment with other Photoshop functions on your own

4. When the dialog opens (with all but the Invert function), experiment with sliders and settings to achieve the effect you want.

5. Use your *History* palette to back up or undo an experiment. Feel free to explore other adjustments and filters to create a high-contrast image. Choose your favorite result to finalize this layer.

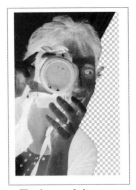

The Invert Adjustment

Filters: Pixelate>Color Half Tone (left) and
Sketch>Halftone Pattern (right)

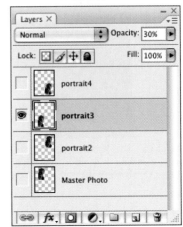

Steps 1–2: Setting up to
experiment on the portrait3 layer.

Outlining and Scribbling

1. Turn the view of the *portrait2* layer off, and turn on the view of the *portrait3* layer. Again, use the eye icon in the *Layers* palette to achieve this.

2. Click on the *portrait3* layer to ensure it is the active layer.

Method 1: Using Filters

1. Choose the following function(s) to alter the image and create an outline-look version:
   o *Filter>Sketch>Photocopy*
   o *Filter>Sketch>Charcoal* combined with *Filter>Brush Strokes>Dark Strokes*

2. Experiment with other Photoshop functions on your own and combine filters as you experiment. The Filter Gallery of Photoshop CS3 or CS4 makes experimentation and combinations of filters very easy. Review the Gallery on page 144.

Filters: Sketch>Photocopy (left) and
Sketch>Charcoal combined with Brush
Strokes>Darken Strokes (right)

Method 2: Outlining by Drawing with a Brush on a Separate Layer
In this technique, you will be drawing your outline on a layer. In order to see the outline more clearly as your work progresses, it is helpful to create and use a *fill layer* of solid white and place this beneath the outline layer so that you can view your outline against a white background. You will need to turn the *fill* layer's view *off* as you draw your outline, and then turn its view *on* when you want to look at the outline. Follow the steps below to draw with a brush on a separate layer.

Step 3: Setting the opacity of the portrait3 layer.

1. Ensure that you are on the current layer. Create a new layer by choosing the **Create a new layer** button at the bottom of the Layers palette. A new layer will appear directly above the *portrait3* layer.

2. Double-click on the *New layer* name to open a dialog and type in a new name for the layer. Use *outline of portrait 3* as your name.

3. Click on the *portrait3* layer and change its opacity to 75%. This will dim the layer so that you can see what you draw on the layer above.

4. In the *Layers* palette choose the **Create new fill or adjustment layer** button at the bottom of the *Layers* palette and select the *solid color* option. When the dialog opens, slide your cursor to the upper-left corner of the palette to choose the color white. Click **OK**. This will create a fill layer of white directly above the *portrait3* layer. Turn its view *off* for now by clicking on the eye icon in the *Layers* palette.

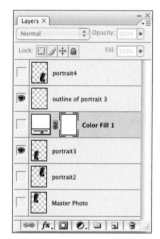

Step 4: Creating a fill layer above the portrait3 layer and beneath the tracing layer.

5. Click on the *outline of portrait3* layer to make it the active layer.

6. Choose the **Brush** tool (or other painting tool). Set a *foreground* color for your drawing by clicking on the foreground icon in the Toolbox and choosing a color from the *Color Picker*, or choose a color from the *Swatches* palette.

7. Draw an outline of the contours of the face, or any other detail you want to accentuate in your portrait. Experiment with the tip of your brush using the *Brush Preset Picker* to choose new tips or alter the diameter and/or hardness of the brush.

8. View the outline by turning the view of the *fill layer* on (click on the eye icon area in the palette well to turn on the eye). This will hide the *portrait3* image layer and place a solid white background beneath the tracing. Continue to work on the tracing, turning the view of the *fill* layer on and off as you work to monitor your progress.

Method 3: Outlining by Creating Selections and Stroking Them
In this method, you create a selection on the portrait layer, then move to a tracing layer and stroke the selection you created on the portrait layer. You can move back and forth between the two layers, creating selections

A sample of tracing with the Brush tool

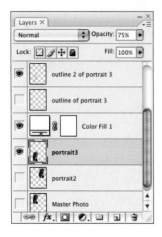

Sample of an outlined image created using the Magic Wand tool on the portrait layer and the Edit>Stroke command on the outline layer

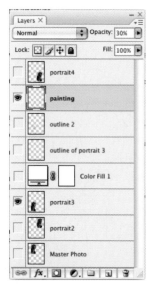

Steps 1–2: Creating a layer for painting and turning on the view of this layer and a portrait layer.

then moving to the new layer to stroke them. Use the *fill adjustment* layer created above to assist you in viewing the stroked selection.

1. Create and name a new layer above the *outline of portrait3* layer. Name the new layer *outline2 of portrait3.*

2. Ensure that the *fill* layer's view is turned off.

3. Click on the *portrait3* layer to make it active.

4. Choose the selection tool of your choice and outline a portion of the face through the creation of a selection. Observe the marching ants.

5. Click on the *outline2 of portrait3* layer to make it active.

6. Choose the *Edit>Stroke* menu command and choose to stroke the selection with a color. Set the stroke width to approximately 2, although you may change this to achieve whatever effect you want. Set the *Location* to *Center.* Click **OK**. The selection will be outlined.

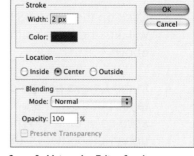

Step 6: Using the Edit>Stroke command to create an outline.

7. Turn on the view of the white *fill* layer to enable you to see the results more clearly.

8. Repeat steps 3 through 6 to continue the outlining process, if you so desire.

Painted Areas with Color

Warhol liked to paint solid or transparent colors in areas of his images. In Photoshop, you can achieve this by painting with a brush, or by creating a selection (geometric or free form) and filling it with color. You may want to do these actions directly on a portrait image, or on a layer you create directly above the image. Painting may be done with full opacity or with partial opacity, which results in a translucent color.

1. Decide which version of the artwork you want to use as your base for painting. The high-contrast images or an outlined version of the artwork are suitable for this section of the exercise. Ensure that the eye is turned on for the layer that has the imagery you want to use.

2. Create a new layer now and name it *painting.* Ensure that this layer is above the outline or portrait layer you want to work with, and that the view of the layer is turned on. Click on this layer to make it the active layer.

Using the Brush Tool

1. Choose the **Brush** tool in the Toolbox.

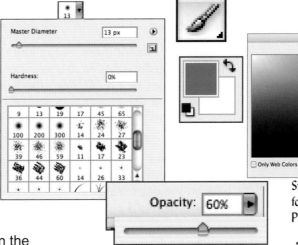

2. Using the *Brush Preset picker*, choose the brush diameter, hardness, and tip of your choice.

3. Click on the *foreground* color in the palette and when the *Color Picker* opens, choose a color to paint with. Click **OK** to close the dialog.

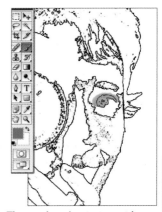

Step 3: Choosing a new foreground color in the Color Picker.

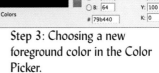

Step 4: Setting the opacity of the Brush tool prior to painting.

4. If you want your painting to be somewhat transparent, change the opacity setting in the options bar.

5. Ensure that you are on the layer you want to paint on. Using your brush, paint over the area of the image you want to add color to.

Creating a Selection and Filling with Color

1. Ensure that you are on the layer you want to paint on (e.g., the *painting* layer).

2. Choose a selection tool of your choice, and select a portion of the portrait you want to fill with color.
   Note: If you are using the **Magnetic Lasso** selection tool, you will need to move to the portrait layer you are tracing with the tool, and then move back to the painting layer before you perform the next step.)

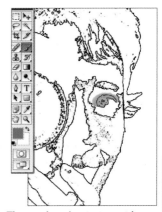

The results of painting with a transparent brush

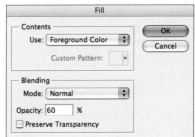

Step 4 (below): Using the Edit>Fill command and setting the opacity to 80%.

3. Click on the foreground color and choose a color to fill with in the *Color* dialog.

4. Choose the *Edit>Fill* menu command. When the dialog opens, ensure that the *Contents* is set to *Foreground* color. Change the opacity if you desire the painting to be somewhat transparent. Click **OK**. Your selection will fill with color.

Creating Colored Shapes

You can use the **Shape** tools and *shape layers* in Photoshop to lay colored areas on your portrait. This is similar to the painting techniques above, except that you have more control over the shape objects in that they can be easily rotated and scaled on their own layer.

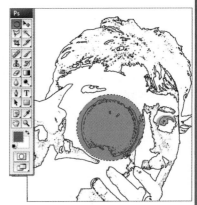

The results of filling a selection with a slightly transparent color

1. Set a new color as the *foreground* color in the Toolbox.

Step 1: Setting a new foreground color.

Step 2: Choosing the Rectangular Shape tool and the Shape Layers option.

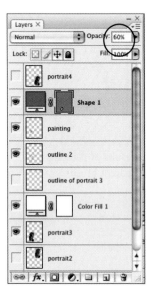

Steps 3 and 4: Creating a shape and thus a shape layer and changing its opacity to 60%.

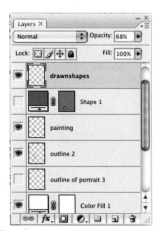

Creating a new layer to draw shapes on, using the Fill Pixels shape mode

Step 2: Choosing the Shape Layers option.

2. Choose the **Rectangular** shape tool in the Toolbox. You can choose to use either the *Shape Layers* or the *Fill Pixels* mode in the options bar. If you choose the *Shape Layers* option, you will be working with vector art. If you choose the *Fill Pixels* option, you will be drawing with raster (pixel) art. The advantage of using Shape Layers is that a separate layer for the shape is created automatically, and shapes can be edited in methods beyond the basic transformations. Read through both options below to decide which one you want to use.

Using Shape Layers Mode

3. With the *Shape Layers* mode selected in the options bar, *click+drag* with the **Rectangle** tool to draw a shape on your image. When you release the mouse, you will see that the new rectangle exists on its own shape layer and it is opaque.

4. You can make the shape object become transparent by changing the *opacity* of the *shape layer* in the *Layers* palette.

5. If you want to edit the shape, you may do so easily by using the **Path Selection** tool (to select the shape so that you may move or transform it) or the **Direct Selection** tool (so that you may reshape the object). Review the use of these tools on pages 105 and 111.

6. You can make the shape object become transparent by changing the *opacity* of the *shape layer* in the *Layers* palette.

The rectangle drawn above was reshaped by using the Direct Selection tool to move one corner point.

The Path Selection (left) and Direct Selection (right) tools

Using Fill Pixels Shape Mode
OR

3. Create a new layer above the portrait artwork you want to work with. Name this layer *drawnshapes*.

4. With the *Fill Pixels* mode selected in the options bar, *click+drag* with the **Rectangle** tool to draw a shape on your image. When you release the mouse, you will see that the new rectangle exists on the new layer you created and it is opaque.

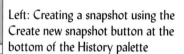

5. You can move the shape using the **Move** tool and you can use transformation functions in the *Edit* menu to alter the shape.

6. You can make the shape object become transparent by changing the *opacity* of the *drawnshapes* layer in the *Layers* palette.

The yellow shape was created using Fill Pixels mode and then was rotated using Edit>Free Transform.

Creating a Backup of a Portrait Image

We are about to embark on using the fourth and last image of your portrait multiples. At this point you may want to do two things to allow flexibility in design in case you want to return to an original photo as you work:

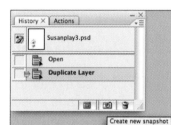

1. Create a *snapshot* of your artwork at this point in time, so you can return to this moment if you need to. To do this, click on the **Create new snapshot** button at the bottom of the *History* palette. The snapshot will appear at the top of the palette. You can rename it if desired.

Left: Creating a snapshot using the Create new snapshot button at the bottom of the History palette

2. Make a *copy* of an untouched original image layer so that you can return to this artwork if you need to. To do this, turn on the view of the *portrait4* layer and make it the active layer. Then choose the *Duplicate Layer* command from the *Layers* palette menu. A dialog will open and you can name the layer if you like. By default, the layer is called *portrait4 Copy.*

Creating a copy of a layer using the Duplicate Layer menu command in the Layers palette menu

Changing the Hue/Saturation of Your Photographic Image

The following steps will walk you through changing the overall colors of a portrait image:

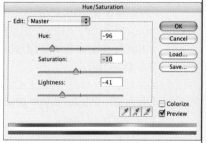

1. Click on the *portrait4* layer in the *Layers* palette to make it the active layer. Turn the *eye* of the duplicate portrait layer off so it is not visible.

2. Choose the *Image>Adjustment>Hue/Saturation* menu command. A dialog will open. Experiment with the various sliders to find a hue you like. Click **OK**. Your image will change.

Using the Hue/Saturation adjustment to alter the color of an image

Using the Paint Bucket to fill in the background area on a layer

Note:

Use Your Snapshot
If you are not happy with the fill, remember that you can use the snapshot you created to return to that point in time. Simply click on the snapshot name in the History palette.

Using a fill layer to create a colored background to an image that sits on a transparent background

Changing the Background of Your Photographic Image

This experiment will teach you how to change the background color that surrounds a portrait. You may use either the **Paint Bucket** tool or a *fill layer*. If you use the **Paint Bucket** tool, the fill will be part of the portrait layer. If you use a *fill* layer, the *fill* will exist on its own layer, which you will arrange to sit behind a portrait layer.

Using the Paint Bucket

1. Click on the portrait layer where you want to add a colored background. Ensure that it is viewable by turning on the *eye* of the layer. Turn off the view of other layers that interfere with the view.

2. Choose the **Paint Bucket** tool.

3. Choose a color to fill with by clicking on the foreground color in the Toolbox and selecting a color from the *Color Picker* dialog. Click **OK**.

4. Move your cursor over to the artwork and position it above the background area. Click with the mouse and the background of the image will fill with color.

Using a Fill Layer

1. Click on the portrait layer where you want to add a colored background. Ensure that it is viewable by turning on the *eye* of the layer. Turn off the view of other layers that interfere with the view.

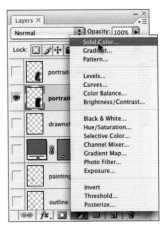

2. In the *Layers* palette choose the **Create new fill or adjustment layer** button at the bottom of the *Layers* palette and select the *solid color* option. When the dialog opens, slide your cursor around the palette to choose a color. Click **OK**. This will create a fill layer of your chosen color directly above the *portrait* layer you selected and it will obscure the view of the portrait.

3. Click on the *fill layer* and drag it beneath the *portrait* layer.

Above: Choosing the Create new fill or adjustment layer button in the Layers palette to create a fill layer. Below: The new colored fill layer is then dragged beneath the portrait layer.

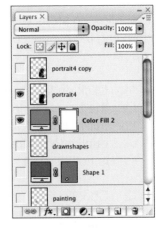

The advantage of a *fill* layer is its independence from other layers and the ease of changing its color. If you want to experiment with other colors, double-click on the color thumbnail on the layer and choose a new color from the *Color Picker* in the dialog that opens. Click **OK**.

4. Save your file.

Combining Layers

At this point, you may choose to move the various layers around, superimposing one portrait or effect on top of another. You will achieve this by dragging layers, turning their view on or off, and using the **Move** tool to reposition the artwork. *Experiment in the following ways:*

o Turn the view of layers on and off as you work.
o Reposition the stacking order of layers by dragging them up or down in the *Layers* palette.
o Reposition artwork on a layer by using the **Move** tool to move the imagery.
o Change opacities of layers.
o Change the color of a color fill layer.

The result of the above may be a viable way to create a final portrait, or you may prefer to start over, building a new portrait that incorporates all the information you learned through experimentation in this part of the exercise.

Example of a final version of a self-portrait

Quick Exercise, Part 3: Building a Self-Portrait à la Warhol (or other artist)

Goal
To utilize the knowledge gained in Part 2 of this chapter to approach the building of a final self-portrait. If you want to use the style of another artist, feel free to do so. Research the artist's style and determine through experimentation (as we did in Part 2) which Photoshop tools work best to achieve the desired results.

Kristin Matoba, in the style of Lichtenstein

Photoshop Tools and Functions
♦ Those already introduced in Parts 1 and 2, or other tools and functions

Quick Overview of the Process
Now, you are ready to build a final portrait utilizing the skills learned to this point.
The steps are as follows:

1. Load, crop, and resize your original photo image to the size you want to work with. If you are planning to create a singular image, try using 5" × 7". If you plan to use multiple images, use a 3-1/2" × 5" size.
2. Set the *Canvas* size up so you have some room to experiment, and create multiple images if you want them. Refer back to Part 1 of this exercise if you need a refresher.
3. Use the knowledge gained in Part 2 of this exercise to create the effects you want with your portrait.
4. Use layers as necessary.
5. Save and print the final image.

Osbaldo Ahumado, in the style of Picasso

New Concepts

o   Translating what you have learned to your own situation, using your own art as the resource and starting point

Source of Imagery

o   Your own personal digital art image

Step-by-Step

Follow the steps introduced in Part 1 utilizing knowledge of techniques created in Part 2 of this exercise.

Melisa Farnsworth

Student Gallery
Self-Portraits
Mesa College Students

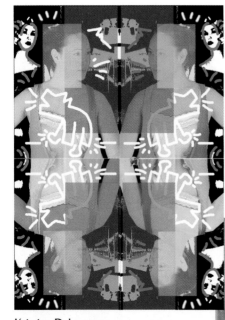

Kristine Delosreyes

Mariel Diaz-Mendoza

June Triolo

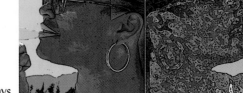

Princess Chanelle Nager

Carmen Solis

Kari Pacheco

Theresa Mays

Painting and Drawing: The Tools

There are two approaches to drawing in Photoshop: painting and drawing. Painting involves tools that are raster-based, and drawing involves vector-based tools. The painting approach is often chosen, as it suits photographs and scanned imagery.

This chapter will walk you through the Toolbox and first discuss the paint-type tools used to create original art, or to retouch existing bitmap art. These tools include the Brush, Pencil, Eraser, Shape tools (in Fill pixels mode), Paint Bucket, and various retouch or image-editing tools. Next will be a discussion of drawing with object-based functions and tools such as the Pen, Path Selection, Direct Selection, Type, and Shape tools. To complete the tour of the Toolbox, a few miscellaneous tools are discussed at the end of the chapter.

Paint and Paint-Type Tools in the Toolbox

This book equates *painting* in Photoshop with working in raster or bit-mapped mode. Therefore, you create art by dealing with individual pixels that are drawn, picked up, or edited, dot by dot. You can move around the document and work in any area without thought of completing an object, so in many ways this is a very free approach to design. The discussion that follows will cover the painting tools used to generate original art followed by the retouching tools used to edit and manipulate raster or pixel-based design.

The following are features of Paint-type tools:
- o Pixels are laid down to create the art.
- o Typically, anti-aliasing (the averaging of edge pixels) occurs, but this can be turned off with some tools.
- o You are free to move around the image, drawing and editing freely without worrying about finishing one section before you start another.
- o Painting is typically done with the foreground color in the Toolbox.
- o Erasing varies according to whether you are working on the background or a layer. One erases to the *background* color if you are on the Background and to transparency if you are on a layer.
- o Each tool has options you may utilize to facilitate the painting process. These are found in the options bar.
- o Tools can be customized with your own choice of settings and saved as a *Tool Preset* in the options bar.
- o Brushes can be customized (by setting the diameter and hardness of your tool's tip) and saved for use in the *Brush Preset Picker*.

The Brush Tool and Pencil Tool   (B)

The **Brush** tool has a soft edge, while the **Pencil** tool has a hard edge. The soft edge of the Brush tool results because anti-aliasing occurs. Painting with these tools is done with the *foreground* color as set in the Toolbox.

The Tool Preset Picker: This allows you to access brushes already preset with given combinations of settings. You may also create new presets or manage existing ones. To create a Tool Preset, first choose all the settings you want for the tool, then save them using the Tool Preset menu.

The Brush (left) and Pencil (right) tools

To use the Brush or Pencil:

1. Choose either the **Brush** or **Pencil** tool.

2. Choose the color you want as your painting color and set it as the *foreground* color in the Toolbox.

3. Select and set the options in the options bar for the tool.

4. *Click+drag* your cursor on the image where you want to paint and release the mouse when you are done with your stroke.

o If you want to draw a *straight line*, press and hold the *Shift* key on the keyboard as you draw.

o If you want to create an *airbrush* effect, click on the airbrush button (the picture of the airbrush) in the options bar, which will cause your painting to work in an airbrush mode.

Brush and Pencil Tool Options

The Brush and Pencil options bar allows you to control the following:

The Brush Preset Picker

This allows you to easily control the diameter and hardness of your current brush tip. You may also choose to use built-in brush tips. If you click and hold on a brush tip you will see its name appear.

To create a custom Brush Preset:

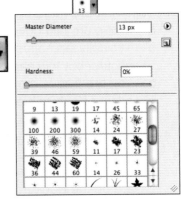

The Brush Preset Picker

1. Choose the **Brush** or **Pencil** tool.

2. Click in the *Brush Preset picker.* A window will open. Customize your settings for the tool in the options bar (diameter and hardness). Further editing of the brush tip can be done using the *Brushes* palette.

3. Either click on the **Create a new preset from this brush** icon in the pop-up, or click on the arrowhead to open the menu and choose *New Brush Preset...* option (both in the upper-right corner of the window). Once the option has been chosen, a dialog opens.

4. Type in a name for your preset and click **OK**.

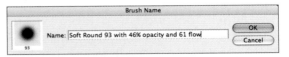

Step 4: Naming a Brush Preset as the last step of creating a Brush preset.

This Brush or Pencil Preset will now appear in the *Brush Preset Picker* window.

Tool Preset menu button

Create a new preset from this brush icon.

The Brush pop-up menu that opens (below)

Mode

Your choice of blending mode dictates how the color you are painting with blends with the artwork beneath it (i.e., with the layers below the layer you are drawing on).

Opacity

This setting controls the level of opaqueness or transparency you are using. As long as you continue to hold the mouse as you paint, you will never exceed the level of transparency set. However, if you *click+release* and then paint some more, you can overlay one paint stroke on top of another and your image will not be as transparent as you might have wanted. Learning how to paint with opacity allows you creative outlet.

Opacity Example Above:
Top stroke: Opacity of 100%
Center stroke: Opacity of 50%
Lower stroke: Opacity of 20%

Flow (Brush tool only)

Flow controls the flow of paint from the tip of the brush. Thus, if you set this option to 50% paint will flow out at a quicker rate than if it were set at 20%.

Airbrush (Brush tool only)

When this button is clicked the airbrush option turns on. This allows you to paint as if you had an airbrush, so that the longer you let your mouse sit in one spot as you pass back and forth, the more paint you lay in that area. Settings for brush tip, opacity, and flow all affect how the airbrush works.

Airbrush example of painting, The cursor was held longer in the darker lower area, resulting in more paint being laid down.

Flow Example Above:
Top stroke: Flow of 100%
Center stroke: Flow of 20%, one stroke
Lower stroke: Flow of 20%, three strokes back and forth prior to lifting the mouse

Auto Erase (Pencil tool only)

When this option is turned on and you draw with the **Pencil** tool, you will be erasing with the current *background* color in the Toolbox (as opposed to the *foreground* color).

The Color Replacement Tool

This tool allows you to *paint* over a targeted color or color range (using Tolerance settings) with a new replacement color.

To use the tool:

1. Choose the **Color Replacement** tool.

2. Adjust the various settings as necessary in the options bar (discussed below).

3. Set the *foreground* color in the Toolbox to the color you want to use to replace targeted colors.

4. Click on the color you want to replace in the image.

5. Drag in the image with the tool to paint your new color over the original color. You may need to test various settings to get the desired results.

Color Replacement Example: Blue is being used to paint over the yellow yarn in this knit example. The tolerance was set to 60, Limits were contiguous, and Sampling was continuous.

Fashion Use: o   Selecting colors in fabrics to change for new
                      colorways (textile design and printing)
                  o   Quick color change for a garment for design
                      and merchandising

Color Replacement Tool Options

*The Color Replacement Tool options bar allows you to control the
following:*

The Brush Preset Picker
This allows you to easily control the diameter and hardness of your
current brush tip as well as choose between preset brushes.

Mode
You can choose between four modes: Hue, Saturation, Color, and
Luminosity. Typically the Color option is used.

Sampling
There are three sampling modes. Your choice dictates how Photoshop
determines the sampled color(s) for replacement. *Continuous* samples
colors continuously as you drag the cursor, *Once* only samples the first
color you click on, *Background Swatch* allows you to replace only areas
on the image that are the same color as the *background* color in the
Toolbox.

Limits
This dictates the outer limit or how far the painting extends as you paint
with the **Color Replacement** tool. *Discontiguous* replaces the sampled
colors under the cursor as you paint, wherever they occur in the image.
Contiguous replaces colors that are contiguous with the color immediately

under the pointer. *Find Edges* allows the painting
of the new color to be replaced in connected areas
that contain the sampled color. The sharpness of the
edges is preserved.

Tolerance
As with the **Magic Wand** tool, *Tolerance* allows
you to broaden the range of colors you choose, by
expanding the targeted color to include a greater
number of shades of the color to either side of the
exact hue you click on. For example, if tolerance is
set to 30 and you sample a color, you are actually
including 60 additional shades in your sample, 30 to
each side of the original. The ability to use tolerance
facilitates work in Photoshop as it is a great way to
deal with subtle shading and anti-aliasing.

Experimenting with Tolerance:
Left: Tolerance is set to 60.   Right: Tolerance is set to 30.

Anti-Aliasing
When this is checked you are able to paint with a smoother edge.

The History Brush and Art History Brush Tools

Both of these tools work in conjunction with the *History* palette. In essence, you select a history state or a snapshot as a reference point, and when you paint with the tools you are painting back to that history state/snapshot as you paint, The difference between the **History Brush** and the **Art History Brush** is that the latter allows you to set various additional options (beyond the history state itself) and thus painting can be more artistic.

To use either tool:

1. Click in the left column of a state or snapshot in the *History* palette. Note how an icon appears in the palette beside the state/snapshot. This sets the state as that to be used for the History or Art History brush.

2. Choose the **History Brush** or the **Art History Brush** in the Toolbox.

3. Set the brush tip size and parameters in the options bar. You may also choose a brush preset. If you chose the *Art History Brush*, choose any additional settings (such as *Style*, *Area,* and *Tolerance*).

4. Paint with brush strokes on your artwork in the area where you want to retrieve some of the history.

Image Size and History Brushes

The image size of the history state/snapshot needs to be the same size as the artwork you are altering.

Setting the history state/snapshot to be used with the history brushes

a   b   c   d

Working with the history brushes:

a. The original art; the Duomo in Florence, Italy
b. After removing the buildings to the left
c. Using the History Brush to commence painting back the building with a 50% transparency
d. Using the Art History Brush to commence painting back the building in an artistic manner. The following settings were used: 81% opacity, Tight Short Style, Area of 50 pixels, and Tolerance of 50

History Brush and Art History Brush Tool Options

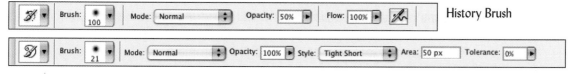

History Brush

Art History Brush

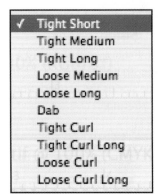

The Style options for the Art History Brush

Both brushes allow you to choose a Brush tip or Brush Presets, and you can select a blending *Mode* and *Opacity* setting. In addition, the History Brush allows you to set the *Flow* and choose to use the *Airbrush* option. These were discussed on page 81 in the Brush discussion. The Art History Brush has several new options. *These are:*

Style

This controls the shape of a paint stroke. Options are shown in the illustration to the left.

Area

Setting the area dictates how large the area covered by a paint stroke will be.

Tolerance

Setting *Tolerance* for the Art History Brush limits the areas in which you can paint. A high tolerance limits your painting to only areas that differ greatly from the color in the history state/snapshot. Lower (or no) tolerance settings let you paint in more areas of the image.

The Eraser Tools   *(E)*

This group of tools includes the Eraser, Background Eraser, and Magic Eraser tools. The general purpose of this tool group is to erase drawn art.

Eraser Tool

This tool allows you to erase or change colored pixels to either the background color or to transparent pixels, If you are working on the *background* or on a *layer with locked transparent pixels*, you will erase to the current background color in the palette, If you are working on a *layer* that does not have transparent pixels locked, you will erase to transparency.

The **Eraser** tool may be used to erase pixels to a *prior state selected in the History palette.* To use this function, you must set a source of history in the palette by clicking on the left column of the point of history in the *History* palette. A *history brush* icon will appear in the check box, and a point in history is established. Choose the Eraser tool and check the *Erase to History* box in the options bar. Now when you use the Eraser tool to erase, as you rub over an area, it changes back to the state it was in when you set the history point.

Background Eraser

The **Background Eraser** allows you to erase pixels on a layer to transparency. The brush has what is known as a *hot spot*, a point in the center of the brush that is used to define the color to delete throughout the area of the brush as it is stamped or dragged around the artwork. Depending on your settings, some pixels will be completely erased (to full transparency) and others will become somewhat transparent. A process of color extraction occurs at the edges of the brush to smooth out the erased areas as they meet the rest of the artwork. As with the **Color Replacement** tool, you can control the sampling and tolerance options.

To use the Background Eraser:
1. Select the layer you want to work on.

2. Choose the tool.

3. Customize your settings in the options bar, if desired.

4. *Click+drag* the cursor on the document to erase or remove pixels from an image.

Magic Eraser

The **Magic Eraser** is somewhat a combination of the Eraser and Magic Wand tools, You have the option to set tolerances, just as you do with the Magic Wand. When you use this tool, it automatically erases or changes all pixels similar in color to those you touch when you begin to erase. Thus, as you touch a green area on the image, all greens similar (and within the tolerance range) to the one you touched will erase. The pixels touched on the background and layers that have transparent pixels locked will erase to the background color in the Toolbox; erasing on layers will erase to transparency.

To use the Magic Eraser:
1. Choose the tool.

2. Set the Brush options in the options bar.

3. Choose your settings in the options bar.

4. Drag on the screen to erase or remove pixels from an image.

     Fashion Use: o   This is a quick way to change multiple colors to the background color set in the palette. This may be needed when reducing colors in print fabrics.

Eraser Tool Options

Many of the settings in the options bar for the Eraser tools are identical to those already discussed with other tools. Thus, for the sake of brevity, only new and unique functions will be covered here.

Eraser Tool options

Modes

There are three new Modes to explore. *Brush* allows you to erase with a soft edge while *Pencil* erases to a hard edge. *Block* is a fixed-size, hard-edged mode with no options for opacity or flow.

Erase to History

When this is checked, you can use a History state or snapshot (set in the *History* palette) and erase to that artwork.

Background Eraser options

> **Quick Erase**
> One way to quickly erase areas on your document is to use the Marquee tool to select an area of the screen or choose the Select>All menu command to select the entire document and then press the Delete/Backspace key on the keyboard, This will erase the selected area to the current background color in your Toolbox.

The options for the **Background Eraser** tool are identical to those for the **Color Replacement** tool (see page 81 for a description). The only new addition is the option to *Protect Background Color*, which allows you to set a color in the palette as your background color; this color will be protected as you erase.

Magic Eraser options

The Magic Eraser options are similar to those for the Magic Wand (pages 33–34).

Alternate Quick Erasing Tip:
Paint to Erase

1. Choose a color as your *foreground* color and white as the *background* color in the Toolbox.
2. Choose a painting tool such as the **Brush** or **Pencil**.
3. Now, when you draw on a white canvas or the background, you can press *X* on the keyboard to exchange the foreground and background colors in the palette, thus moving between the painting color and an erasing white. This allows you to draw and erase without having to switch tools.

   Note: This technique also works when you are touching up images and working in areas where there are primarily two colors you are working between. Set one color as the foreground and the other as the background and alternate.

The Shape Tools   (U)

The **Line** and **Shape** tools can be used to paint in a pixel-based manner (as opposed to drawing with objects). When you choose any of these tools, ensure you have chosen the *Fill pixels* mode in the options bar. If

you do not, you will be drawing with paths (creating shape or line objects) and these cannot be edited in the same manner as painted pixels.

The **Line** tool in particular will become one of your most-used tools when drawing in a pixel-based mode. Other Shape tools include shapes such as the **Rectangle**, **Rounded Rectangle**, **Ellipse**, **Polygon,** and **Custom Shapes**.

The following is true of the Shape tools and their options:

o A line or shape is drawn with the set *foreground* color in the Toolbox.
o The *opacity* may be changed allowing you to draw lines or shapes that are more transparent.
o If the *anti-alias* option is turned on, the lines or edges of a shape will be softened through the use of pixels that average the line color with the background color it is being drawn on.
o You can *constrain* a line to be perfectly straight (horizontally,

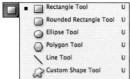

The Shape tools in the Toolbox. Click and hold to view the pop-up and select the tool of your choice.

Fill pixels mode for painting

vertically, or diagonally) by holding the *Shift* key down as you draw. In the same manner, press and hold the *Shift* key to draw a square (with the rectangle shape) or a perfect circle (with the ellipse shape). If you want a hollow circle or rectangle, you will need to use a **Rectangular Marquee** selection tool to create a shaped selection and then stroke it with color (using the *Edit>Stroke* menu command.

o   Each tool has its own set of options found in the *Geometry options* pop-up menu in the options bar. Click on the down arrow to the right of the tool strip to access the pop-up options.

o   The **Custom Shape** tool allows you to choose a shape from the Shape pop-up in the options bar and draw with that shape. Choose the shape, then *click+hold+drag* your mouse on the screen to create and size the desired shape. You can choose from various shape libraries found in the Shapes menu of the shape library in the options bar.

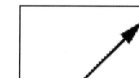

o   You may specify the *weight* of a line. You can do this by simply typing a number followed by in (inches), px (pixels), or cm (centimeters) in the options bar.

o   Arrowheads can be added to a line by clicking on the *Geometry* options in the options bar and choosing your arrowheads options.

Adding an arrowhead at the end of the Line using the Geometry options pop-up

o   You can draw curved lines by creating a series of straight lines in your drawing. This works well for the neckline and armhole areas of garments.

To use a line or shape tool:

1.   Choose the tool and set the color you want to draw with as the foreground color in the Toolbox.

2.   In the options bar, click on the *Fill pixels* mode. Choose the settings you want. Set the *Mode*, *Opacity,* and determine if you want *Anti-alias* on or off. If you are drawing a line, set the line *Weight.*

3.   *Click+hold* on your document to set the starting point of the line. Drag to the position where you want to end the line or shape. Release the mouse. If you *press+hold* the *Shift* key as you draw you will constrain the shape.

Line and Shape Tools Options

The settings for the various line and shape tools are typically similar. All have options for blending *Mode*, *Opacity,* and *Anti-alias*. The *Geometry Options* pop-up differs slightly between tools, so do check this. Some have options that are unique to the tool. For example, the **Line** tool has a setting for *Weight*. The **Custom Shape** tool has a *Custom Shape picker* pop-up for choosing the specific custom shape.

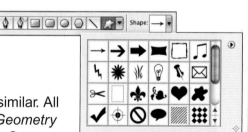

Custom Shape picker pop-up for the Custom Shape tool

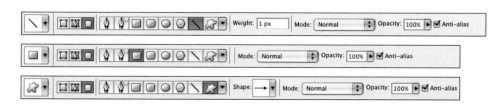

Line options

Rectangle options

Custom Shape options

The Paint Bucket　　　(G)

The **Paint Bucket** tool fills adjacent pixels that are similar in color. *Tolerance* settings are used to assist in defining what range of color should be filled. The Paint Bucket tool icon in the Toolbox looks like a paint can being tipped over. The "hot spot" or active spot of the cursor (which must be placed carefully over the pixels you want to fill when you are working in small areas) is the lower tip of the paint being poured out of the can.

To use the Paint Bucket tool:

1. Choose the tool in the Toolbox and set the color you want to paint with as the *foreground* color in the Toolbox. If you want to fill with pattern, choose the *Pattern* option and select a pattern (in the options bar).

2. In the options bar, set the *Mode, Opacity,* and *Tolerance* settings. Determine if you want *Anti-alias, Contiguous,* or *All Layers* options on or off.

3. Place your cursor on the screen, carefully positioning the hot spot where you want it. When you click, Photoshop looks at the pixel under the hot spot of the tool to determine the targeted color and then looks at your various tolerance and other settings to determine how far to spread the color in the image.

Note: Deselect
If a selection is active on the document you must deselect it if you are trying to use the Paint Bucket tool in another area of the image.

a　　　　　　　b　　　　　　　c　　　　　　　d

Working with the Paint Bucket fills:
a. The original art: a knit ensemble
b. Foreground Fill: Left side is filled with 100% Opacity, Right size is filled with 50% opacity, Tolerance = 40, Blending mode = normal.
c. Foreground Fill: Both sides use 50% Opacity and Tolerance of 40. Left side uses Color Burn blending mode and right side uses Hue blending mode.
d. Pattern Fill: Both sides use 50% Opacity and Tolerance of 40. Left side uses Normal blending mode and right side uses Color Burn mode.
The fill color for b and c is shown as it was in the foreground of the palette.

In *Normal* mode, Photoshop will fill with a consistent set of pixels, maintaining the same opacity setting throughout the area. If you choose some of the other blending modes, you will retain some of the shadowing. Work with selections and image adjustments to experiment with your art.

Paint Bucket Tool Options

The settings for the Paint Bucket tool are common settings shared by numerous tools, but particularly, the Magic Wand tool. *A quick review follows:*

Fill Type
This allows you to choose between the *foreground* color in the toolbox or a pattern. If you choose to use a *Pattern* fill, you can choose the pattern from the library of patterns accessed through the pattern pop-up list.

Mode
Mode dictates how the fill on the current layer interacts or blends with the layers beneath it.

Opacity
This setting allows you to control how opaque or transparent your fill will be in the image.

Tolerance
Tolerance allows the Paint Bucket to fill pixels with the color you click on with the tool and a specified number of shades to either side of that color (according to the number you set in the options bar).

Anti-alias
If you choose to use the anti-alias mode, your fill will create blending pixels at the edge of the fill, thus creating a smoother transition between the fill and the colors it touches at its edges.

Contiguous
The contiguous option allows you to control the fill so that it only extends until it hits a colored boundary. If contiguous is not checked your fill will extend to all colors on the image within the specified tolerance range of the color you click on. If you are filling solid color into a top outlined with black, using contiguous will allow the color to contain itself within the boundary of the garment.

The Gradient Tool   (G)
The **Gradient** tool allows you to create a color spread between two or more colors. You begin by defining the colors to be included in the spread and then dragging the Gradient cursor on the screen. The beginning and end points of the dragging operation set the angle and distance of the color spread. If a selection is active on the document, the gradient will fill only that area; otherwise it will cover the entire document.

Note:
Gradients
Gradients do not work with bitmap or index color images.

Note: **Color Modes**
Since a color gradient is used on a grayscale image, the color mode must be either RGB or CMYK.

To use the Gradient tool:
1. Choose the **Gradient** tool.

2. Choose a Gradient preset in the options bar or set the *foreground* and *background* colors in the Toolbox to the two colors you want to work with. Choose other settings in the options bar such as *Gradient Direction, Mode, Opacity, Dither,* and so on.

3. *Click+drag+release* your gradient cursor on the screen. The starting and end points of your cursor (i.e., the click and release points) will define the direction of the gradient. You do not need to start at one end or corner of the document.

a
Original art

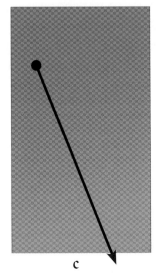

b

c

d

The foreground and background colors used in the gradient

Working with the Gradient Fill:
a. The original art; a concrete statue, Burgundy, France
b. Cropped image, converted to grayscale and then back to CMYK, with increased contrast
c. The gradient between a blue-gray and an orange, with 70% transparency. This was placed on its own layer. The "drag" occurred where the arrow illustrates, between the dot and the arrowhead.
d. The gradient as it sits over the background layer

Gradient Tool Options

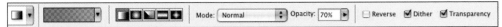

The following are available options for the Gradient tool:

Gradient Picker
This pop-up allows you to choose a preset gradient or to edit or build a new gradient.

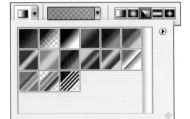

The Gradient Picker, opened by clicking on the down arrow. Through the Picker's menu you can access additional gradient libraries.

Gradient Direction
Click on the appropriate button to choose between *Linear, Radial, Angle, Reflected,* and *Diamond* gradients.

Mode
Mode dictates how the fill on the current layer interacts or blends with the layers beneath it.

Opacity

This setting allows you to control how opaque or transparent your fill will be in the image.

Reverse

This check box allows you to reverse the gradient from *background* to *foreground* colors instead of *foreground* to *background* colors.

Dither

When *Dither* is checked, a smoother gradient results.

Transparency

When this is checked you can use a transparency mask for the gradient (which allows you to have varying transparencies within the gradient). See below and Adobe's Help for instructions.

Gradient Editor

If you want to build more advanced gradients, you will need to learn about the **Gradient Editor**. This is accessed by clicking inside the gradient spread bar in the options bar. When you do this the *Gradient Editor* dialog window will open.

At the top of the window you see an assortment of *presets* (including any new gradient you have just built using the foreground/ background colors in the palette as discussed above). You may click on any of these to edit and its color spread will appear in the horizontal bar.

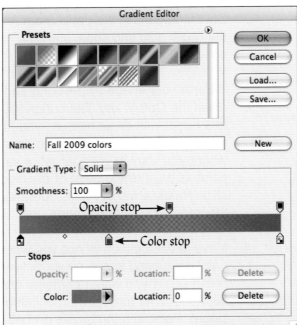

The Gradient Editor (above) allows you to edit and create new gradients. The menu (right) allows you to access gradient libraries.

There are two types of stops in the dialog: *color stops* (located beneath the color spread) and *opacity stops* (located above the color spread). You can add new colors to the gradient simply by clicking underneath the bar at the position you want to add the stop. Then, you can choose to use the *foreground*, *background,* or a *user-defined* color. Simply clicking in the *color stop* (once a color appears there) will open the *Color Picker.* An opacity stop can be added by clicking above the color strip where you want the stop to appear. Then, with the stop active, you can control its opacity. Thus it is possible to have varying opacities in a gradient that go from, as an example, opaque to transparent and back to opaque.

The different gradient fill directions, as labeled to the left of each illustration. An opacity of 60% was used for all.

Other controls in the Gradient Editor include *Gradient Type* and *Smoothness*. You may name the gradient and include it in the *Editor* by typing in a name and clicking on **New**. In addition, click on the arrowhead in the Editor window to open the menu, which displays the various gradient presets and libraries that already exist.

The Clone Stamp Tool　　　(G)

This tool allows you to paint or touch up areas of an image by taking sampled pixels and painting them over other pixels in the artwork. It differs from the **Healing Brushes** and **Patch** tools in that no blending occurs between the sampled pixels and the artwork you are stamping on; thus this tool falls into both the *Painting* and *Retouch* realms.
To use the tool:

1. Select the tool.

2. Set the options in the options bar (e.g., the brush size and edge, blending mode, opacity, flow, align, etc.).

3. Sample your image by pressing and holding down the *Opt/Alt* key. The cursor will change to a target with cross hairs as you hold down the keys. Move to a location on your image where you want to set a target or sample point as the starting point of the clone and click. Release the key. This operation will put the target point into memory.

4. Move to the location where you want to paint the cloned image pixels. Adjust the brush size if you want (a smaller brush tip allows for finer tuning when painting in the clone). Paint with the brush, and observe that as you do, you can view a reference point that shows you what part of the original you are painting. If aligned was checked in the options bar, you can *click+release* as you paint, which allows you to work in short spurts and makes an "undo" a quick fix for the last little bit you painted (but don't forget that you have a *History* palette). Understand that when you paint, you can keep extending the artwork far beyond the original target point.

The original image is above. Below, using the Clone Stamp tool, two new twirls are added to the garment.

Above: Observing the reference point as you draw the clone can assist in knowing where to paint.

Experiment
Many of these tools won't make great sense until you actually put them to work, so experiment.

Cloning Process: (right)
a. Preparing to set the target point by positioning the cursor
b. Pressing the Opt/Alt key and clicking to set the target
c. Painting the clone in a new location

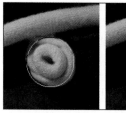

a　　　　　b　　　　　c

Clone Brush Tool Options

The following are available options for the Clone Stamp tool:
The **Brush Preset Picker**, **Mode**, **Opacity**, **Flow**, and **Airbrush** all behave as discussed on pages 80–81 with the **Brush** tool.

Align
The **Align** check box significantly affects your painting of the clone. When it is checked, you may click and release your mouse as you are drawing the clone and you will always be able to continue out from the source point. If it is unchecked, each time you click with the mouse, you start a new clone.

Sample
This allows you to control where you are sampling from: the current layer, current and below, or all layers.

When the Align checkbox is left unchecked, you start a new clone each time you release the mouse while painting. This allows you to stamp multiple images in a cluster.

Fashion Use:
- o To add more embellishment, buttons, or similar elements to a garment, cloning from one location to another
- o To edit and correct imperfections in an image
- o To introduce elements from one garment to another

The Clone Source Palette
This is a palette that works with all cloning tools. It is accessed by choosing the *Window>Clone Source* menu command. The palette allows you to set up multiple clone sources so that you may pick and choose between them as you work on an image. It also allows you to resize, rotate, offset, and change the opacity of the clone as you create it. This is handy as you do not always want the clone to look exactly like the original.

The Pattern Stamp Tool   (G)
The **Pattern Stamp** tool is similar to the **Clone Stamp**. Instead of sampled pixels, however, painting is performed with a predefined pattern image. You can create a new pattern or use one from the *Pattern* library.

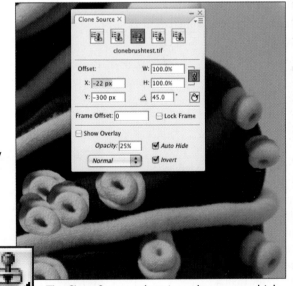

The Clone Source palette is used to store multiple sources and to provide flexibility in creating clones.

To create a new pattern:
1. Choose the **Rectangular Marquee** tool (with feathering set to 0) to select artwork.

2. Choose the *Edit>Define Pattern* menu command. A dialog will open.

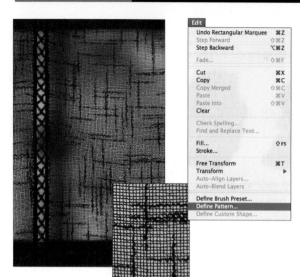

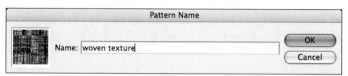

Photograph of a curtain and the
pattern that was extracted

3. Name your pattern and click on **OK**. This will now
be part of your pattern library, and you can access
the image at any time.

Pattern Name		
	Name: woven texture	OK
		Cancel

Creating a Custom Pattern: A photo of a curtain was loaded and a small
piece was extracted, lightened, and sharpened. It was then reduced in
size (Image Size) and a portion was selected. The Edit>Define Pattern
menu command was used to create the pattern which was named "woven
texture". This became part of the pattern library and was used to paint
the garment below with the Pattern Stamp tool.

To use the Pattern Stamp tool:

1. Choose the tool.

2. Choose the pattern you want to work with in the *Pattern Preset*
library.

3. Set the brush options in the options bar. Set the blending mode,
alignment, and other options.

4. *Click+drag* on your artwork to paint with the repeating tile of
the pattern. Alignment is an important option. Make sure you
understand how it works (see below).

Note:

Airbrush
Explore the airbrush
option, which allows for
fading on the edges of the
pattern stamp as stamped in
place.

Fashion Use:

o   To place hatch marks in illustrations
o   To paint a partial pattern or texture on a
dress to suggest the fabrication
o   To quickly paint a new fabric or pattern in
place

The white blouse on the left image
was selected using primarily the
Quick Selection tool. The selection
was then painted with the Pattern
Stamp tool using the woven texture
pattern created from the drapes
above. The results are shown on the
image to the right.

Retouch Tools

Photoshop's retouching tools, often called image processing tools, allow you to edit images as if working in a darkroom. A large number of tools exist in this group. They are: Healing Brush, Spot Healing Brush, Patch, Red Eye, Blur, Sharpen, Smudge, Dodge, Burn, and Sponge. In many ways, the tools previously discussed, the Clone Stamp, Pattern Stamp, Eraser, Background Eraser, and Magic Eraser, are often considered retouching tools as well depending on their use (painting vs. retouch).

The primary Retouch tools in Photoshop's palette. Hidden tools exist beneath each of these tools.

Healing Brush   (J)

The **Healing Brush** allows you to correct imperfections in an image. It is a cloning tool and it allows you to sample a portion of the image (i.e., pick up pixels) and stamp them down in a different area. In many ways it is similar to the **Clone Stamp** tool, so experiment between the two to determine which works best for your situation. The Healing Brush differs from the Clone Stamp in that when you lay down sampled pixels over the area you are touching up, the new pixels are averaged with the colors of the artwork you are repairing. Thus the Healing Brush matches the lighting, transparency, texture, and shading of the sampled pixels to the pixels being repaired or healed. The end result usually is seamless.

To use the tool:

1. Examine the image *around* the area you want to correct to determine where you want to sample pixels from.

2. Select the **Healing Brush** tool and choose your settings in the options bar. Remember that you can set the size of your tip quickly by pressing the [and] keys on the keyboard.

In the image above, the white marks between the statue's hand and body attracted too much attention. The Healing Brush was used to tone down this whiteness without losing the general sense of some texture in the background. This is why the Healing Brush is better in this situation, as it attempts to blend the lighting, texture, and so forth. Results are below.

3. Sample your image by *Opt/Alt+clicking* on your artwork in the area you want to pull pixels from. This sets the sampling point. If you want to set more than one sampling point, choose the *Window>Clone Source* menu command to open the *Clone Source* palette. This allows you to set up to five different sampling points. The sampling process essentially picks up pixels from the artwork.

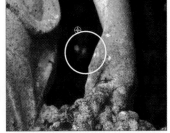

Step 3: Sampling (above) and
Step 4: Healing (below).

4. *Click+drag* your cursor over the area you want to correct. Sampled pixels are melded with the pixels you have dragged over when you release the mouse. Experiment with the length of stroke and the results.

Fashion Use: o To touch up imperfections in skin, hair, and so on
                 o To correct flaws in art of all types without major alteration to the texture and shading of the original area

Healing Brush Tool Options

If you choose to use a soft-edge brush when using the Healing or Spot Healing Brush, choose the Replace blending mode to preserve the general texture at the edges of your brush stroke.

a

b

c

d

Working with the Spot Healing tool
a. The original art; model with bindi
b. Stamping with the Spot Healing tool
c. Results of the stamping
d. Final image after a few more operations with the Spot Healing tool, followed by the Smudge tool to smooth the edges

Brush
Click on this to access the brush pop-up that will allow you to set parameters of your brush tip including the size, hardness, spacing, and so on.

Mode
Select the blending mode you want to work with (between layers).

Source
There are two options to choose from when choosing your source for *healing* or repairing artwork. The *Sampled* option allows you to use pixels from the current image and the *Pattern* option allows you to choose pixels from the Pattern pop-up menu (in which case you want to choose a pattern).

Aligned
The aligned option allows you to release the mouse button without losing the current sampling point (thus sampled pixels are applied continuously, regardless of how many times you start and stop your painting). If Aligned is deselected, the sample pixels are applied from the initial sampling point each time you stop and start painting. Experiment with this operation for full understanding.

Sample
This pop-up menu allows you to choose whether you want to sample from the current layer only, current and layers below, or all layers.

Adjustment Layer button
This button allows sampling to ignore the effects of adjustment layers. If you click on the icon, adjustment layers will be ignored.

Spot Healing Brush Tool   *(J)*
This tool is similar to the **Healing Brush** tool in that it heals by painting with sampled pixels, matching the lighting, texture, transparency, and shading of the original artwork. The only difference is that you do not need to sample as the tool automatically looks around the surrounding areas and creates the healing pixels itself.

To use the tool:

1. Select the **Healing Brush** tool and choose your settings in the options bar. Try to choose a brush tip size that is slightly larger than the imperfection you are trying to fix.

2. Click on the area you want to fix or *click+drag* your cursor over the area where you want to smooth the pixels. Experiment with both *clicking* and *clicking+dragging* to see the difference.

Fashion Use: o To touch up facial imperfections such as blemishes

Spot Healing Brush Tool Options

Brush, Mode, and **Sample** are the same as the **Healing Brush**.

Type
The *Proximity Match* option looks at the pixels around the edge of your brush tip (when you stamp) to determine what to use as a patch. *Create Texture* uses all the pixels under the brush tip when you stamp to create a texture to use to fill the area. Experiment with the two options, and also try dragging through the area a second time if you choose the texture option.

Patch Tool   (J)
The **Patch** tool allows you to repair images by working with a source and destination. In essence you select two areas: one that needs repair (the source) and the other that you want to use as your sample or patch (the destination). As with the Healing Brushes, the Patch tools use sampled pixels that match the lighting, texture, transparency, and shading of the original artwork. *To use the tool:*

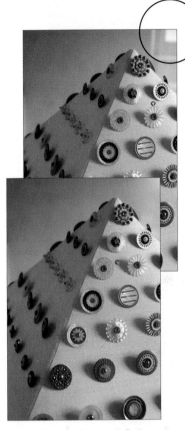

1. Select the tool.

2. Move the cursor to the image and drag around the area that you want to repair. Then select *Source* in the options bar. The cursor behaves much like the *Lasso* tool.

3. Now drag the cursor around the area you want to sample or use as your patch. Choose *Destination* in the options bar.

4. Drag the selection created in Step 3 over to the area you want to patch. The pixels of the source will be averaged with the pixels of the destination. Be careful not to overlap areas of the image you do not want to alter as these too will change.

The Button Pyramid: Before (above) and after (below) using the Patch tool

Step 2	Step 3	Step 4	Results
Setting the Source	Setting the Destination	Dragging the Destination over Source	

Fashion Use:
- o To correct areas of fashion art where you want to retain some of the original lighting, textures, transparency, and so on
- o For creative effect

Patch Tool Options

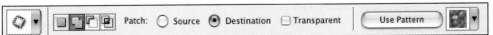

A pattern patch is put over the entire image of the statue (above) using the Transparent option. The pattern is shown above (center right).

As with many tools that involve selections, you have the typical selection options (*Add to, Subtract from, Intersect with*).

Source and **Destination**
These buttons allow you to define your selection as a source or destination.

Transparent
When the *Transparent* box is checked, the patch is placed with transparency.

Pattern
Once you have a selection made you can access the **Pattern** button. Choose your pattern first, then click on the button. The area will be patched with the pattern. Experiment with this feature, as many creative effects can be achieved combining transparency and pattern.

The Focus Tools: Blur, Sharpen, and Smudge

There are three "focus" tools in Photoshop used to retouch images: Blur, Sharpen, and Smudge. The **Blur** tool serves to soften edges, reducing clarity, whereas the **Sharpen** tool creates a harder edge in the areas you touch. The **Smudge** tool allows you to pick up color where the painting begins and drag it through other parts of the image (much like finger painting). These tools are commonly used in touching up digital camera and scanner images.

Blur

Sharpen

Smudge

To use the tools:
1. Select the appropriate tool.

2. Set your options in the tool's options bar.

3. *Click+drag* your cursor in a painting manner over the area you want to blur, sharpen, or smudge. Repeat as necessary as the effect is continued with each stroke.

The Blur tool was used to soften the enlarged image of the model's face in the upper-left corner of the image. This image appears on its own layer, which was set to a transparency of 50%.
Model: Kendra Brown

Fashion Use:

- o Use Blur to soften a harsh line in make-up on a model's face.
- o Blur and Smudge work well in smoothing out edge lines that occur when correcting and editing artwork.
- o Sharpen works well to define the lines of hand-drawn line arts, once scanned and brought into Photoshop.
- o For creative effect, particularly when working with tools to simulate traditional art materials such as watercolor, charcoal, and so on.

Blur, Sharpen, and Smudge Tool Options

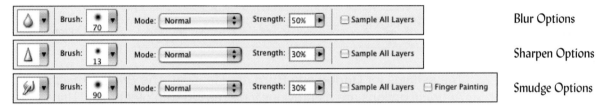

Blur Options

Sharpen Options

Smudge Options

The various settings for the **Blur**, **Sharpen**, and **Smudge** tools are identical with the exception that the Smudge tool provides an extra *Finger Painting* option. *Strength* is an option for all tools that allows you to dictate the strength of the action. When the *Fingerpainting* option of the Smudge tool is checked, the smudge will begin with the foreground color in the Toolbox. If it is not checked, it will begin with the color under the cursor when you start your action.

The Darkroom Tools: Dodge, Burn, and Sponge

These next three tools allow you to perform edits similar to what photographers do in a darkroom. Traditionally, light is sent by the enlarger through the negative, which exposes the image onto light-sensitive paper. When trying to correct flaws in the work, or for creative effect, a photographer will withhold (dodge) or add (burn) light onto areas of the image. Thus, the **Dodge** tool lightens, and the **Burn** tool darkens the area you are painting over. Continued painting will heighten the results. The **Sponge** tool allows you to change the saturation levels of the image where you are painting.
To use the tools:

 Dodge

 Burn

 Sponge

1. Choose the tool.

2. Set the brush tip with the size, diameter, and edge hardness of your choice in the *Brush Preset* pop-up.

3. For the **Dodge** or **Burn** tools, choose any additional options (tonal, exposure, airbrush) in the options bar. For the **Sponge** tool, choose saturate to heighten the color and desaturate to soften or lessen the color's intensity, and adjust the flow.

4. Paint with the tool over the area you want to change. Continue stroking with your brush until you get the desired effect.

Fashion Use:

o The Dodge tool can be used to lessen the visual impact of an area of the image that should remain, but not pull the eye toward it.
o Burn is a great tool for creating shadows in your artwork.
o Sponge can be used to intensify makeup color such as lipstick on a model.

Dodge, Burn, and Sponge Tool Options

Dodge Options

Burn Options

Sponge Options

The settings for **Dodge** and **Burn** are identical. The *Brush Preset* and *Airbrush* options are as previously discussed with other tools. Use the *Range* pop-up to choose to work on the Shadows, Midtones, or Highlights. The *Exposure* pop-up allows you to lessen or increase the effect of what you are doing with each stroke. The *Mode* setting of the **Sponge** tool lets you choose whether you want to saturate or desaturate. *Flow* and *Airbrush* are as previously discussed with other tools.

The Burn tool is used to enhance color.   Aya Saito

Above: The Burn tool was used to bring out detail on the fingers of the model playing the guitar. Original is to the left and burned image is to the right.
Model: Blake Lazear

Right: The Dodge tool was used to lighten the darkened areas of the model's face. Original is to the left and dodged image is to the right right.
Model: Kendra Brown

Draw and Object-Based Tools in the Toolbox

Photoshop provides you with the ability to create and utilize vector objects. The use of anchor points, Bezier curves, and vector editing tools facilitate the process. The vector tools in Photoshop are not as abundant or flexible as those found in Illustrator, yet these tools serve a function in Photoshop and will be discussed briefly. The topic of vector art in Photoshop is rather detailed and complicated, so read carefully, consult the Help files when necessary, and plan to reread and experiment in order to understand these rather foreign concepts. Review the brief discussion comparing raster (pixel-based) painting and vector (object-based) drawing on pages 6–7. It will also be helpful to understand the role of the *Paths* palette in working with vector art.

Vector-based tools

Overview of Paths and the Vector Thought Process

♦ Paths are vector objects that contain no pixels, unlike the various painting tools such as the **Brush**, **Pencil**, and so on. In a sense, a path is a "guide," and not a physical object, until you make it so.

The Pen and related tools

♦ Paths are created using the **Pen** or **Shape** tools (in Path mode). One draws a path by setting/creating a series of anchor points. These join straight lines and curves.

The Type tools

♦ As you draw with the **Pen** or **Shape** tool in *Path* mode, a *work path* appears in the *Paths* palette. This work path is a temporary storage in the *Paths* palette that allows you to keep track of the paths you have drawn. *Work paths* must be saved as *paths* in order to have them for future reference.

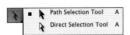

The Selection tools

♦ If you create a working path, then deselect it in the *Paths* palette and start a new work path, the original one will be lost. The only way to keep a path for future reference is to save it (using the *Save Path* menu command in the *Paths* palette).

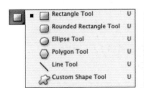

The Shape tools

♦ Paths drawn in Photoshop must have another operation performed to them (e.g., *filled* or *stroked*) in order to be printed.

Typical Flow of Work

The following is the typical flow of steps of working with paths:

Step	Purpose
1. Draw with the Pen tool	This creates a work path (as seen in the Paths palette).

Work path in Paths palette

| 2. Edit the Path | Work paths can be easily edited and transformed (using Pen-related Path Selection tools and the *Edit>Transform* menu commands). |

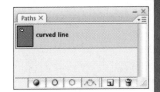

Saved path in Paths palette

| 3. Save a Path | If you want to keep it when you start a new working path. |

| 4. Convert the Path | To something you can utilize or print in other areas of Photoshop. Paths can be stroked, filled, turned into a selection, and turned into a clipping path. |

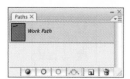

Work path in Paths palette

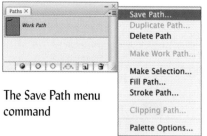

The Save Path menu
command

Saved path in Paths palette

What Can You Do with a Work Path?

Once you have created a work path, you can:

1. *Save the path*—which allows you to manage your work, and keep track of what you are doing. To save a path, double-click on the *Work Path* in the *Paths* palette to open the *Save Path* dialog. Type in a name for the path and click **OK**. You may also choose the *Save Path* menu command in the *Paths* palette.

2. *Edit the path*—by moving anchor points (with the **Direct Selection** tool), altering the type of anchor point (with the **Convert** tool), and altering the arc of a curve through the use of the directional lines

3. *Fill the path* with the foreground color in the Toolbox, which paints the inside and thus creates a bitmap image.

4. *Stroke the path*—which paints color along the path. You can either use the **Stroke path with brush** button in the *Paths* palette (which strokes the path with the current brush), or use the *Stroke Path. . .* menu option in the *Paths* palette, in which case you are presented with more options.

5. *Convert the path to a selection*—which converts the path to a selection which can be used in all the traditional ways in Photoshop.

6. *Convert the path to a clipping path*—which clips the image or prevents areas from displaying in publishing packages.

Once you have stroked or filled a path, you will have a raster image on your document. This may be altered in typical raster ways. Note that the path still exists and if it is altered (with vector tools), the stroked or filled version does not change. Thus a path can be used repeatedly to generate art for use in Photoshop.

The examples to the right show you various operations you can perform to a path in order to make it printable in Photoshop.

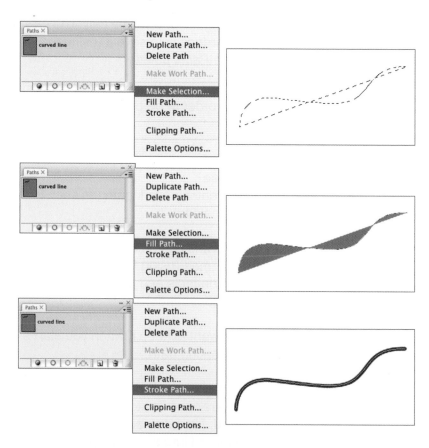

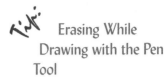
Why Use Vector Tools?

Vector objects serve several functions:

o   To allow quick resizing and editing of shapes and nonphotographic artwork without loss of clarity or resolution as vector paths and shapes are resolution independent

o   As a means to easily tweak the shape of a drawing through the use of anchor points and direction lines

o   As a starting point to generate a shape, which can then be converted to a selection, filled, or stroked

o   As a clipping path to make part of your artwork transparent when exporting it to a layout program. This is typically what is done with catalogue work where garments are shot digitally, then a clipping path is created around the garment to allow the background of the image to be transparent in InDesign®, Quark®, or some other layout program. See Fashion Exercise #14.

o   As a vector mask to hide areas of a layer

There are several tools which are used for drawing in Photoshop. These are the **Pen** and **Shape** tools, and the **Path Selection** tools. The **Type** tools are also vector based and will be discussed in this section.

The Pen and Related Tools

This group of tools allows you to draw and edit paths using *anchor points* and *segments*. Each tool performs a slightly different function as briefly outlined below. Detailed discussion of vector terminology and basic concepts follows on pages 106–110.

Pen Tool (P)

The **Pen** tool allows you to draw a path with the greatest precision, setting anchor points and creating straight and curved segments as you draw, as dictated by the way you use your mouse. If you want to preview the line segments as you draw, you can click on the *Geometry options* pop-up in the options bar and check the *Rubber Band* option.

o   To draw a straight segment   *click+release* as you set points
o   To draw a curved segment   *click+hold+drag* as you set points
o   To end an open object   Cmd/Ctrl+click with the mouse
o   To end with a closed object   *click* on the starting anchor point

The Pen tool will be utilized in Fashion Exercise #6.

Pen options include the Rubber Band, which allows you to preview
line segments as you draw.

Erasing While Drawing with the Pen Tool

While drawing, you can press the Esc key on the keyboard once to erase the last set anchor point, or twice to delete the entire path.

Vector-based tools

The Pen and related tools, which are stacked beneath the Pen tool

The Pen tool

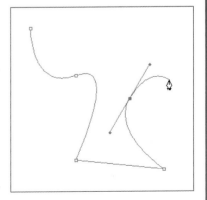

The open path drawn with the Pen tool, which consists of straight and curved segments and anchor points

Freeform Pen tool

Freeform Pen (P)

The **Freeform Pen** allows you to draw paths in a manner that is more similar to working with pencil and paper. If you click on the magnetic check box in the options bar, the tool looks for contrast between imagery and snaps to an edge. To close the path, double-click anywhere over the shape, or click on the starting point. Once you trace your image, you create a work path that can then be saved, and then edited, stroked, filled, and so on.

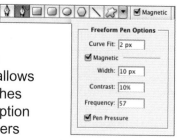

If you click on the *Geometry options* pop-up in the options bar, you can access the Freeform Pen options. The *Curve Fit* allows you to control how closely your path matches the movement of the mouse. The *Width* option controls the width in pixels the pen considers as it is moved. The *Contrast* option controls the contrast needed by the Pen between shapes and the *Frequency* setting controls the number of anchor points that are set.

Freeform Pen tool options

 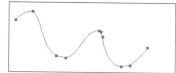

The process of drawing freehand with the Freeform Pen (left) and the resulting path with anchor points (right)

The Freeform Pen tool in Magnetic mode was used to quickly trace the model's head. This created a path with anchor points that was saved in the Paths palette.

Add Anchor Point and Delete Anchor Point Tools

These two tools allow you to add anchor points to, or delete them from an existing path. You must have an existing path prior to using these tools. Once you have chosen either tool, you must position your cursor over a segment (to add an anchor point) or over an existing anchor point (to delete an anchor point).

Add Anchor Point tool

Delete Anchor Point tool

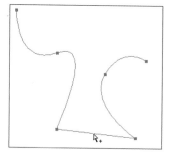 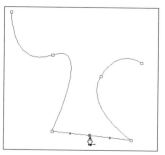

Adding an anchor point (left) and deleting an anchor point (right)

Convert Point tool

Convert Point Tool

The **Convert Point** tool allows you edit a path and change corner anchor points to smooth anchor points (and vice versa). The basic action for using this tool involves positioning the tool cursor over an existing anchor point and *clicking+holding+dragging* the mouse to convert the point.

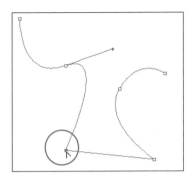 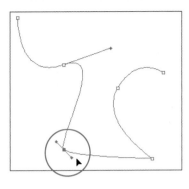

The Convert Point tool is positioned over an anchor point on the left image, and then a click+hold+drag operation is performed to convert the corner anchor point to a smooth anchor point as seen in the right-hand image.

The Selection Tools

The Selection tools allow you to edit paths, to select or move the entire path **(Path Selection tool),** or to edit a portion of the path **(Direct Selection tool).**

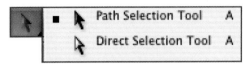

The Selection tools

Path Selection Tool

This tool allows you to select an entire path. All anchor points will appear solid, which indicates that all points are selected. *Once you have selected a path, you may:*

 o   Move the path
 o   Transform (scale or rotate) the path using transformation functions
 o   Delete the path

The Path Selection tool

Direct Selection Tool

This tool allows you to select specific areas of a path. *You can:*

 o   Select segments by clicking on the segment
 o   Select anchor points by clicking on the point, or dragging a box around a point or group of points

The Direct Selection tool

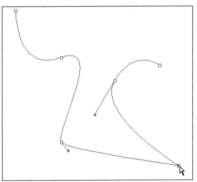

Moving a selected point (above) and transforming the path (below)

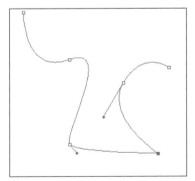 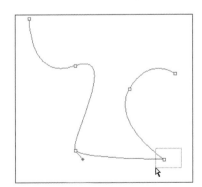

Selecting the lower segment (left) and click+hold+drag to select an anchor point (right)

Once you have selected points or segments you can:

 o   Move the point
 o   Delete the segment selected or attached to the selected points
 o   Transform the selected segment

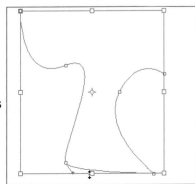

Vector Terminology and Concepts

The initial learning curve of drawing with vector objects is somewhat steep as you will need to study and understand numerous concepts foreign to the typical process of drawing by hand. The object-based design world has its own unique language. Understanding the language and concepts that follow will serve you well. Drawing in Photoshop, as we have defined it, is performed with the **Pen** tool or **Shape** tools.

Vector Terminology

The following is a list of vector terms that you should understand. If you read on to the *Concepts* in the next section, you will see these terms illustrated.

Object—A vector-based element of design, created through the drawing of paths.

Paths—The outer edge of an object, composed of anchor points and segments. Paths are easily edited after drawing.

    Working Path—A temporary path, illustrated in gray, which can be saved using the *Paths* palette. Work paths do not print.

    Path—A saved path in Photoshop, displayed in the *Paths* palette. A path does not need to be one connected series of segments; it can be any combination of path components.

    Path Component—A connected series of segments.

    Closed Path—An object that has the same beginning and ending anchor point (e.g., a full circle).

    Open Path—An object that has different beginning and ending anchor points (e.g., an arc).

Bounding Box—The box that surrounds a path (if the *Show Bounding Box* option is checked) when working with the **Path Selection** tool. The Bounding Box has eight handles around its edge. You may perform quick transformations by moving the entire box or its handles. Transformations include *Scale*, *Rotate*, *Move*, and so on.

Anchor Point—A single point on the drawing or a point that joins two segments of a path, represented by a small square on the screen.

End Point—The beginning or end point of an open path.

Corner Point—A Corner Point joins two straight segments or a sharply curved path that has a direction line on one side only. It is represented by a small square on the screen.

Smooth Point—This joins two curved segments, represented by a square on the screen with two direction lines, one arm for each curved segment.

Direction Line—An antenna (or pair of antennae) that projects from an anchor point and thus defines the arc of the curve of the segment it is attached to. The length of this line and its angle control the shape of the curve.

Direction Point—The circle at the end of a *Direction Line*. Click and hold on the circle to drag and reshape the Direction Line and thus the curve.

Segments—A straight or curved drawing or path.

Straight Segment—The segment between two corner points.

Curve Segment—The segment between one corner point and a smooth point, OR, the segment between two smooth points.

Stroke—The outline or edge of a path/object. In Photoshop, once you stroke a path, it becomes a raster image. When you apply the stroke, you can control its color, thickness and style by your choice of stroking element (Pen, Brush, etc.).

Fill—The color, pattern, or gradient assigned to the inside of an object. Again, once something is filled, it becomes a raster image.

Selections/Select—The process of highlighting an object or points on an object to make them active. One must select an object or path in order to edit it. Photoshop's two vector selection tools are the **Path Selection** and **Direct Selection** tools. A complete object is selected by clicking on it with the Path Selection tool. Individual segments or points are selected (for editing) by choosing the **Direct Selection** tool and performing any of the following operations:
* Clicking on the segment itself
* *Dragging+selecting* around the desired segment(s)
* Clicking on an anchor point to select it

Concept 1: Objects
When you draw in vector mode, you create objects or shapes composed of one or more segments.

Three straight segments

A circle composed of four curved segments

Two curved segments

Concept 2: Segments, Paths and Path Components
Segments are the lines (straight or curved) used to create an object. A path component is made up of one or more continuous segments. A path is any combination of path components, not necessarily connected to each other. So, as you draw, you are building a path composed of objects or path components, which are composed of one or more segments.

One straight segment and three curved segments create the path shown here.

Concept 3: Open and Closed Paths/Objects
The paths you create may be either *open* (as in the case of an arc), or *closed* (as in the case of a circle where the beginning and end points are the same).

An open path (left) and a closed path (right)

Concept 4: Anchor Points and End Points

Anchor points define the beginning and ending points of each segment. End points are the two outer anchor points of an open path. Therefore, closed paths are composed of multiple anchor points, and open paths are composed of two end points and anchor points (if there is more than one segment). You control the shape of a path through its anchor point type (see Concept 6 below); thus the manner in which you set or edit anchor points dictates the shape of your object.

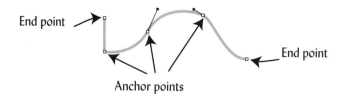

Concept 5: Curved vs. Straight Segments

Straight segments are created by simply *clicking+releasing* the mouse button as you set your anchor points. Curved segments are created by *clicking+dragging* the mouse as you place an anchor point. A *direction line* will appear and extend from the anchor point and *direction points* appear at the end of the direction line. The angle of the direction line and the distance of the direction points from the anchor point together dictate the arc of the curve. You can move the direction points at any time to change the shape of the curve.

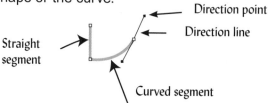

Concept 6: Corner vs. Smooth Anchor Points

There are two types of anchor points: corner and smooth. At a *corner* anchor point, a path will abruptly change its direction (think of a rectangle). At a *smooth* anchor point, two curved paths are connected as a continuous curve (think of a circle). Thus a corner anchor point connects two straight segments, or two sharp curves and a smooth anchor point connects two gentle curves. The smooth anchor point has two direction lines, whereas the corner anchor point has one or no direction lines. You may change corner points to smooth points and vice versa at any time using the **Convert Anchor Point** tool. When you move a direction line on a smooth point, the curved segments on both sides adjust. When you move a direction line on a corner point, only the one side is affected.

The Convert Anchor Point tool

One direction line controls the segment to the left of the anchor point. The other direction line controls the segment to the right of the anchor point.

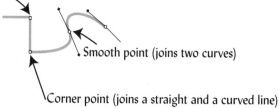

Concept 7: Selecting Points

In order to edit anchor points, you need to select them. This is done by using the Selection tools. The **Path Selection** tool (black arrowhead) selects all points in an object and allows you to move it or transform it by scaling, rotation, and so on. The **Direct Selection** tool allows you to select only the points you click on, or drag around, providing greater editing control. You can move selected points, convert them to a different type of anchor point, or perform other transformations on them such as rotate, scale, and so on. Selected anchor points appear as a solid square, whereas nonselected points appear as a hollow square. The **Direct Selection** tool also allows you to select a segment by clicking on it. The end anchor points will not become solid, but you can move the segment.

The Path Selection tool

The Direct Selection tool

A nonselected point is hollow.

A selected point is solid.

There are two ways to select chosen points with the **Direct Selection** tool:

Click—Using the **Direct Selection** tool, click on a point to select it. It will become solid. Be careful not to shake or jiggle your hand as you select a point as you could inadvertently move it. If you want to select multiple points, press and hold the *Shift* key down as you click on additional points. The first time you click on a point it is selected (solid). If you click elsewhere, it becomes deselected (hollow).

Drag+select—Using the **Direct Selection** tool, click and hold your mouse *near* an anchor point and then drag a box around it to select it. To select multiple points, *drag+select* around a group of points.

Concept 8: Mouse Actions

There are two mouse movements you will use when *drawing* with the Pen tool:

Click+release—used to set an anchor point with no direction lines (curve control arms).

Click+hold+drag—used to set an anchor point with curve control (and thus direction lines).

There are two mouse movements you will use when *selecting anchor points* for editing (using the Selection tools). *These are:*

Click+release—used to select an object (with the Selection tool) or a chosen point or segment on an object (with the Direct Selection tool).

Click+hold+drag—used to select multiple points by dragging a box around them. This action will be referred to as *drag+select* throughout this text.

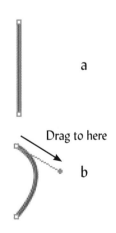

a

Drag to here

b

Various Mouse Actions and Results
a. click+release
b. click+hold+drag

Concept 9: Ending an Open Path

If, when you are drawing an open object/path (with the **Pen** tool), you want to end the object prior to closing it, *there are two ways to achieve this:*

Click away – Press and hold the *Cmd/Ctrl* key and click away from the object. While depressed, this modifier key changes the cursor and thus the tool to the most recently used **Selection** tool (either Path Selection or Direct Selection). Using this approach allows you to keep the **Pen** tool handy for drawing the next path component, without going to the Toolbox to choose a different tool and then back again to reselect the **Pen** tool. If you are using a Selection tool, you simply click away from the object.

Select a different tool – The selection of a different tool while drawing with the **Pen** tool ends the drawing of the current object. You will need to move to the Toolbox to do this (or use a keyboard shortcut for a different tool). You will need to choose the **Pen** tool once again to continue drawing a new object.

End open paths by either clicking away or selecting a different tool.

Concept 10: Drawing Straight Segments

Holding down the *Shift* key on the keyboard as you draw causes the drawn line to be perfectly horizontal, vertical, or diagonal (45 degrees), according to how you position and drag the mouse.

Concept 11: Learning to Nudge

If you want to move a segment and/or anchor point(s) in a controlled manner, use the **Direct Selection** tool to select the desired points/segments, and then press and tap the appropriate *arrow key* on the keyboard, which will *nudge* the selected points/segments in the direction of the arrow. You can continue tapping the key until you have moved the selection the desired amount.

Constrained segments result in lines that are perfectly horizontal, diagonal, or vertical.

Concept 12: Understanding the Use of Direction Lines

You can use direction lines to alter the shape of a curve. Extending the length of a direction line deepens the arc of the curve. Changing the angle of the direction line affects the shape of the curve. Remember that when you select and edit a direction line of a smooth anchor point, both arms of the direction line are affected.

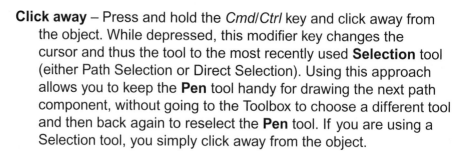

The left image is the original curve. The image to the right shows you how extending the direction line deepens the arc of the curve.

The left image is the original curve. The image to the right shows you how repositioning the angle of the direction line affects the arc of the curve.

Concept 13: Stroke and Fills

Once you choose to stroke or fill a path, the result will become raster art on the layer. The path still remains but is a separate entity to the stroked/filled element you just created.

Shape Tools (in Path Mode)

The line and shape tools can be used to draw in a vector manner (as opposed to painting with pixels). When you choose any of these tools, make sure you have chosen the *Path* mode in the options bar. If you choose *Fill pixels* mode you will be painting with pixels, and if you choose *Shape Layers* you will create a vector mask using the shape.

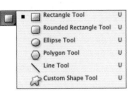

The Shape tools

When you draw with any of the **Shape** tools you create path objects, which can be freely edited using any of the vector editing tools (such as the **Selection** tools and various **Pen** tools). The vector logic of work paths, paths, and vector editing applies to shapes created in paths just as it does to drawings created with the **Pen** and related tools.

Drawing a Rounded Rectangle and the work path that is created

Shape Tools

Shape tools include the **Line** tool and shapes such as **Rectangle**, **Rounded Rectangle**, **Ellipse**, **Polygon**, and **Custom Shapes**.

The Shape tools

The following are features of the Shape tools and their options:

o   A line or shape is drawn as a work path and must be saved to become a path. While a work path or path, it is easily edited using the vector editing tools. Paths can then be stroked, filled, or turned into a selection, or made into a clipping mask.

o   You can *constrain* a line to be perfectly straight (horizontally, vertically, or diagonally) by holding the *Shift* key down as you draw. In the same manner, you can press and hold the *Shift* key to draw a square (with the rectangle shape) or a perfect circle (with the ellipse shape). If you want a hollow circle or rectangle, you will need to use a Marquee selection tool to create a shaped selection and then stroke it with color (using the *Edit>Stroke* menu command).

o   Each tool has its own set of options found in the *Geometry options* pop-up menu in the options bar. Click on the down arrow to the right of the tool strip to access the pop-up options.

o   The **Custom Shape** tool allows you to choose a shape from the Shape pop-up in the options bar and draw with that shape. You may choose the shape, then *click+hold+drag* your mouse on the screen to create and size a path of the desired shape. You can choose from various shape libraries found in the shapes menu of the shape library in the options bar.

o   Different shape tools have different option settings in the options bar, so always check what is available.

o   The options bar contains *Pathfinder* functions, which allow you to work creatively with multiple paths/shapes on a document. Read up on these operations in Photoshop's Help files.

Pathfinder function in the options bar

To use a Line or Shape tool:

1.   Ensure that the *Paths* palette is open.

2.   Choose the **Shape** tool of your choice and make sure that you are set on *Paths* mode in the options bar.

Path mode in the options bar

3. *Click+hold* on your document to set the starting point of the line. Drag to the position where you want to end the line or shape. Release the mouse. If you *press+hold* the *Shift* key as you draw you will constrain the shape.

4. Save the work path created to become a path.

5. Convert the path for whatever purpose you need it (e.g., edit it, fill it, stroke it, etc.).

Vector Tools and Shape Layers

When drawing in this mode, shapes are created on a separate layer. The layer itself is composed of two parts, which are linked: a fill layer, which defines the fill color, and a vector mask that defines the shape's outline. Both **Pen** and **Shape** tools can be used to draw in this mode. The *Path* palette displays the paths (outlines) of your objects. Shape layers are used to generate art for Web pages (i.e., buttons, bars, etc.).

Type Tools

The **Type** tools in Photoshop allows you to add titling and labeling to fashion presentations. When you use the **Horizontal Type** or **Vertical Type** tool, a layer is created in the *Layers* palette. This type layer allows you great freedom to edit and manipulate your type.

The Type tools

Typically, you work with various options in the options bar, or you may open the *Character* and *Paragraph* palettes. The type you create can be edited while it is in vector mode. If you want, you can rasterize it using the *Layer>Rasterize>Type* menu command, and then the type behaves as a graphic.

With vector type you can:
- o Edit the content and style (font, point size, style, color, alignment, etc.).
- o Transform the type using *Edit>Transform* or the *context* menus (*Ctrl+click* on the Mac and *right mouse click* on Windows).
- o Apply a layer effect.
- o Change its opacity.
- o Change the Blending mode between layers.

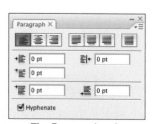

The Character palette

The Paragraph palette

To rasterize vector type:
1. Choose the *Layer>Rasterize>Type* menu command. You can only revert back to vector type through the History palette (if you want to). There is no going back once the file is saved.

With rasterized type you can:
- o Fill it with a gradient or pattern.
- o Apply filters or paint strokes.

layer

A Drop Shadow effect

layer

Transforming type

textile

Pattern and gradient fills applied to rasterized type

textile

Horizontal and Vertical Type Tools

The **Horizontal Type** tool allows you to insert type horizontally on the document and the **Vertical Type** tool enters the type vertically.

There is a Change text orientation button in the Type options bar that allows you to alternate between the two tools simply by clicking on the button.

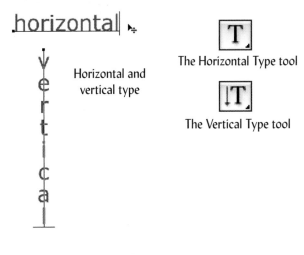

Horizontal and vertical type

The Horizontal Type tool

The Vertical Type tool

There are two ways to insert text after you choose the tool:

1. *Point Type* - Click and release the cursor to set an insertion point
2. *Paragraph Type* - *Click+hold+drag* with the type cursor to drag a box for large blocks of text.

Point Type Insertion

Fashion is always chang- ing, and for this we are glad, as life would be too static if nothing

Paragraph Type Insertion: Click+drag to create a text box, then begin to type in the box. Press the Cmd/Ctrl+Return/Enter keys when you are through.

The following is true of type:

o It sits on its own layer. Multiple layers of text can be linked so that they act as one layer.
o It can be edited by choosing the Text tool again, clicking on the text layer, placing the cursor, and changing the text. You can highlight the text, and edit it, just as in a word processor.
o It can be moved (using the **Move** tool).
o It can be transformed.
o You can control the Type orientation by changing the **Text orientation** button in the options bar or using the *Layer>Type>Horizontal or Vertical* menu command.

The Type Mask Tools

The **Horizontal Type Mask** or **Vertical Type Mask** tools create a selection in the shape of type. *You can work with that selection in various ways*:

o Stroke the selection
o Fill the selection with pattern, gradient, or other
o Paste imagery into the selection
o Create a layer mask

A Type layer is created when type is added to a document.

The Horizontal Type Mask tool is used to create a selection of text.

Viewing Fonts

If you want to explore what different fonts look like in your text, do the following:

1. Create the type on your document and then highlight it.
2. Double-click on the font name in the options bar to highlight it.
3. Press and tap the up or down arrow on the keyboard and view the type on the screen as it changes with each font.

The Process of Type

The process of adding type to a document is simple. *The steps are as follows:*

1. Click on the **Type** tool of your choice.

2. Choose desired font and settings in the options bar, *Character* palette, or *Paragraph* palette. These include the font, point size, font style, color, and so on.

3. Place the type cursor on the screen. Click where you want to place the text if you want **Point** type, or *click+hold+drag* to create a text box if you want **Paragraph** type.

4. Begin to type. When you are done, click on the **Commit** button in the options bar or press the *Cmd/Crtl+Return/Enter* keys on the keyboard to confirm the text and finish the process. The text appears on its own layer.

To learn more about working with type, consult Adobe's Help files. Presentation Exercise #2 explores using type in creative ways.

Other Tools in the Toolbox

There are additional tools in the Toolbox. *These are:*

Notes Tool

This is used to add notes to a document. Notes will not print, but will be saved with the document for future reference.

Audio Annotation Tool (CS3)

With the use of a microphone, this tool allows you to create audio annotations.

Eyedropper Tool

This tool is used to sample colors in the artwork and move the color to either the foreground or background color in the Toolbox (depending on which is the active color at the time). Click on the tool, and then use the Eyedropper icon to click on a color in your artwork.

The Eyedropper tool is used to sample colors from the artwork and place them in the foreground or background color of the palette, among other things.

The Notes tool is used to record information.

Color Sampler

The *Color Sampler* **tool** works in conjunction with the *Info* palette. You can use this tool to sample up to four colors on an image. As you click on each color a marker appears on the document, and the color information appears in the *Info* palette.

The Color Sampler lets you sample up to four colors and record their color formulas in the Info palette.

Ruler Tool

The **Ruler** tool aids in positioning imagery with precision. When you use the tool, it draws a nonprinting line between your beginning and ending points. The *Info* palette provides various types of information about the line drawn, including length, angle, and so on.

The Count Tool (Photoshop Extended)

This tool counts the number of objects on a document by recording each click you make as you count (clicking once for each object). It also counts the number of selections on a document and logs this information in the *Measurement Log* palette.

The Ruler tool allows you to measure and record various types of information, which will allow you to position imagery with precision.

The Measurement Log palette

Hand Tool

This tool allows you to pan around an image. It only works if you are zoomed into the point where scroll bars exist on the document. Select the tool, then *click+hold* the hand icon in place and drag with the mouse to move the image around on the screen. In CS4, the Hand tool also appears in the Application Bar at the top of the workspace.

The Hand tool allows you to pan an image, moving it around within the document.

Zoom Tool

This tool allows you to zoom into an area of your image. When you click on the tool for use, you will see a magnifying glass cursor. Position this on the document in the area you want to zoom into and click with the mouse. You may also drag a box around the area you want to magnify, and when you release the mouse you will zoom into this area. Pressing the *Opt/Alt* key on the keyboard will change the plus icon into a minus icon, which will allow you to zoom out. In CS4, a Zoom pop-up appears in the Application Bar.

The Zoom tool allows you to magnify an area (lower left) to zoom in (upper right).

For Fun....

In Photoshop CS4 the Toolbox (or Tools palette) is now called the Tools panel. The position of several of the tools has changed, and in the Extended version, 3D tools are added. See page vii of the Preface for general information on this.

Using the Clone Stamp tool to remove an unwanted tourist from a photograph. Carlo the cyclist, delivered a suitcase via scooter to the author, enabling her to bring Italian art and fashions home from Verona, Italy. A good portion of this book was written, in retreat, in Verona. Grazie, Carlo Your art and service to fashion were greatly appreciated.

Servigio?

Ma, senz'altro.

Photoshop's Menus

If you examine the Menu Bar positioned at the top of the Photoshop window, you will see the many menu options available. These are organized according to function. Each menu has numerous commands; some open a dialog (those ending with ...) and some have submenus (those ending with a black arrowhead). When you examine the menus, you will see that various items have keyboard shortcuts shown to the right of the command name. These generally begin with the *Command* (Apple) key on the Macintosh, and the *Ctrl* key on Windows, but other keys are used as well. Some menu functions may be accessed through the palette menu functions, but many are unique and found only in the main Menu Bar.

Note:
CS4 Menus
The menus in Photoshop CS4 have changed only slightly, with some reshuffling, a few new commands, and the addition of a 3D menu in the Expanded version. This chapter will discuss the menus as they appear in CS3. New CS4 menu changes and additions are discussed in the Preface on pages vii and viii.

| | **Photoshop** | File | Edit | Image | Layer | Select | Filter | Analysis | View | Window | Help |

| File | Edit | Image | Layer | Select | Filter | Analysis | View | Window | Help |

Photoshop's Menu Bar: Macintosh (upper), Windows (lower)

Your use of Photoshop will dictate which menus you use most. Photographers will use different features than textile designers. You have the ability to customize your menus using the *Edit>Menus...* command to access the dialog. Here you can create your own custom menu set, choosing which commands to display and selecting color options if you want.

This discussion of menus will not cover each and every menu command. Rather, it will focus on menu items used in the various exercises included in this book. If you want to understand the commands not covered here, invest in a general Photoshop book, or use the built-in Help files to assist you. Much of the information on the *Select* and *Layers* menus is covered in Chapter 2 and you will often be cross-referenced back to those pages.

Basic Maneuvering through the Menus

To use Photoshop's menus, click on the appropriate menu title in the Menu Bar. The full menu with submenus will open. Release the mouse and move down to the submenu function of your choice. If dots appear beside the command, there is yet another level of submenus to choose from and this will open once you click on the submenu. Move the mouse to the desired command and click and release. This activates the menu command.

If a menu command appears dimmed (or grayed out), this means the menu is currently unavailable. Typically, in this situation, it is necessary to perform a function in the program prior to selecting the menu. More often than not, this involves selecting an object or objects.

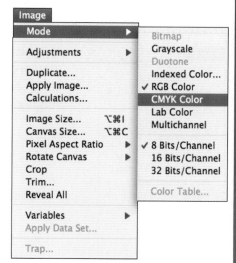

Photoshop's Image menu with dimmed items, keyboard shortcuts, and menu items ending in ..., which indicates a dialog will open.

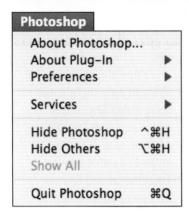

The Macintosh Photoshop menu

The Macintosh Preferences dialog with General options displayed. Access the various preferences by clicking on the name of the set you want (on the left side of the dialog).

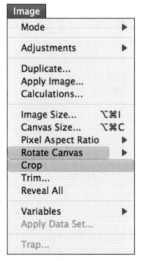

Using the Show Menu Colors option. The above are in the Painting and Retouch group.

In the discussion that follows, each main menu and its commands will be covered, moving from left to right across the Menu Bar.

Photoshop Menu

The Photoshop menu is available to Macintosh OSX users, but Windows users, do read on, as Preferences information is covered here. The first two commands, About Photoshop... and About Plug-In, provide credits, serial number, and related information about the program and plug-ins.

Preferences

The Preferences command appears in the **Photoshop** menu on the Macintosh and in the **Edit** menu on Windows. It will be discussed at this point in time for both Macintosh and Windows platforms. Photoshop CS3 and CS4 have rearranged some of the Preferences locations, so if you are using an earlier version, you may have to look in other areas for the options.

Preferences allow you to choose settings for various functions in the program such as the display, tools, units, exporting, and so on. These typically go into effect immediately (although some won't occur until you next open the program) and will be remembered for future documents. When you choose a *Preference* option and open the *Preferences* dialog box, you can move from one Preference group to another by clicking on the appropriate name along the left side of the dialog (Mac) or selecting them through the drop-down list (Windows). You may also click on the **Previous** and **Next** buttons to step through the various Preference groups.

Most options are chosen by clicking on a check box to turn the function on. Some options require you to type in a number field. Work your way through the various options and click **OK** when you are finished adjusting your settings. Specific discussion of altering some Preferences settings may be covered more fully in the design exercises where a specific task requiring a preference change is used. The following list contains a brief discussion of the most commonly used and more interesting Preference settings.

General
- *Color Picker* allows you to choose the color mixer of your choice.
- *Use Shift Key for Tool Switch* allows you to press the *Shift* key and the keyboard shortcut to toggle between all the hidden tools. If you uncheck this, you can simply press the keyboard shortcut to toggle between the tools... a handy setting to know about.
- *Export Clipboard*, when checked, allows the contents of the clipboard to remain even if Photoshop is closed.

Interface
- *Show Tool Tips* allows the name of a tool to be displayed when you place your cursor over a tool.
- *Save Palette Locations* causes the palettes' positions to be remembered upon closing and opening the program.

- *Show Menu Colors* will display menu commands in color if you set this up using the *Edit>Menus...* command.

File Handling

- *Image Previews* allow you to see a thumbnail of your image when loading images.
- *Append File Extensions* allows you to choose whether to have these added automatically or not.
- *Ask Before Saving Layers on TIFF Files*, when checked, will remind you that there are layers and give you the option to cancel, flatten the image, and save the TIFF file again.

Performance

- You may allot what percentage of your RAM you want available for Photoshop. Your decision will depend on how much RAM you have, and how many programs you want open at the same time.
- *History States* allows you to choose the number of states to display before the first item falls off the list. The more memory states you use, the more memory you will need.
- Photoshop uses RAM memory as you work and a chunk of your hard drive stores data temporarily. If you have more than one hard drive, you can direct Photoshop to use a secondary *scratch disk* when it needs more memory.

Performance Preferences

Display and Cursors

- Options here allow you to choose how you want your cursors displayed while working.

Unit options for Rulers

Transparency and Gamut

- The main control here allows you to change the size and color of the transparency grid.

Units and Rulers

- *Ruler* units allows you to set the display of your rulers choosing between inches, pixels, points, picas, millimeters, centimeters, and percent.
- *Type units* control the measurement unit for how type/text is measured. Most people prefer to use points, but other options include millimeters or pixels.
- *New Document Preset Resolutions* allow you to control both the print and screen resolutions of new documents. These can be set in pixels per inch or centimeter.

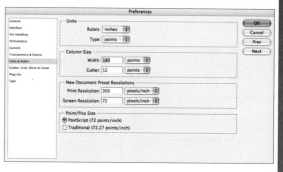

Units & Rulers Preferences (above) and Guide, Grid, Slices & Count Preferences (below)

Guides, Grid, and Slices

- Choose the *Guide* color and style (lines vs. dots) for your guidelines, which are pulled out from the rulers on the outer edge of your

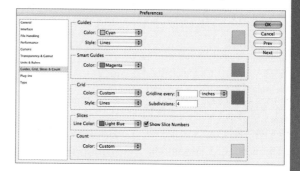

document. Clicking on the colored square opens the *Color Picker* and allows you to choose the Guide color.

- Choose the *Grid* color and style (lines vs. dots) for the grid whose display is accessed through the *View>Show Grid* menu command. You may also set the frequency of the grid (e.g., per inch) and the number of subdivisions displayed. Fashion Exercise #6 uses a grid as a tool.

Plug-Ins

- If you purchase or download numerous additional *Plug-Ins* for Photoshop, you can create and assign additional folders for Photoshop to look at when loading the Plug-Ins.

Type

- You can choose to have a visual display of each font displayed in small, medium or large scale. This is handy when choosing fonts for use in design.

Services (Macintosh only)

This is an interesting menu that offers various services such as screen capturing and mail options. Check out the many offerings.

Hide Photoshop/Hide Others/Show All (Macintosh only)

You can choose to temporarily hide all of the Photoshop documents, palettes, and tools by choosing the *Hide Photoshop* command from the **Photoshop** menu. To return to the program, either press and hold the *Cmd* key and then tap the *Tab* key repeatedly until you see the Photoshop icon appear. This keyboard shortcut allows you to toggle between open programs, and is a handy shortcut to know. You may also click on the Photoshop icon in the task bar to return to the program. *Hide Others* allows you to hide all other applications. *Show All* will bring all programs and documents back for use.

Quit Photoshop (Mac)   *Cmd/Ctrl+Q*

Use this command to quit/exit and close the program. Many new users assume that closing all documents closes the program, when in actuality, only the documents are closed. If you have been working in Photoshop for a long time, it is wise to completely close the program and reopen it again to refresh memory. Software and computers, like humans, need a break now and then in order to refresh.

File Menu

The **File** menu contains commands that allow you to create, open, save, and manage your files.

New   *Cmd/Ctrl+N*

This command allows you to create a new document. You may choose a preset document, or set up your own document settings by choosing the size, units, resolution, and color mode. You can choose to have the *Background Content* be white, the *background* color in the Toolbox, or transparent. Once you have chosen the parameters of your document,

The File menu, CS3 (Macintosh)

you have the option to save these as your own preset by clicking on the **Save Preset** button and naming the preset. If you type in a name for your document, don't assume that the file is saved. You must still use the *Save* or *Save As* command to actually save the file. Advanced settings let you control the pixel aspect ratio and the color profile of the image.

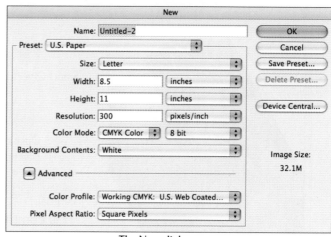

The New dialog

Open...   *Cmd/Ctrl+O*
The *File>Open* command presents you with the *Open* dialog that allows you to locate files on your hard drive and open them.

Browse...   *Opt/Alt+Cmd/Ctrl+O*
The *File>Browse* command allows you to open Adobe's **Bridge** or the *Browse* window (CS1). The **Bridge** is a control center for the entire Creative Suite, whereas the *Browse* window works within Photoshop CS1 itself. Use *Browse* to locate, view, and organize files. You can rename images, or delete them. You can also rotate an image if it was taken with a digital camera in the portrait orientation.
The following tips are helpful to know:
- o You can open multiple images by pressing the *Cmd/Ctrl* key as you click on the desired images.
- o Clicking on an image with *Ctrl/right mouse button* opens a pop-up context menu with options for renaming, rotating, and so on.

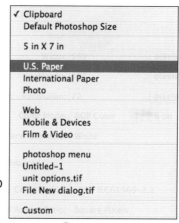

Preset options

Open as Smart Object...

Smart Objects are layers that allow you to edit vector or raster art, yet retain the original image's content without altering it. Thus, work you do is considered to be "nondestructive." This is a new feature as of CS3.
Smart Objects allow you to:
- o Perform transformations and use filters in a manner that does not destroy the original image.
- o Work with Illustrator vector files without rasterizing them.

Smart Objects are created by:
- o Loading an image as a Smart Object (*File>Open as Smart Object...*).
- o Placing a File (*File>Place*).
- o Converting a Photoshop layer into a Smart Object (*Convert to Smart Object* in the *Layers* palette menu).
- o Pasting in a vector image from Illustrator (*Edit>Paste*).

Adobe's Bridge program and window

When you open or place a file as a Smart Object, you will have the option to transform the image when you open it. Once you are happy with the settings you choose (if any), click on the **Commit Transform** button in the options bar. If you look at the *Layers* palette, you will see the new layer with a *Smart Object* icon displayed to remind you that you are working with a Smart Object layer.

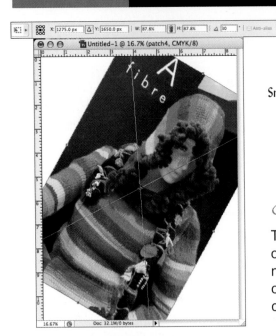

Smart Object icon

Opening or Placing artwork as a Smart Object. Note the icon in the Layers palette, which indicates that the layer is a Smart Object layer.

Open Recent

This command allows you to view recently saved files and open them directly. This is handy if you don't recall the exact name and/or location of the file you last saved. At the bottom of the recent file list is a menu command that allows you to clear the list of recent files (*File>Open Recent>Clear Recent*).

Device Central

This command allows you to set up for exporting content to mobile devices.

File Close and Save Commands

There are several commands in the **File** menu that provide control over closing and saving your files. The main ones we use in this book will be discussed here.

Close Cmd/Ctrl+W   Close All Opt/Alt+Cmd/Ctrl+W

Use the *Close* command to close your document. Understand that closing all documents does not mean that you have closed the program. You must use the *Photoshop>Quit Photoshop* (Mac) or *File>Exit (Windows)* command to close the program. The *Close All* command is handy as it closes all documents with one operation on your part.

Save, Save As..., Check-In, Save for Web & Devices

Various save commands exist in Photoshop. The *Save* command opens a *Save* dialog that allows you to save your file and choose the location (on your hard drive) and format (AIL, PDF, etc.) of the file. Learn to use the keyboard shortcut (*Cmd/Ctrl+S*) to save your files often. Each time you use the menu or the command you are updating the saved version of your file. Get into the habit of saving, and you will avoid the frustration of losing work if the computer crashes or Photoshop shuts down unexpectedly.

File>Save—saves changes to the current file.
File>Save as...—saves changes to a new file.
Check In.. (CS3 and CS4) or Save a Version (CS2)—involves the turning on of Version Cue in Preferences and is designed to aid workgroups sharing files or to increase personal productivity.

Save for Web & Devices—opens a dialog that allows you to optimize an image for the Web, resulting in a file that is smaller in size and thus loads quickly on the Internet. The name of this command varies slightly between CS versions.

Revert

Although *Revert* is a common command in many programs, most people do not use it to best advantage. This command allows you to return (or revert) to the last saved version of your file. If you are about to try something you are unsure about, save the file and then proceed. If you are not happy with the results, you can use the *Revert* command to return to the saved version. Of course, you can use the *History* palette for this, but there are times when Revert is simply faster.

Place

The *Place* command allows you to *import* artwork into Photoshop as Smart Objects, which can be altered without degrading the original file. When you choose the Place command and select your image, it will come in and the options bar will have settings available for resizing, rotating, and so on. Choose the settings (if any) and confirm.

Import and Export Commands

Use the *File>Import* and *File>Export* command to import and export files in a variety of formats. Exporting *Paths to Illustrator* is a common command used in this set.

Automate

This menu command offers several wonderful functions, each of which simplifies a series of typically complex steps by combining them into one (or more) dialog boxes. Some of the most valuable *Automate* commands are summarized below:

o   The *Batch* command allows you to run *actions* on an entire folder of files, setting source and destination folders.
o   The *PDF Presentation...* allows you to create a multiple-page PDF document of selected images and run a slideshow if you choose.
o   The *Create Droplet...* option allows you to create a droplet icon tied to an action. Then, you may drag a folder of files onto the droplet and the action will be applied to all images inside the folder.
o   The *Crop and Straighten...* command allows you to take a scanned file of multiple images and break them into separate files automatically.
o   *Contact Sheet II* allows you to build a contact sheet (thumbnails) of images within a given folder. You can save and print the sheet. If there are numerous images in the folder, Photoshop will build multiple contact sheets. These files tend to be rather large.

Save for Web or PowerPoint

If you are publishing your fashion images on the Web, or creating Powerpoint presentations, it is best to use the Save for Web command to save the files. Once this command is chosen, you view the image in up to a 4-up display, each showing slight differences in quality, file size, and loading time as dictated by the speed of the modem. You may choose to save files as .jpg or .gif. The .jpg files are preferable for photographic images. Use .gif files for line art graphics. Prepping images using the Save for Web command is helpful, as reducing image size for PowerPoint allows you to use more images in a presentation and at the same time keep the file size smaller. To understand all the features available through this command, read Photoshop's Help files. See also Exercise #5 in the Presentations section of the book.

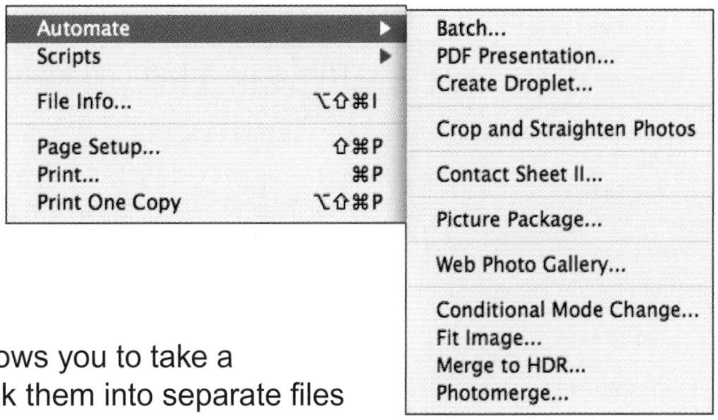

Automate	▶
Scripts	▶
File Info...	⌥⇧⌘I
Page Setup...	⇧⌘P
Print...	⌘P
Print One Copy	⌥⇧⌘P

Batch...
PDF Presentation...
Create Droplet...
Crop and Straighten Photos
Contact Sheet II...
Picture Package...
Web Photo Gallery...
Conditional Mode Change...
Fit Image...
Merge to HDR...
Photomerge...

The Automate menu commands

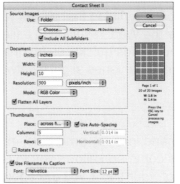

The dialog for building a contact sheet, accessed through the File>Automate>Contact Sheet II menu command

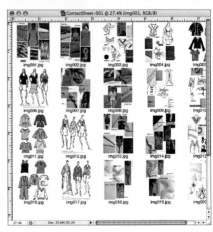

A contact sheet built from a folder of files

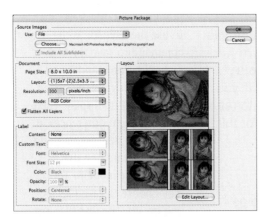

The Picture Package dialog allows you to choose how to lay out your image for printing multiple photos of the same image.

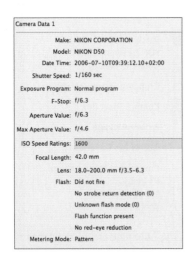

A photo gallery, built in HTML format, ready for publishing on the Web

o   The *Picture Package* command builds a picture page (similar to photography studios) of multiples of the same image. You can control the number of images per page (e.g., two 5 × 7, four 3 × 4, etc.).

o   The *Web Photo Gallery* command allows you to build a web gallery (in HTML format) of all the images in a folder. The command generates thumbnails and web images, with links between the two.

o   The *Fit Image* command allows you to specify either a width or height, and Photoshop will automatically resize an image based on whichever of the two parameters is greater, still maintaining the aspect ratio of the image. This is handy for prepping PowerPoint presentations where you want to control the size of the image so that there is room for text, or that it doesn't roll off the page and thus have to be resized. It is also good for building thumbnail web images of garments (among other things), so that there is a consistency of height and the images work well within a table.

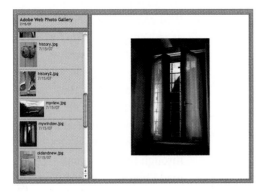

Viewing digital camera settings for an image loaded into Photoshop using the File Info menu

Scripts
This is an advanced feature that allows users to utilize scripts to automate tasks.

File Info   *Opt/Alt+Shift+Cmd/Ctrl+I*
Numerous features of value can be accessed through this file command. If your artwork was taken with a digital camera, you can see the camera settings used, as the camera's JPG and RAW files save this information with the image. If you want to attach your name to the file you are creating electronically, you can use the *Origin* options and fill in your information.

Page Setup   *Shift+Cmd/Ctrl+P*
This command opens the *Page Setup* dialog, which allows you to alter

settings for the document including the format for the printer, paper size, orientation, and scale. Choose your settings and click **OK** to finalize the changes. The use of *scale* is handy, in that you can temporarily change the printout size without changing the document size. This is a handy way to proof and save ink. *Note*: Scale can also be accessed in the print dialog that opens with the *File>Print* command.

Add file origin information using the File Info menu.

Adding Ownership to Your Artwork
Use the Origin options of the File Information dialog to include your name, copyright, and anything else you want saved with a file. The keyboard shortcut for creating the copyright sign is Opt/Alt+G.

The Print dialog on the Mac (below)

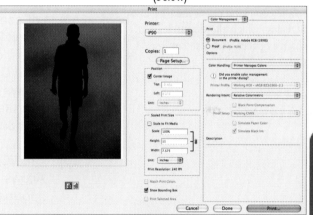

Print with Preview (CS2)   Opt/Alt+Cmd/Ctrl+P
This command opens a more advanced print dialog that allows you to choose from among various settings including positioning, scale, color management, and output settings. These are found in the regular print dialog of CS3 and CS4.

Print...   Cmd/Ctrl+P
The *File>Print* command allows you to choose the print settings for your document and print the file. There are various options to choose from.

Print One Copy
This option sends the image to your printer directly, and prints one copy, without offering any options. You might see warnings regarding oversized files and other messages, but no print dialog will open.

Exit   (Windows Only)   Ctrl+Q
Use this command to quit and close the program on Windows. As stated in the Mac discussion, many new users presume that closing all documents closes the program, when in actuality, only the documents are closed. If you have been working in Photoshop for a long time, it is wise to completely close the program and reopen it again to refresh memory.

The Edit menu on the Mac

Edit Menu
The **Edit** menu is comprised of standard editing commands used in the Windows and Macintosh worlds. In addition to the undo and clipboard functions, you will also find specialized Photoshop functions.

Undo Cmd/Ctrl+Z   Redo Shift+Cmd/Ctrl+Z
The *Undo* command allows you to undo or cancel the last operation performed. The actual wording of the undo may change to become more specific about the task just performed (e.g., Undo Rectangular Marquee). The *Redo* command allows you to undo an undo.

Step Forward and Step Backward in the History palette are the same as the Edit menu commands.

The Fade command opens the Fade dialog, which allows you to change opacity and blending mode.

Paste Into

When using selections and Paste Into, it is helpful to ensure that all your files are in the same resolution. If they aren't, you can use the Transform functions to assist in getting the scale of imagery between documents accurate.

Step Forward   *Shift+Cmd/Ctrl+Z*

Step Backward   *Opt/Alt+Cmd/Ctrl+Z*

These two menu commands allow you to progressively step forward or backward through the history states. These commands also exist in the *History* palette.

Fade...   *Shift+Cmd/Ctrl+F*

The *Fade* dialog's exact name will change depending on which tool you are using. For example, if you just painted with the brush, the menu name will change to *Fade Brush Tool...* The menu command opens a *Fade* dialog that lets you adjust the *Opacity* and blending *Mode* of the last function just performed.

Clipboard Functions

The next group of commands pertain to the clipboard, which is an invisible holding tank for imagery, text, objects, and so on. Only one item at a time can be held on the clipboard at any given point in time.

Cut   *Cmd/Ctrl+X*

Allows you to take selected imagery/objects/text or other information, remove it from its source, and send it to the clipboard until another piece of information replaces it.

Copy   *Cmd/Ctrl+C*

Allows you to take imagery/objects/text or other information and send a *copy* of it to the clipboard.

Copy Merged   *Shift+Cmd/Ctrl+C*

Creates a merged copy of all the visible layers that are in the document. If a selection exists, it copies all imagery on all visible layers within the selection.

Paste   *Cmd/Ctrl+V*

Allows you to bring clipboard information into the document you are working on. In Photoshop, art pasted in from the clipboard and placed on a new layer. Text can only be pasted between text boxes.

Paste Into   *Shift+Cmd/Ctrl+V*

Allows you to paste the clipboard imagery into a selection. This will be used in laying fabrics into garments. The imagery on the clipboard is pasted into its own layer in the shape of the selection, and the selection on the current layer is turned into a layer mask.

Clear

Allows you to delete selected art.

Fashion Use: o   Paste Into is used to bring fabric to a garment.
                o   The clipboard can be used as a means of transporting colors from one document to another.

Check Spelling   Find and Replace Text

These two commands allow you to check spelling of all text (on Text layers) used in Photoshop. You can also perform typical search and replace functions.

Fill...   *Shift+F5*

Fill works in conjunction with selections. Once you have created a selection and chosen the command, the *Fill* dialog opens. Here you may choose to have the contents of your fill be the *Foreground Color, Background Color, Color* (which opens the *Color Picker*), *Pattern, History, Black, 50% Gray,* or *White*. You can also choose the *Blending Mode* and the *Opacity*. Lastly, you can choose to *Preserve the Transparency* of the layer the selection was made on as the fill is made. See the discussion on pages 44–45.

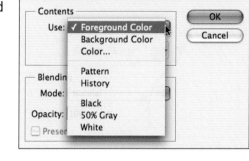

The Fill dialog allows you to choose the way you want to fill your selection.

Fashion Use:
- o Selecting the pixels inside a garment and filling them with color or pattern as a quick means to fill a garment
- o Filling text converted to a graphic with pattern for special effects

Stroke

A stroke is an outline, and is a term typically used with object-based software. The *Stroke* command works in conjunction with selections. Once you have created a selection and chosen the command, the *Stroke* dialog opens. Here you may choose the width and color of the stroke as well as its location in relation to the marquee (*Inside, Center,* or *Outside*). You can choose the *Blending Mode* and the *Opacity*. Lastly, you may choose to *Preserve the Transparency* of the layer the selection was made on. See page 45 for further discussion on *Stroke*.

The Stroke dialog allows you to choose the manner in which you want to stroke your selection.

Fashion Use:
- o Creating a quick line art image by selecting the perimeter of artwork, moving to a new layer, and then stroking it
- o Outlining artwork for emphasis

Free Transform   *Cmd/Ctrl+T*

This menu allows you to perform transformations in one easy set of operations. The transformations include: *Scale, Skew, Rotate, Distort, Warp,* and so on. When you create a selection and then choose the menu command, a *Bounding Box* appears around the selection. This box has eight anchors on it. The position of your cursor in relation to the bounding box provides you with different transformation options, and you can tell which one is available to you by the cursor.

Rotate—The curved double arrow cursor appears when you move the cursor outside of the bounding box.
Scale, Skew—The straight double-arrow cursor appears when you place the cursor on an edge of the bounding box.
Move—The arrow cursor appears when your cursor is inside the bounding box. This allows you to move the selection.

The bounding box

↶ Rotate cursor

↖ Scale cursor

► Move cursor

The Transform
options bar

Once you have chosen the command, you will see transformation options available in the options bar. *The following operations can be performed with Free Transform, the bounding box, and options bar:*

o   You may perform more than one operation before finalizing the art.

o   **Rotations** may be made by typing a number in the options bar, or placing the cursor outside the bounding box, waiting for the curved double arrow, then *click+hold+drag* to create the rotation.

o   **Scaling** may be performed by typing in the options bar, or by clicking on an anchor or a side of the bounding box and dragging the box to resize it.

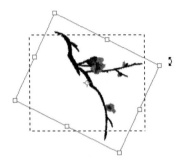

A rotation in process using the bounding box. Note the curved double-arrow cursor, which is the rotation cursor.

o   If you want to keep the same *aspect ratio* in scaling, either click on the lock in the options bar, or press and hold the *Shift* key on the keyboard as you *drag+scale* with the bounding box.

o   There are two ways to **distort** a selection. In the first, you press the *Opt/Alt* key and drag a handle of the bounding box, which will distort the image relative to the center. In the second method, you press the *Cmd/Ctrl* keys and drag a handle to distort freely.

o   To **skew**, press the *Shift+Cmd/Ctrl* keys on the keyboard and drag a side handle. You can also enter the degree of distort in the options bar.

o   To apply perspective, press the *Shift+Cmd/Ctrl+Opt/Alt* keys and drag a corner handle.

Buttons in the Transform options bar:
Left to Right: Switch Between Free Transform and Warp Modes, Cancel Transformation, and Commit Transformation

o   If you want to warp the image, click the **Switch Between Free Transform and Warp Modes** button on the options bar and drag any of the points on your bounding box to warp the image.

o   When you are finished with all your transformations, you must click on the **Commit** button in the options bar or press the *Cmd/Ctrl+Return/ Enter* keys on the keyboard. If you want to cancel what you have done, click on the **Cancel** button.

Content-Aware Scaling

CS4 has a new feature called Content-Aware Scaling. See the brief discussion on page vii in the Preface.

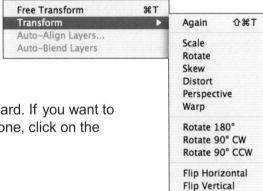

Transform

The *Transform* command provides many of the same options as the Free Transform, but also adds a *Flip Horizontal* and *Flip Vertical* plus an *Again* command. You must perform each command one at a time, which is the advantage of learning to use *Free Transform* (where more than one operation can be done in a quick session).

Examples of Transformations

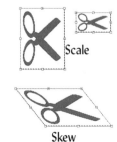

Original image

Scale

Skew

Distort

Rotate

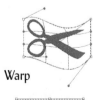

Warp

Perspective

Auto-Align Layers

This feature allows you to automatically align layers by looking at the similar content in the layers. You create or load all the layers into one document, and then assign a reference layer by locking it (or let Photoshop do it). Select the layers you want to align and choose the menu command. An **Auto-Align Layers** dialog will open. Choose the option of your choice, click **OK,** and let Photoshop do the work. The *Perspective* command performs the traditional "stitching" function that scanner software uses to create a panorama of multiple images by finding the common imagery and aligning it by overlapping as necessary. This new function definitely deserves some exploration as creative effects can be achieved. Be prepared, however, as the operation takes a long time to process.

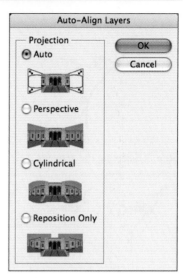

The Auto-Align Layers dialog

Auto-Blend Layers

The *Auto-Blend Layers* function is useful in working with composites. Its primary task is to blend layers with different exposures and lighting, creating *Layer Masks* as needed to blend the imagery together in the best way possible.

Define Brush Preset

This command gives you the ability to select artwork to use as a brush tip. *To create a Brush Preset, the steps are as follows:*

1. Choose the **Rectangular Marquee** tool. Ensure that feathering is not checked or being used in the *Refine Edges* dialog. If it is, the menu will remain dimmed.

2. Select the art that you want to use as a brush tip. Attempt to keep the selection small, as most brushes work best if the tips are smaller.

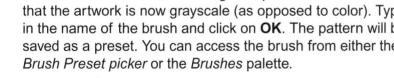

Step 2: Selecting the artwork.

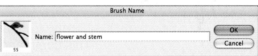

Step 3: Naming the brush.

3. Choose the *Edit>Define Brush Preset* menu command. A *Brush Name* dialog will open. Note that the artwork is now grayscale (as opposed to color). Type in the name of the brush and click on **OK**. The pattern will be saved as a preset. You can access the brush from either the *Brush Preset picker* or the *Brushes* palette.

We will use Brush Presets in the Textile Design Exercises.

Fashion Use:
- o As a means of creating a quick motif for textile design to be used with the Grid function
- o As a means to create fashion details such as zipper teeth, overlock stitch, and so on

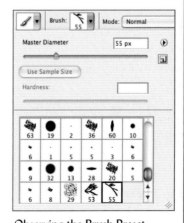

Observing the Brush Preset

Define Pattern

The *Define Pattern* command is used when creating patterns for use as fills. Patterns are stored in a pattern preset library. *To create a pattern, the steps are as follows:*

1. Choose the **Rectangular Marquee** tool. Ensure that feathering is not checked or being used in the *Refine Edge*s dialog. If it is, the menu will remain dimmed.

Step 2: Selecting the artwork.

2. Select the art that you want to use to create a pattern.

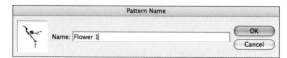

Step 3: Naming the pattern.

3. Choose the *Edit>Define Pattern* menu command. A *Pattern Name* dialog will open. Type in the name of the pattern and click on **OK**. The pattern will be saved in the Pattern Preset library.

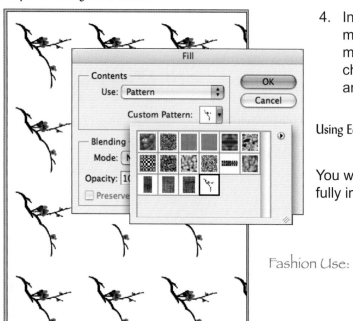

4. In order to apply this pattern to your artwork you must create a selection and choose the *Edit>Fill* menu command (discussed on page 127). Then, choose the *Pattern* option from the pop-up menu and select your pattern from the library.

Using Edit>Fill and choosing the pattern just created

You will explore defining and using patterns more fully in the Textile Design section of this book.

Fashion Use:
  o Creating fabric prints or rendered textures to insert into garments
  o Drawing repetitive patterns quickly

Utilizing a pattern to fill the document

Define Custom Shape

This command gives you the ability to select a path (work path, saved path, or a vector mask for a shape layer), and create a custom shape with it.

To create a custom shape, the steps are as follows:

1. Using vector tools, build a path. You may want to open the *Paths* palette to track your work. Keep the object as its own path (i.e., remove any other artwork that should not be on the path).

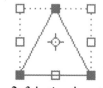

Step 2: Selecting the artwork.

2. Choose the **Selection** tool and select the artwork, or choose the path in the *Paths* palette.

Step 3: Naming the shape.

3. Choose the *Edit>Define Custom Shape* menu command. A *Shape Name* dialog will open. Type in the name of the shape and click on **OK**. The shape will be saved as a preset. You can access it in the *Custom Shape* picker.

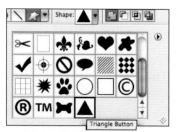

Observing the custom shape in the Custom Shape picker

Fashion Use: o   To build buttons and similar detail
                      shapes as part of a library

Purge

The *Purge* menu command allows you to remove or purge
stored data such as history, the clipboard, and undo information.

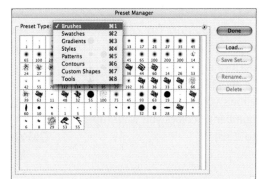

The Edit>Purge command

Adobe PDF Presets...

This menu command allows you to create, edit, or delete
presets for creating Adobe PDF files.

Preset Manager

The *Preset Manager* allows you to create, edit, or delete any
of the presets that exist in Photoshop. Through the *Preset
Manager* dialog that opens, you have access to all the presets
including Brushes, Swatches, Gradients, Styles, Patterns,
Contours, Custom Shapes, and Tools.

The Adobe Preset Manager
accessed through the Edit menu

Keyboard Shortcuts   *Shift+Cmd/Ctrl+Opt/Alt+K*

Choosing this menu command opens a dialog that allows you to edit the
various keyboard shortcuts used in Photoshop.

Menu...   *Shift+Cmd/Ctrl+Opt/Alt+M*

Photoshop allows you to hide and color menu items. You may also use
the presets Adobe has created for menu sets or build your own custom
sets.

The balance of the menu commands in the **Edit** menu pertain to color
management. Read Adobe's Help files for information on these.

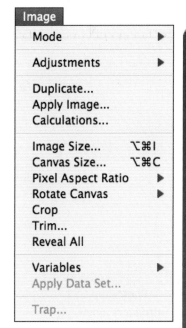

The Image Menu

Items in this menu pertain to operations you would perform on the
image as a whole (as opposed to a selection).

Mode

Photoshop offers you various color modes to work with.
These are as follows:

Bitmap—This is the black and white mode and it has one channel.
Images are displayed in black and white only. To convert a color
image to Bitmap, you must go through Grayscale mode.
Filters do not work on Bitmap images.

The Macintosh Image menu

Grayscale—Grayscale mode uses shades of gray to
display the image. In 8-bit mode you can have 256
shades of gray. (This is calculated by $8 \times 8 \times 8 = 256$, and
since 0 is considered a value the range is from 0 to 255).

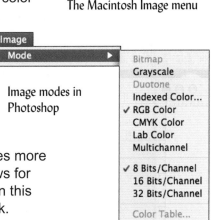

Image modes in
Photoshop

Duotones—This is a mode often used for printing as it provides more
shades and better results than Grayscale. Photoshop allows for
monotones, duotones, tritones, and quadtones. Read up on this
mode in the Help files if you need to print in single-color ink.

Tip   Color
Reduction Tip
Indexed Colors is one way of performing a color reduction, as choosing the command allows you to specify the number of colors you want (up to 256).

Indexed Color—This is a mode used to limit colors to 256 or less, and it is often used for Web pages as file sizes are kept small. When converting files, Photoshop looks at the colors, and indexes up to 256 colors for the image. If it can't find a good match within the 256 colors chosen, it often dithers other colors to simulate the color it needs.

RGB—This mode has three color channels, one each for red, green, and blue. In 8-bit mode, each channel can have an intensity range from 0 to 255. The RGB mode is the most common for video display. In 8-bit mode, a pure black has a formula of 0-0-0 and pure white has the formula of 255-255-255. The color theory involved with RGB is known as additive color.

CMYK—This mode ties to press printing, as four colors, Cyan, Magenta, Yellow, and Black, are used to create the full color spectrum. There are four channels in this mode. In 8-bit mode, pure black has the formula of 255-255-255-255 and pure white has the formula of 0-0-0-0. The color theory involved with CMYK is known as subtractive color.

Lab Color—Lab color mode is based on human perception of color and therefore is very device dependent.

Multichannel—This mode is a specialized mode for printing and contains 256 shades of gray in each channel. It is not commonly used for our purposes in fashion design.

8-Bit vs. 16-Bit vs. 32-Bit

The number of bits in each channel dictates how many shades of each color you have to work with. As the number of bits increases, so does file size. In an 8-bit mode you have a range of 256 shades per channel ($8 \times 8 \times 8$). In 16-bit HiColor mode you have 65,536 mixed colors as you use 5 bits to represent both red and blue and 6 bits to represent green. Thus the total available is calculated by multiplying $32 \times 64 \times 32$. The term 32-bit is generally a misnomer with regards to color depth, as the use of 10 to 11 bits per channel produces 4,292,967,296 distinct colors. Yes, it is confusing.

Note: CS4 Adjustments
Photoshop CS4 introduces a new Adjustments panel, which simplifies the creation of adjustment layers. See page vi in the Preface for a quick overview.

Adjustments

The adjustments of Photoshop are one of the real powerhouse areas of the program. It is through these that you can improve the quality of color and tonality in an image or create special effects. Traditionally, colors were altered by photographers using special films, lens filters, and darkroom techniques. Photoshop offers users electronic means to alter images.

The following is true of adjustments:

o   Adjustments serve to alter the color and tonality of images. Color refers to the hue. Tonality refers to the shadows, midtones, and highlights of an image.

o   Some adjustments are geared more to the tonal changes and others more toward color changes.

o   Using adjustments through the *Image* menu results in a permanent change, whereas using an *Adjustment Layer* allows you to make a temporary change that you can commit to later if you choose.

o   Adjustments can be made to the entire layer or to a selection.
o   Most adjustment dialog boxes allow you to preview the change that is about to happen.
o   The *Histogram* palette is helpful when working with adjustments as it allows you to see the changes graphically.

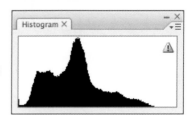

A photo (below) and its histogram (above)

There are a number of adjustments you can perform, and not all will be covered in detail here. Photoshop has automated many of the adjustments (e.g., Auto Levels, Auto Contrast, Auto Color, etc.) and most dialog boxes have an **Auto** button in them as well. Yet, the best control for your own purposes is to learn how to employ the mechanisms offered to you in the various Adjustment dialogs.

Prior to discussing adjustments it is important to understand what a *histogram* is, and how reading it can assist you. A histogram is a pictorial reading or graph of the tonal range of pixels in an image. The *Levels* histogram can show you, for example, what percent of the pixels are in the shadows, the midtones, and the highlights. The goal would be to have a good balance, although special effects can be achieved through creative play with this concept. Using the Levels adjustments, you can redefine what you want to consider the Shadow, Midtone, and Highlight colors.

The most important adjustments (for our purposes) will be discussed below. Exercises #3 and #4 in the Basic Exercises will walk you through the performance of several adjustments to an image.

Levels

Levels allow you to adjust and control the *tonal range* of an image through the adjustment of intensity levels. You may perform separate operations on the shadow, midtone, and highlights of an image. A histogram will show you an analysis of the image's tones/colors. Three sliders appear underneath the histogram. They represent the *Shadows* (black slider), *Midtones* (gray slider), and the *Highlights* (white slider).

Level adjustments were applied to the photo to improve its colors.

There are two ways to make adjustments:
1. Dragging Sliders
Drag the black slider (the shadows) on the left so it is under a portion of the histogram that starts to have some height. Observe the changes that occur in your image. Now, drag the white slider (the highlights) on the right so it is under a portion of the histogram that has some height. Again, observe the results. Finally, move the center slider (the midtones) back and forth in the center until you feel you have the best results in the image.

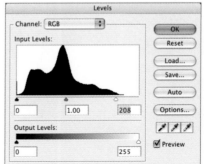

2. Using the Eyedroppers
In this approach, you click on the different *Eyedropper* tools in the *Levels* dialog and then click on a color in the image itself to set the tone. For example, click on the black eyedropper and then move the cursor to the blackest black in your image (or the black you want to define as the shadow). When you click on the image with the cursor, the levels will change. Repeat the process to define

The Levels Eyedropper tools

your highlight color (with the white eyedropper) and the midtones (with the gray eyedropper).

The black Eyedropper tool is used to sample black from the model's shirt.

Working with the Histogram palette and the Brightness and Contrast adjustment. The upper image shows the histogram of the original file. The second image shows the histogram after the brightness slider has been moved to the right (increasing brightness). The bottom image shows you the results of moving the Contrast slider to the left (decreasing contrast).

Fashion Use:

o To correct imagery so that better tonal values exist. Level adjustments are some of the most common adjustments made to imagery of all types, including fashion imagery.

Curves

Curves is a more advanced technique for adjusting the tonal balance in your image. Whereas *Levels* gave you three adjustments (shadows, midtones, and highlights), Curves gives you up to 14 points. Refer to Adobe's Help files for instructions on using Curves.

Brightness/Contrast

This command allows you to make quick and simple changes to the tonal range of your artwork. Most people prefer to use *Levels* as more control exists. The *Brightness/Contrast* dialog offers you two sliders to work with:

o As you are moving the brightness slider, you are shifting the arrangement of pixels toward the highlights (if moving to the right) or the shadows (if moving to the left).

o The contrast slider adjusts (expands or shrinks) the tonal values in your artwork.

Working with the Curves dialog

Before   After

Color Balance

This adjustment changes the overall color mixture in your artwork. If you want to warm the image up, add yellow. If it needs more red, simply move the slider.

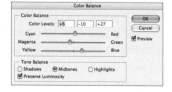

Adjusting the color balance of an image that has too much yellow in it

Fashion Use: o   To correct images taken with fluorescent lighting (which are too yellow) such as window displays of mannequins at night

Black and White

Using the black and white adjustment is superior to changing an image to grayscale, as you can control various subtleties of the tonal changes as you make the shift. You can adjust all color values of the image and if you check the *Tint* option at the bottom of the dialog you can easily create sepia-tone type images and choose any color you want. An additional advantage to using the Black and White adjustment is that you remain in a color mode (e.g., RGB or CYMK), which would not be the case if you shifted to grayscale color mode.

Using the Black and White adjustment to create a sepia-toned look from a color image

Fashion Use: o   To convert color images to black and white for publishing
o   To apply quick sepia-tone or colorizing effects

Hue/Saturation

This adjustment allows you to change the hue, saturation, and lightness of your image. If you choose to check the *Colorize* option, you are essentially colorizing a grayscale image with the current *foreground* color in the Toolbox, and interesting effects can be achieved. In all cases the tonal values are retained, which allows you to keep depth and shadows in your imagery.

In the example to the right, the original file was loaded (shown to the left). A selection of the right mannequin's dress was made. With the selection active, the *Hue/Saturation* settings were changed to turn the dress coral. Then the selection was inversed (*Select>Inverse*) and further Hue/Saturation adjustments were made to the background, this time with *Colorize* turned on.

Intermediate image

Final image

Original image

Using Black and White Color Mode

Use the Black and White adjustment to create grayscale images and remain in RGB or CMYK color mode (instead of Grayscale).

The settings used in the Match Color dialog

Fashion Use:

- o To recolor images maintaining the shadows and tonal value differences of the original art
- o To recolor areas of fabric to create new colorways, retaining the tonal values of the original color

Match Color   (RGB images only)

This function allows you to match the color from one document to another, or from one layer to another within the same document. You may also match colors between selections, either in the same document or on different documents. Basically you work between a *target* and a *source* and control the color conversion of the target by moving *Luminance, Color Intensity,* and *Fade* sliders. This adjustment only works on RGB imagery.

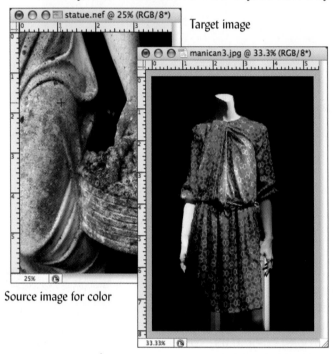

Target image

Source image for color

The new image created using the statue's colors

Fashion Use:

- o To create colorways for fabric from imagery that is nontextile in source
- o To facilitate the process of creating coordinate colorways

Replace Color

The *Replace Color* adjustment allows you to choose colors in an image using an Eyedropper tool, and replace them with a new hue. There are actually three Eyedropper tools for you to choose from. The *Add Eyedropper* lets you continue to add shades of the color you want, and the *Subtract Eyedropper* lets you remove colors, if necessary. It is helpful to choose the replacement hue at the bottom of the dialog early in the process so you can see the change that is occurring. As you work, you can see what is selected in the *Preview* window. Tonal values are kept in this mode.

Fashion Use:

- o To create alternate colorways for fabric and garments
- o To quickly exchange a color in a garment

Using Replace Color to replace the reddish tones on the skirt with green. This adjustment allows you to sample the color you want to replace from the image itself.

Original image

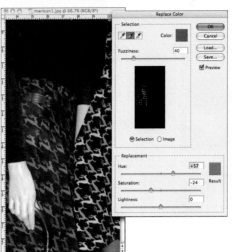

Working with Replace Color

New art

Other Adjustments

There are numerous other adjustments available for your exploration. Take the time to simply play. Many can be used for creative effect. Examples of some of the additional adjustments appear below.

Original image

New art

Exposure used to create a dramatic effect

Original image

New image

Posterize, set at 4 levels to simplify the image and create a poster effect

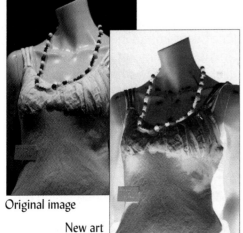

Original image

New art

Invert used to create a "negative" or inverse color effect

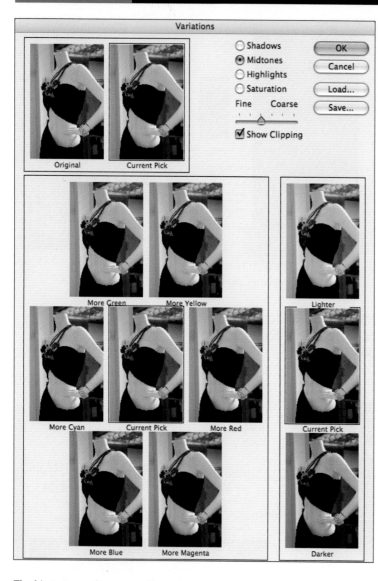

This completes the discussion of the *Adjustment* options. Although not all were discussed, you should have a good idea of the type of things that are possible using adjustments functions.

Duplicate
The **Duplicate** menu allows you to quickly duplicate an image. This is not saved until you actually perform the *File>Save* or *File>Save As...* command.

Apply Image
This command allows you to work with two images: a source and destination. You can blend a layer and channel of the source with a layer and channel of the active image (the destination). See Adobe's Help files for further information.

Calculations
This command allows you to blend two individual channels. They may be from the same or different sources. If you use two different images, they must have the same pixel dimension. Read Adobe's Help file for more info.

The Variations adjustment allows you to choose from multiple options, each with a different color tone.

Image Size
This is a highly used function in Photoshop. It allows you to analyze the file you already have and to resize your artwork with great control. Once you select this menu command, the *Image Size* dialog will open. You can examine the information provided to learn about your image. At the top of the dialog you can see how large the current file is and as you make changes, this information will update.

Through the Image Size dialog, you can adjust the following:
- o   The *Pixel Width* and *Height* of your image in pixels or percent.
- o   The *Print Size* in percent, inches, centimeters, millimeters, points, picas, or columns. If you click on the *Constrain Proportions* check box, any change you make in width or height will automatically alter the other dimension keeping the file's original proportion.
- o   *Resolution* in pixels per inch or centimeter. The resolution of an image greatly impacts its file size.
- o   *Scale Styles* is an option that when checked ensures that any styles that were created in the image will also scale.
- o   *Resample Image*, if checked, allows you to choose which method of interpolation you want (from the pop-up).

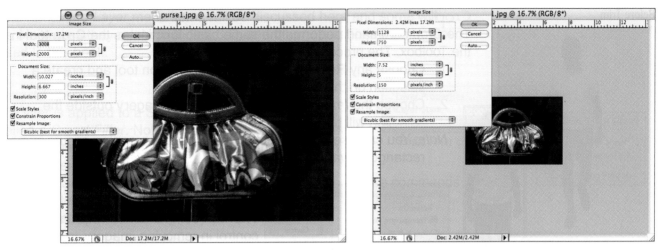

An image of a purse was opened and resized in both resolution and in image size (inches). The file size was reduced from 17.2 megs to 2.42 megs.

Canvas Size

This command allows you to add (or remove) canvas or working space to your artwork with great control. You can look at the current file size, width, and height, and then *you can alter the following:*

Taking the 7.52 x 5 inch image and adding canvas to create a 10 x 8 inch document

- o The *New Size* of the canvas in inches or centimeters, and where you want to position the current art relative to the canvas to be added or removed. The latter is controlled by clicking on the appropriate anchor (which controls the position of your current art relative to the change).
- o The *Relative* option, when checked, allows you to enter how much canvas you want to add or subtract from the perimeter of the image. You may use positive or negative numbers.
- o The *Canvas extension color.* You may choose between black, white, foreground, background, or transparent in the *Canvas extension color* pop-up. If you want a custom color, click on the little colored square to the right of the popup.

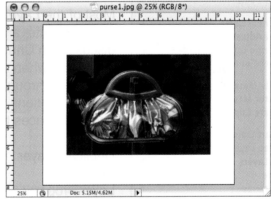

White canvas was added to the purse image. The purse was anchored to the center, so canvas was added evenly around it.

Pixel Aspect Ratio

You have the ability to control the aspect ratio of the display of pixels in Photoshop. By default the pixel is square, but other options exist. Note that this menu command has been moved to the View menu in CS4.

Rotate Canvas

This command allows you to actually rotate the canvas (without really rotating the saved image). Many people like this since they use a stylus (in lieu of a mouse) and feel like they are working on a piece of paper that is rotated, as they would be if they were working by hand. In CS4, a Rotate View button has been placed in the new Applications Bar at the top of the screen.

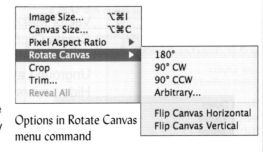

Options in Rotate Canvas menu command

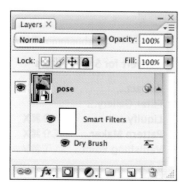

Viewing Smart Filters in the Layers palette

3. Perform filter operations. You will be able to edit these at any time by double-clicking on the filter effect name in the *Layers* palette (which appears under the Smart Object icon). This will open the filter gallery and allow you to edit or change the filter.

Extract

This is a filter that looks at artwork and attempts to isolate the foreground from the background of the image. It then erases the background.

1. Choose the layer that contains the artwork you want to perform an extraction on. If you choose the background it will become a layer when you are through, and if there is a selection in the layer, only the selection will be considered in the extraction process.

2. Choose the *Filter>Extract* menu command. The *Extract* dialog will open.

3. Use the tools in the dialog to assist Photoshop in knowing which part of the image you want to extract. There are numerous tools and the discussion of how to use them will not be presented here. Consult Photoshop's Help files. You can preview the extraction prior to committing, but when you are done, click the **OK** button to finalize the extraction.

The original image (above) and the new image (below) after the Cutout and Spatter filters were applied

The Filter Gallery   *(RGB only)*

The Filter Gallery allows you to apply multiple filters to an image in one set of operations. In a sense you create layers of filters in the gallery dialog, observing the result of each, turning the view of each on and off as you experiment. You may adjust the options for each filter as you work and see the effect. Most of the filters are special effect filters.

When you first open the *Filter Gallery*, you will see your image on the left and a listing of filter families in the center, filter options in the upper right, and a panel for active filters you create on the lower-right side.

The Filter Gallery dialog

Zooming and Panning

- o You may zoom in and out of your image and pan using the controls found on the lower-left side of the dialog.
- o To change the *magnification* of your image, click on the plus or minus buttons in the lower left of the image, or click on the magnification pop-up and choose the magnification level of your choice.
- o Use *Cmd/Ctrl++* or *Cmd/Ctrl+-* to zoom in or out.
- o To *pan*, place your cursor over the image, press the *Shift* key, and drag the mouse to pan, or you may use the scroll bars.

To Apply Filters

- o To choose a filter group, click on the down arrow of a filter group in the center of the Filter Gallery dialog.
- o To choose a specific filter, click on the icon for a filter in an open filter group, or click on the filter pop-up, and access the full list of filters available. If you know the name of the filter you want, you can press the first letter of the name of the filter. Note how the filter name appears in the list of active filters in the lower-right side of the dialog.
- o To experiment with options for each filter, move sliders, click on check boxes, or select other choices from the pop-ups available. The options will differ from filter to filter.
- o To create a second filter, click on the **New effect layer** button in the lower-right side of the dialog. Note how a second filter item appears in the list.
- o To delete a filter, click on the name of the filter in the filter list and then click on the **Delete effect layer** button in the lower-right corner of the dialog.

When you close the gallery and thus apply the filters, you will find that the next time you open the gallery, it will return to the last set of filters you used.

Liquify

This filter distorts the image by various methods so that the end results look like you have pushed and pulled, bloated, and distorted. This tool is used for both retouching and artistic effects.

The Liquify filter was run on an image of a sculptural knit.

Patternmaker

This is a filter that assists with creating patterns. We will explore this filter in the Textile Design section of the book. See Exercise #1 in the Textile Design section. *Note*: This filter has been removed from CS4.

Accented Edges
Angled Strokes
Bas Relief
Chalk & Charcoal
Charcoal
Chrome
Colored Pencil
Conté Crayon
Craquelure
Crosshatch
Cutout
Dark Strokes
Diffuse Glow
Dry Brush
Film Grain
Fresco
Glass
Glowing Edges
Grain
Graphic Pen
Halftone Pattern
Ink Outlines
Mosaic Tiles
Neon Glow
Note Paper
Ocean Ripple
Paint Daubs
✓ Palette Knife
Patchwork
Photocopy
Plaster
Plastic Wrap
Poster Edges
Reticulation
Rough Pastels
Smudge Stick
Spatter
Sponge
Sprayed Strokes
Stained Glass
Stamp
Sumi-e
Texturizer
Torn Edges
Underpainting
Water Paper
Watercolor

Filters and CMYK
The following filters do not work on CMYK files:
- Artistic
- Brush Strokes
- Sketch
- Texture
- Video

The same is true of miscellaneous filters in the Distort, Render, and Stylize groups.

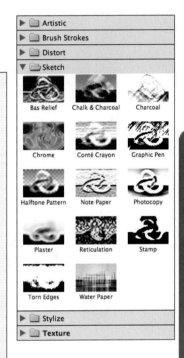

The New effect layer button (left) and Delete effect layer button (right)

New Filter Shortcut
When you are in the Filter Gallery, you can use the Cmd/Ctrl+N keyboard shortcut to add a new filter to the working list.

Artistic Filters   *(RGB only)*

The *Artistic* filters are a group of filters that simulate and create effects similar to what one can create using various art mediums (e.g., pencil, pastels, watercolor, etc.). Each has its own set of options for you to explore. All are available through the *Filter Gallery* as well. Explore some of these filters in Fashion Exercise #11.

Artistic ▶	Colored Pencil...
Artistic filter options	Cutout...
	Dry Brush...
	Film Grain...
	Fresco...
	Neon Glow...
	Paint Daubs...
	Palette Knife...
	Plastic Wrap...
	Poster Edges...
	Rough Pastels...
	Smudge Stick...
	Sponge...
	Underpainting...
	Watercolor...

Original Image   Palette Knife   Colored Pencil   Neon Glow   Cut-Out

Samples of Artistic Filters

Blur Filters

This group of filters serve to assist both with retouching and with special effects. They are used to retouch through a softening of the image by averaging pixels. We will use this in Fashion Exercise #8. Experiment with the entire group, but do explore the following in particular:

Blur ▶	Average
Blur filter options	Blur
	Blur More
	Box Blur...
	Gaussian Blur...
	Lens Blur...
	Motion Blur...
	Radial Blur...
	Shape Blur...
	Smart Blur...
	Surface Blur...

Original image

Gaussian Blur

Samples of Blur Filters

Smart Blur
This filter gives you a lot of control over the blur process.

Average
Average determines what the average color in the image/selection is, and then proceeds to fill your work area with the color. This is a great technique for doing color reduction and finding the average color of a group of pixels. It works well for creating a single-color background to an image.

Blur and Blur More
These reduce or eliminate what is known as "noise." In areas where there are a lot of color transitions, *Blur* serves to smooth the transition by averaging pixels next to hard edges. *Blur More* does the same thing as Blur, but with a much greater (three to four times) strength.

Gaussian Blur
Gaussian Blur allows you to blur a selection by an adjustable amount.

Lens Blur
Lens Blur produces an effect similar to having a low depth-of-field setting with your camera. The foreground is left sharp while the background becomes blurred.

Brush Strokes Filters   *(RGB only)*

This group of filters is similar to the *Artistic* filters in that you
are given tools that allow you to simulate the fine arts. The
Brush Strokes group filters provide ink stroke and brush effects through
the use of texture, noise, grain, edge detail, and so on. These filters are
all available for use through the *Filter Gallery*.

Brush Strokes ▶	Accented Edges...

Brush Strokes filter options

- Accented Edges...
- Angled Strokes...
- Crosshatch...
- Dark Strokes...
- Ink Outlines...
- Spatter...
- Sprayed Strokes...
- Sumi-e...

Samples of
Brush Strokes
Filters

Original image   Accented Edges   Ink Outlines   Dark Strokes

Distort Filters

This group of filters does exactly what the name implies: distort the
original art. There are a variety of options, some of which are available
through the *Filter Gallery*.

Distort ▶

Distort filter options

- Diffuse Glow...
- Displace...
- Glass...
- Lens Correction...
- Ocean Ripple...
- Pinch...
- Polar Coordinates...
- Ripple...
- Shear...
- Spherize...
- Twirl...
- Wave...
- ZigZag...

Samples of
Distort Filters

Original image   Ocean Ripple filter   Twirl filter

Noise Filters

This group serves to locate pixels
with random color levels and blends
them into the other pixels. Noise can
be added or removed, and we will
use this filter to assist in generating
rendered textiles (see Exercise #9
in the Textile Design chapter). The
Despeckle filter is used in Fashion
Exercise #8 to remove noise that
resulted from scanning a textured
paper.

Noise ▶

Noise filter options

- Add Noise...
- Despeckle
- Dust & Scratches...
- Median...
- Reduce Noise...

Original
image (left)
with contrast
heightened

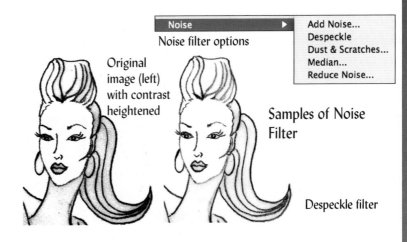

Samples of Noise
Filter

Despeckle filter

Pixelate

The *Pixelate* group of pixels looks at the pixels in an image/selection and clumps them together into cells or units of color.

Pixelate filter options

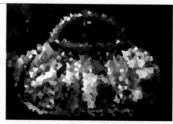

Pixelate ▶
Color Halftone...
Crystallize...
Facet
Fragment
Mezzotint...
Mosaic...
Pointillize...

Samples of Pixelate Filters

Original image

Mosaic filter

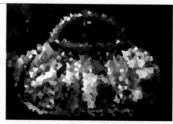

Crystallize filter

Render Filters

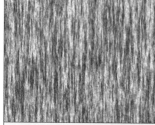

Render filter options

Render ▶
Clouds
Difference Clouds
Fibers...
Lens Flare...
Lighting Effects...

Although this group of filters is not used often for fashion, there is one filter of interest, the *Fibers* filter. You can use this in the *Rendered Fabrics* exercise (Exercise #9 in the Textile Design Chapter).

Sharpen Filters

The *Sharpen* filters are used

Sharpen filter options

Sharpen ▶
Sharpen
Sharpen Edges
Sharpen More
Smart Sharpen...
Unsharp Mask...

to increase the contrast of adjacent pixels. These are commonly used filters, particularly for photography, as an added crispness can be achieved in the image. Sharpen changes are subtle, but obvious to the eye up close.

Two versions of the Fibers filter: In the above example, a single color render was created. The lower example shows the rendering performed on a layer, above a solid color layer.

Sharpen, Sharpen More, and *Sharpen Edges* will be used in this book. *Sharpen* improves the clarity, and *Sharpen More* does the same, but more strongly. *Sharpen Edges* looks for where significant color changes occur and sharpens there.

Samples of Sharpen Filters

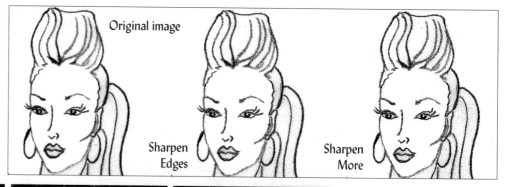

Original image

Sharpen Edges

Sharpen More

Original image

Sharpen Edges filter

Sharpen More filter

Samples of Sharpen Filters on a Photographic Image

Sketch Filters   *(RGB only)*

This group of filters can be used to add a hand-drawn look
or texture to your artwork. Many of the filters utilize the foreground and
background colors, as set in the Toolbox, and use them to redraw the
image. You will find all the *Sketch* filters in the *Filter Gallery*.

Sketch ▶	Bas Relief...
Sharpen filter options	Chalk & Charcoal...
	Charcoal...
	Chrome...
	Conté Crayon...
	Graphic Pen...
	Halftone Pattern...
	Note Paper...
	Photocopy...
	Plaster...
	Reticulation...
	Stamp...
	Torn Edges...
	Water Paper...

Samples of Sketch Filters

Original   Bas Relief   Water Paper   Graphic Pen   Conte Paper

Note: the foreground and background colors used are shown to the right.

Foreground and background colors
used with Sketch filters

Stylize Filters

These filters create interesting effects either by shifting pixels
or by finding and increasing the contrast in the artwork. Not all of the
filters are available through the Filter Gallery, so you must access them in
the *Stylize* section of the **Filter** menu. The controls are quite different on
these filters.

Stylize ▶	Diffuse...
Stylize filter options	Emboss...
	Extrude...
	Find Edges
	Glowing Edges...
	Solarize
	Tiles...
	Trace Contour...
	Wind...

Samples of
Stylize Filters

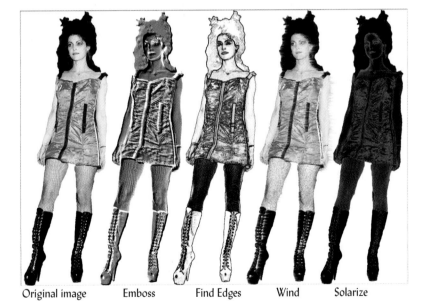

Original image   Emboss   Find Edges   Wind   Solarize

Texture Filters   *(RGB only)*

This group of menus adds the illusion of depth to imagery.
It also allows for creative effects. The Texturizer filter adds a
texture to your image, either one you select or one you create.
It can be used to simulate a textured paper upon which your image is set,
and thus, you can create art that looks hand-drawn.

Texture ▶	Craquelure...
Texture filter options	Grain...
	Mosaic Tiles...
	Patchwork...
	Stained Glass...
	Texturizer...

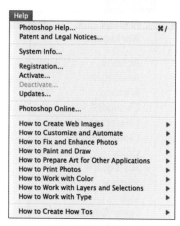

The Help menu

Help Menu

The **Help** menu serves primarily as a means to access the *Help* files of Photoshop (both built-in and online). At the lower end of the CS3 and CS4 Help menu, you will see a series of *How to's.* Use these as a means of learning how to perform commonly used functions and tasks in Photoshop.

This completes the discussion of the Menu Bar and menu functions in Photoshop.

Photoshop's Key Palettes

Photoshop has numerous palettes available. These are accessed through the **Window** menu and the *palette dock* on the right side of the screen.

A palette is a floating window that contains functions according to a theme. Palettes allow you to modify images, or to monitor your work status. If a palette is open, a check mark appears beside the palette name in the **Window** menu. The choice of which palettes to use will vary, user to user, and from project to project. Any given palette window may contain multiple functions, each organized like a manila folder with a tab.

The *Toolbox* and *Options Bar* are slightly different from the majority of the palettes, yet, they are considered palettes. In this book, the most commonly used palettes in Photoshop are the *Toolbox, Options Bar, Layers, History, Color, Swatches, Paths,* and *Brushes* palettes. Some of these are discussed elsewhere in this book and cross-references will be given to those areas to avoid redundancy. Since not all palettes will be covered here, refer to Photoshop's Help files to read up on those not discussed.

Photoshop's Workspace

A workspace is a combination of palettes, bars (both Menu and Option), and windows. The arrangement of these elements is called a *Workspace*, and you have the option to customize/create your own workspace. You may indeed create several, to suit the needs of different types of projects, or how you choose to view a project at different points in time. Photoshop also offers you a variety of preset workspaces, created according to project type. Quick access to workspaces is found in the options bar.
To create a custom workspace:

1. Open the palettes you want to use (either through the *Window* menu or by opening them in the Palette dock). Position them where you like for best efficiency in your work.

2. If you want to change the font size of text displayed in the options bar, palettes, and tool tips, change these in the *General Preferences*.

3. Choose the *Menu* and *Keyboard* set you want to work with (in the **Edit** menu).

4. Choose the *Window>Workspace>Save Workspace* menu command. A *Save Workspace* dialog will open.

5. Choose the options you want to include and type in a name for the workspace. Click **OK**.

Note: Palette vs. Panel
As of version CS4, Photoshop is now using the term panels. All prior versions used palettes. This book will use palettes as it was written prior to the release of CS4.

Note: Photoshop's Key Palettes
The key palettes used throughout this book are:
- o Toolbox
- o Options Bar
- o Layers
- o Navigator
- o History
- o Color
- o Swatches
- o Paths
- o Brushes

Note: Palette Layout in Memory
Photoshop will remember your most recent palette layout when you reopen the program.

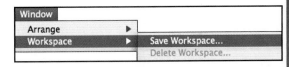

Choosing the menu command used to create a workspace (above) and naming the workspace (below)

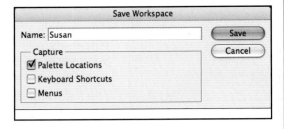

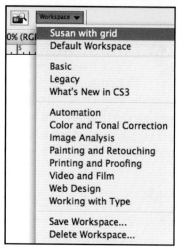

Choosing your workspace from the options bar

The workspace will be saved. You can recall it at any time by choosing the *Window>Workspace* menu and locating your workspace in the menu list. You can also choose a workspace from the options bar (CS3) or Applications Bar (CS4). To revert back to the default workspace, choose this option from the *Window>Workspace* menu or the options bar/Application Bar.

The Layout and Language of Palettes

Photoshop has a myriad of palettes, and thus, your workspace can become quite cluttered. There are ways to organize palettes for improved efficiency. It is important to develop an understanding of all the language revolving around the palette world. Note that CS3 and CS4 differ somewhat from prior versions and the discussion below refers primarily to CS3.

Hide/Show Palettes

Pressing the Tab key on the keyboard hides all palettes from view. Pressing the key a second time returns them to view. Pressing the Shift+Tab keys hides the palettes but leaves the Toolbox; and, of course, pressing the Shift+Tab a second time returns palettes to view.

Palettes (defined)

A palette (panel) is a collection of functions and commands pertaining to a common theme, arranged into a window. *Typically, the following are components of a palette:*

Title Bar—which displays the name of the palette (on a tab) and contains the minimize and maximize buttons. You can collapse a palette to its title bar only, by clicking on the bar, or by double-clicking on the palette tab. Docked palettes contain double arrows that allow you to collapse (to icon view) and expand the palette (to full view).

Window—which displays and contains the primary functions or options of the palette. The contents vary greatly from palette to palette.

Palette Menu—Most palettes have a menu, accessed by clicking on the downward pointing arrow (CS3 and CS4) or the arrowhead (CS1 and CS2). These menus contain additional commands pertinent to the function of the palette. For some palettes, many of the options in the menu can also be found in the correlating menu of the Menu Bar at the top of the Photoshop window.

Palette Buttons—Numerous menus have a bar of buttons across the bottom, which serve as shortcuts to key functions of the palette.

The palette title bar (above) and the button bar (below)

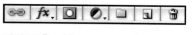

Double arrows used to collapse a palette to icon view

The History palette as a free-floating palette

Window
Title Bar   **Palette Menu**

New Layer...   ⇧⌘N
Duplicate Layer...
Delete Layer
Delete Hidden Layers

New Group...
New Group from Layers...

Lock All Layers in Group...

Convert to Smart Object
Edit Contents

Layer Properties...
Blending Options...

Create Clipping Mask   ⌥⌘G

Link Layers
Select Linked Layers

Merge Down   ⌘E
Merge Visible   ⇧⌘E
Flatten Image

Animation Options   ▶
Palette Options...

Palette Buttons

Free-Floating Palettes

These are palettes that sit by themselves on the workspace. All Creative Suite versions of Photoshop have free-floating palettes. When you select a palette via the ***Window*** menu, it will become free-floating.
The following is true of free-floating palettes:
- o   They can be moved anywhere on the document, and thus offer the advantage of being placed nearer to where you are working on the art.

- o They can be resized by dragging and moving any side of the palette, or by dragging the size box in the lower-right corner of the palette.
- o They can be collapsed to the title bar to reduce the clutter in your workspace. This is achieved by clicking once in its title bar, or double-clicking on the palette tab.
- o Free-floating palettes can be **grouped**, **stacked,** or **docked**. This is typically done to simplify the workspace and organize the palettes by shared function.

Palette Group

A *palette group* is a collection of palettes arranged *horizontally* in a window. This is generally done with palettes that are related in function such as the *Color, Swatches,* and *Styles* palettes. The result is an efficient workspace. The group becomes a unit, which has advantages.
The following are features of palette groups:
- o You can move a palette into a group by dragging the palette by its tab into the highlighted blue drop zone at the top of the group.
- o Clicking on a palette tab will bring the palette to the front of the group.
- o If you want to rearrange the palettes within the group, drag a palette (by its tab), left or right, to its new location.
- o To move an entire group, *click+hold* on the group's title bar and drag it to a new location.
- o Palette groups can float anywhere on the document, or they may be docked.

Palette Stack

This is a collection of free-floating palettes or palette groups that are joined *vertically*, top to bottom. One would stack palettes when it is desirable to organize or move the palettes as a unit.
The following are features of palette stacks:
- o You can stack palettes by dragging the top of one palette (by its tab) under another palette, and moving it until you see the highlighted blue strip. When you release the mouse, the palettes will be stacked.
- o Palette stacks can float anywhere, or they may be docked.

Palette Dock

A palette dock is a collection of palettes or palette groups displayed together, typically vertically, and arranged in the *docking area* to the right side of the workspace. You can tell when you are in a dock by the blue highlighting that appears as you drag the palette around. This indicates that you are in what is known as the *drop zone*.
The three views of docked palettes are:
1. **Icon View** – the most compressed view (called an icon dock), which displays the icon of the palette only, and no working functions. You would use this view when you do not need the palette, but want to keep it handy.
2. **Icon with Title View** – a view that contains the icon and the title, but no working functions. To move between Icon View and Icon with Title view, click and hold on the gripper bar and drag it left or right.

Palette Tip
In the User Interface Preferences, you have the option to Auto-Collapse Icon Panels. When this is checked, palettes will auto-collapse when you click outside the palette.

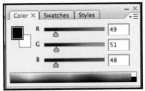

A palette group

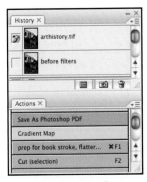

A palette stack

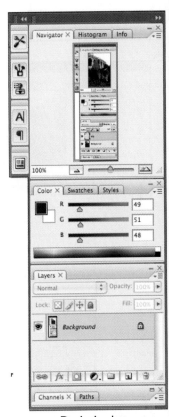

Docked palettes

The three
views of
docked
palettes:
icon,
icon plus
title, and
expanded

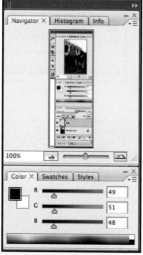

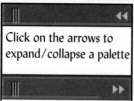

Click on the arrows to
expand/collapse a palette

3. **Expanded View** – This view of the docked palette shows you the
   entire palette with all its functions ready to use.

The following are features of the palette dock and its palettes:

o   To *expand* from icon view to expanded view, click on the double
    arrows (left-pointing) at the upper right of the palette.
o   To *collapse* from expanded view to icon view, click on the double
    arrows (right-pointing) at the upper right of the palette.
o   If you drag a palette or palette group into an icon dock, the
    palettes will automatically collapse to icons.
o   Palette icons or icon groups can be dragged vertically up and
    down in the dock.
o   As you drag a palette up or down in a dock you will see blue
    highlighting, which indicates that you are in a *drop zone*. If you
    drag the panel outside the drop zone, it becomes free-floating.
o   To *dock* a free-floating palette, drag it by its tab into the dock.
    You can position it at the top, bottom, or between other palettes.
    Palette groups can be docked by dragging the group by its title bar
    into the dock.
o   To *undock* a palette, drag the palette by its tab, or the palette
    group by its title bar, out of the dock. You can drag a palette or
    palette group into another dock, or onto the screen (in which case
    it is free floating).
o   If all palettes are removed from a drop zone, the drop zone will
    disappear.
o   To create a *new palette dock*, move a palette to the drop
    zone, next to an existing dock or at the outer right edge of the
    workspace. When you drag and see the blue vertical highlight you
    know you are creating a new dock.
o   Docked palettes can be *resized* horizontally by dragging the
    gripper in the title bar of the palette.

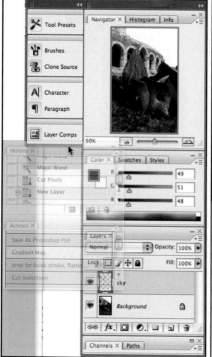

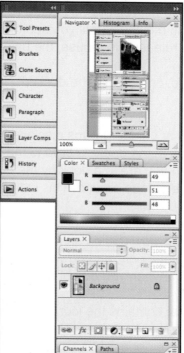

Docking Zones and Drop Zones
These are the areas where panels
can be docked and they are
indicated by the blue highlighting you
see as you are dragging a palette in
the zone. There is a drop zone at the
top and at the bottom of a palette.

The Process of Docking
a Palette Stack
On the left, the History and Actions palette
stack are dragged over to the docked palettes
and under a stacked group that includes the
Layer Comps palette. You can see the blue
highlighted line, which means that you are
in the drop zone. The right image shows you
how the History and Actions palettes have
become icons in the dock.

The Toolbox

The Toolbox in Photoshop is technically a palette (and now panel in CS4). It can be opened and closed using the **Window** menu. Most of the functions of the Toolbox are discussed in other chapters of this book. The *Selection* tools are discussed in Chapter 2. The *Painting*, *Retouching*, and *Drawing* tools (including Type) are covered in Chapter 4.

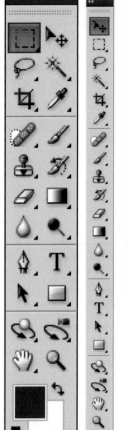

The following are features of the tools in Photoshop's Toolbox:

o Tools that have arrows in the lower-left corner have **additional tools** stacked or hidden beneath. You can access these tools by clicking and holding on the top tool, and sliding over to the desired tool. This tool will remain on top until you select a different tool. All tools in a stacked group that have a shortcut share the same keyboard shortcut.

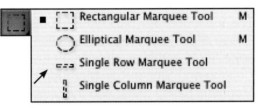

Above: The arrowhead in the lower-right corner of the Rectangular Marquee selection tool indicates that there are further tools stacked beneath.

Tool Tips: Place your cursor over a tool and wait to see its name and keyboard shortcut.

o **Tool tips** exist. Placing your cursor over a tool and waiting allows you to see the name of the tool and the keyboard shortcut for that tool.

o When you select a tool, the **options bar** displays the various options available for use with that tool.

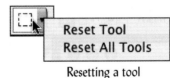

The options bar for the Rectangular Marquee tool

Photoshop's CS4 (double-wide) and CS3 (single-wide) Toolbox.

o Tools can be **reset** to their original default setting by holding the *Ctrl key/right mouse* click (Mac/Windows) and clicking on the tool's icon in the options bar. Choose the *Reset* tool menu command.

o **Tool Presets** can be accessed, created, and saved. These are user-defined combinations of settings (from the options bar, such as mode, opacity, and flow for the **Brush** tool) and they are created and used to save time if you use the same combination of settings often as you work.

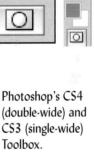

Resetting a tool

o To *access a preset*, click on the *Tool Preset picker* in the options bar. When the pop-up opens, choose the preset of your choice.

o To *create a preset*, click on the *Tool Preset picker* and slide over to the **Create new tool preset** button and click. A dialog will open. Name your Preset and click **OK**. The next time you access the Tool Preset pop-up menu for the tool, you will see your preset.

Various tools in Photoshop already have presets available. You can access these presets by clicking on the Tool Preset Picker in the options bar. The *Tool Preset* menu allows you to manage your presets and access the various libraries of presets.

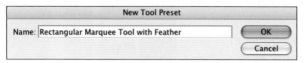

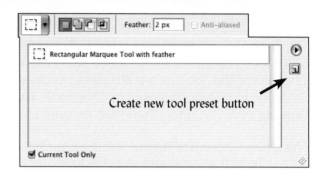

Creating a Tool Preset: First choose all the settings you want for the tool, then name and save it using the Tool Preset menu.

Create new tool preset button

The Selection tools

Selection Tools

The top four tools (plus hidden tools) are the Selection tools in Photoshop. These allow you to create selections, either by shape, by painting, or by color. Tools in this group include the Rectangular, Elliptical, and Single Column and Single Row Marquee tools; the Lasso, Polygonal Lasso, and Magnetic Lasso tools; and the Quick Selection, Magic Wand, and Move tools. A full discussion of these tools is given in Chapter 2, pages 28–34.

Crop and Slice Tools

This tool group allows you to crop an image or slice it for Web pages. Tools in this group include the Crop, Slice, and Slice Select tools.

The Crop and Slice tools

Crop Tool   (C)

This tool allows you to select areas of your image and remove the outer nonselected area. This is an easy way to remove unwanted portions of an image.

To use the tool:

1. Choose the **Crop** tool.

2. *Click+hold+drag* the mouse as you surround the portion of the image you want to keep. You do not need to be precise as you can adjust this later. The outer areas of the image will be dimmed once the mouse button is released. You will see the cropping marquee surrounding the image.

3. If you like, resize the marquee by dragging the handles of the selection. You can move the marquee around on the image by clicking and holding inside the selection and dragging it to a new position. The marquee can be rotated by moving the cursor to the outside of the bounding box, and when you see the rotation cursor, clicking and dragging on the document to rotate the cropping bounding box.

4. Double-click inside the marquee to finalize the crop or click on the **Commit** button (the check mark) in the tool options bar.

Note: **Alternate Ways to Crop Images**
In addition to the Crop tool, you may use the Image>Crop or Image>Trim menu commands to crop. Each option has its own unique approach.

Note: **CS4 Tools**
The Tools panel of CS4 has rearranged the tools somewhat. See page vii of the Preface for a quick overview.

Crop Tool Options

Two sets of tool options are available, depending on whether or not you have selected a cropping area.

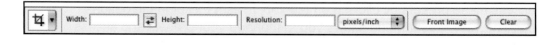

Cropping in Process:
Left: The original image
Center: Cropping in process
Right: The cropped image

Before   During   After

Prior to using the tool you will have the following options:

Width and Height
Setting these options allows you to crop the image in a specified finished
size. You enter the width and height of your image, and your cropping
selection will become that size once you click on the document. If you do
not enter any numbers here, but set a resolution (discussed next), your
selection will be in the same aspect ratio as your original image. Type "in"
or "cm" after your number to set inches or centimeters.

Resolution
Setting the resolution allows you to define the ultimate pixels per inch or
centimeter resolution of the finished cropped piece. When the cropping
is complete, the resolution will change automatically. Recall that high
resolutions (e.g., 300 dpi) are used for printing and lower resolutions
(e.g., 72 dpi) are used for Web graphics.

> *Note*: Using the Width, Height, and Resolution options allows you to
> combine *image size* functions with the *cropping* function. Your
> image will be resampled according to your specifications. If you
> check the *Image Size* after you crop, you will see that it has
> become the numbers you set in Width, Height, and Resolution.
> You do not need to set all three items; you can choose width and
> height or resolution.

Front Image
Clicking on this button allows you to see the settings (width, height,
and resolution) of the current image. If you want, you may load another
image and use its settings as the guide. Simply choose the **Crop** tool,
click on the **Front Image** button, then switch to the document you want to
crop. (Note that you have the settings of the other image.) Perform your
cropping functions, resampling thus, from another document.

Clear Front Image Settings
Remember to clear the
settings of the Front Image
if you do not want to apply
them to the cropping of
the current image, as front
image settings remain as you
toggle between documents.
Click on the Clear button to
remove all information.

Clear

After a cropping area is selected, clicking on this button clears all numbers. Once a cropped selection is made, with or without width/height/ resolution settings, the tool options change. You will then see new options in the options bar. *These are:*

Cropped Area: Delete/Hide

If the *Delete* option is active, the cropped area (i.e., the area outside the cropping marquee) will be deleted or removed from the image. If the *Hide* option is active, the cropped area remains part of the image and you can move the view of the cropped image with the **Move** tool.

> *Note*: The Delete/Hide options will be dimmed if you are working on a *background*. Convert the background to a layer (using the *Layer>New>Background from Layer* menu command or by double-clicking on the *Background* name, as this turns the background into a layer.

Cropping Shield Options

A cropping shield masks or shades the area of the image outside the cropping marquee. You can change the *color* by clicking once on the color box, and choosing a new color from the *Color Picker* that opens. Change the *opacity* of the shield by typing in a new number or clicking on the arrow of the opacity pop-up and moving the slider that appears.

The Slice and Slice Selection tools
(plus hidden tools)

Slice Tools   (K)

Slice tools are used to prepare images for the Web. You can slice a large image into sections, which speeds up the process of loading a large image on the Web. Although the user sees no difference between the full image and a sliced image, the loading time is sped up tremendously, as each slice of the image loads simultaneously. This tool will not be used nor addressed further in this book as it is a Web design tool.

The Retouch tools
(with hidden tools)

Retouching Tools

The next group of tools are used for retouching your artwork. These tools, often called image-processing tools, allow you to edit images as if you were working in a darkroom. A large number of tools exist in this group. They are: Spot Healing Brush, Healing Brush, Patch, Red Eye, Clone Stamp, Pattern Stamp, Eraser, Background Eraser, Magic Eraser, Blur, Sharpen, Smudge, Dodge, Burn, and Sponge. These are covered in Chapter 4, pages 95–100.

The Painting tools
(with hidden tools)

Painting, Drawing, and Type Tools

The **Painting** tools are used to paint with pixels and include the Brush, Pencil, Color Replacement, History Brush, Art History Brush, Gradient, and Paint Bucket. **Drawing** and **Type** tools serve to draw and edit vector images, and create type. They include the Pen and its variants (Add, Delete, and Convert Anchor Point tools; Horizontal and Vertical Type tools and type Masks; Path and Direct Selection tools; and various Shape tools). Note that the Shape tools may be drawn as raster images by simply choosing the mode in the options bar before you begin drawing.

The Drawing and
Type tools
(with hidden tools)

Annotation, Measuring, and Navigation Tools

The **Note** and **Audio Annotation** tools allow you to create annotations as you work. The **Eyedropper** and **Color Sampler** allow you to sample colors, and the **Ruler** and **Count** allow you to measure. The lower two tools allow you to maneuver around your document either by zooming in or out (**Zoom** tool) or by panning around the document (**Hand** tool). The Zoom and Hand tools are discussed on page 15.

Annotation, Measuring, and Navigation tools

Foreground and Background Colors

The *Foreground* and *Background* icons are positioned beneath the tool groups. You use them to set the current foreground or background colors simply by clicking on the chosen option and picking a color from the *Color Picker* or by choosing a color in the *Swatch* or *Color* palette. You may also use the **Eyedropper** tool to sample a color from artwork. The upper color selection box is the foreground color and the lower color selection box is the background color.

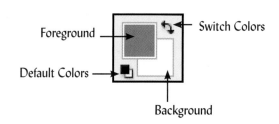

Foreground · Switch Colors · Default Colors · Background

There are two icons that assist with color selection and management. The **Switch Colors** icon (or *X* on the keyboard) allows you to reverse the foreground and background. The **Default Colors** icon (or *D* on the keyboard) allows you to return to the default black foreground and white background.

Standard Mode vs. Quick Mask Mode

This icon, positioned near the bottom of the Toolbox, is a "toggle" in that it changes according to whether you are in *Standard Mode* or *Quick Mask* mode. Quick Mask assists you in painting selections. See Chapter 2, pages 37–39 for a fuller discussion.

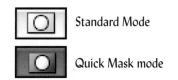

Standard Mode · Quick Mask mode

Screen Modes   (F)

The lower icon in the Toolbox allows you to choose which screen display you want. When you click and hold on the icon, you may choose between Standard Screen Mode, Maximized Screen Mode, Full Screen Mode with Menu Bar, and Full Screen Mode. *Clicking+holding* on the current mode will open a pop-up menu and allow you to change modes. CS4 allows access to screen modes from the Application Bar.

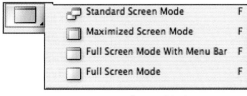

Screen Modes

The Options Bar

The **options bar** is typically located at the top of your workspace; however, it can be moved anywhere you want. This bar allows you to view all options for the tool currently selected in the Toolbox. Thus, when you switch tools, the options change to reflect those available for the tool. Tool presets are located to the left side of the bar and you can access custom workspaces through the *Workspace* pop-up on the right side of the bar (CS3 only). A discussion of the basic features of the options bar is presented in Chapter 1, pages 15–16.

The options bar

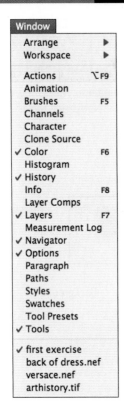

The check marks in the Window menu indicate which palettes are open.

The Navigator palette shows you what part of the image you are actually seeing in the document.

The next group of palettes are the most commonly used palettes in this book.

The Navigator Palette

The *Navigator* palette allows you to see what portion of the document you are viewing on the screen. This is particularly helpful if you are zoomed in, as you can see where you are in relation to the full image. A red box in the palette shows you the *Proxy Preview Area*. If you *click+hold* inside of this area, you can drag the hand cursor that appears and move the Proxy Preview area around on the document, thus controlling what portion of the image appears in your view on-screen. You may also control the magnification or zoom level by moving the **Zoom Slider** at the bottom of the palette or by typing in a new number in the number field in the lower-left corner of the window. You can also click on the **Zoom In** or **Zoom Out** buttons, which appear to either side of the Zoom slider.

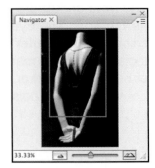

To navigate, pan by dragging the Proxy Preview Area (the red box). Zoom using the various controls at the bottom of the palette.

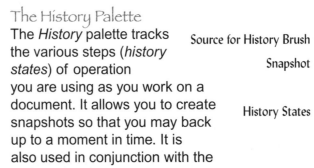

Palette options exist and may be accessed by clicking on the palette menu arrowhead in the upper-right corner of the window.

The Layers Palette   *F7*

The *Layers* palette is one of the most used palettes in the program (along with the Toolbox and options bar). Layers are used to isolate imagery and allow you to work with various elements of your artwork more independently. There are different types of layers (adjustment layers, fill layers, type, masking layers, etc.). A full discussion of layers and the *Layers* palette is given in Chapter 2, pages 47–59.

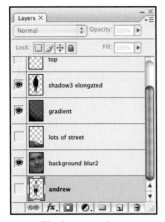

The Layers palette

The History Palette

The *History* palette tracks the various steps (*history states*) of operation you are using as you work on a document. It allows you to create snapshots so that you may back up to a moment in time. It is also used in conjunction with the **History Brush** tool (see pages 83–84). Certain operations, such as tool changes, are not recorded in the palette. A discussion of the *History* palette, history *states,* and *snapshots* is given in Chapter 1, pages 22–23, and is used elsewhere in the book.

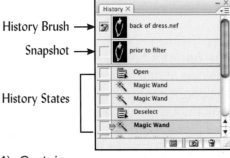

Source for History Brush

Snapshot

History States

The History palette

The Color Palette   F6

The *Color* palette displays a strip of colors, called a *Color Ramp* or *Spectrum*, used to select, edit, or mix colors. You may click on either the *Foreground* or *Background* icon in the palette, and then select/create the color you want as the current working color. On examination of the palette, you will see the default black and white colors appear along the left side of the palette window. In the palette menu you may choose from various color modes (e.g., RGB vs. CMYK). You can move these sliders to mix custom colors.

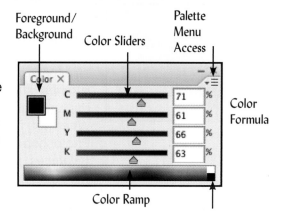

Foreground/Background   Color Sliders   Palette Menu Access

Color Formula

Color Ramp

Default white and black boxes

To choose/create a custom color:

1. Choose or change the color *mode*, as desired, by selecting the color model of choice from the palette menu (click on the arrowhead in the upper-right corner of the palette to view the menu).

2. Click on the *Foreground* or *Background* icon in the *Color* palette. This will place a dark outline around the icon, indicating that it is the active box.

3. *Click+hold+drag* your cursor over the Color Ramp and note it has changed to an eyedropper. As you move the eyedropper around the color strip, the color changes in the *foreground or background* icon that is active. Once you release the mouse button, the color remains and will become the current color for the *foreground/background*. If you want to mix the color manually or edit the color slightly, move the individual color sliders (e.g., CMYK) to the left or right as shown in the example below.

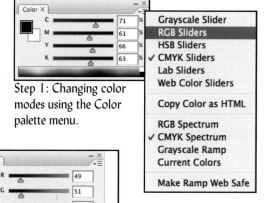

Step 1: Changing color modes using the Color palette menu.

| Grayscale Slider |
| RGB Sliders |
| HSB Sliders |
| ✓ CMYK Sliders |
| Lab Sliders |
| Web Color Sliders |
| Copy Color as HTML |
| RGB Spectrum |
| ✓ CMYK Spectrum |
| Grayscale Ramp |
| Current Colors |
| Make Ramp Web Safe |

Step 3: Explore colors by moving the eyedropper icon over the Color Spectrum bar.

Creating a deeper shade of pink. The palette on the left shows the original pink. The palette on the right shows how the black slider was moved to the right to create a deeper shade of pink. This technique is commonly used for adding shading in fashion drawings.

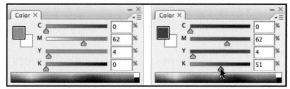

Documenting Color Formulas
Record color formulas (in RGB or CMYK) to quickly reproduce the color later in a different project. You can also drag an image, transporting the color from one document to the next. You may also use the clipboard and copy/paste artwork to transport colors.

Recording Color Formulas

It is often helpful to record a color formula so that you can mix the color in another file or program (although you can simply copy and paste imagery with the color into the destination file and retrieve the color with the Eyedropper tool). Simply record the Red-Green-Blue components (if RGB), or the Cyan-Magenta-Yellow-Black components (if CMYK). As an example, the pink above has a CMYK formula of 0-62-4-0, and this is altered by adding black to create a formula of 0-62-4-51.

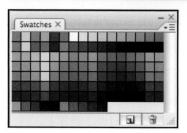

The Swatches palette in thumbnail view

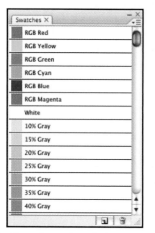

The Swatches palette in list view

The Create new swatch of the foreground color button (left) and the Delete button (right)

The Swatches Palette

The *Swatches* palette stores colors and allows you to save custom libraries as well as access other color libraries (such as the Pantone libraries). When you first open Photoshop and the *Swatches,* palette, you will see a default set of swatches, which includes a spectrum of colors. The first two rows are composed of the various RGB or CMYK basic colors and a full range of grayscale. The other colors provide a nice spread of the basic hues. If you move and hold your cursor over a color, you will see its name. Across the bottom of the palette you will see two buttons. The left button allows you to *create a new swatch from the foreground color*. Clicking on this button will take the current foreground color and add it to the palette. The second button (the *Trashcan*) allows you to *delete* a swatch by dragging the swatch over the icon.

The palette menu allows you to access various commands that provide the ability to create swatches, load and save libraries, reset libraries, and change the view of the *Swatch* palette between differing sizes of thumbnails and the list view.

The following describes the steps of various operations involving the Swatches palette:

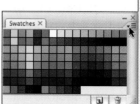

The Swatches palette menu showing view and library options

To switch between thumbnail and list view of swatches:

1. Access the *Swatches* palette menu and choose the view you want by sliding over it. When you release your mouse button, the view of the swatches in the palette will change.

To add a swatch to the palette:
Using the Swatches palette button bar:

1. Click on the **Create a new swatch of foreground color** button at the bottom of the *Swatches* palette. The current *foreground* color in the Toolbox will now appear at the end of the palette and it will be called *Swatch 1*.

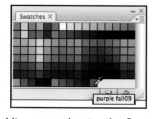

Adding a swatch using the Create new swatch of the foreground color button (above) and naming the swatch (below)

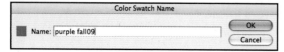

2. Double-click on the swatch in the *Swatches* palette to open the *Color Swatch Name* dialog.

3. Name your swatch and click **OK**.

OR
Using the Swatches palette menu:
1. Choose the *New Swatch* command from the *Swatches* palette menu. The *Color Swatch Name* dialog will open showing the current foreground color.

2. Name your swatch and click **OK**. The swatch will appear at the end of the color strip in the palette.

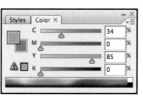
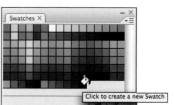

Adding a new swatch using the palette menu

OR
Using the Color palette or the Foreground color in the Toolbox:
1. Make either the foreground or background color the active color in the *Color* palette, or simply use the foreground color that is active.

2. Place your cursor in a gray area of the *Swatches* palette. It will turn into a paint bucket icon.

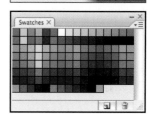

Adding a new swatch using the Color palette or the foreground color and the paint bucket cursor

3. Click with the cursor, and the new color will fill the first open palette spot at the end of the color strip in the palette. You will have to rename it as above.

OR
Using the Color Picker in CS3 and CS4:
1. Click on the *Foreground* or *Background* icon in the Toolbox to open the *Color Picker* dialog.

2. Either use the color that was in the Toolbox, or choose a new color in the *Color Picker*.

3. Click on the **Add To Swatches** button. The *Color Swatch Name* dialog will open showing the current color in the *Color Picker*.

4. Name your swatch and click **OK**. The swatch will appear at the end of the palette.

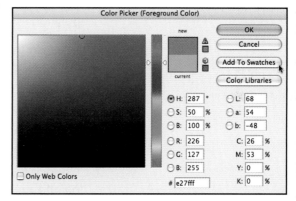

Adding a new swatch using the Color Picker and the Add to Swatches button

To delete a swatch:
Do one of the following:
o Drag the swatch you want to remove over the **Delete** button at the bottom of the palette (the trash can icon).
OR
o Press and hold the *Opt/Alt* key on the keyboard. The cursor will turn into a pair of scissors. Move over the swatch you want to delete and click.

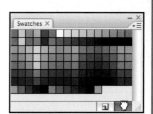

Dragging a swatch over the Delete button (trash can) to remove it

OR

o   Position your cursor over the swatch you want to delete and *Ctrl/Right+click* to open the context menu. Slide down to the *Delete Swatch* option and release the mouse.

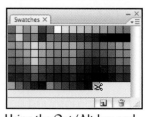

Using the Opt/Alt key and the scissor icon to remove a swatch

In CS1 and CS2 you can select multiple swatches by pressing the *Cmd/Ctrl* key on the keyboard as you click on each swatch and add it to the selected group. Then you can perform the deletion process as above.

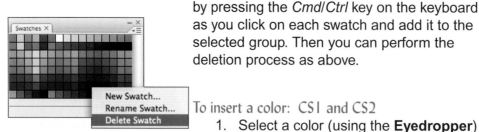

Using the Context menu to remove a swatch

To insert a color: CS1 and CS2

1. Select a color (using the **Eyedropper**) in the *Color* palette or create a new foreground color in the Toolbox.

2. Hold down the *Shift+Opt/Alt* keys and position the pointer over a swatch in the middle of the palette (the pointer will turn into a paint bucket cursor). Click with the mouse to insert the color. All colors to the right of the current position move over one.

To reposition swatches: CS1 and CS2

1. *Click+hold* on the swatch you want to move and drag it to a new position.

2. Release the mouse button and all swatches will shuffle as necessary.

To save a swatch library:

1. Organize your swatches in the palette. Give them meaningful names and, if you have CS1 or CS2, reposition them.

2. Choose the *Save Swatches...* command from the *Swatches* palette menu. When the dialog opens, type in a name for your library and click on **Save**. The swatch library should be saved in the *Color Swatches* folder found in the **Presets** folder of

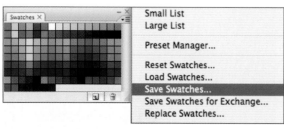

Saving a Swatch Library

the **Photoshop** folder on your hard drive. If the file requester that opens does not direct it there, you may want to manually direct the file there to retain consistency with other saved libraries.

You would want to build a custom swatch library if you are working with specific colors for a given collection or season. For example, once you create and mix the colors of your upcoming Fall collection, you would want to save this library for use as you develop the collection, and as a means of archiving the data.

To load a built-in swatch library:

1. Open the *Swatches* palette menu and slide down to the palette you wish to open. Release the mouse.

2. A dialog will open, asking if you want to replace or append. Make your decision and click **OK**. If you chose to append, the library will appear beneath the existing library.
   If you chose to replace, you will see only the new library.

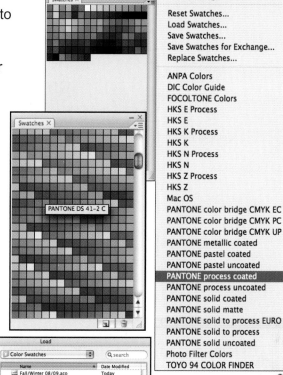

The process of loading a built-in library of swatches such as a Pantone collection

To load a previously saved custom swatch library:

1. Open the *Swatches* palette menu and choose the *Load Swatches...* command.

2. A file requestor dialog will open. Locate the library, which should be in the *Color Swatches* folder found in the **Presets** folder of your **Photoshop** folder. Click **OK**. The custom library will load.

To restore the default Photoshop Swatches palette:

1. Choose *Reset Swatches...* from the *Swatches* palette menu.

2. A warning dialog will open, asking if you want to replace the current swatches with the default swatches. If you click **OK,** you will exchange libraries. If you click **Append**, the default library will appear beneath the existing library.

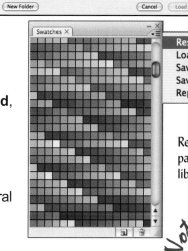

Resetting the Swatch palette to the default library

Adobe's Color Picker

Although the *Color Picker* is not a palette, it is integral to working with color in the *Color* and *Swatches* palettes and thus it deserves some discussion.

The following is true of the Color Picker:

o Clicking on the foreground or background color in the Toolbox opens the *Color Picker*.

o You may work with color in one of four models: HSB, RGB, Lab, and CMYK.

o The color formulas of all four models are displayed for your use and information.

o You can view the *current* color (i.e., the original color) as you choose your *new* color.

Note:

Append?
You will often be given the chance to "append" a palette. Append means to "add" colors to the existing palette instead of replacing the existing palette. This way you can work with two palettes; the original and the new one loaded.

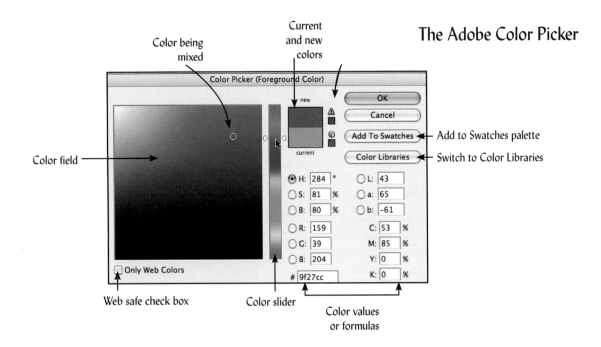

Color being mixed

Current and new colors

The Adobe Color Picker

Add to Swatches palette

Switch to Color Libraries

Color field

Only Web Colors

Web safe check box

Color slider

Color values or formulas

The Out of Gamut Alert

The Web Safe Alert

o The *color slider* appears as a vertical bar in the center of the picker. Move your cursor up and down this bar to choose the hue.

o The *color field* for the selected hue shows you the value scale for the hue and a small white circle icon allows you to see where you are in the range of values.

     o There are two warning alert icons that may appear in the *Color Picker*. The **Alert Triangle** (which looks like a Yield sign) indicates that the color is out of gamut for printing. The **Alert Cube** icon indicates that the color is not a Web-safe color. If you click on either of these icons (should they appear), Photoshop will choose the closest safe color.

o To view only Web-safe colors, click on the *Only Web Colors* check box in the lower-left corner of the dialog.

o In CS3 and CS4, clicking on the **Add to Swatches** button will add the color to the *Swatches* palette and return you to the *Color Picker*. You will be asked to name the color in the *Color Swatch Name* dialog that opens.

o Clicking on the **Color Libraries** button takes you to the *Color Libraries* dialog where you can select a color library using the Book pop-up. Then, you can simply type a color name/number appropriate to the numbering system of the library to take you to that area of the library.

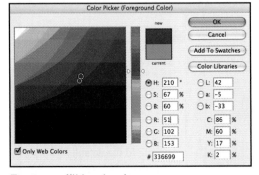

Turning on Web-safe colors

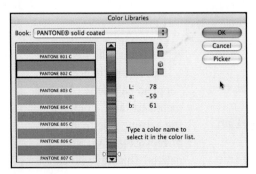

Using the Color Libraries

Naming a color in the Color Swatch Name dialog

Name: mint green

OK

Cancel

The Brushes Palette

The *Brushes* palette allows you to change the setting of your brushes, customizing them as needed to suit your purposes. You may save your brushes.

The *Brushes* palette allows you to customize the brush tips for a variety of tools including the Brush, Pencil, History Brush, Art History Brush, Eraser, and other tools that use a brush tip.

- o You can open the palette by choosing the *Windows>Brushes* menu. Clicking on the *Toggle* palette icon on the right side of the options bar toggles the palette on and off.
- o You may dock the palette by dragging its tab into the Palette Well (CS1 or CS2) or dragging it into the dock of CS3/CS4.

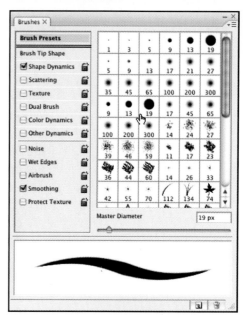

Various Brush Presets

To customize your brush tip:

1. Open the *Brushes* palette by choosing the *Windows>Brushes* menu.

2. Select a drawing tool, such as the **Brush** or **Pencil** tool.

3. Click on the various check boxes to explore. As you select a check box, various options appear to the right, enabling you to change settings. The diameter of the tip may be changed by clicking on the *Brush Preset* option at the top of the left side and moving the diameter slider. As you work, a preview appears in the bottom of the window.

4. Test the tip by drawing on your document.

Editing and Creating Custom Brush Presets

A *Brush Preset* is a combination of brush settings that have been saved. Various presets already exist in Photoshop and are accessed by clicking on the *Brush Presets* option in the *Brushes* palette. You may either edit an existing preset, or build your own. Presets can be saved and utilized in the future.

1. In the *Brushes* palette, click on the *Brush Preset* option.

2. Scroll down through the various preset options. Test draw a sample of the preset on the screen.

3. If you want to change the tip, click on any of the options in the left column in the Window (e.g., Shape Dynamics, Scattering, etc.). Each option may be set separately, but the check box must be checked in order to access the various options.

The Brushes palette menu (above)

Editing the brush tip (left)

4. Observe the brush tip as you make changes to the options.

5. Test draw on your document.

Saving a Brush Preset

When you create a *Brush Preset* that you like, you may save it by clicking on the arrowhead in the upper right of the *Brushes* palette and choosing the *New Brush Preset* option (or you can click on the Tool Preset Picker in the options bar). A window will open and you can save your preset brush. This will then appear in the Presets library for your use at any time.

Try to create the following looks with brushes

o   Watercolor
o   Charcoal
o   Pastels (hit, use smudge tool)
o   Oil with thick loaded brushes (thus showing the hairs of the brush)
o   Stippling
o   Blotting
o   Airbrush

Fashion Exercise #11 utilizes brushes to create fashion art that simulates fashion art mediums such as watercolor, charcoal, and so on.

Can you figure out a way to make...

o   Top stitching
o   Fake fur

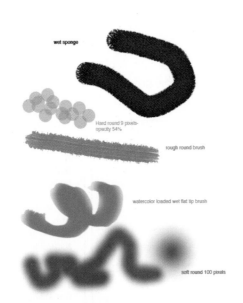

Experimenting with Brushes
Sandra Gonzales

Experimenting with Brushes
Rachael Soares

The Paths Palette

The *Paths* palette allows you to monitor and work with vector art. As you create with the **Pen** tools and various **Shape** tools (in *Paths* or *Shape Layers* mode), you will see thumbnails appear for the following:

> *Work Path*—a temporary storage that allows you to keep track of the paths you have drawn.
>
> *Path*—a working path that has been saved and thus is available for future reference as you work.
>
> *Vector Mask*—which appears when you are drawing with the *Shape Layers* mode. Masks created allow you to hide and reveal portions of layers below the vector mask layer.

If you deselect a working path and then start to draw a new path, the original path will be lost. The only way to retain a working path as you select and deselect work is to save it as a path.

Paths may be:

o   *selected* by clicking on the name of the path in the palette.

o   *deselected* by clicking in the blank area of the palette (beneath all the path names) or by pressing the *Esc* key on the keyboard.

o   *reorganized (in stacking order)* by dragging the path to a different position in the palette.

The flow of work typically goes as follows:

Create the Path ↓	Drawing with the **Pen** tool or **Shape** tools in *Path* mode creates a working path.
Edit the Path ↓	Paths can be easily edited and transformed (using Pen-related Path Selection tools and the *Edit>Transform* menu commands).
Save the Path ↓	Use the *Save Path* command in the *Paths* palette.
Convert the Path	Convert a path to something you can utilize or print in other areas of Photoshop. Paths can be stroked, filled, turned into a selection, and turned into a clipping path.

A working path or saved path may have more than one path object. If you create a working path, then deselect it (by clicking on another path or in the *Paths* palette), and start a new work path, the original one will be lost. The only way to keep a path for future reference is to save it (using the *Save Path* menu command in the *Paths* palette).

Paths can be edited by moving anchor points (with the **Direct Selection** tool), altering the type of anchor point (with the **Convert** tool), and altering the arc of a curve through the use of the directional lines.

Paths Palette Menu Commands

The *Paths* palette menu allows you to perform a variety of operations on a working path or path.

You can:

o   *Save a Path*—which allows you to manage your work, and keep track of what you are doing. To

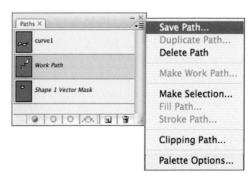

The Save Path command

save a path, double-click on the Work Path in the Paths palette to open the Save Path dialog. Type in a name for the path and click OK. You may also choose the Save Path menu command in the Paths palette.

o *Duplicate a Path*—to create a second copy of it.

o *Delete a Path*—to remove it.

o *Create a Work Path*—from a selection.

o *Convert to a Selection*—from a work path.

o *Fill the Path*—with the foreground color in the Toolbox, which paints the inside of the path and thus creates a bitmap image.

o *Stroke the Path*—which paints color along the path. You can either use the Stroke Path as a Brush button in the Paths palette (which strokes the path with the current brush), or use the Stroke Path... menu option in the Paths palette, in which case you are presented with more options.

o *Convert to a Clipping Path*—which hides areas of the image so that they are not visible when the art is taken to publishing packages.

Fashion Exercise #6 (Drawing Flats with a Grid using Paths and Vector Tools) and Fashion Exercise #14 (Working with Clipping Paths) both work with the *Paths* palette.

Photoshop's new CS4 introduces a new panel called the Applications Bar. This houses many handy functions in a convenient locations. See the Preface, page v for a quick overview. Also read the discussion on the Applications Frame on page vi. This allows you to group all panels, documents, etc., into one frame, which can easily be resized or moved on the screen. It is a great feature. Other palettes exist in Photoshop, but these will not be discussed here. Refer to Adobe Help for information on all other palettes.

Basic Exercises

This chapter includes a series of exercises that will teach you basic Photoshop skills needed for all types of design. These skills are the building blocks for the fashion exercises later in the book. As you work your way through each exercise, attempt to understand the steps and be able to repeat them without referring to the instructions. The goal is to understand the concepts covered so that you may apply them to all types of design later.

The exercises below will teach you the basics of setting up documents, working with document size and resolution, improving imagery, and working with adjustments and adjustment layers. You will also learn how to create selections in a variety of ways, and how to work with layers. Lastly, you will learn how to reduce the number of colors in an image, and how to recolor your art.

Recoloring a garment, Exercise #9

The exercises are as follows:

Exercise # 1   Setting up a Document and Workspace
Exercise # 2   Image and Document Settings: Working with Resolution, Image Size, Cropping, and Canvas Size
Exercise # 3   Improving the Quality of a Digital Image
Exercise # 4   Working with Adjustments and Adjustment Layers
Exercise # 5   Working with Layers and the Layers Palette Button Bar
Exercise # 6   Creating and Working with Selections
Exercise # 7   Using the Quick Mask to Build or Improve Selections
Exercise # 8   Techniques for Reducing the Number of Colors in an Image
Exercise # 9   Recoloring Images

On the accompanying DVD, there is a folder called **Basic Exercises**. Inside this folder are exercise folders containing sample files. Most of the exercises in this section utilize artwork found on the DVD. Since you will be asked to save files on occasion, it is suggested that you create a folder on your hard drive and move the **Basic Exercises** folder to that folder so that you can load and save files at will. *To do this:*

1. Create a folder on your hard drive called **PSExercises**.

2. Drag the **Basic Exercises** folder from the DVD into this folder.

When the instructions in an exercise direct you to your Art DVD, you can move to the folder you created on your hard drive. This will be more convenient and you will be able to save your work to this folder as well.

File Access

To simplify loading and saving files while performing the various exercises in this book, drag the entire contents of the DVD (less the portfolio folder) to your hard drive.

Student Gallery
Composite Built
Using Basic Skills
Angel Beckwith-Malone

Adjustments made, filter run to create line art, and enlarged

Selection made and filter run, then enlarged

Level Adjustment performed on selection, transformed to flip, and enlarged.

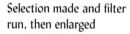

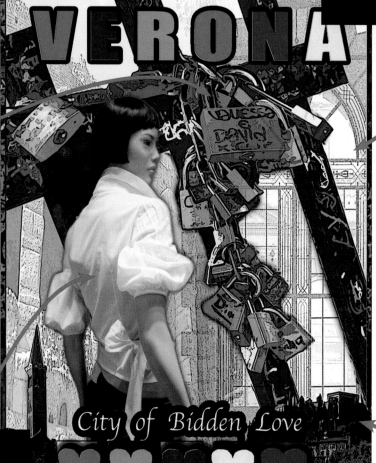

City of Bidden Love

Level Adjustment performed, art filter applied, and selections made

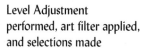

Exercise #1: Setting up a Document and Workspace

Goal

The goal of this exercise is to set up a typical document and workspace.

Photoshop Tools and Functions

- ◆ *File>New* menu
- ◆ Various palettes such as *Navigator*, *History*, *Layers*, *Colors,* and *Swatches*
- ◆ *Foreground* and *background* colors in the Toolbox

Quick Overview of the Process

When you first open Photoshop, it does not open with a document window, so you must create a document prior to starting work. In this exercise you will create a new file and choose its width and height, resolution, color mode, and background contents. You will then open and organize the palettes you want to use while you work and set the *foreground* and *background* colors in the Toolbox. The assumption is that you have the default set of palettes in your workspace. If you do not, choose the *Window>Workspace>Reset Palette Locations* to get to Photoshop's default workspace, which is what will be used here.

Note: Naming vs. Saving a File
Naming a file in the File>New dialog does not save the file. You must perform a separate File>Save operation to actually save the file.

Step-by-Step

Setting up

1. Create a new document. Choose the *File>New* menu or press the *Cmd/Ctrl+N* keyboard shortcut. The *New* dialog will open.

2. In the *Preset* pop-up, choose the *U.S. Paper preset* option (CS3) or set the document to 8.5 inches wide by × 11 inches high. Note that the default *Resolution* for the U.S. Paper size is 300, the *Color Mode* is RGB Color, and the *Background Contents* is set as White.

3. Change the *Resolution* to 150 as this will keep your file size smaller. Leave the *Color Mode* as RGB, but if you are planning to press print your work, change the mode to CMYK. Leave the *Background Contents* as White and turn off the *Advanced* options by clicking on the arrow next to the word *Advanced*. Type in a name for your document, and click **OK**. The document will open and the name will appear in the Title Bar of the document.

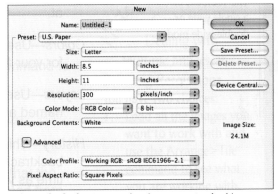

Steps 2-3: Setting up the document in the New dialog. Above, you see the Preset settings. Below, you see the resolution has been altered.

Opening Palettes for Use

Ensure that the following palettes (which are the most commonly used palettes) are open and available for use: *Toolbox, Applications Bar (CS4), Options Bar, Navigator, Colors, Layers,* and *History.* You will find several of these already open (if you have reset the palette locations). Save the document using the *File>Save* menu command.

Exercise #3: Improving the Quality of a Digital Image

Goal
The goal of this exercise is to teach you how to improve photos and scanned artwork using two key image-enhancing functions in Photoshop: the *Levels* adjustment and the *Sharpen* filter.

Photoshop Tools and Functions
- *Image>Adjustments>Levels*
- *Filter>Sharpen* (various options)

Quick Overview of the Process
In this exercise you will perform two very common image enhancements. The photo image used is a little dark and not completely crisp (as a result of the photography). *The basic steps are as follows:*
1. Open the photo image.
2. Adjust the levels using the *Image>Adjustments>Levels* menu command.
3. Adjust the sharpness of the image using the *Filter>Sharpen>Sharpen* and the *Filter>Sharpen>Sharpen Edges* commands (plus others if you choose to experiment).

New Concepts
- *Levels* adjustments
- *Sharpen* filter

Note: **Filters and Color Mode**

All filters work with RGB files, but not all filters work with CMYK files.

Sources of Imagery
- Digital images of artwork or photographs

Review pages 133–134 for the discussion on *Levels*, and page 148 for a discussion on the *Sharpen* filter.

Step-by-Step
Loading the Photo File
1. Choose the *File>Open* menu. Direct the file requestor to the companion DVD or to the location on your hard drive where these files have been moved and stored. Move to the **Basic Exercises** folder and then the **Ex 3** folder to view the files inside. Select one file to work with. The example used in this exercise is **dpose.jpg**.

2. Observe the *Layers* palette. Note that the image is the *Background*.

3. Ensure that the *History* palette is open (*Window>History*) so that you may undo operations or back up to a prior point in time, should you choose. Open the *Navigator* palette so that you can see where you are in the image as you work.

4. Observe the *Title Bar* of the document and note that the image is in RGB color mode.

dpose.jpg

5. Choose the *Image>Image Size* menu command to learn about the image. You will see that the image size is approximately 3.5 × 9 inches in size and that the resolution is 150 dpi.

6. If you zoom into the image, to the face, you will see that it is not focused sharply. You can also see that the brightness and contrast could be improved.

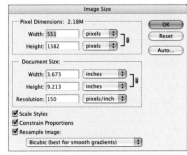

Altering the Levels

Levels is an adjustment that allows you to adjust and control the tonal range of an image through the altering of intensity levels. Operations are performed on the shadow, midtone, and highlights of an image.

The Image Size dialog provides information on file size.

1. Zoom into the image so you can see the face more closely. You can use the *Navigator* palette to do this. If you want, create a snapshot (using the *History* palette) at this time so you can compare the original image and the one you are about to create through the adjustment of *Levels*.

2. Choose the *Image>Adjustments>Levels* menu command. The *Levels* dialog will open. Observe the histogram and the triangular sliders under it.

The Navigator palette allows you to zoom into an area of the image and view where you are in relation to the whole.

3. Drag the left black slider (the shadows) to the right until it is under a portion of the histogram that starts to have some height. Observe the changes made to the image. Now, drag the white slider on the right (the highlights) so it is under a portion of the histogram that has some height. Again, observe the results. Finally, move the center slider (the midtones) back and forth in the center until you feel you have the best results in the image. Click **OK** to finalize the changes.

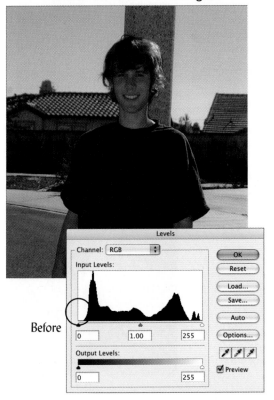

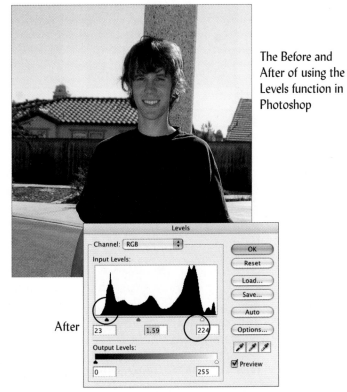

The Before and After of using the Levels function in Photoshop

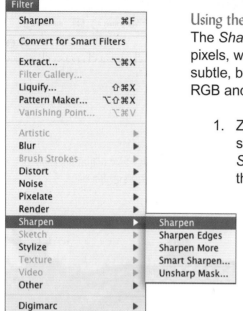

Filter	
Sharpen	⌘F
Convert for Smart Filters	
Extract...	⌥⌘X
Filter Gallery...	
Liquify...	⇧⌘X
Pattern Maker...	⌥⇧⌘X
Vanishing Point...	⌥⌘V
Artistic	▶
Blur	▶
Brush Strokes	▶
Distort	▶
Noise	▶
Pixelate	▶
Render	▶
Sharpen	▶
Sketch	▶
Stylize	▶
Texture	▶
Video	▶
Other	▶
Digimarc	▶

Sharpen
Sharpen Edges
Sharpen More
Smart Sharpen...
Unsharp Mask...

The Filter>Sharpen commands

Using the Sharpen Filters

The *Sharpen* filters are used to increase the contrast between adjacent pixels, which adds a crispness to the artwork. The changes are generally subtle, but obvious to the eye close-up. The *Sharpen* filters work in both RGB and CMYK color modes.

1. Zoom into the image so that you can see the face, which is somewhat fuzzy. Observe the image carefully. If you like, make a *Snapshot* of the image prior to running any *Sharpen* filters (using the *History* palette).

2. Choose the *Filter>Sharpen>Sharpen* menu command. You will see slight changes in the edges around the hair and face. If you like, you can run the sharpen function again, or choose the *Filter>Sharpen>Sharpen Edges* filter.

3. Explore the other *Sharpen* filters and see if any assist you in obtaining what you want. Be prepared to "undo" if the results are not good.

The results of the *Sharpen* filters vary according to the artwork. Sometimes you will see instant results, and other times you can't detect any significant change.

Prior to Sharpening

After Sharpen

After Sharpen Edges

This is an alternate image (called photoshoot.jpg) that you may use in this exercise to learn more about improving artwork through Levels and Sharpening.

Before   After

Exercise #4: Working with Adjustments and Adjustment Layers

Goal

This exercise will teach you how to use *Adjustments* and *Adjustment Layers* to improve the quality of an image or experiment creatively.

Photoshop Tools and Functions

- ◆ Image adjustments
- ◆ Layers and adjustment layers
- ◆ **Selection** tools

Quick Overview of the Process

In this exercise you will load an image and perform different adjustments on it using the *Image>Adjustment* commands and *Adjustment Layers*. You will compare both approaches, as the former creates a permanent change while the latter creates a temporary change.

The general approach is as follows:

1. Load an image to be adjusted and save it twice.
2. On the first file, duplicate the background multiple times to create several layers. Each will have the same artwork.
3. Perform different adjustments on each layer, using the eye icon to turn other layers off, thus placing them out of view.
4. On the second file, reproduce the adjustments using *Adjustment Layers*. Experiment with viewing multiple adjustments, turning some off and on, and so on to experience how adjustment layers offer greater flexibility.

Review the concepts in Chapter 5 on Adjustments (pages 132–133) if necessary.

Original art (above)
and altered art (below)

New Concepts

- o Using *Adjustments* to improve the color and tonal quality of an image
- o Using *Adjustment Layers*

Sources of Imagery

- o Digital photographs of artwork needing adjustment

Step-by-Step

Loading Your Artwork

1. Choose the *File>Open* menu. Direct the file requestor to the companion DVD or to the location on your hard drive where these files have been moved and stored (e.g., PSExercises). Move to the **Basic Exercises** folder and then the **Ex 4** folder and load the file called **andrew walking.jpg.** The image was shot at twilight, with low light. The goal of shooting the image was to obtain a walking pose that could be used in design (see page 192 for the final fashion image developed from this starting artwork).

The original file

2. Using the *File>Save As...* menu command, save the image as a TIF file. Remember to choose the TIF option using the pop-up at the bottom of the *Save* dialog. Choose the new location in your work folder (as you cannot save to the DVD) and name the new file **Andrew walking2.tif.** Click **OK** to complete the operation. Repeat the operation, saving another version of the file as **Andrew walking3.tif**.

3. Load the **Andrew walking1.tif** file. This is necessary since saving it with the new name in step 2 above essentially closed the old file.

4. Ensure that your *Layers* palette is open.

Step 5: Turning the Background into a layer and naming it.

5. Double-click on the *Background* name in the *Layers* palette. This will open a *New Layer* dialog and you will type **Andrew** in for the layer name. You have just converted a background to a layer.

Step 6: Creating multiple layers (above) using the Duplicate Layer command of the Layers palette menu (right).

6. Choose the *Duplicate Layer* command from the *Layers* palette menu. Do not worry about changing the layer name, as we will do this later. Repeat this process to create a total of three new layers.

Step 2: The before (above) and after (below) of using Levels to adjust your image.

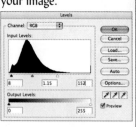

Creating Adjustments Using the Image>Adjustment Menu Commands

1. Hide all layers but the *Andrew copy* layer. You can achieve this by clicking on the "eye" icon to the left of each layer name. This turns the eye off, and thus the display of the layer off. Note that you can *click+hold+drag* up the *Edit well* and turn multiple layers off in one sweep. Click on the *Andrew copy* layer to make sure it is the active layer.

Step 1: Prepping the layers.

2. **Using Levels.** Levels allow you to adjust and control the tonal range and color balance of an image through the adjustment of intensity levels. You may perform separate operations on the shadow, midtone, and highlights of an image. Choose the *Image>Adjustment>Levels* command. The *Levels* dialog will open. Observe the dialog. You will

see a histogram. Drag the black slider on the left beneath the histogram over slightly, so that it is under where some height exists in the histogram. Drag the white slider on the lower-right side of the histogram to the left until it is under an area of the "mountain" where some height exists. As you perform these operations, you will see the image improving. Click **OK** when you are happy with your results. The layer thumbnail will actually look lighter.

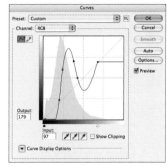

Step 4: Experimenting with Curves to create a solarized effect in the result. Adjust the highlight, shadow, and midtone points, add points by clicking near the baseline, and then drag these to experiment.

3. Now, double-click on the layer name for the layer you just changed and rename it to *Levels*. Turn the eye of this layer off and turn on the display of the next layer (*Andrew copy2*).

4. **Using Curves.** Curves provide a more complex yet more advanced means of dealing with tonalities in an image. Read up on them in Adobe's Help files, and be willing to explore. Choose the *Image>Adjustment>Curves* command. The *Curves* dialog will open. There you see a histogram with a diagonal line moving from lower left to upper right. Drag the upper-right highlight point (at the upper end of the diagonal baseline) along the line to just above the point in the histogram where some height of pixels is starting to occur. Now, click near the baseline to add a point and drag it around. Experiment with adding points and try to achieve a solarized effect. The examples here show you where the points were added or moved and the results.

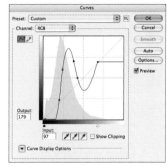

The results of experimenting with Curves

5. Double-click on the layer name for the layer you just changed and rename it to *Curves*. Turn the eye of this layer off and turn on the display of the next layer (*Andrew copy3*).

6. Choose an adjustment in the *Image>Adjustment* menu to experiment with. The example below used two adjustments, first **Brightness/Contrast**, followed by **Hue/Saturation.**

7. Double-click on the layer name for the layer you just changed and rename it to *BC and HS*.

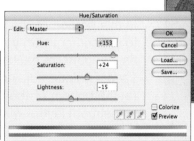

8. Look at the various results of your adjustments by turning the eyes of each layer on

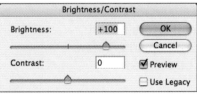

Step 6: The results of experimenting with two adjustments: Brightness/Contrast and Hue/Saturation. The settings can be seen in the dialogs.

and off. You will not be able to see through the layers as opacity for each is set to 100%.

Step 9: Creating a snapshot.

9. If the *History* palette is not visible, open it now. Save a snapshot of where you are at this time. Achieve this by clicking on the **Snapshot** button at the bottom of the *History* palette. Name your snapshot by double-clicking on it and typing in its name prior to conducting further experiments.

10. Just for fun, turn on the view of the three layers with adjustments, and experiment with *Opacity* settings for each, and with the *Blending Modes*. The *Opacity* setting will allow you to see through one layer down to the next, and the blending mode will cause different effects to occur as the layers blend.

11. Save the file.

Experimenting with Saturation blending applied between the BC and HS layer and the Levels layer

Experimenting with Opacity settings. A 41% opacity was used on the BC and HS layer and a 62% opacity was used on the Curves layer. The image to the left was flattened so you could see the results.

Experimenting with Hue blending applied on the top layer

Step 1: Loading andrew walking2. tif (above) and the Layers palette that results (below).

Creating Adjustments Using the Image Adjustment Layers

In this portion of the exercise, you will now work with *Adjustment Layers* to experiment with your image. You do not create multiple layers. Rather, as you perform each adjustment via the *Layers* palette adjustment layers button (at the bottom of the *Layers* palette), new adjustment layers will be created.

1. Using *File>Open...* load the file called **andrew walking2.tif** that you saved earlier. You will see that the image is a *Background* in the *Layers* palette.

Step 2: Creating an adjustment layer.

2. **Using Levels.** *Click+hold* on the **Create new fill or adjustment layer** button on the lower strip of the *Layers* palette, and slide

up or down to the *Levels* option. Release the mouse. The *Levels* dialog will open and the settings in this dialog will be exactly as they were when you chose the *Image Adjustment>Levels* menu command. If you want, you can alter the settings as you did on page 189. Click **OK**. A *Levels* adjustment layer will now appear in your *Layers* palette and the image will look improved. Leave the view of this adjustment layer on as you continue to work.

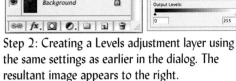

Step 2: Creating a Levels adjustment layer using the same settings as earlier in the dialog. The resultant image appears to the right.

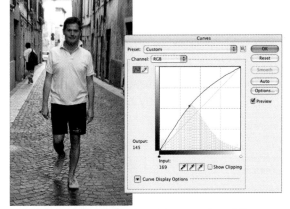

3. **Using Curves.**
   Once again, *click+hold* on the **Create new fill or adjustment layer** button on the lower strip of the *Layers* palette, and slide up or down to the *Curves* option. Release the mouse. The *Curves* dialog will open. Experiment with the curve settings by dragging points around the diagonal line. What you are viewing on your document is a result of both the *Levels* adjustment and the *Curves* adjustment. When you are happy with the results, click **OK**. You will now see another adjustment layer in the *Layers* palette.

Using a Curves adjustment layer on top of the Levels layer results in the image above. The layers palette shows all adjustment layers.

Step 3: Creating a Curves adjustment layer.

The Layers palette showing both adjustment layers

4. Experiment with other types of adjustments. The example to the left shows you the result of adding an *Invert* adjustment layer. The example to the right turns the view of the *Invert* adjustment layer off and adds a *Threshold* adjustment layer.

The Layers palette with various adjustment layers

The Flexibility of Adjustment Layers

Using adjustment layers offers flexibility in several ways:

o Adjustment layers are not permanent and can easily be edited or removed.

o To edit an adjustment layer, double-click on the layer thumbnail and the adjustment dialog will open and be available for editing.

o   To remove an adjustment layer, select the layer and click on the **Delete Layer** button (the trash can) in the lower-right corner of the *Layers* palette. You will need to do this twice, the first time to delete the *Layer mask*, and the second time to delete the *layer* itself.

To Merge Adjustment Layers

To merge adjustment layers with the rest of your image, choose from the various options in the *Layers* palette (Merge Down, Merge Visible, etc.). In most cases, you will need to make sure that the layer you want to merge is the active layer. The *Merge Down* option will not be available unless you have selected the visible layers directly above the *Background*. Remember that you can select multiple layers by pressing and holding the *Shift* key as you select layers.

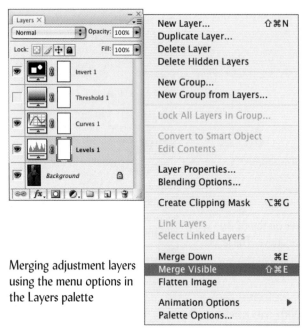

Merging adjustment layers using the menu options in the Layers palette

The Layers palette after the visible adjustment layers were merged with the Background

The image after the adjustment layers were merged

For Fun...

The image **andrew walking.tif** used in this exercise was developed to create the graphic below, which involves three distinct layers: a shadow, a gradient, and a blurred facial image.

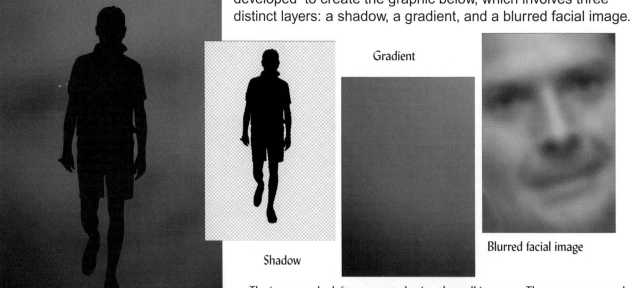

Gradient

Shadow

Blurred facial image

The image to the left was created using the walking pose. The pose was turned into a shadow and elongated. It was then placed over a transparent gradient layer, which was positioned over a face layer that was blurred for visual effect.

Exercise #5: Working with Layers and the Layers Palette Button Bar

Goal
The goal of this exercise is to teach you how to use functions of the *Layers* palette, specifically those found in the bottom button bar of the palette.

Photoshop Tools and Functions

- Various layer functions including *New Layers, Adjustment Layers, Layer Styles, Linked Layers,* and *Layer Groups*
- *Linking* layers and *Layer Groups*
- *Opacity* settings for layers
- Placing artwork (*File>Place*) and Smart Object layers
- **Type** tool and **Vertical Type** tool

The final image (above) and the Layers palette (below) showing the various layers created in the exercise (below)

Quick Overview of the Process
In this exercise you will create a composite/collage, beginning with a blank document, and adding an image of a statue. Throughout the exercise you will use most of the layer *functions* accessed through the button bar at the bottom of the *Layers* palette.
The steps are as follows:

1. Create a blank document and change the background color in your Toolbox.
2. Place a digital image called **statue.jpg**. Copy the image to the clipboard and then perform a *layer adjustment* to the layer.
3. Paste the image from the clipboard back into the document and perform a scaling transformation on it. Recopy the image to the clipboard.
4. Paste in multiple copies of the scaled image. Position the new layers as desired. Delete any unwanted layers.
5. Name all layers at this point.
6. Change the opacity of each of the new layers, then link the layers of the smaller statue.
7. Flip the linked layers (using *Edit>Transform>Flip Horizontal*).
8. Create a *Layer group* and drag the statue head layers into it. Rename the group.
9. Using the **Type** tools, create text and place it on the image.
10. Add a *layer style* to the type layers.

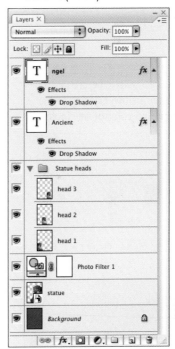

New Concepts
o Using functions on the *Layers* palette button bar
o Using *Opacity* settings on layers
o Placing artwork and Smart Object layers
o Linking and group layers

Sources of Imagery
o Digital images of artwork on the DVD

Step-by-Step
Creating the Document and Changing the Background Color

1. Choose the *File>New* menu command. When the dialog opens, set the document size to 8 × 10.5 inches and choose a *Resolution* of 120. You can use an RGB or CMYK *Color Mode* and let the *Background Contents* be white. Name the file **Layers Exercise** and click **OK**. The document will open.

Step 1: Creating the new document.

2. Immediately save the file in your working folder, as simply naming the file in the prior step does not save it.

3. Observe the *Layers* palette at this time and note that you have a *Background* and no layer.

The Layers palette before (above) and after (below) clearing to the Background color of the Toolbox

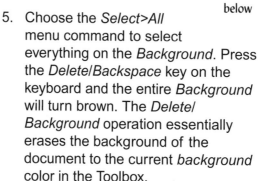

4. Double-click on the *Background* icon in the Toolbox to open the *Color Picker*. Choose a brown color in the *Color Picker* and click **OK**. This will now be the background color in the Toolbox.

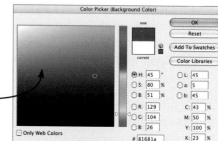

Setting the background color and "erasing" to this color in the Background as shown below

5. Choose the *Select>All* menu command to select everything on the *Background*. Press the *Delete/Backspace* key on the keyboard and the entire *Background* will turn brown. The *Delete/Background* operation essentially erases the background of the document to the current *background* color in the Toolbox.

Introducing the Art to the Document

1. Choose the *File>Place* menu command. Direct the file requestor to the companion DVD or to the location on your hard drive where these files have been moved and stored. Move to the **Basic Exercises** folder and then **Ex 5** and choose the file called **statue.tif**. Click on **Place**. The file will appear in your current document and you will see an "X" through it. This is because it is a *Smart Object*. Double-click inside the document and the image will become a layer in your document. Note that the new layer thumbnail contains a Smart Object icon. If you double-click on the thumbnail, you will open the original image. Any adjustments made to the original image will update in the current file.

Step 1: Placing an image into the document.

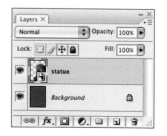

The placed file is now on its own layer.

2. Observe the *Layers* palette. Note that the image is now on its own layer called *statue*.

3. Click on the *statue* layer to make it the active layer.

4. Choose the *Select>All* menu command to select the entire contents of this layer. Choose the *Edit>Copy* menu to copy the art to the clipboard.

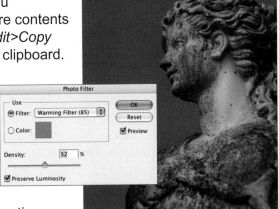

5. With the *statue* layer still active, move to the *Layers* palette and click and hold on the **Create new fill or adjustment layer** button at the bottom of the palette. Slide up to the *Photo Filter* option and release. A dialog will open. Ensure that the *Preview* check box is checked. Experiment with the different photo filters (the pop-up menu) and the *Density* setting. Click **OK** when you like what you see in the *Preview*. The image will update and a new *Photo Filter* adjustment layer will appear above the *Statue* layer.

Step 5: Using a Photo Filter adjustment layer.

The Photo Filter dialog and the resultant image and layer

Note: CS4 users can use the Adjustments panel for Step 5.

6. Save the file to update it.

Adding Composite Imagery

You are now ready to add more layers and continue building the composite of this statue image.

1. Choose the *Edit>Paste* menu command. The original image of the statue that you sent to the clipboard is still there, and will now paste into the document on its own layer.

2. Choose the *Edit>Free Transform* menu command and a box will appear around this new image. Either *click+drag* on a corner of the bounding box to scale the image (holding down the *Shift* key to constrain the proportions), or use the options bar and type in the new scale of the image. Once the image is resized to your satisfaction, move it to the upper-left corner of the document by dragging it there with the cursor.

Step 2: Transforming the scale of the new image and repositioning it.

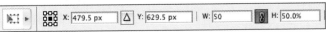

The Transformation controls in the options bar

3. Ensure that you are on the new layer (currently called *Layer 1*). Choose the *Select>All* menu and copy the smaller version of the statue to the clipboard (using *Edit>Copy*).

Steps 4–5: Pasting in the copies of the statue head and positioning them.

Steps 6–7: Deleting one layer (the original head) and adjusting the transparency levels of the remaining head layers.

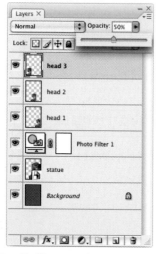

Step 7: Changing the opacity of the head layers.

4. Choose the *Edit>Paste* menu and a copy of the smaller statue will paste into the document on its own layer. Paste in a total of three images noting that each goes to its own layer. Initially, all three heads will be directly on top of each other, but you will move them in the next step. Your new layers will be *Layers 2, 3,* and *4.*

5. Choose the **Move** tool, and position each of the images on layers 2, 3, and 4, across the bottom of the document. You will need to click on the layer that holds the imagery you want to move prior to moving it. Once you have positioned the heads, rename the three layers with an appropriate name (such as *head 1, head 2,* and *head 3*). To rename a layer at this point, you must click on the layer name and when the text box appears, retype the name. Sometimes it takes a couple of attempts at clicking until you can get the text box ready to receive the new name.

6. In the *Layers* palette, select *Layer 1* and click on the **Delete layer** button (the Trash can) in the lower-right corner of the palette. You will be asked if you are sure. Click **OK** and the layer will disappear.

7. Now, in turn, choose each of the head layers and alter the *Opacity* setting of each layer so that the heads become lighter as you move to the right.

We are now going to link three layers so that they act as a unit.

8. Press the *Shift* key on the keyboard and click on the three head layers. They will all be highlighted. Now, click on the **Link layers** button at the bottom-left side of the *Layers* palette. A link will appear beside all three layers.

9. Click on any of the three linked layers to select it, and then choose the *Edit>Transform>Flip Horizontal* menu command. The three heads will flip. Use the **Move** tool to position the heads where you would like them. If you want, change the *Opacity* settings of the head layers. You can use varying degrees of opacity for each of the layers.

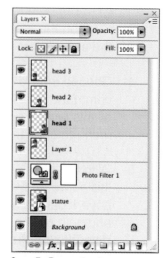

Step 5: Renaming layers.

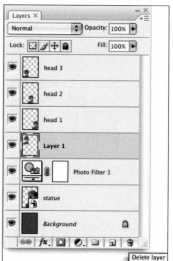

Step 6: Deleting a layer.

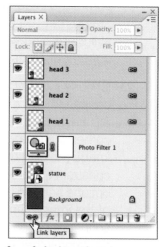

Step 8: Linking three layers.

Creating a Layer Group

1. Click on the *head 3* layer to select it. Doing this will ensure that the *layer group* will appear **above** the *head 3* layer.

2. In the *Layers* palette, click on the **Create a new group** button at the bottom of the palette. A layer called *Group 1* will appear at the top of the palette.

3. In turn, *click+hold+drag* each of the three head layers over the *Group 1* layer. You will see that the head layers become indented and that the *Group 1* layer now has an arrowhead on the left side of the layer to indicate that it has contents. Clicking on this arrowhead opens and closes the view of the layers in the group.

4. Click on the *Group 1* layer name and rename this layer *Statue heads*. You can close the expanded view of the group by clicking on the down arrow, thus condensing the viewable layers into a compressed view.

The image after the three head layers have been flipped

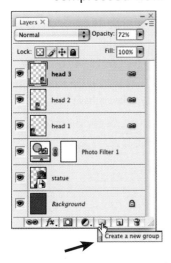

Step 2 (left): Clicking on the Create a new group button creates a layer group.

Steps 3–4 (right): The head layers are now positioned in the group and the group layer has been renamed. The far right image shows you the Statue head layer group in its compressed state.

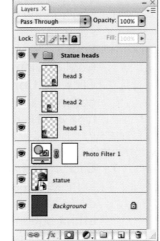

The statue heads group in closed view position

Adding a Type Layer and Layer Effects

At this point, we will add some text to the upper-left corner of the image. When text is added, it creates its own *type layer*. We will then create a *layer effect* by adding drop shadow to the type layer.

1. Double-click on the *foreground* color in the Toolbox and when the *Color Picker* opens, choose a color as your text color. We will use a dark gray.

Step 1: Setting the foreground color for the Type.

2. Click on the *Statue heads* layer group to select it. This will ensure that your Type layer will appear above all the head layers.

3. Click on the **Type** tool in the Toolbox. Move to the options bar, and choose a font family and a font size. Start with a large font size of about 60 to 72 points.

The Type options bar

4. Place the cursor on your document in the upper-left corner and click to set the initial point of typing. A type cursor will appear.

Steps 4–6: Adding text to the image (above and below).

Type in the word *Ancient*. You can reposition the text by clicking on it and dragging it to a new location. You can also click on the text to highlight it, preparing it for editing or typing additional text.

5. While the cursor is still blinking (and active), highlight the text. Then click once in the Font family pop-up to highlight the type name. You can now use the *up arrow* or *down arrow* keys on the keyboard to scroll through the various fonts and see the text update instantly on the screen. Make your final font decision and then click on the **Confirm** check mark in the options bar. You will now see a *Type* layer with the words you typed.

Step 5: Experimenting with different fonts.

6. Choose the **Vertical Type** tool (which is stacked beneath the regular **Type** tool). Position the cursor on the image once again, and type *ngel* (borrowing the "A" from the word *Ancient*). Position this new word to align with the "A" of Ancient. Click the **Confirm** check mark in the options bar. You now have two type layers in the *Layers* palette.

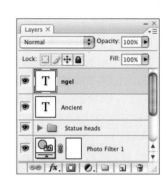

The Layers palette after both type layers have been added

Adding a Layer Effect

1. Click on the *Ancient* type layer to make it the active layer. Now *click+hold* on the **Add layer effect** button at the bottom of the *Layers* palette and slide to the *Drop Shadow* option. The *Layer Effect* dialog will open.

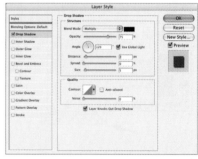

2. Experiment with different settings in this dialog, watching the preview of your image. The default drop shadow color is black, which is the color used in our image. Experiment with the *Distance*, *Opacity*, and *Size* options. Take note of your final settings and click **OK** to approve them.

The Layer Style dialog (above) and the final image (below)

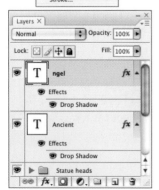

Adding a layer effect to the Type layers

3. Repeat the layer effect with the second type layer, using the same settings.

This completes the Layers exercise. You have used all but the **Add layer mask** button. A discussion of this can be found on page 57.

Exercise #6: Creating and Working with Selections

The original image to be utilized in this lesson

Goal

The goal of this exercise is to allow you to practice creating selections by shape and color.

Photoshop Tools and Functions

♦ *Shape Selection* tools (**Marquees** and **Lasso**)
♦ *Color Selection* tools (**Magic Wand** and **Quick Selection**)
♦ **Move** tool
♦ Layers

Quick Overview of the Process

You will load an art image and will practice making selections using first, the various *Shape Selection* tools, and then the *Color Selection* tools. Review pages 26–33 in Chapter 2, which discuss how to use the various selection tools.

The steps are as follows:

1. Load a digital image called **images.jpg**. Analyze the images on the page and determine which selection tools would work best on which images.
2. Create a duplicate layer of the artwork so that you can come back to the original if you need to.
3. Using the various **Shape** selection tools, select artwork and copy/paste it to a new layer, then position it in the nonimage area of the document.
4. Using the various **Color** selection tools, select artwork and copy/paste it to a new layer, then position it in the nonimage area of the document.

New Concepts

o Analyzing artwork to determine which *selection* tool will work best.
o Using the clipboard to transport selections to new layers.

Sources of Imagery

o Digital images of artwork

Step-by-Step

Loading the Start File

1. Choose the *File>Open* menu. Direct the file requestor to the companion DVD or to the location on your hard drive where these files have been moved and stored (e.g., **PSExercises**). Move to the **Basic Exercises** folder and

Images.jpg

then the **Ex 6** folder and load a file called **images.jpg**. You will see several images placed on a black background.

Tool Summary

o The Rectangular Marquee works best when you want a rectangular or square selection. You may choose to use feathering.

o The Elliptical Marquee tool works best when your selection would be more round or oval-shaped.

o The Lasso tool allows you to draw freehand around an image to select a portion of it. This tool works well in busy areas that have no other alternative.

o The Polygon Lasso works well on images where the edges of what you want to select are more angular.

o The Magnetic Lasso works best on images that have a high-contrast edge. You can assist the contrast of the edge by creating a temporary Adjustment layer and increasing the contrast.

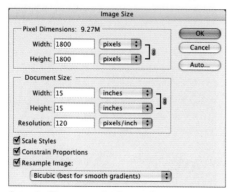

Step 4: Observing the Image Size.

2. Observe the *Layers* palette to note that the image is the *Background*.

3. Ensure that the *History* palette is open (*Window>History*) so that you may undo operations or back up to a prior point in time, should you choose. Open the *Navigator* palette so that you can see where you are in the image as you work.

4. Choose the *Image>Image Size* menu command to learn about the image. You will see that the image size is large, measuring 15 inches square and using a resolution of 120 dpi.

5. As a back-up of the original art, open the *Layers* palette menu (click on the arrowhead in the upper-right corner of the palette), and choose the *Duplicate layer* option. For now, turn the view of this layer off by clicking on the eye icon in the *Edit* well on the layer. Click on the *Background* layer to make it active.

The Layers palette after creating the duplicate layer and hiding it from view

Selection Basics

As preparation for creating selections with this image, refer back to Chapter 2 to the discussion on the *selection* tools. Before you begin to actually create a selection, read and attempt to understand the following basics of selections. You may choose to experiment a little with the artwork as you read through this section.

Creating a selection (left) and erasing it by pressing the Delete/ Backspace key on the keyboard

Erasing Areas of the Image

1. Using a selection tool of your choice, select an area of the image that you want to remove from the image. Once you have created the selection you will see the marching ants.

2. On the keyboard, press the *Delete* key (Mac) or the *Backspace* key (Windows) and the selection will disappear and become white (the current *background* color).

Deselecting a Selection

1. Using a selection tool of your choice, select an area of the image. Once you have created the selection, you will see the marching ants.

2. Press *Cmd/Ctrl+D* on the keyboard, and the selection will go away. As an alternative to the keyboard, choose the *Select>Deselect* menu command.

Selecting the bread (upper image) and then deselecting it (lower image)

Moving a Selection

1. Using a selection tool of your choice, select an area of the image. Once you have created the selection you will see the marching ants.

2. Choose the **Move** tool in the Toolbox. Place your cursor inside the selection marquee and *click+drag* with the mouse to move the *selection* to a different location on the document. Note that the imagery does not move.

Creating a selection (left) and moving it while it is still active

Transforming a Selection

1. Using a selection tool of your choice, select an area of the image. Once you have created the selection, you will see the marching ants.

2. Choose the *Edit>Free Transform* menu command. A rectangular box with square corners and sides will appear around the selection.

3. Move your cursor around the perimeter of the box and note how the display of the cursor changes. The cursor icon will tell you if you can continue to scale or rotate the image.

- To scale in proportion, *click* on a corner point, press the *Shift* key on the keyboard, and then *drag* the image inwards or outwards.

- To stretch the image, *click+hold* on any corner or side point and *drag* the mouse.

- To rotate the image, move your cursor outside a corner of the image until it turns into the rotate cursor (a curve with two arrowheads). Then, *click+hold+drag* and rotate the image.

- To skew the image, press the *Cmd/Ctrl key* while you select a corner anchor and move it.

The Move tool

The Rotate (left) and Scale (center and right) Transformation cursors

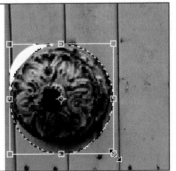

Creating a selection (left), setting up to transform it (center), and scaling the selection larger (right)

Adding to and Subtracting from a Selection

1. Using a selection tool of your choice, select an area of the image.

2. Click on the **Add to selection** button in the options bar to make it active.

3. Select another area of the image, and continue to create selections, observing how you are adding to the current selection.

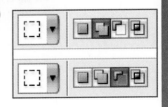

The Add to selection (above) and Subtract from selection (below) buttons found in the options bar

4. Click on the **Subtract from selection** button in the options bar to make it active.

5. Select an area of the current selection and notice how it is removed from the selection.

Add to Selection

a. A selection is created using the Lasso tool.
b. A new selection is started to the left of the first selection.
c. Both selections are now active and merge as they overlap.

a   b   c

Analyzing the Artwork and Creating Selections

The following discussion leads you through the use of the various selection-by-shape tools. Attempt to understand how each selection tool works, then look at the images on your document to determine which image or part of an image best suits each tool. As you create a selection you will copy it to the clipboard and then paste it back into the document. It will paste into its own layer, which gives you great control over the artwork.

The Rectangular Marquee tool

Rectangular Marquee

Selections made with this tool will be rectangular or square. Look for a section of artwork that suits this type of shape.

1. Choose the **Rectangular Marquee** tool in the Toolbox.

2. Move the cursor to the artwork, and *click+hold+drag* to select the artwork. If you want the selection to be square, press and hold the *Shift* key as you drag the mouse. Release the mouse and observe the marching ants.

Steps 2–3: Selecting a rectangular shape (above), and pasting it into its own layer, and moving it to one side (below).

3. Choose the *Edit>Copy* menu command (or press *Cmd/Ctrl+C* on the keyboard). Now choose the *Edit>Paste* menu command (or press *Cmd/Ctrl+V* on the keyboard). The selected artwork will now appear on its own layer, but directly above the original selection and thus you won't necessarily know it is there. If you observe the *Layers* palette you will see that a new layer has formed.

Step 5: The Layers palette after renaming the rectangular selection layer.

The Move tool

4. Choose the **Move** tool, and move the selection over the black background area of the image.

5. Rename the new layer *rectangular selection* and click on the *Background* to make it active for the next selection.

The Elliptical Marquee tool

Elliptical Marquee

1. Choose the **Elliptical Marquee** tool in the Toolbox and locate artwork on the document that suits an elliptical or circular selection.

2. To try something new, set the *Feathering* option in the options bar to 5. This will create a soft edge when the image is pasted into its own layer.

3. Move the cursor to the artwork, and *click+hold+drag* to select the artwork. If you want the selection to be perfectly round, press and hold the *Shift* key as you drag the mouse. Remember that you can move the selection once you have made it, either by dragging it or by using the arrow keys on the keyboard to nudge it.

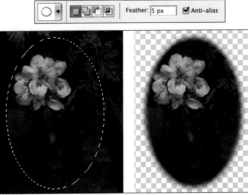

Creating a selection with feathering turned on (left) and the results (right).

4. Choose the *Edit>Copy* menu command (or press *Cmd/ Ctrl+C* on the keyboard). Now choose the *Edit>Paste* menu command (or press *Cmd/Ctrl+V* on the keyboard). The selected artwork will now appear on its own layer, but directly above the original selection. If you observe the *Layers* palette you will see that a new layer has formed.

5. Choose the **Move** tool (*V*), and move the selection over the black background area of the image. If you zoom in, you will see the feathered edges. You may also turn off the view of the *Background* in order to see the feathering more clearly.

6. Rename the new layer *elliptical selection* and click on the *Background* to make it active for the next selection.

The Layers palette after renaming the elliptical selection layer and clicking on the Background to make it active

Lasso

1. Choose the **Lasso** tool in the Toolbox and locate artwork on the document that suits a selection that is irregular in shape and can be easily traced by hand.

The Lasso tool

2. Move the cursor to the artwork, and *click+hold+drag* to surround the area of the imagery that you want. Release the mouse when you are through.

3. Choose the *Edit>Copy* menu command (or press *Cmd/Ctrl+C* on the keyboard). Now choose the *Edit>Paste* menu command (or press *Cmd/ Ctrl+V* on the keyboard). The selected artwork will

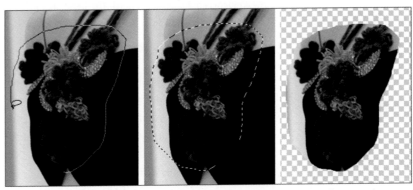

Creating the Lasso selection (left), the final selection (center), and the pasted-in selection (right)

Eraser

You can use the Eraser tool to erase parts of a selection that you do not want. Since the selection is on its own layer you do not need to worry about erasing the master image.

The Polygon Lasso tool

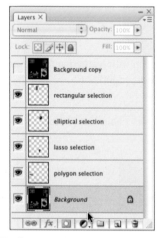

The Layers palette after renaming the polygon selection layer

now appear on its own layer. If you observe the *Layers* palette you will see that a new layer has formed.

4. Choose the **Move** tool, and move the selection over the black background area of the image. You may temporarily turn off the view of the *Background* layer in order to see the selection more clearly.

5. Rename the new layer *lasso selection* and click on the *Background* to make it active for the next selection.

Polygon Lasso

1. Choose the **Polygon Lasso** tool in the Toolbox. Locate artwork on the document that suits a selection that is irregular in shape and can be easily outlined as a polygon through a series of clicks with the mouse as you set outlining points around the image.

2. Move the cursor to the artwork, and *click+hold+release* to set points as you outline the image. You don't actually see points, but they do define the outer edge. To complete the polygon you either need to end at the first point, or double-click with the mouse.

3. Choose the *Edit>Copy* menu command (or press *Cmd/Ctrl+C* on the keyboard). Now choose the *Edit>Paste* menu command (or press *Cmd/Ctrl+V* on the keyboard).

4. Choose the **Move** tool, and move the selection (which sits directly above the original art) over the black background area of the image. You may temporarily turn off the view of the *Background* layer in order to see the selection more clearly.

5. Rename the new layer *polygon selection* and click on the *Background* to make it active for the next selection.

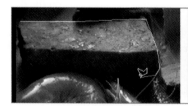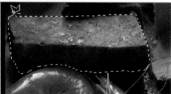

Creating the Polygon Lasso selection (left), the near-final selection (center), and the pasted-in selection (right)

Magnetic Polygon Lasso

1. Choose the **Magnetic Polygon Lasso** tool in the Toolbox. Locate artwork on the document that suits a selection that is irregular in shape and has high contrast between the shape and its background. The Magnetic Lasso tool uses contrast to determine the edge of a shape, and thus it works best with contrasting edges. You can change the contrast setting in the options bar to create cleaner selections.

The Magnetic Polygon Lasso tool

2. Move the cursor to the artwork, and *click+hold+drag* around the image. You may also *click+release* as you move. You will see anchor points on the image. You can press the *Delete/Backspace* key to back up and reset additional points. Surround the area of the imagery that you want. To complete the polygon you either need to end at the first point, or double-click with the mouse. The example below utilized the **Subtract from selection** function in the options bar (once the initial outlining selection was created) and removed the area between the arm and the body from the selection.

3. Choose the *Edit>Copy* menu command (or press *Cmd/Ctrl+C* on the keyboard). Now choose the *Edit>Paste* menu command (or press *Cmd/Ctrl+V* on the keyboard).

4. Choose the **Move** tool and move the selection (which sits directly above the original art) over the black background area of the image. You may temporarily turn off the view of the *Background* in order to see the selection more clearly.

5. Rename the new layer *magnetic polygon selection* and click on the *Background* to make it active for the next selection.

> **Adjustment Layer to Aid Selections**
> You can create a temporary adjustment layer above the artwork to heighten the contrast of the image. This can often aid in creating selections with the Magnetic Polygon tool.

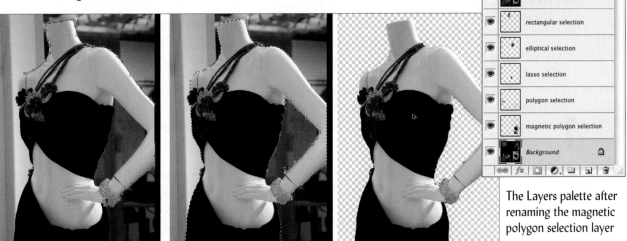

The Layers palette after renaming the magnetic polygon selection layer

Creating the Magnetic Polygon Lasso selection (left), using the Subtract from selection option to remove the area between the arm and body (center), and the pasted-in selection (right)

As you create selections with each tool, note how easy or difficult it is to be accurate. Paying attention to how the tools work will help you choose the proper tool for the task in future projects.

Working with Color Selection Tools

The **Magic Wand** and **Quick Selection** tools are used to create selections by color and color range. In many cases, the selections that can be made are very intricate and could never be achieved by a shape selection tool. Review the discussion of these on pages 33–36. You can experiment with changing the settings of various functions (such as *Tolerance* for the Magic Wand) in the options bar to increase the accuracy of your selection.

The Magic Wand tool

Magic Wand

1. Choose the **Magic Wand** tool in the Toolbox and locate an area of artwork on the document that is in a narrow color range. Our examples will use the floral arrangement, first the leaves (a relative simple challenge) and then the hydrangea flowers (a more complex challenge). The **Magic Wand** works best when selecting colors that border contrasting adjacent pixels. The existence of contrast will simplify the selection process. Examine the options bar. Note that the default *Tolerance* setting is 32. Don't change this yet. Make sure that the *Anti-alias* and *Contiguous* settings are checked (and thus turned on). The hydrangea flowers have lots of shades of purple, so they will be a challenge to select; click on the **Add to selection** button in the options bar so that you can continue to add to your selection with each mouse click.

Add to selection

Magic Wand options

  Magic Wand Selection Tips

- Work slowly until you understand how selections work.
- Be prepared to undo and redo.
- Change the Tolerance setting in the options bar.
- Become familiar with the various options in the Select menu (such as Select>Similar).

2. Zoom into the floral arrangement on the art so that you can see more clearly.

3. Move the cursor to the artwork and over the green leaves in the center of the arrangement. *Click+release* the mouse over a leaf. You will see a selection occur. Continue to click and add to the selection, attempting to add more of the leaves in the area that you want. Be prepared to "undo" if you add too much. If necessary, utilize the **Subtract from selection** function in the options bar (once the initial outlining selection is created) and carefully remove an area of unwanted selection.

4. Choose the *Edit>Copy* menu command (or press *Cmd/Ctrl+C* on the keyboard). Now choose the *Edit>Paste* menu command (or press *Cmd/Ctrl+V* on the keyboard). The selection will paste into its own layer.

5. Choose the **Move** tool, and move the selection (which sits directly above the original art) over the black background area of the image. You may temporarily turn off the view of the *Background* layer in order to see the selection more clearly.

6. Rename the new layer *magic wand selection* and click on the *Background* to make it active for the next selection.

a. Starting the selection of leaves

b. Adding to the selection

c. The pasted-in selection

Note how detailed a selection can become when it is selected by color.

7. For additional practice, attempt to select the hydrangea flowers using the **Magic Wand**. You will definitely want to have the **Add to selection** button active, and you will want to be clicking over the light, medium, and dark shades of the purple color that forms the petals of the flower. You will find that selecting the flowers is a greater challenge and it will require more patience. *Consider using some of the following aids in creating your selections:*
   - *Select>Grow*
   - *Select>Modify>Expand*
   - *Select>Modify>Contract*
   - Changing the *Tolerance* level as you work
   - Undo (*Cmd/Ctrl+Z*) and Redo (*Shift+Cmd/Ctrl+Z*)

8. Save the file if you have not done so recently.

      a   b   c

a. The first phase of creating a selection of the hydrangea flowers using the Magic Wand

b. Adding to the selection while utilizing various Select menu commands and altering the Tolerance setting

c. The final selection moved to the center area of the document

Quick Selection Tool (CS3 and CS4 only)

The **Quick Selection** tool is a wonderful addition to Photoshop. It allows you to create selections in a painterly way. As you drag your mouse, the selection expands outwards to find the defined edges of the artwork. We will return to the hydrangea flowers with this tool to show you how easy the selection becomes when you have the right tool.

The Quick Selection tool

1. Choose the **Quick Selection** tool in the Toolbox. It is stacked under the **Magic Wand** tool.

Quick Selection options

2. Observe the options bar. Choose a brush tip in the *Brush Picker* pop-up. A tip size of 10–15 is good. Make sure that the **Add to selection** button is active, so you can continue to build your selection.

3. Move over to the flower arrangement on your file. Make sure you are on the *Background*. Zoom in as necessary to see your work.

4. Place your cursor over the petals of the hydrangea and *click+hold+drag* and move the cursor over the flower, observing the selection you create as you move the mouse. *Try the following as you experiment:*
   - Try clicking and releasing often with the mouse as you paint.
   - Increase and decrease the brush tip size for fine-tuning, using the keyboard shortcuts (*Shift+Cmd/Ctrl+]* to increase and

Shift+Cmd/Ctrl+[to decrease.
- Switch back and forth between **Add to selection** and **Subtract from selection** modes as set in the options bar.

a   b   c

a. The first phase of creating a selection of the hydrangea flowers using the Quick Selection tool
b. Using the Subtract from selection option to remove some of the greenery that was picked up in the selection
c. The final selection

Select	
All	⌘A
Deselect	⌘D
Reselect	⇧⌘D
Inverse	⇧⌘I
All Layers	⌥⌘A
Deselect Layers	
Similar Layers	
Color Range...	
Feather...	⌥⌘D
Modify	▶
Grow	
Similar	
Transform Selection	
Load Selection...	
Save Selection...	

Functions of the Select menu

You will find that the selection is easy to create with great accuracy, and certainly, much easier than the one made with the **Magic Wand**. Thus, you should recognize the value of choosing the right tool for the task.

Other Selection Functions that Warrant Attention

There are several selection functions found in the *Select* menu that warrant attention when creating selections. These are discussed at length on pages 40–43 of Chapter 2. *A quick summary follows:*

> *All*—selects the entire image
> *Deselect*—removes the current selection
> *Reselect*—returns you to a selection that was just deselected
> *Inverse*—inverts the selection
> *All Layers*—allows Photoshop to create selections on all the layers, not just the current layer
> *Deselect Layers*—allows you to deselect layers that are selected
> *Similar Layers*—selects all layers of the same type
> *Color Range*—allows you to create a selection based on color
> *Refine Edge*—allows you to change several things from one central control center. Changes can be made using Radius, Contrast, Smooth, Feather, Contract/Expand, Modify, and Grow.

As a final note for this exercise, remember that selections can be saved (*Select>Save*) and reloaded later. They can also be transformed.

In the next exercise you will learn how to use the **Quick Mask** to assist with creating and fine-tuning selections.

The various selections created in this exercise

Exercise # 7: Using the Quick Mask to Build or Improve Selections

Goal

This exercise will teach you how to use the *Quick Mask* to assist in creating selections of complicated imagery.

Working in Quick Mask mode

Photoshop Tools and Functions

- ♦ **Selection** tools
- ♦ *Quick Mask* mode and *Standard* mode
- ♦ **Brush** tool

Quick Overview of the Process

Adobe's *Quick Mask* allows you to essentially paint your selection using the **Brush** tool. You can begin to create your selection using any of the selection tools, and then tweak and improve the selection using the *Quick Mask* functions, or you can simply paint the entire selection in *Quick Mask* mode. Review pages 37 to 40 in Chapter 2 to prepare yourself for the use of Photoshop's Quick Mask.

In this exercise we will be performing the following actions:

1. Load a digital image that is somewhat complex in its nature with regards to creating a selection.
2. Choose a selection tool and begin to select a portion of the image (the water in the case of the artwork used in this exercise).
3. Move into *Quick Mask* mode, and use the **Brush** tool to add to the selection through a painting process.
4. Move back and forth between *Standard* and *Quick Mask* modes to monitor your progress.
5. Exit *Quick Mask* mode to view your final selection.
6. Save the selection.
7. Create an adjustment layer to alter the color of the selection.

New Concepts

- o *Quick Mask* operations
- o *Quick Mask* vs. *Standard* modes

Sources of Imagery

- o Digital images of artwork that are somewhat complex with regards to creating selections

Step-by-Step

Loading Your Artwork

1. Choose the *File>Open* menu. Direct the file requestor to the companion DVD or to the location on your hard drive where these files have been moved and stored. Move to the **Basic Exercises** folder and then the **Ex 7** folder. Load the file called **sea play.jpg**.

2. Using the *File>Save As...* menu command, save the image as a TIF file. Remember to choose the TIF option using the pop-up

Note: **Quick Mask in CS4**
Photoshop now combines the Standard and Quick Mask mode buttons into one button in the Toolbox. The name for the button toggles between Edit in Quick Mask Mode and Edit in Standard Mode.

Note: **Mask Mode Confusion**
People are often confused by Quick Mask instructions, with reference to the Mask Mode button in the Toolbox. This is because the mode you are actually in (Standard vs. Quick Mask) and the name of the button (Edit in Quick Mask Mode vs. Edit in Standard Mode) seem to be at odds with each other. Keep in mind that the name of the button refers to the mode you will move into, if you activate the button.

at the bottom of the *Save* dialog. Choose the new location in your work folder (as you cannot save to the DVD). Click **OK** to complete the operation.

3. Examine the image. The goal will be to select the water only, so that its color can be changed. This will prove to be a challenge, as there is not much contrast between the model's skirt and the water near it. Likewise, there is not much contrast between the sky and the water in the upper-left side of the image.

The original photograph, Banu Tavlasoglu, Mesa College student

Create the Initial Selection

You will begin the selection process by selecting as much water as you can using a color selection tool.

1. Choose either the **Magic Wand** tool or the **Quick Selection** tool in the Toolbox. Ensure that the **Add to selection** button is clicked in the options bar. This exercise will use the **Magic Wand** as it is

available in all versions of the Creative Suite. Set the *Tolerance* in the options bar to 24 and ensure that *Anti-alias* and *Contiguous* are checked.

Setting options for the Magic Wand tool

2. Move to the image and begin to create your selection on the left side. You will have to be careful in the area where the water meets the sky. The **Add to selection** button will assist you in building the selection. Do not worry if you get a bit more than you need in some spots, or if you have areas that are not selected, as you will use the **Quick Mask** to assist you.

3. Move your **Magic Wand** cursor over to the right side of the image and click in the water area. You will find that the model's skirt wants to be included in the selection, as it is very similar in hue/saturation/ value to the water that surrounds it. Do not worry if you get some of the skirt in the selection. Continue to add to the selection, being careful in the areas of the hair. If necessary, use the **Subtract from selection** button in the options bar to remove some of the selection, but do not become overly concerned about doing this, as the *Quick Mask* functions will aid you in building a good selection.

Selecting the water on the left side of the image

Adding to the selection by selecting the water on the right side of the image

4. Once you have created a reasonably good selection, click on the **Edit in Quick Mask Mode** button in the Toolbox, which will put you into *Quick Mask* mode. Note how the *foreground* and *background* colors in the Toolbox change to white and black, respectively. Note also how the *Quick Mask* button now becomes active and slightly red. If you look at the document, you will see that the nonselected areas are now red, and that the selected areas of the image are true to the original image.

Standard Mode (left) and Quick Mask mode (right)

5. Double-click on the *Quick Mask* button in the Toolbox to open the *Quick Mask Options* dialog. Here you can see that red is the color used, and so masked areas (that is, the nonselected areas) will be shown with red. Review page 38 for a more detailed discussion on changing the settings, color of the mask, and so on. Click **OK** to exit the dialog.

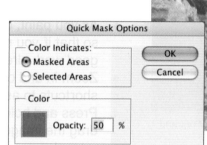

Quick Mask Options

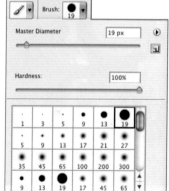

Working in Quick Mask mode

6. Choose the **Brush** tool in the toolbox, and choose a brush tip from the *Brush Preset pop-up* in the options bar. You will want to choose a hard-edge brush. Since the first area you will be working on is the water in the lower-left corner, choose a fairly large tip size (e.g., 19).

Step 6: Choosing a brush tip from the Brush Preset.

7. Move over to the document and begin painting the water areas that are red with the brush. As you paint, you will be removing red (and thus adding to the selection). As you work, you can use the keyboard shortcuts for increasing or decreasing your brush tip size. These are the square bracket keys, *[* and *]*. Get used to adjusting the size of the brush tip as you work, using the keyboard to assist you.

8. When you want to monitor the selection, click on the *Edit in Standard Mode* button in the Toolbox to move back to *Standard* mode and view the selection on your image. Click on the *Edit in Quick Mask Mode* button to move back into *Quick Mask* mode and continue your painting.

Painting with the Brush while in Quick Mask mode to build a proper mask and thus selection

Checking the selection as you go

The Layer palette showing the Background

Adjustment Layer
Tip for Selections

You can experiment with adding a Levels adjustment layer to the image in order to increase the contrast between the hat and the T-shirt vs. the background of the image. This often facilitates the process of creating a selection.

2. Observe the *Layers* palette to note that the image is the *Background*.

3. Make sure that the *History* palette is open (*Window>History*) so that you may undo operations or back up to a prior point in time, should you choose.

Using the Hue/Saturation Command

For this first image we will use the **Magic Wand** tool to create a selection of the T-shirt and the **Quick Selection** tool to create a selection of the hat. The *Hue/Saturation* command will be accessed through the *Image>Adjustments* menu for the T-shirt and through an *Adjustment layer* for the hat. Once the file is saved, the T-shirt color changes will be permanent while the hat color changes can be easily edited.

1. Choose the **Magic Wand** tool in the Toolbox. In the options bar, set the *Tolerance* to 32. Make sure that *Contiguous* and *Anti-alias* are checked. Click on the **Add to selection** button to make this option active.

Step 1: Magic Wand settings in the options bar.

2. On the **hatpose.jpg** image, click on an area of the blue T-shirt. Continue to add to the selection by clicking elsewhere in the T-shirt area. Zoom in and out, as necessary to see what you are selecting. If you select too much, back up in the *History* palette, or use the **Subtract from selection** button in the options bar to deselect areas.

The hatpose.jpg image
Model: Anjali Samant

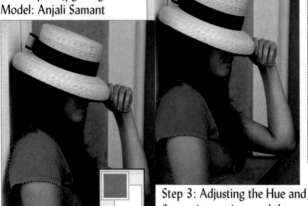

Step 2: Creating the selection of the T-shirt using the Magic Wand.

Step 3: Adjusting the Hue and Saturation settings and the result.

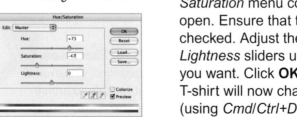

3. Choose the *Image>Adjustment>Hue/Saturation* menu command. A dialog will open. Ensure that the *Preview* check box is checked. Adjust the *Hue, Saturation,* and *Lightness* sliders until you create the color you want. Click **OK** and the selection of the T-shirt will now change. Deselect the selection (using *Cmd/Ctrl+D*).

Using the Colorize option to force the hue to the foreground color in the Toolbox

Note: As an alternate to using the Hue/Saturation and Lightness sliders, click on the **Colorize** option in the *Hue/Saturation* dialog. Observe how the current foreground color in the Toolbox will be used as your hue.

You will now select the hat. This will be more challenging because the contrast between the hat and the background is more subtle and selections become more difficult to make. If you have CS3, the **Quick Selection** tool works better than the **Magic Wand** in areas like this. If you do not have CS3 or greater you might need to use the **Magic Wand** in combination with **Quick Mask** functions to assist you in getting a clean selection of the hat. Review pages 36–39 and Basic Exercise #7. The **Magnetic Polygon** tool is another tool worth exploring for this task.

Save Selections
If a selection was particularly difficult to make, you may choose to save it using the Select menu so you can always access the selection in the future.

4. Choose the **Quick Selection** tool in the Toolbox. In the options bar, choose a *Brush* tip size of approximately 10 pixels. Click on the **Add to selection** button to make this option active.

Step 4: Quick Selection settings in the options bar.

5. Click on an area of the hat and drag the cursor. Release the mouse and observe your selection. You can continue to add to the selection by clicking and dragging the **Quick Selection** tool over areas of the hat. *The following tips will assist you:*
   o Zoom in and out as you work.
   o Change the *Brush* tip size. The smaller the tip, the easier it is to select narrow areas.
   o Change the selection mode to **Subtract from selection** when too much is selected to back up slightly, and alternate between the **Add to** and **Subtract from** options.
   o Quick *click+release* operations work well for fine tuning a selection.

a    b    c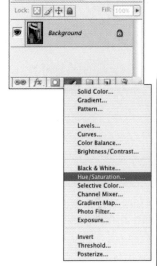

Creating the selection of the hat using the Quick Selection tool
a. Subtracting from the selection   b. The final selection
c. Adding to the selection

Step 6: Creating an adjustment layer for Hue/Saturation (above), the settings used (lower left), and the results (below). The Layers palette now shows the adjustment layer.

6. Once you have created a clean selection of the hat, move to the *Layers* palette and *click+hold* on the **Create new fill or adjustment layer** button at the bottom of the palette. Slide up to the *Hue/Saturation* option and release the mouse. A dialog will open. Adjust the *Hue, Saturation,* and *Lightness* sliders until you create the color you want. Click **OK** and the color of the hat selection will now change. Deselect the selection (using *Cmd/Ctrl+D*).

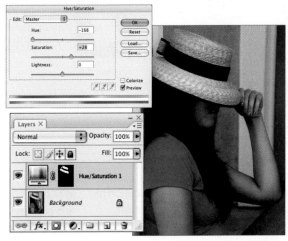

7. Observe the *Layers* palette and you will see the *Hue/Saturation* adjustment layer.

You have completed the color changes of this image. The recoloring of the T-shirt is permanent once you save the file, but the hat color may be changed simply by removing or altering the *Hue/Saturation* adjustment layer.

Using the Replace Color Command

This **Replace Color** adjustment command allows you to create a mask to select specific colors in an image and then replace them with a new color. It suits images where the color you want to change can be changed throughout the entire image. You do not create a selection in advance; rather you create your selection while in the *Replace Color* dialog. This function is only accessed through the *Image>Adjustment* menu and cannot be used as an adjustment layer.

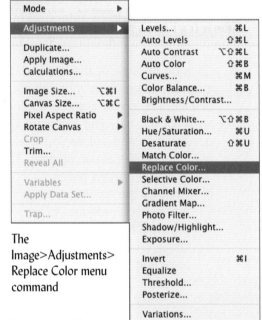

The Image>Adjustments> Replace Color menu command

The toppose.jpg image
Model: Isabelle Bright

1. Move to the **toppose.jpg** image. If you have not opened it, do so at this time. The goal will be to change the color of the blue top worn by the model.

2. Choose the *Image>Adjustments>Replace Color* menu command. A dialog will open.

3. Ensure that the *Preview* box is checked.

4. Select the *Display* option to *Selection,* which will show you a mask of the image in the preview area. The black areas are masked and the unmasked areas are white. Areas that are partially masked will appear as varying levels of gray. You can use the cursor to click on areas of your textile/design to have those areas be the color that is selected and nonmasked (and thus ready for change). You can use either of the following techniques to create the sampled area of colors from your artwork.

Using the Eyedropper

Use the *Shift+click* function or use the *Add to Sample* eyedropper to add to the sampled area.
Use the *Subtract Sample* eyedropper to remove colors from the sampled area.

Steps 2–6: Using the Eyedropper option to select the mask and changing the color.

Using the Selection Swatch

Double-click on the *Selection Swatch* (at the top of the window), which will open the *Color Picker.* Here you can click directly on the color in the image that you want to change and it will become selected in the Mask area.

Steps 5–6: Using the Selection Swatch option to create the mask.

5. Adjust the tolerance of the mask by moving the *Fuzziness* slider back and forth to adjust the sampled area.

6. Select the new color by performing one of the following:

    a. Drag the *Hue*, *Saturation*, or *Lightness* sliders,

    OR

    b. Double-click on the *Result Swatch* in the lower palette and use the *Color Picker* to select the *Replacement* color.

Your choice of which adjustment function to use will vary according the artwork you want to alter and how the color is used in the image. Understand that the *Hue/Saturation* and *Replace Color* functions differ in the following ways:

o   *Hue/Saturation* works well when you want to create a selection of the area to alter and change its color.

o   *Replace Color* works well when you want to change the same color consistently throughout the entire artwork. This suits changing colors in garments that appear in an isolated color and in textile prints where you want to change the color throughout the entire image.

Step 6: Choosing the new color by double-clicking on the Result Swatch and choosing the color from the Color Picker.

More Thought...

As a challenge, load the **blackwhitepose.jpg** image and alter some of the garment colors, choosing the best option between *Hue/Saturation* and *Replace*. This image presents some thought challenges as the black and white garment colors you want to change appear elsewhere in the image. Have fun!

The blackwhitepose.jpg image
Model: Isabelle Bright

A Blank Page...

time to make notes before the fashion exercises begin

Fashion Exercises

This chapter includes a series of exercises that focus on the creation of fashion artwork that is commonly used to express a mood or illustrate a fashion garment. The first several exercises will involve the process of building a composite (known as collage in the art world). Through these exercises you will advance your skills of working with selections and layers. Next, you will learn how to draw fashion flats, through the use of a fashion croquis and then using a grid and drawing freehand. SnapFashun, a commercial fashion clip art collection, will be explored as an alternative to original drawing. Exercises pertaining to fashion illustration will teach you how to translate your hand drawings to Photoshop and how to color these. You will also learn to work with digital art to create fashion poses and illustrations and how to use various tools that simulate art mediums such as watercolor, charcoal, and markers. The final group of exercises will teach you how to lay fabric into your garments using a variety of techniques.

Illustration by Mariel Diaz-Mendoza

The exercises are divided into groups based on the type of fashion drawing: composite building, drawing garment flats, and creating fashion illustrations.

Exercises include:

Selection Exercises: Composite Building

Exercise #1   Composite: Working with Selections on the Background
Exercise #2   Composite: Working with Selections Using the Clipboard and Multiple Layers
Exercise #3   Creating a Promotional Composite
Exercise #4   Building a Color Trend Composite Utilizing Travel and Fashion Imagery

Flats by Cynthia Martinez

Fashion Flats

Exercise #5   Drawing Flats on a Fashion Croquis
Exercise #6   Drawing Flats on a Grid Using Paths and Vector Tools
Exercise #7   Working with the SnapFashun Library of Flats

Fashion Illustrations

Exercise #8   Translating a Hand-drawn Fashion Pose to Digital Format
Exercise #9   Coloring Line Art Images
Exercise #10   Extracting a Pose from a Fashion Photo
Exercise #11   Illustrating Fashion with Art Medium Brushes

Deco Rose

Laying Fabric into Garments

Exercise #12   Laying Fabric into Garments
Exercise #13   Laying Fabric into a Fashion Pose Using Color Mapping
Exercise #14   Working with Clipping Paths

Cotton Dress
$59.99

Photo Styling and Clipping Masks by Mary Drobnis

Illustration by Natalie Richardson

Sketches drawn by hand were brought into Photoshop and scanned fabric was laid in the garments. Valentina Tiurbini, artist

Note:

Fill Mode vs. Object Shapes

There are two modes by which lines and shapes can be drawn in Photoshop. The Fill Pixel mode creates raster or pixel drawings whereby the Shapes mode creates vector objects.

Fashion Design in Photoshop

There are various approaches you can take when designing with Photoshop. Your choice of approach will vary according to your art skills and your knowledge of the various tools and functions available. Collage-type projects will require experimentation with composite-type images, heavily utilizing selections and image processing. Some illustration-type projects will require that you start your drawing from scratch. Others will start with a digital image that you will utilize as a design source to be traced, edited, or manipulated.

The following are options for creating fashion art in Photoshop:

1. Imagery Work in the Realm of Composites (Collage)

Photoshop excels in the building of composite imagery, which involves combining multiple images to create a piece of art. In the fashion industry, this falls into the area of theme boards used to set a mood or inspire design teams to think and focus in the same manner. Composites are also used as background art for presentation boards. This type of work relies heavily on an understanding of working with digital images and using selections and layers.

2. Drawing by Hand and Translating the Art to a Digital Form

If you are comfortable drawing by hand but not yet comfortable with drawing freehand in Photoshop, your best approach to creating fashion art is to use a scanner or digital camera to translate your hand-drawn work to a digital format ready for use in Photoshop. Once you bring the artwork into Photoshop, it becomes a pixelated image ready for editing. The quality of the art (from a digital standpoint) will dictate how much clean-up work you need to do.

Advantages
- o   You can pull from your personal collection of drawings.
- o   You can create drawings at any point in time, without a computer, and later translate them to digital form.

Disadvantages
- o   If the quality of the original art is not good, you will have to spend time performing clean-up work in Photoshop.
- o   Art papers with texture may translate with extraneous pixels when scanned; therefore you may have to spend some time performing clean-up work in the digital form of your drawing.

3. Drawing Freehand in a Painterly Mode
(using Paint-oriented tools)

Designing from scratch in Photoshop is an approach whereby you use the various paint-type tools such as brushes, lines, and shapes (in *Fill Pixel* mode), erasers, paint bucket, and so on. Imagery is laid down as pixels that are easily drawn, erased, and redrawn.

Advantages
- o   This is a very free-form approach to design.
- o   You can move from one part of the image to the other without worrying about completing one object/area before you start another.

Disadvantages
- o Drawing freehand takes some art skill and a sense of proportion.
- o If you work in low resolutions, your drawing will be pixelated and thus print with jaggies. Working in higher resolutions improves the results.

4. Drawing Freehand in a Vector Mode (using object-oriented tools)

Photoshop contains vector drawing tools such as the Pen, Shapes, Selection tool, and so on. These tools allow you to create drawings with objects. All vector drawing tools found in Photoshop exist in Illustrator. If you are used to working in Illustrator, you will find that many of the tools are the same. Photoshop does not contain the depth of tools that Illustrator does, and thus certain operations are more difficult to perform, which proves frustrating to a user who knows Illustrator (or similar software).

Advantages
- o Output is smoother (no jaggies).
- o Vector shape/objects can be resized without loss of clarity.
- o Clipping masks are easily created and edited.
- o Editing is often simpler, once you understand the tools.

Disadvantages
- o The learning curve is steeper.
- o The set of tools available for use in Photoshop is limited compared with those in Illustrator and other vector-style programs, and thus using these tools in Photoshop can be more frustrating.

Rendering with medium brushes
Sandra Gonzales

5. Utilizing Fashion Clip Art

In this approach you can utilize predrawn computer fashion art. The images become your starting point, and you can either trace portions of them or simply edit and redraw as necessary. Your choice of tools will be dictated somewhat by the type of computer clip art you start with. For example, if you import a vector-based clip art drawing of a garment, you can either continue in the vector mode or switch to a pixel (raster) mode. SnapFashun is one example of the fashion "clip art" libraries available to companies and individuals (see sidebar for information).

Advantages
- o This is a good starting point for people with minimal drawing skills.
- o The time needed to create or draw a garment is greatly reduced (assuming minimal editing is necessary).

Disadvantages
- o You must concern yourself with copyright infringement if you are selling your work.

Edited SnapFashun image by Cara Marks

6. Tracing an Existing Digital Image as a Starting Point

In this approach, you trace an existing photo or pose that is brought into the program digitally. This works well to translate a photograph of a fashion model into line art that can then be used in various ways. You may choose to work in either a pixel or vector mode of drawing.

Note:

SnapFashun
Contact Information
SnapFashun/BGA
8581 Santa Monica Blvd.,
#515, Los Angeles, CA
90069-4120
Phone: (310) 659-5956
Fax: 323-882-6712
SnapFashun inquiries
sales@snapfashun.com
http://www.snapfashun.com

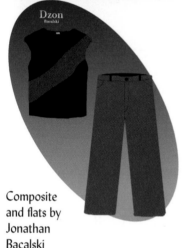

Composite
and flats by
Jonathan
Bacalski

Advantages
o   You don't need great drawing skills to produce good
    fashion drawings.
Disadvantages
o   You must beware of copyright infringement if you are
    selling your work.

7. Editing Digital Imagery

In this approach to design, you work with scanned imagery (e.g.,
photos, fabrics, etc.) and alter it according to your needs (as opposed to
tracing or redrawing). Fabrics can be scanned for use and easily scaled,
recolored, simplified, and so on and ultimately laid into drawn garments.

Advantages
o   One does not need to draw the artwork from scratch.
o   Artwork and fabrics are quickly transferred to a medium that can
    be altered for various end uses.
Disadvantages
o   If the digital imagery is of poor quality, a lot of editing work may be
    necessary to create a satisfactory result.
o   You must concern yourself with copyright infringement if you are
    selling your work.

Flats by Osbaldo Ahumada

Rendering with an art
medium by Samantha Song

Classic Car Show
Collection

Style #0201
Spring 2004

Style #0202
Spring 2004

Composite and
fashion flats to
match by Nadia
Lopez

The Fashion Composite (Collage)

Collage is a technique commonly used to build story or theme boards for presentation. These are used within the fashion industry to aid in conveying a theme or mood to the intended audience. In large companies, theme boards may be used to help designers from various departments retain focus so that although they design their lines independently, the company's total collection works as a unit and may be merchandised in stores together. Collage techniques are also used to present trends, color stories, and develop artwork for publication and the Web.

Paris Composite by Kanae Otaka

Essentially, a collage is an assemblage of images, placed together to suggest a theme or mood and to aid in communicating an idea. This was traditionally done by cutting and pasting photos, clippings, and other mediums onto a mat board. In Photoshop and in the computer world, the term **composites** is used in lieu of the traditional term collage. A composite is thus the assemblage of images (*backgrounds* and *elements)*, using selections, layers, transparency, filters, and other creative effects to create an artistic piece. If you use a digital camera to gather your imagery, you will soon learn how to look at the world in terms of backgrounds, textures, and elements, and gather your imagery accordingly.

The first four exercises in this section of the book will focus on creating composites. Each exercise will focus on teaching a new skill.

Rome Composite by Ksenia Galyga

Photoshop Tools and Functions

- ◆ *Selection* tools
- ◆ **Move** and **Crop** tools
- ◆ Clipboard functions such as *Cut* and *Paste*
- ◆ Layers, adjustment layers, and layer effects
- ◆ Feathering
- ◆ Transparency (of images and layers)
- ◆ Type
- ◆ Gradients
- ◆ *Shape* tools

General Process:

1. Collect imagery that pertains to your theme.
2. Prepare images if they are not already in a digital format.
3. Evaluate and alter images, as necessary, for color, resolutions, and so on.
4. Prepare a document to be the main collage document/background.
5. Build the composite.

Retro Composite by Paula Tabalipa

Sources of Imagery

- o Digital camera images

Note: Copyright?
If you sell the work you create, you must be aware of copyright infringement, so choose your art carefully. Remember, it is more creative to be original.

New Concepts:

- o Using *Opt/Alt+drag* to copy an image from one place to another on the **same** layer.
- o Understand that the order you bring imagery to the composite area dictates what sits on top and what is underneath. Imagery stacks bottom to top as it is introduced.
- o Working with transformations

Sources of Imagery

- o Art provided on the DVD

Step-by-Step

The original artwork composed of window shots of mannequins and a blank off-white area for your composite

Loading the Initial Work File and Setting up

On the accompanying DVD (or the location on your hard drive you moved the files to), you will find a folder called **Fashion Exercises.** Inside this folder is a folder called **Composite Art**.

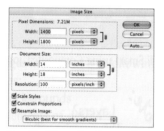

Step 2: Observing image size and information.

1. Using the *File>Open* menu, load one of the following images: **Composite1.jpg** or **Composite2.jpg.** These files contain imagery taken of store windows in Europe. The example here is **Composite1.jpg**.

2. On the image you will see that there are fashion poses around the left side and the top and there is an off-white rectangular box to the center right. You will build your collage in the off-white area. Consider it your art paper. Choose the *Image>Image Size* menu command. This will open the *Image Size* dialog and show you information about the file. Observe the file size, the document size, and the resolution. This is a very good habit to get into, anytime you load art. You will see that the resolution of the current image is relatively low (100 dpi) and that the document size is large (14 inches by 18 inches).

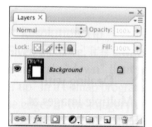

Step 3: Observing the Layers palette.

3. Observe the *Layers* palette to note that the image is the background. We will not be using layers in this exercise, so realize that you cannot change the background opacity or fill.

4. Make sure that the *History* palette is open (*Window>History*) so that you can undo operations or back up to a prior history state, should you choose.

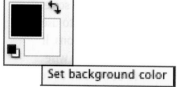
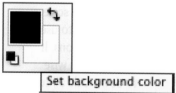

Step 5: Setting the background color as the off-white color used in the artwork.

5. Ensure that the background color in the Toolbox is the same color as the off-white color of your composite area. Click on the background color icon in the Toolbox. The *Color Picker* will open. Move the cursor off the *Color Picker* window and onto your artwork. The cursor will become an eyedropper. Place it over your off-white color and click; the background color icon in your Toolbox will become the off-white color of your artwork. Now, when you erase in this area, you will erase to the off-white color.

6. Save the file as *collage1.psd*. Do this by using the *File>Save As* menu command and change the file format to Photoshop by choosing the *Photoshop* option from the *Format* pop-up menu.

The discussion that follows introduces various techniques that you may use to build the composite. The first section discusses techniques used after you have created a selection. The second section discusses additional techniques that do not necessarily need to have a selection made prior to performing them.

Build the Composite: Working with Selections

Using the techniques below, build your composite in the center of the document in the space provided. As you work through the following steps, refer back to Chapter 2 and the discussion on the *Selection* tools. Attempt to understand and use the following tools and functions:

The top level of Selection tools (above) and Selection options (below)

- **Rectangular** and **Ellipse** Marquee
- **Lasso** tools (Lasso, Polygon Lasso, and Magnetic Lasso)
- **Move** tool
- Deselect (*Select>Deselect*) menu or *Cmd/Ctrl+D* on the keyboard
- Selection modes in the options bar (Add to Selection, Remove from Selection)
- Copying a selection on the same layer using *Opt/Alt+Drag*

Study the following list of tools and techniques you can use in this exercise. Page references to additional discussion of each tool/function are provided. Prior to starting the composite, it is always wise to set the background color in the Toolbox as the color of the area into which you are laying your images.

The top level of Selection tools (above) and Selection options (below)

Note: All examples of techniques below assume a selection of imagery exists.

Erasing Areas of the Image (pages 26–27)
- o Press the *Delete/Backspace* key (Mac/Windows) and the selection will disappear and become the background color.

Deselecting a Selection (page 28)
- o Press *Cmd/Ctrl+D* on the keyboard and the selection will disappear or deselect.

Moving a selection (above) and copying a selection (below)

Moving a Selection (pages 26–27, 33)
- o Choose the **Mover** tool. Place your cursor inside the selection and *click+drag* with the mouse to move the selection to a different area of the document.

Copying a Selection on the Same Layer (page 26)
- o Choose the **Move** tool. Place your cursor inside the selection and then press and hold the *Opt/Alt* key on the keyboard as you *click+drag* with the mouse to move (and copy) the selection to a different area of the document.

Selection modes in the options bar

Adding to or Removing from a Selection   (page 32)

o   Observe the options bar at the top of the screen, and click on the appropriate selection option to add or remove from a selection as you work.

Transforming a Selection Using Free Transform   (pages 127–128)

1. Press *Cmd/Ctrl+T* on the keyboard (or choose the *Edit>Free Transform* menu command). A rectangular box with anchor points will appear around the selection.

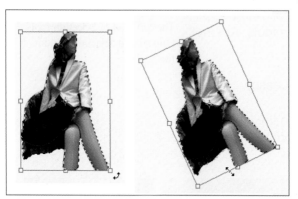

2. Move your cursor around the perimeter of the box and note how it changes. The type of cursor icon will tell you if you can continue to scale or rotate the image.

•   To scale *in proportion*, click on a corner point and press the *Shift* key on the keyboard and then drag the image inwards or outwards.

•   To stretch the image, *click+hold* on any corner or side point, and drag the mouse.

•   To rotate the image, move your cursor outside a corner of the image until it turns into the rotate cursor (a curve with two arrowheads). Then, *click+hold+drag* and rotate the image.

3. Click on the **Commit** button in the options bar (the check mark button), or double-click inside the image to confirm the transformation.

Transforming a Selection Using Edit>Transform Menu Functions
(page 128)

1. Choose the *Edit>Transform* menu to observe your options (Scale, Rotate, Skew, Flip, etc.). Once you have selected an option, the bounding box with anchor points appears around your selection.

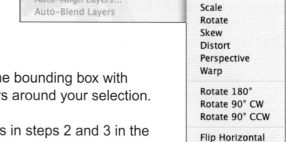

2. Perform operations as in steps 2 and 3 in the Free Transform discussion above.

Understanding Lasso Selections   (pages 30–32)

1. In turn, choose each of the **Lasso Selection** tools, and select an area of the image. As you are creating the selection, note how easy or difficult it is to be accurate.

Lasso

2. When you use the **Polygon Lasso**, experiment with backing up by using the *Delete/Backspace* key on the keyboard.

Polygon Lasso

3. When you use the **Magnetic Lasso**, experiment with changing the Contrast settings in the options bar. This will often increase the contrast on the edges and assist in using the tool.

Magnetic Lasso

The following tools and functions may also be used. These do not require that you have a selection made prior to use, although several of these will also work in a selected area of the image if one exists.

Eraser Tool   (page 84)

When working on a Background image (as opposed to a layer), the Eraser tool will allow you to erase to the background color as set in the Toolbox.

1. Make sure that the background color in the Toolbox is the color you want to erase with.

2. Select the **Eraser** tool in the Toolbox.

3. On the background image, *click+hold+drag* the Eraser icon over the image in the area you want to erase. You will erase the imagery to the current background color in the Toolbox.
Note: You may increase or decrease the eraser size by pressing the *[* or *]* keys on the keyboard.

Using the Eraser tool to erase to the background color

Paint Bucket Tool   (pages 86, 88–89)

The Paint Bucket tool lets you fill an area on your image with the current foreground color. The fill extends over the color you clicked on from the point under the cursor (when you click) to a different color boundary. You can use tolerance settings in the options bar to expand the range of colors your fill extends over.

1. Select the **Paint Bucket** tool in the Toolbox. This is typically stacked under the **Gradient** tool.

2. Click on the foreground color in the Toolbox and select a color from the *Color Picker* (or choose a color from the *Swatches* palette).

3. Move the **Paint Bucket** cursor over the area you want to fill with color and click. Color will spread to a boundary.

Using the Paint Bucket tool to fill the area in the lower left with the off-white background color

Eyedropper Tool   (page 114)

The **Eyedropper** tool is used to aid you in selecting a color from the artwork and moving this color to the foreground color in the Toolbox (or the background color if this was the selected icon).

1. Select the **Eyedropper** tool in the Toolbox.

2. Move the Eyedropper tool icon over the color on your document you want to sample. Click with the mouse. The color you just sampled will become the foreground color of the palette.

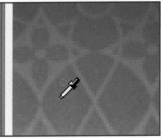

Note: When you click on either the *Foreground* or *Background* icon in the Toolbox, the *Color Picker* opens. You can move to the **Eyedropper** tool so that you can choose a color from the palette in the *Color Picker,* or from the image on your document. Once you have selected the color and clicked **OK** in the *Color Picker* dialog, you move back to the tool you were using prior to changing colors.

Using the Eyedropper tool to sample a purple color from the artwork

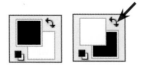

Clicking on the Switch Foreground and Background Colors icon in the Toolbox allows you to swap the colors.

Switch Foreground and Background Colors   (page 86)

There will be times when you want to swap your foreground and background colors as you work with your graphics. You can do this by clicking on the **Switch Foreground and Background Colors** icon in the Toolbox, or by pressing *X* on the keyboard.

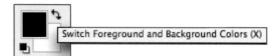

Crop Tool   (page 160)

When you have completed building your composite, you will use the **Crop** tool to isolate the final artwork from all the surrounding artwork. *To use this tool:*

1. Click on the **Crop** tool in the Toolbox to select it.

2. Move over to your document and *click+hold+drag* to frame off the portion of the image you want to keep. Note that the area outside of the image turns dark gray to assist in viewing the area you are intending to keep.

3. Either double-click inside the cropped area, or click on the **Confirm** check mark in the options bar to finalize the crop. All other imagery will disappear. You may also press the *Cmd/Ctrl+Return/Enter* keys on the keyboard.

Composite by Jodi Smart

Begin now to build your composite using any combination of the functions discussed above. Remember that you are to work on the Background only with no use of the clipboard or layers. When you are through, use the **Crop** tool to crop your image to show only the final artwork.

Kristin Matoba

Banu Tavlasoglu

Student
Gallery
Composites
Mesa Fashion
Students

Jeanne Reith

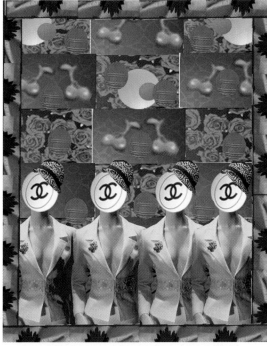

Mariel
Diaz-
Mendoza

Melisa Farnsworth

Osbaldo
Ahumada

Pontus Wickbom Burevall

Collage in process by
Karol Topete

Exercise #2: Composite: Working with Selections Using the Clipboard and Multiple Layers

Goal

This exercise explores the process of creating selections and building more sophisticated artwork using the clipboard, layers, and transformations.

Photoshop Tools and Functions

- **Marquee** selection tools (rectangular and ellipse)
- **Lasso** selection tools (Lasso, Polygon Lasso, and Magnetic Lasso)
- Feathering (to soften edges of a selection)
- **Magic Wand** and **Quick Selection** (CS3) tools
- **Move** tool
- Transform functions (*Edit>Transformation*)
- Clipboard functions (*Edit>Copy, Edit>Paste*)
- Layers
- Layer opacity

Overview

You will begin with the same artwork as Exercise #1 and, using additional functions in Photoshop, you will build a more advanced composite. You will be adding new Photoshop skills to your repertoire.
These include the use of:

- the **Magic Wand** and the **Quick Selection** tools to create selections by color and by painting over a color
- **layers** so that you can easily organize and manipulate your artwork
- the **clipboard** and copy and paste functions to easily move artwork into your work area on separate layers
- **feathering** (when making a selection) to soften the edges of your selection when it is pasted into the document
- the use of layer **opacity** levels to make imagery somewhat transparent

Review the concepts of creating selections by color and painting on pages 33–36 and the use of layers on pages 47–57.

New Concepts:

- o Using alternate methods of creating selections such as the **Magic Wand** tool (to select by color) and the **Quick Selection** tool (to select by painting over a color)
- o Using layers to isolate and organize your imagery, control the stacking order of what sits above and below, and allow for transparency of imagery
- o Using feathering function to soften the edges of selected artwork

Sources of Imagery

- o Art provided on the DVD; **Composite1.jpg** or **Composite2.jpg**

Step-by-Step

Loading the Initial Work File and Setting up
On the accompanying DVD (or the location on your hard drive you moved the files to), you will find a folder called **Fashion Exercises.** Inside this folder is a folder called **Composite Art**.

1. Using the *File>Open* menu, load one of the following images: **Composite1.jpg** or **Composite2.jpg.** The example here will use **Composite2.jpg**.

2.–5. Follow steps 2 through 5 on page 232.

6. Save the file as **collage2.psd.** Do this by using the *File>Save As...* menu command and change the file format to Photoshop by choosing the Photoshop option from the *Format* pop-up menu.

Composite2.jpg, one of the sample files used for this exercise

The discussion that follows introduces various new techniques that you may use to build this second composite. Page numbers refer you to further discussion of the tool or function.

Magic Wand Tool   (pages 33–36)
The **Magic Wand** tool allows you to create selections by color.
1. Click on the **Magic Wand** tool in the Toolbox to select it.

2. Set the *Tolerance* level in the options bar. The higher the number, the broader the range of colors selected once you click on the artwork. The lower the number, the narrower the range of color selected. You will need to experiment.

The Magic Wand in action

3. Move the cursor to your artwork, over the area where you want to make a selection and click. Observe the selection.
   - If you want to *deselect* the selection, choose the *Select>Deselect* menu command or press *Cmd/Ctrl+D* on the keyboard.
   - If you want to **add** to the selection, click on the **Add to selection** button in the options bar. Conversely, if you want to subtract from the selection click on the **Subtract from selection** button in the option bar. You may also press and use the *Shift* key on the keyboard as you click on your selection.

4. Once you have created your selection, you may continue in various manners such as:
   - move the selection with the **Move** tool
   - perform an *adjustment* or run a *filter* on it
   - copy the image to the clipboard and paste it into the document
   - delete the selection by pressing the *Delete/ Backspace* key on the keyboard

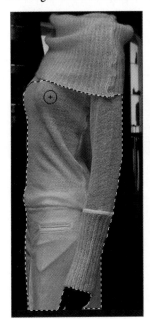

The Quick Selection tool in action

Quick Selection Tool   (pages 36–37)
The **Quick Selection** tool allows you to paint over an area and create a selection by color. *Tolerance* levels

Creating and naming layers

The Copy and Paste commands in the Edit menu

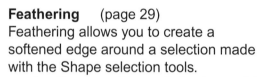

Two images: The right image has feathering of 5 pixels applied and the example on the left has no feathering.

Feathering options and the Refine Edge button

can also be used with this tool. Follow the steps above (for the Magic Wand), increasing or decreasing the brush tip size as you work.

Use of Layers   (pages 47–57)
Adding the use of layers to your work process will give you amazing freedom. One of the main advantages of layers is that artwork can be isolated from the rest of the imagery; thus you can easily edit and transform it. You can change the stacking order of your layers, which allows you to organize the imagery, front to back, on the document.

Copy and Paste Clipboard Functions   (pages 5–10)
Using the **Edit** menu and clipboard functions allows you to copy and paste imagery from one location to another. This provides great freedom in that the original artwork is retained and the copy you paste into the document appears on its own layer. This provides great flexibility for editing.
To use the clipboard:

1. Create a selection of artwork.

2. Choose the *Edit>Copy* menu command. This will copy the artwork to the clipboard, which is an invisible holding tank for information.

3. Choose the *Edit>Paste* menu command. This will paste the artwork into your document from the clipboard and onto its own unique layer. Typically, the pasted-in artwork positions itself directly above the copied artwork, so you will have to use the **Move** tool to reposition it.

Feathering   (page 29)
Feathering allows you to create a softened edge around a selection made with the Shape selection tools.

Moving the pasted-in artwork (on its new layer) to a new position on the document

1. Choose a Shape Selection tool (e.g., the **Rectangular** or **Elliptical Marquee**, or any of the **Lasso** tools).

2. Set the feathering amount by typing a number in the *Feather* field in the options bar. The higher the number, the softer your edge will become once it is pasted into its new location.

3. Create the selection.

4. Either move or copy the selection to a new location and you will see the feathering that occurs. You can use the **Move** tool to move a selection, and add the *opt/alt+drag* keyboard functions to copy the selection on the same layer. If you use the clipboard to copy and paste the artwork, the new feathered selection will appear on its own layer.

Note to CS3 and CS4 Users: If you forget to set the feathering amount prior to making a selection, use the **Refine Edges** button in the options bar to add feathering after the selection is made.

Layer Opacity   (page 49)
You may change the opacity level of a layer by clicking on and dragging on the *opacity slider*. This allows you to create artwork that is translucent; thus you can see through it to the layers below.
1. Click on the layer you want to make transparent.

2. *Click+hold* on the *opacity slider* in the *Layers* palette, and drag the slider until you get the opacity level you want. Release the mouse.

Applying a 70% opacity setting to the master garment layer and the resulting transparency

Begin now to build your composite using any combination of the functions discussed above.

Tips to Assist in Composite Building

o   It is possible to use multiple *Selection* tools as you work. For example, start with the **Magic Wand**, and then switch to the **Magnetic Lasso Polygon** tool to continue creating a selection using the **Add to selection** function in the options bar.

o   When you are selecting artwork from the original image, remember to first click on the *Background* to make it active.

o   Remember to name your layers as this will assist you in quickly identifying what is on each layer.

o   Remember to deselect a selection when you want to proceed with another task. Use the *Cmd/Ctrl+D* keyboard shortcut.

o   Remember to select the layer you want to work on by clicking on it in the *Layers* palette. If you forget to do this, the operation you are attempting to perform will not work properly.

Karol Topete

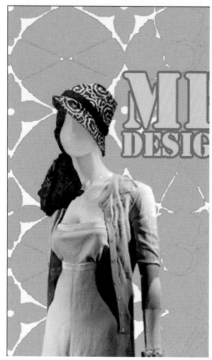

Melisa Farnsworth

Nania Pongpitakkul

June Triolo

Kari Pacheco

Pontus
Wickbom Burevall

Exercise #3: Creating a Promotional Composite

Goal

This exercise will teach you how to prepare a fashion promotional composite that includes imagery and type. You will learn how to incorporate a gradient using a layer mask.

Photoshop Tools and Functions

- **Selection** tools
- Cut/Paste (**Edit** menu)
- Layers and adjustment layers
- Transformation functions such as *Scale* and *Rotate* (**Edit** menu)
- Touch-up tools such as **Clone Stamp**
- *Gradient* in a *Layer Mask*
- *Stroking* a selection (*Edit>Stroke*)

Sample Promotional Composite

Quick Overview of the Process

You will work with two images of a knit sweater, one of the full garment and one that is a detail shot. You will choose one to be the background and the other to be the small insert. You can use any portion of the imagery you want.

The general approach is as follows:

1. Load the images and observe image information.
2. Determine which image will become the background. Prep the file as your background image so as to have the imagery fade away to nothing (to allow for a type area that can be easily read). Target the image to fit on an 8" × 10" page.
3. Determine which portion of the second image will be your insert art. Prepare this as a rectangular piece and copy it via the clipboard into the main image.
4. Resize the inset image and stroke it to give it a border. Rotate it using *Edit>Transform commands.*
5. Build a gradient, pulling colors from the image if you like.
6. Create a *Layer Mask* and insert the gradient into the mask.
7. Add **Type** with promotional content.

Review the following discussions:
Selections and Layers: Chapter 2, pages 28–37 and pages 51–57
Transformations: Chapter 5, pages 127–128
Gradient: Chapter 4, pages 79–82
Clone Stamp: Chapter 4, pages 92–93

New Concepts

- o *Gradients* and *Layer Masks*
- o *Stroking* a Selection
- o **Type** and *Type Layers*

Sources of Imagery

- o Two images on the accompanying DVD: **sweater.jpg** and **sweaterdetail.jpg**

Note:

Image Size

You must always be aware of the resolution and image size of the artwork you are using, as this will assist you in making decisions and knowing how to handle the art. Use the Image>Image Size menu to gather this info.

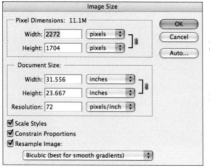

Step 2: Adjusting the image size, the before (above) and after (below).

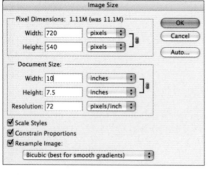

Step 3: Setting the Fixed Ratio.

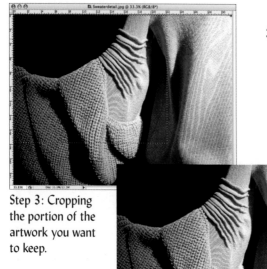

Step 3: Cropping the portion of the artwork you want to keep.

Step-by-Step

Loading the Initial Work File and Setting up

On the accompanying DVD or the location on your hard drive to which you moved the files from the DVD, you will find a folder called **Fashion Exercises.** Inside this folder is a folder called **Composite Art**.

1. Using the *File>Open* menu, load one of the following images: **Sweater.jpg** or **Sweaterdetail.jpg.** The images were taken of a sweater (from Grignasco Group) at the Pitti Filati Trend Show in Florence, Italy.

2. Make sure that you have the *Layers*, *History*, *Navigator*, and *Colors* palettes open and ready for use.

3. Choose the *Image>Image Size* menu command and learn what you need to know about each image. Do not worry if the document sizes of the images are large, as you may want to crop from the image to get what you need.

Creating the Background Art

1. Determine which image you want to work with as your art background and bring this document to the front. Determine if you are going to crop an area of it, or if you want to work with the entire image. We will work with the detail image to create the background art.

2. Conduct a quick test to see if the artwork is in a proportion relative to 8 × 10. Choose the *Image>Image Size* menu again, and enter 10 in the larger of the two document size measurements and press the *Tab* key on the keyboard. The other dimension in the dialog will change to show the constrained proportion change. You will see that this image, if reduced to 10 inches wide, would be 7.5 inches tall, and you have to decide if that is ok for your purposes. Cancel if you don't want to alter the size, but this little trick is handy. If you do rescale the image, you may need to zoom into your image after altering its size.

3. We will use the **Rectangular Marquee** tool to crop the part of the image we want (as opposed to the **Crop** tool). The reason we do this is because the Rectangular Marquee options will allow us to set a *Fixed Ratio* for a selection. Choose the **Rectangular Marquee** tool. In the options bar, choose the *Fixed Ratio* option from the *Style* pop-up menu and set it at 10 wide by 8 tall. Now, when you click on the screen and drag, your marquee will always be in this proportion. Select an area of the image, and remember, you can move the marquee while it is active by nudging it on the keyboard. You can deselect (*Select>Deselect* menu or *Cmd/Ctrl+D* on the keyboard) and reselect at any time. Select the area of the imagery you want for your background. You will see marching ants surrounding the area.

4. Choose the *Image>Crop* command and the artwork will crop to your selection. While it is on your mind, you may want to return the selection *Style* to *Normal* in the options bar.

5. Now, choose the *Image>Image Size* menu, and change the image size to 10 wide and press the *Tab* key. You will see the height become 8 (or very close to it). If you want to keep some pixel size in the image, change the resolution to 150 or higher. Click **OK** and the image will resize. Now you have a background image that is a standard size.

The cropped artwork

6. Perform any image adjustments you see fit (if any) and save the file as a Photoshop file. This example was saved as **promobackground.psd.** Remember to change the file format in the pop-up list in the *Save* dialog.

Creating the Insert Image

You now have two images of differing resolution and document size. You can choose to get them closer in scale now, or perform transformations later; the decision is yours. We will employ an interesting approach using the **Crop** tool.

1. Using the *File>Open* menu command, locate and open the **Sweaterdetail.jpg** image. Examine the image and plan what portion of it you want to keep, and how large you ultimately want it to be in the composite you are building.

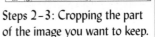

Step 2: Setting the Crop options.

2. Choose the **Crop** tool in the Toolbox. In the option bar, set the resolution to 150 (or the same as the background image), and again, think of the size you would like the insert to be in relation to the 10 × 8 of the background image. You don't have to be exact, but you can get close. Our setting will be 4 inches wide by 5 inches tall (taking into consideration the proportions of the imagery).

Steps 2–3: Cropping the part of the image you want to keep.

3. Now, *click+drag* on the artwork with the **Crop** tool. It will keep the 4 × 5 proportions as you drag the box. Frame off a portion of the imagery that you want to use. The area outside the bounding box will darken with a shield color. You can change the opacity of the shield if it helps you visualize the cropping better. The example here used an opacity of 100%. You can also move the cropping box by *clicking+dragging* inside it. When you are happy with your cropping, click on the **Commit** button in the options bar, or double-click inside the box.

4. The artwork has some text in the upper-left corner that you may or may not want in the final art. To remove it, choose the **Clone Stamp** tool. Zoom into the area where the text exists. Set the brush tip size to approximately 30. Then, press and hold the *Opt/Alt* key down as you sample an area of the solid background. Release the *Opt/Alt* key and drag the

Step 4: Using the Clone Stamp tool to remove unwanted art.

Clone Stamp
Refer to pages 92–93 for a review of the Clone Stamp tool.

Steps 2–3: The Layers palette after the insert artwork is pasted in from the clipboard,

Step 3: Using the Eyedropper tool to sample a color from the artwork and setting it as the current foreground color.

Step 5: Using the Edit>Stroke command to outline the insert artwork.

sampled background over the text. Continue to sample and stamp background until the text is removed.

Moving the Insert Art into the Background, Stroking It, and Rotating It

You are now ready to bring the insert art to the background image. We will do this via the clipboard.

1. On the *insert* image document, choose the *Select>All* menu to create a selection of the entire image. Choose the *Edit>Copy* menu, which will copy the image to the clipboard.

2. Move to the *background* file and choose the *Edit>Paste* menu, which will paste the insert image into the file on a separate layer. Rename *Layer 1* to *Insert* (double-click on the layer name and type in your new name).

The insert artwork is pasted into the artwork of the main image.

3. We are going to create a colored outline around the insert imagery. This will be achieved by stroking it. First, we need to pick a color to use as the outlining color. Choose the **Eyedropper** tool, and click on the artwork to pick up a color you want to use for the outline. You can continue to sample colors until you find the one you want. Observe the *foreground* color in the Toolbox as you work.

4. Choose the **Magic Wand** tool. On the *Insert* layer, click outside the imagery. Everything but the insert will be selected. Now, choose the *Select>Inverse* menu command to invert the selection so that only the insert imagery is selected.

The insert artwork is now stroked with a pale coral color that was sampled from the artwork using the Eyedropper tool.

5. Choose the *Edit>Stroke* command. A *Stroke* dialog box will open. Set the *Width* to 15 px and check that your color is correct. Make sure that *Preserve Transparency* is not checked. Click **OK**. You will now see a colored outline around your insert image. Deselect the marquee (*Cmd/Ctrl+D*). Do not worry about placement yet; we will come back to this.

Setting up the Gradient and Layer Mask

The plan is to create a gradient that will be used on the background image with some transparency. You will need to pick a color to use at one end of the gradient, and use white at the other end.

1. This is probably an ideal time to take a snapshot of the artwork. In the *History* palette, click on the **Create new snapshot** button at the bottom of the palette. Rename the snapshot (which will appear at the top of the palette) to *after adding stroke*. Slide up to the top of the *History* palette to see the snapshot.

Step 1: Taking a snapshot.

2. Click on the *foreground* color in the Toolbox. When the *Color Picker* opens, choose a color for your gradient. A light green will be used in this exercise. Leave the background color as white.

Step 3: The Gradient Picker.

3. Click on the **Gradient** tool in the Toolbox. Click on the down arrow of the *Gradient Picker* in the options bar to observe the gradients. Your colors will appear in the upper-left corner of the *Gradient Picker pop-up*. There will be two gradient options in your colors, one with transparency and one without. Choose the one with transparency.

4. Ensure that the *Background* is the active layer in the *Layers* palette.

5. Click on the **Create new fill or adjustment layer** button at the bottom of the *Layers* palette. Slide up to the *Gradient* option. The *Gradient Fill* dialog will open. Experiment with the various options and watch your image as you do. Click **OK** when you have a setup you like. If you look at the *Layers* palette you will see that there is now a new layer with two thumbnails. One is a *layer* thumbnail, and the other is the *Layer Mask* thumbnail.

Steps 4–5: Creating a Gradient Fill layer.

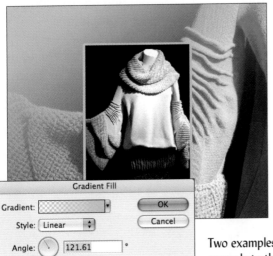

Two examples of gradient fill layers. The example to the left uses a Linear style, and the example on the right uses a Reflected style of fill.

6. If you want to experiment again, hide the *Layer Mask* layer (by turning the eye off) and click on the *Background*. Repeat step 5, trying a different gradient option in the dialog.

7. Finalize your decision and turn on the view of the chosen gradient layer mask. Hide the other gradient layer by ensuring that the eye is turned off.

8. Save the file to update it.

Transforming the Insert

At this point, we are going to rotate the insert image to create more interest in our art.

1. Click on the *Insert* layer to make it the active layer.

2. Choose the *Edit>Free Transform* menu command. A box will appear around the insert image.

3. Position your cursor just outside a corner of the box and wait for the cursor to become the rotation cursor (a curved segment with two arrowheads). *Click+drag* with the cursor to rotate the image. Release when you are happy with the rotation. You may reposition the image as you are working with rotation, by placing your cursor inside the image and *clicking+dragging* it to a new position. You may also rotate the image further (by moving the cursor outside a corner of the image, waiting until you see the rotation cursor, and *clicking+dragging* some more). When you are happy with the image, click on the **Commit** button in the options bar (or double-click inside the image). The transformation is complete.

Note: If you want, you can also scale the image while performing the transformation.

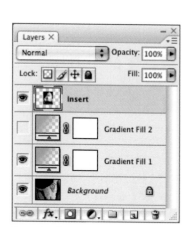

Step 1: Clicking on the Insert layer to make it the active layer.

Step 3: Note the rotation cursor in the lower-left corner of the bounding box, which appears around the artwork after you choose the Free Transform menu command.

The Commit button, which appears in the option bar

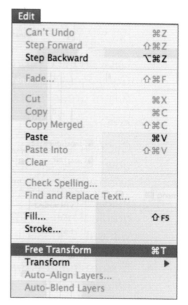

Step 2: Choosing the Edit>Free Transform menu command.

Adding Type

The last step of our project is to add some type to the image. Type will appear on its own type layer. You do not need to set up a layer, as the **Type** tool, when used, creates its own type layer. Observe your image and determine where you want to place some text and what color you want the text to become.

The artwork after the rotation is made

1. Click on the **Type** tool to select it.

2. Choose your initial font, font size, and font color in the options bar. You can change your mind later, so feel free to experiment.

3. Move to the artwork, and *click+drag* to create a text box in the area you want to type. Begin typing the text you want for the promotion. When you are through, click on the **Commit** button in the options bar.

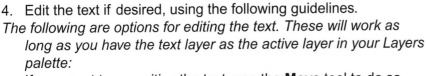

Font settings in the options bar

4. Edit the text if desired, using the following guidelines.
The following are options for editing the text. These will work as long as you have the text layer as the active layer in your Layers palette:
- If you want to *reposition* the text, use the **Move** tool to do so.
- If you want to *change the color* of the text, select the **Type** tool, then highlight the text and change the font color in the options bar.
- If you want to change the *font style* or *size*, change these in the options bar.

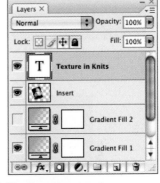

A Text layer is created once the Type tool is used.

If you want to correct a typing error:
1. Make sure you are on the *Type* layer.
2. Choose the **Type** tool, then *click+hold+drag* on the existing text to highlight what you want to change.

Adding a Layer Style to Type
A drop shadow will now be added to the *Text* layer to polish the look of the promotional piece.

Adding type

1. Ensure that the text layer is the active layer.

2. Click on the **Add a layer style** button at the bottom of the *Layers* palette and choose the *Drop Shadow* option from the pop-up menu. A dialog will open. Experiment with settings in the dialog. Choose a new color for the drop shadow, as the default black will not stand out against a dark background on the artwork. Click **OK**. A drop shadow will appear behind your text.

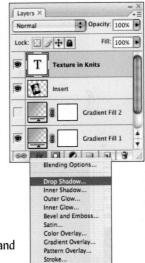

Experimenting with type and adding a drop shadow

Reposition Artwork
As the final step on the project, reposition and rescale (if necessary) any of the components of your artwork.

This completes the exercise.

Kristin Matoba

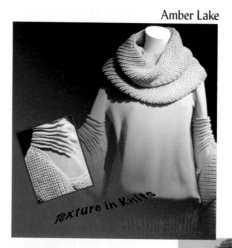

Amber Lake

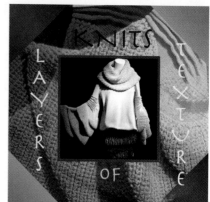

Jodi Smart

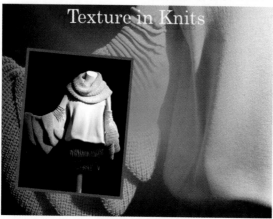

Matthew
Gilroy

Osbaldo Ahumada

Angel Beckwith-Malone

Jeanne Reith

Kristine Delosreyes

Student Gallery
Promotional Composite
Mesa Fashion Students

Exercise #4: Building a Color Trend Composite Utilizing Travel and Fashion Imagery

Goal

To develop a *Color Trend* composite that includes imagery and forecast colors illustrated creatively on the artwork.

The Color Trend composite built in this exercise

Photoshop Tools and Functions

- ♦ Various **Selection** tools
- ♦ Cut/Paste (***Edit*** menu)
- ♦ Layers and adjustment layers
- ♦ Adjustments and filters
- ♦ Transformation functions such as *Scale* and *Rotate* (***Edit*** menu)
- ♦ Feathering
- ♦ *Swatch* palette
- ♦ **Shape** tools
- ♦ Other Photoshop tools as needed

Quick Overview of the Process

You will work with an assortment of images collected from different countries and provided on the Art DVD. The images include scenes from the various cities, fashion windows, art of the area, and so on.

The general approach is as follows:

1. You are to build a composite/collage of images from one of the countries. Use the various tools and functions you practiced in Fashion Exercises #1 through #3 to develop the composite.
2. Plan a color theme using the necessary filters or adjustments to assist your imagery in communicating the color forecast. Using **Shape** or similar tools, create five swatches or blocks of color to include in this trend forecast.
3. Label the composite and individual colors using the **Type** tool.

New Concepts

- o   Shape tools
- o   Layer opacity
- o   Type

Sources of Imagery

- o   Multiple images supplied on the accompanying DVD

Review page 229 for tips on creating collages/composites. Review Fashion Exercises #1–#3.

Step-by-Step

Analyzing Artwork and Prepping the Document File

On the accompanying DVD you will find a folder called **Fashion Exercises.** Inside this folder is a folder called **TravelPics**.

1. Using the *File>Browse* menu, locate and determine which group of files you want to use from the **TravelPics** folder. Adobe Bridge will open and allow you to review the images in each travel folder. If you click on an image to select it, detailed information is shown on the right. Note each image's resolution and image size.

If you use the *File>Open* command to view the images in a folder, you can view initial information by clicking once on the image and observing the info provided in the dialog. You can also open an image and choose the *Image>Image Size* menu command to learn

Adobe's Bridge (above) is used to browse folders of imagery. Detailed info can be obtained by clicking on an image and observing the data provided (as shown below).

what you need to know about each image. Do not worry if the document sizes of the images are large, as you may want to crop from the image to get what you need. For the purposes of this exercise, images from the **Verona** travel folder will be used. These files vary between 240 and 300 dpi resolution. This is a relatively high resolution and will result in a large file for the composite. To economize somewhat on file size, without great loss to detail, a resolution of 150 dpi will be used in this exercise.

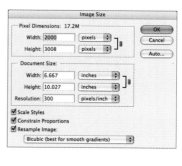

Photoshop's File>Open dialog (above) is used to view images in a folder. Clicking once on a file (while in icon view) provides you with file size and dimension data. Using the Image>Image Size menu command in Photoshop (once the file is open) will allow you to see document size and resolution.

2. Ensure that you have the *Layers, History, Navigator, Swatches,* and *Colors* palettes open and ready for use.

3. Decide which image will serve as your background image.

Note:

Adobe Bridge vs. File>Open

You may also use the File>Open command to view files in folders. Adobe Bridge was introduced in CS2.

I used the image of the Adige River in Verona (**DSC_8874.jpg**). Load this one first and save the file with a new name pertinent to the project (e.g., **Veronacollage.psd**). Make sure that you save in Photoshop's native PSD file format, so all layers will be maintained. Other file formats that conserve layers are TIFF and PDF. Make sure that the *Layers* palette is open and available for use. Since this image will be the base image, you want to adjust its size to the proper dimension for your artwork. This may entail a change of resolution, cropping and altering the document size.

The image to be used as the base image for the collage

4. Choose the *Image>Image Size* menu. The dialog that opens will show you the resolution, document size, and file size (in pixels and in megs) of the image. Change the document width to 10.5 and the resolution to 150. Note how the height of the image adjusts automatically (as *Constrain Proportions* is checked and active). Click **OK** and the image will resize.

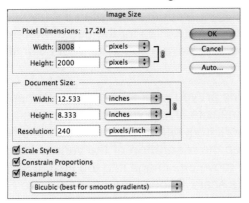

Step 4: Adjusting the resolution and document size in the Image Size dialog. Left: Before the adjustment. Right: After the adjustment.

5. Adjust the *Levels* of your image using the *Image>Levels* menu command. Drag the white *Highlights* slider to just under the beginning height of the histogram (on the right). Move the center *Midtones* slider back and forth to establish the right amount of contrast. The black *Shadows* slider is positioned well. Click **OK** and the image will adjust and improve in appearance.

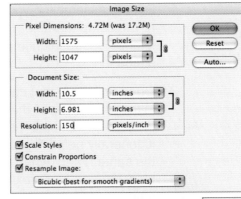

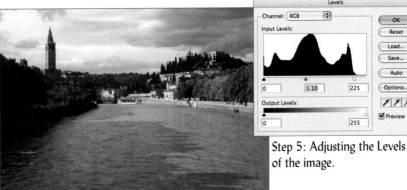

Step 5: Adjusting the Levels of the image.

6. Note the *Layers* palette at this time. No layers exist, only a *Background* image, which is the river image.

7. Save the file again to update it.

The image is now ready for you to build your composite.

Step 6: Observing the Layers palette.

Building the Composite

You are now ready to build your composite. Use the techniques covered in the first three exercises. The difference this time is that you are working with multiple files/images. To broaden your Photoshop knowledge, try working with *adjustment layers* (as opposed to the *Adjustment* options in the **Image** menu). This will allow you to turn adjustments on and off at will, and to combine various adjustments creatively. Review the discussion on adjustment layers on pages 56–57.

There are two ways to bring your images into the main collage file:

♦ using the **clipboard** (*Edit>Copy* in one document and *Edit>Paste* into the other document)

♦ using **drag and drop** between documents (drag a layer from one document into another document, or drag a selection from one document into another)

The instructions below utilize the *clipboard* in moving files from one document to another. These instructions are general in nature and do not detail the how-to's of creating selections. This has already been covered in the prior exercises and in Chapter 2.

1. Prior to assembling your images, **evaluate and plan** the layout of the components of the composite. Plan for the use of mood images and fashion images, and leave a space for your color story shapes.

2. Open an image that contains art you want to use as an element in the master file of the composite. If you want to simplify the process of combining artwork from different sources into one file, it generally helps if you keep the **resolution** of the various images the same. Then, when you move one image into the next, it should be in the same approximate scale. Choose the *Image>Image Size* menu to alter the resolution of your artwork. The image size of any given image will be tied directly to its resolution, so the image sizes will be different.

3. Adjust the *Levels* of your artwork, attempting to keep the level of contrast similar between all images you plan to use in the composite.

4. Using the various *Selection* tools, outline or define the areas of the image that you want to use. Remember, if you want a soft edge, enter a value in the feather field in the options bar. Once the marquee is in place, copy the selection to the clipboard using the *Edit>Copy* command.

5. Move to the main image (using the **Window** menu and sliding down to the proper file) and choose the *Edit>Paste* command to bring the new image to the main background of your composite file. When the image pastes into the document, it will appear on its own layer, which will be positioned directly above the layer that was active prior to pasting in the artwork.

6. Continue to bring in additional artwork by creating selections and transferring them via the clipboard to the main collage document.

Note:

Scaling the Art

It is not critical that you change the resolution of an image prior to bringing it into another document. You may use the Transformation functions to scale artwork once it is in another file. The transformation occurs on the layer you have selected prior to choosing the Edit>Transform>Scale menu command.

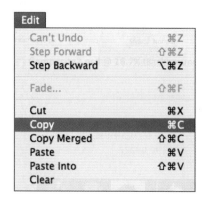

Using the clipboard to move images from one document to another

As you bring images into the main document (via the clipboard), new layers will be created. Use the layers to assist in developing an interesting assemblage of artwork. The following is a short list of some of the functions you may perform on the artwork to assist in building the composite.

- Transform the new image using the *Edit>Transform* menu and choose the type of transformation you want.
- Move the image using the **Move** tool.
- Adjust the *opacity* of the image by changing the opacity of the layer it is on.
- Soften the edges of the imagery you paste into the main document by turning feathering on in the options bar (enter a value in the field).
- Use *Gradients* to create interest.
- Use a *Layer Mask* and a *Gradient* with two images so that one image blends into another (review pages 57 and 58).

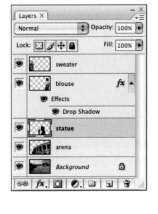

The various layers created for this exercise

Creating a Layer Mask

The steps below use the background of the Adige River in Verona and the Arena layer, which sits directly above the background.

1. In the *Layers* palette, select the layer you want to create the mask on (the arena layer in our example).

2. Click once on the **Add layer/vector mask** button at the bottom of the *Layers* palette. A **layer** mask will be created. This is represented by a new white thumbnail that appears to the right of your layer thumbnail. A link will appear to indicate that the mask is linked to the layer. You may now click on either the imagery thumbnail or the mask thumbnail. This dictates what you are making a change to as you *work on the layer* (i.e., the imagery), or the layer mask.

Step 2: Setting up the layer mask in the Layers palette.

3. Make sure that you are on the layer mask thumbnail. Click on the **Default Foreground and Background Colors** icon in the Toolbox to set black and white as the colors you will use in the mask.

Step 3: Choosing the default colors in the Toolbox.

4. Choose the **Gradient** tool in the Toolbox. Choose the solid black to white option in the *Gradient picker* in the options bar. Choose the *Linear* gradient option and ensure that the opacity setting in the options bar is set at 100%.

Step 4: Setting up the gradient.

Step 5: Creating the layer mask gradient, which will allow you to look through the arena image into the river image.

The layer mask shows the gradient.

Adjustment Tip

Try selecting a portion of your artwork and altering the hue/saturation of that, allowing it to sit against the original colored background.

5.   Place your cursor in the document, and *click+drag* it diagonally on the image. A gradient will appear on the layer mask thumbnail and you will see the results on your image. You can see through the arena image where black exists in the gradient. You cannot see through the white areas. Undo your results and experiment more with the gradient. It makes a difference where you place the cursor, and how much of the image you drag over. You can achieve many different effects with your art depending on the sweep of your hand as you create the gradient itself.

New Skills: Working with Color

Since you are building a composite that will communicate a color story, it may be necessary to alter the colors of some of the original artwork. The following are a few Photoshop functions that can assist you with changing the color of your artwork without losing the shadows and highlights. Do explore other areas of the program in addition to those listed below. If you choose to use adjustment layers, all layers beneath the adjustment layer will be affected by the color change. You will have the ability to turn the adjustment on or off. If you choose to use the adjustment options in the *Image* menu, the adjustments will only occur on the selected artwork. The *Image>Adjust* menu options will be used in this exercise so that you can isolate the adjustments to selected artwork.

Using Color Adjustments: Hue/Saturation

The *Hue/Saturation* color adjustment can be used to change the color of an area of your artwork, and yet maintain the shading and detail of the image.

To create a Hue/Saturation adjustment layer:

1.   Select the area of the artwork you want to alter using the selection tool(s) of your choice. Remember you can combine the use of various selection tools as you work and you can also use the **Add to Selection** and **Subtract from Selection** buttons in the options bar.

A hue adjustment is made to the blouse, changing the original cream color to a pink.

2.   Choose the *Image>Adjustments>Hue/Saturation* menu command. A dialog will open.

3.   Click on the *Colorize* check box to turn Colorize on. Drag the *Hue* slider back and forth to choose the new color hue. Drag the *Saturation* and *Lightness* sliders around to tweak the color. Click **OK**.

Step 3: Setting adjustments in the Hue/Saturation dialog.

Notice how an adjustment layer appears directly above the layer that contains the artwork you were adjusting. You can turn the view of this adjustment layer on or off as you work.

An adjustment layer appears above the blouse layer.

Using Color Adjustments: Color Balance

The *Color Balance* adjustment lets you add or remove color components from an image, thus tweaking the overall color tone.

1. Select the area of the artwork you want to alter using the **Selection** tool(s) of your choice.

2. Choose the *Image>Adjustments>Color Balance* menu command. A dialog will open.

3. Drag the *color* sliders back and forth to alter the color. Click **OK**.

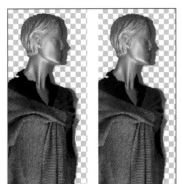

Step 3: Experimenting with the color by dragging the sliders in the Color Balance dialog. The original brown-tone image is changed to a green-tone image.

Creating a Color Story and Moving the Colors to the Swatches Palette

Hopefully, as you have been working with your imagery, you will have developed a plan for a color story of five colors. Ideally, these colors exist in your imagery, but if they do not, you can tweak the colors of the artwork so that the composite and color story work tightly with each other. Use the color adjustment suggestions given above.

As you choose the five colors you want for your forecast presentation, move them to the *Swatches* palette. The techniques discussed below will assist you.

Note: Swatch Palette Review
Review the Swatches Palette discussion in Chapter 6, pages 166–169.

Using the Eyedropper Tool to Sample Colors

You can use the **Eyedropper** tool to pull colors from the artwork itself and place them in the foreground color of the Toolbox.

1. Select the **Eyedropper** tool in the Toolbox.

The Eyedropper tool

2. Move the Eyedropper cursor over an area of the image and *click+hold+drag* your cursor around. As you move the cursor, you will see colors being sampled and displayed in the foreground color in the Toolbox. When you find the color you are looking for, release the mouse and the color will be displayed in the foreground color of the palette.

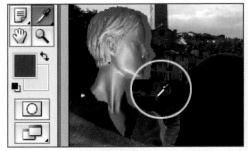

Sampling color with the Eyedropper tool

Moving Foreground Colors to the Swatches Palette

1. Make sure that the *Swatches* palette is open and viewable (*Window>Swatches*).

2. Click on the **Create a new swatch of foreground color** button at the bottom of the *Swatches* palette. The current foreground color in the Toolbox will now appear at the end of the palette and it will be called *Swatch 1.*

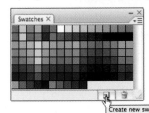

Moving colors into the Swatches palette

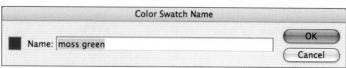

Step 4: Naming a color (above) and the color in the Swatches palette (below).

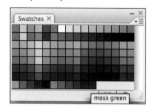

Moving a color from the foreground color of the Toolbox to the Swatches palette

The Shape tool (above) and the Shape Layers mode in the options bar (below)

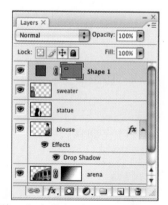

Step 6: A Shape layer is added above the current layer once a shape is drawn.

3. Double-click on the swatch in the *Swatches* palette to open the *Color Swatch Name* dialog.

4. Name your swatch and click **OK**.

Using the Color palette or the foreground color in the Toolbox:

1. Make either the foreground or background color the active color in the *Colors* palette, or simply use the foreground color that is active.

2. Place your cursor in a gray area of the *Swatches* palette. It will turn into a *paint bucket* icon.

3. Click with the cursor, and the new color will now appear at the end of the palette. You will have to rename it as above.

Select and move five colors for your trend report into the *Swatches* palette. Make sure that they are all named.

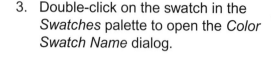

The five new colors are added to the Swatches palette.

Adding the Color Swatches to Your Artwork Using Shape Layers

At this point, you are ready to use shapes on your artwork to communicate the color story. *Shape Layers* will be used as you can easily manipulate and move the shapes as you work. This exercise will use rectangles to illustrate the color story.

1. Choose the **Rectangular** Shape tool in the Toolbox.

2. Click on the **Shape Layers** button in the options bar.

3. Click on the down arrow of the *Geometry Options* pop-up. When the window opens, type the size you want each rectangle to become in the *Fixed Size* fields.

Step 3: Setting a fixed size for the Rectangle tool.

4. Choose one of your trend colors in the *Swatches* palette. This will move the color into the foreground color of the Toolbox.

5. Click on the topmost layer in the image (the *sweater* layer in our example). The shape layer you are about to create will thus be positioned above this.

6. Move to your document and click in the area where you want to position one of the color boxes. A rectangle will appear on the document. If you look at the *Layers* palette you will see that you have a new Shape layer.

7. Change the color in the foreground of the Toolbox by clicking on the next color in the *Swatches* palette. Click back on the *sweater* layer to make it the active layer.

8. Using the **Rectangle Shape** tool, click on the document to create the next color square.

9. Repeat the process (choosing a new color for the foreground color, moving back to the sweater layer, and clicking with the **Rectangle Shape** tool to set a new shape) until you have created five squares on the document. You will have five shape layers in the palette.

10. Choose the **Path Selection** tool in the Toolbox. Using this tool, click on each square in turn, as necessary, and position the five squares on the image. The first time you click, you choose the layer. The second time you click, you select the object. The following tools can assist you in arranging your shapes:
    *   **Guidelines** (pulled from the rulers, *View>Rulers*), used to allow you to see how things are being aligned.
    *   **Snap** (*View>Snap*), which causes movement on the image to snap to the grid, guideline, or whatever else is selected.
    *   Transformations that allow you to rotate, scale, or perform similar operations (*Edit>Transform*).
    Note: As you position the squares, you may find it necessary to resize some of your artwork in order to have a nice balance.

Adding the rectangular shapes and positioning them with the Path Selection tool

Steps 10 and 11: Positioning the color squares and adding a black box behind the group.

11. If you want your colors to stand out, create a black rectangle and position it beneath all the color swatches. This can be achieved by clicking on the *sweater* layer, choosing black as the foreground color, and then *clicking+dragging* a rectangle that is slightly larger than all the colored squares. You will need to remove the fixed size dimensions in the *Geometry Options* pop-up first.

12. Group the *Shape layers* by *shift+clicking* on all the shape layers to select them, and then choosing the *New Group from Layers* menu option in the *Layers* palette menu.

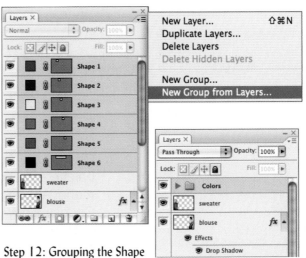

Step 12: Grouping the Shape layers.

Adding Type

You are now ready to add type to your document. You will need a title for the composite to indicate your theme, and you will label each colored swatch with a name or number. You do not need to set up a layer, as the Type tool, when used, creates its own type layer. Observe your image and determine where you want to place some text and what color you want the text to be.

1. Click on the **Type** tool to select it.

2. Choose your initial font, font size, and font color in the options bar. Feel free to experiment as you can change your mind later.

3. Move to the artwork, and *click+drag* to create a text box in the area you want to type. Begin typing the text you want for the promotion. When you are through, click on the **Commit** button in the options bar.

4. Edit the text if desired, using the following guidelines. *The following options for editing text will work as long as you have the text layer as the active layer in your Layers palette:*

• If you want to *reposition* the text, use the **Move** tool.

• If you want to *change the color* of the text, change the font color in the options bar.

• If you want to change the *font style* or *size*, change these in the options bar.

If you want to correct a typing error:
1. Ensure you are on the *Text* layer.
2. Choose the **Type** tool, then *click+hold+drag* on the text to highlight what you want to change.

Adding a Layer Style to Type

A drop shadow will now be added to the *Text* layer to polish the look of the promotional piece.

1. Ensure that the *Text* layer is the active layer.

2. Click on the **Add Layer Style** button at the bottom of the *Layers* palette and choose the *Drop Shadow* option from the pop-up menu. A dialog will open. Experiment with settings in the dialog. Choose a new color for the drop shadow as the default black will not stand out against a dark background on the artwork. Click **OK**. A drop shadow will appear behind your text.

Student Gallery
Trend Composite
Mesa College Fashion Students

Pontus Wickbom Burevall   Sweden Influence

Alana Rillo   Peru Influence

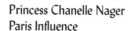
Princess Chanelle Nager
Paris Influence

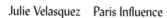
Julie Velasquez   Paris Influence

Jeanne Reith   Rome Influence

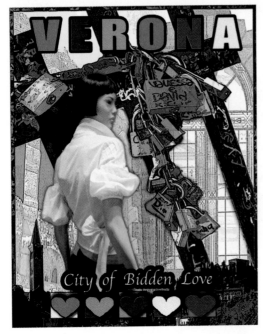

Student Gallery
Trend Composite with Flats
Mesa College Fashion Students

Angel Beckwith-Malone　Verona, Italy Influence

Kari Pacheco
Denmark Influence

Melanie Bruce
Florence Influence

Drawing Flats and Illustrations

The drawing and illustrating of apparel and fashion illustration in Photoshop can be achieved in a variety of ways. You may draw freehand using either painting or drawing tools in Photoshop's toolbox. This approach requires some level of skill in recognizing good proportion and design. Working with painting tools such as the **Pencil**, **Brush**, and **Line** (in *Fill pixels* mode), you can sketch a garment in traditional manners. If you use vector drawing tools such as the **Pen** and **Line** (*Path* mode) tools, you can create drawings that are easily edited through the tweaking and reshaping of objects. The learning curve for this latter approach is greater, and the tools are good, but not as flexible as those offered by Adobe Illustrator.

There are many shortcuts you can take when drawing garments and illustrations. The first is to scan your hand-drawn art and then clean it up in Photoshop. Of course, this approach requires some level of hand-drawing skills. If you do not have those skills at this point in time, you can choose to work with fashion photos and trace the fashion pose or illustration.

Illustration by Kathy White

The first three exercises in this section of the book (Exercises #5 through #7) focus on the creation and editing of fashion flats. You will first learn how to paint flats using the **Line** tool (Exercise #5), and then you will draw flats using the **Pen** tool (Exercise #6). In Exercise #7 you will be introduced to the concept of working with fashion clip art. Images from a commercial fashion library known as SnapFashun will be utilized.

Exercises #8 through #11 will teach you how to create and work with fashion illustrations, utilizing hand drawings and digital imagery as starting points. You will learn how to clean up your scanned art (Exercise #8), and how to color it (Exercise #9). You will also learn how to trace a pose from a fashion photo of a live model (Exercise #10). In Exercise #11, you will learn how to paint a fashion pose by using simulated art mediums.

The next two exercises in this section of the book will teach you how to lay fabric into your garments. You will learn the simple and quick approach, whereby fabric is laid in a linear manner (Exercise #12). Then you will learn how to color map a drawing and lay your fabric in, utilizing rotations that will result in a more realistic and accurate result (Exercise #13). Exercise #14 will teach you how to work with clipping paths to prepare artwork by cropping a busy background away from an image.

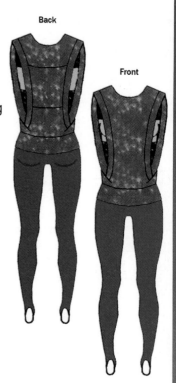

Flats drawn by Kristine Delosreyes

Student Gallery
Flats and Illustrations
Mesa College Fashion Students

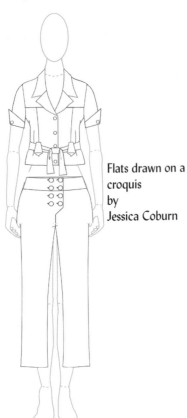

Hand-drawn sketch, scanned and colored in Photoshop
by Misty Frank

NINA

NONA

NINAP

NONAP

ALPARGATAZ

Flat drawn freehand by
Elizabeth Wilkens

Flat drawn on croquis
by Kari Pacheco

Flats drawn on a
croquis
by
Jessica Coburn

Denim Daywear

Flats by Carol Newland

Illustration by
Osbaldo Ahumada

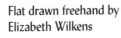

Exercise #5: Drawing Flats on a Fashion Croquis

Goal
In this exercise, you will learn how to draw fashion flats in Photoshop utilizing a fashion croquis as a template for proportion.

Photoshop Tools and Functions
♦ *File>Place*
♦ Smart Objects
♦ Layers and fill layers
♦ Rulers and guides
♦ *Paint* tools for painting
♦ **Line** tool in *Fill pixels* mode

Quick Overview of the Process
In this exercise you will work with a predrawn croquis that was created in Adobe Illustrator. You will place this vector image as a *Smart Object*. Then, you will set up your layers and draw garment flats using the **Line** tool in *Fill pixels* mode.

The general approach is as follows:
1. Create a new document using a custom size of 12 × 16 inches.
2. *Place* the croquis file (found on the art DVD) and scale it up.
3. Set up layers for the garments you will draw.
4. Use the **Line** tool to draw your flats.
5. Color the garments using the **Paint Bucket** tool.

New Concepts
o **Smart Object**, which allows you to preserve vector information from Illustrator, while working in Photoshop (review page 141)
o Placing art

Sources of Imagery
o Adobe Illustrator file of an eight-head croquis

Example of the garments drawn using a croquis to assist in judging proportions

Step-by-Step

Setting up
The file we want to use as a template is an Illustrator file. We want to open it in Photoshop, so do NOT double-click on the file to open it, as this will open it in Illustrator. You will be *placing* the file into an existing Photoshop document. Since this exercise works with the **Line** tool in *Fill pixels* mode, you will work with a large document and a high resolution. Then later, if you want to resize your bitmap drawing, you will be able to keep a smoother appearance to the line art.

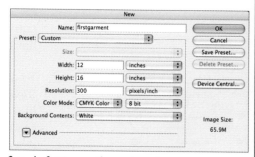

Step 1: Setting up the custom document.

1. Choose the *File>New* menu. When the *File New* dialog opens, set a custom size of 12 x 16 inches, a resolution of 300, and a white background. The color mode can be either CMYK or RGB. In the *Name* field, type **Firstgarment**. Click **OK**. The document will open.

The Place command in the File menu (above) and the Place dialog that opens (below)

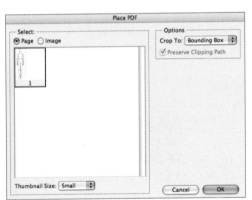

2. Choose the *File>Place* command and direct the file requestor to the accompanying DVD (or the location on your hard drive where you moved the files). There you will find a folder called **Fashion Exercises**, and inside that is a folder called **Flats**. Inside this folder is a file called **8headtemplatemaster.ai**. Choose the file. A *Place PDF* dialog will open. Make sure that the *Page* button is active. Click **OK**. The image will load as a *Smart Object* and you will see a large "X" over the art.

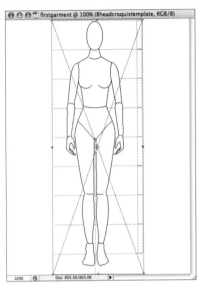

Step 2: Placing the Croquis image.

3. Rescale the art to fill the document. *Click+hold* your cursor inside the image and drag it down to the bottom of the document. Then, move your cursor and place it over the upper-right anchor point. When you see the scaling cursor, *click+hold+drag* the art until you have rescaled it to fill the page. Double-click inside the image to commit to the object placement and resizing (or click on the **Confirm** button in the options bar).

4. Save the file.

Note:

CS4 and Rulers Body

CS4 users may turn on the view of the Rulers from the Application Bar.

Placing a Guideline and Setting up Layers

1. In the *Layers* palette, double-click on *Layer 1* and rename it to *Croquis.* Note that the area behind the croquis is transparent (which you can see if you turn off the view of the background layer). Note also that you have a *Smart Object* icon on the *Croquis* layer, which simply communicates to you that you have a Smart Object.

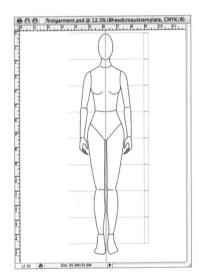

Step 2: Creating the center guideline.

Step 3: Changing the opacity of the Croquis layer and locking the layer.

2. To create a center guideline on the document, choose the *View>Rulers* menu command (or press *Cmd+R*). Make sure that *Snap* is not active or checked in the *Window>Snap* menu. Move your cursor over the numbers on the left vertical ruler. *Click+hold+drag* and move the mouse toward the center of the document. A blue guideline will appear as you drag and move the mouse. Position the guideline over the center of the croquis and release the mouse.

3. Click on the *Croquis* layer and change its opacity to 50%. Lock the *Croquis* layer so that you cannot alter it. Do this by clicking on the

layer name and clicking on the *Lock* in the area above the named layers in the *Layers* palette.

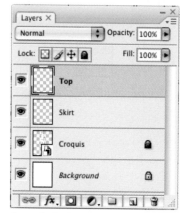

4. Create a new layer for the skirt. Do this by clicking on the arrowhead in the *Layers* palette and sliding over to the *New Layer* option (or choose the *Layer>New>Layer* menu command). Name the layer *Skirt*.

5. Create a new layer for the top in a manner similar to step 4. Name the layer *Top*.

If you need further layers for garment details, you can add these later.

Drawing the Garments

We are going to use the **Line** tool in *Fill pixels* mode for drawing. The Line tool can be used with anti-aliasing on or off. We will experiment with drawing the skirt with anti-aliasing on, and drawing the top with anti-aliasing off. This will allow you to see how anti-aliasing works and how the **Fill Bucket** interacts with anti-aliased lines.

The Line tool

Fill pixels mode

Drawing the Skirt

1. Click on the *Skirt* layer to make it the active layer.

2. Click on the **Line** tool. Go up to the options bar and click on the *Fill pixels* option so that you can draw in a raster approach. Set the *Pixel Width* to 2 or 3 (as the resolution is high and you need to be able to see the lines). Leave *Anti-alias* on (make sure that it is checked).

Step 3: Setting the default colors of black and white.

Anti-alias is active.

3. Click on the *default colors* icon in the Toolbox, which will set black as the foreground color and white as the background color.

4. Move over to the document and begin drawing the right half of the skirt. It is best to start at the center guideline. You must *click+hold+drag* to draw the lines. Click and release as you draw, repeating this action to create a series of joined lines. You will soon sense how your movements affect the continuity of the line. The goal is to draw the line so that it is continuous with no holes between one segment and the next. This will take some practice. To draw curves, draw with a series of short lines. The *Fill pixels* mode of the line tool allows you to draw as if you are using a pencil in your hand. You can move anywhere on the document to draw, and touch up as necessary. If you want to erase areas, use the **Eraser** tool, but ensure that the background color is white. Choose the **Line** tool once again to draw. Finish drawing the right half of the skirt.

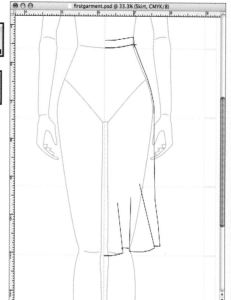

Step 4: Drawing the right half of the skirt using the Line tool.

The Rectangular Marquee tool

The Move tool

Tips:

o　Turn the view of the *Croquis* layer off and on as you work to see how the skirt is progressing.

o　If you want to hide the guideline temporarily, press the *Cmd/Ctrl+H* keys on the keyboard to hide the *Extras*. Pressing the same keys will bring the Extras (the guideline in this case) back into view.

5.　You are now ready to select and copy the right half of the skirt to create the left side. Using the **Rectangular Marquee** selection tool, carefully select the left side of the skirt. Use the guideline as a reference for the selection.

6.　Choose the *Edit>Copy* command to copy the half garment to the clipboard.

7.　Choose the *Edit>Paste* command to paste the half garment back into the garment. Note that a new layer called *Layer 1* is created. Use the **Move** tool to move the new skirt half away from the original.

8.　Choose the *Edit>Transform>Flip Horizontal* command to flip the skirt.

9.　Choose the **Move** tool in the Toolbox, and place the cursor over a black line area of the pasted image on its new layer. Move the flipped piece over to the right, aligning the centers.

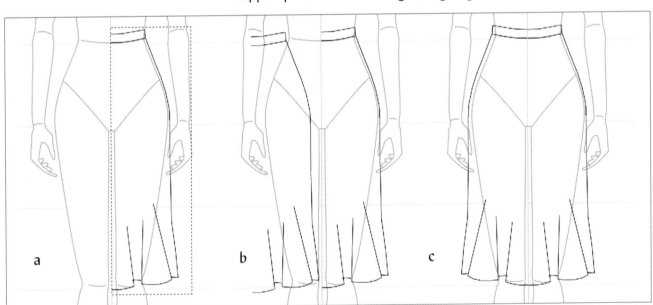

a

b

c

Creating the Second Half of the Skirt, Steps 5 through 9

a.　Steps 5 and 6: Selecting the right side of the skirt and copying it to the clipboard.

b.　Step 7: Pasting in the copy and moving it over to the left with the Move tool.

c.　Steps 8 and 9: Flipping the skirt half and positioning it with the Move tool.

10.　Merge the two skirt layers (*Skirt* and *Layer 1*) by clicking on the *Layer 1* layer and choosing the *Merge Down* option from the *Layers* palette menu. Ensure that there are no holes in the drawing.

11. Perform any touch-ups, as necessary. In particular, zoom in and attempt to find any holes that might cause color to leak when you later add color to the skirt using the **Paint Bucket** tool.

Step 10: Merging the two halves of the skirt.

Drawing the Top

1. Click on the eye icon of the *Skirt* layer to turn its view off. This will make drawing the top easier.

2. Click on the *Top* layer to make it the active layer.

3. Choose the **Line** tool, and this time, turn anti-aliasing **off** by clicking on the *Anti-alias* check box on the right side of the options bar to turn the check off.

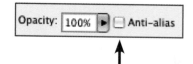

Step 3: Anti-alias is turned off.

4. Draw the top, using the same procedures you used for the skirt (step 4 in skirt instructions).

5. Select and copy the right side of the top, then paste, flip, and position the right side of the garment (steps 5 through 10 in skirt instructions).

6. Merge the new layer with the *Top* layer (step 10 in skirt instructions).

Turn the view of the skirt back on. Zoom in at this point to see the difference in drawing with anti-aliasing *on* (skirt) and *off* (top). Note that the anti-aliased lines look softer, since gray pixels were created next to the black pixels as you drew.

The effect of anti-aliasing is shown above. The lines on the left are drawn with anti-alias turned on, and the line on the right is drawn with anti-alias turned off. You can see the gray pixels that appear on an anti-aliased drawing (color-averaged between the black and white of the drawing). These help to soften the line, but they add a slight level of complexity when it comes to erasing and redrawing.

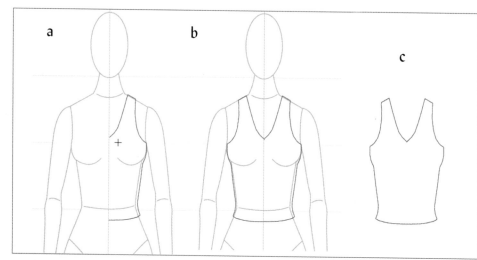

Drawing the Top
a. The right side of the top is drawn.
b. The right side is copied and pasted in, flipped, and positioned.
c. The view of all layers except the Top layer is turned off.

Adding Details

If you wish to add some details to your basic drawings, this is typically best achieved on a separate layer.

1. Click on the *Top* layer to make it the active layer.

Steps 1–2: Adding a layer for drawing garment details.

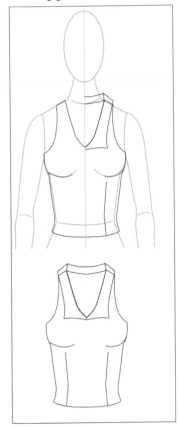

Details are added to the top drawing on a separate layer.

The Paint Bucket tool

Filling the collar of the top with the color used in the skirt

2. Create a new layer by clicking on the arrowhead in the *Layers* palette and sliding over to the *New Layer* option (or choose the *Layer>New>Layer* menu command). Name the layer *Details*.

3. Turn on the view of the garments you want to add details to.

4. Choose the **Line** tool. Turn the anti-alias option on or off, according to your preference.

5. Draw in any details you want to add to your garments.

Correcting Holes in the Line Art

Prior to filling the garments with color, you should do a quick but thorough analysis of your line art drawing. Make sure that there are no holes (breaks in the continuity of the line) in the line art; if a hole exists, the paint will leak through the hole and bleed until it hits a boundary.

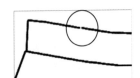

A hole exists in the waistband of the skirt. This needs to be corrected by filling in the gap with the line tool and using black as the foreground color.

1. Zoom in to the garment area using any of the zooming techniques.

2. Press and hold down the *Spacebar* key and *click+hold* on the document, then pan around the image to make sure no holes exist. If they do, then use the **Line** tool and a *foreground* color of black to correct the line so no hole exists.

Filling the Garments with Color

You will be using the **Paint Bucket** tool to add color to the skirt and top. This tool is generally stacked under the **Gradient** tool. The Paint Bucket has various options that you can use, including an anti-alias option.

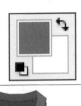

1. Click on the *foreground* color in the Toolbox and select a color for the skirt from the *Color Picker* dialog. Click **OK**.

2. Choose the **Paint Bucket** tool in the Toolbox.

3. Click on the *Skirt* layer to make it the active layer.

4. Move the paint cursor over to the skirt and place it inside the skirt. Click once. The skirt should fill with color. If the color bleeds outside the skirt area, this typically means that you have a hole in your black outline, which you will need to correct.

5. Fill in any other parts of the garment that will utilize the same color. Remember to

click on the layer that contains the drawing of the garment you want to fill.

6. Create and use a new color for the top, should you desire to utilize a second color.

7. Continue to fill with the tool, choosing the appropriate layer prior to filling a bound area.

8. If you want, you can change the order of your layers so that the top sits under the skirt. This is easily achieved by clicking and holding on the *Top* layer and dragging it beneath the *Skirt* layer.

You have completed the creation and coloring of two garments using the **Line** tool and the *Fill pixels* mode as your drawing tool. You probably now can appreciate the value of using layers for this task.

For the greatest success in drawing garments, understand the following:

♦ Layers allow you to easily separate garment pieces and to manipulate each one independently.

♦ Layers allow you to add details to a garment that can easily be removed from view.

♦ You do not need to draw the entire garment; rather you can copy and paste half a garment to build the whole.

♦ Drawing with the **Line** tool in *Fill pixels* mode is a lot like drawing by hand with a pencil in that you can move freely from place to place and you can easily erase and redraw areas.

♦ You may choose to use *anti-aliasing* to soften the lines as you draw with the **Line** tool and fill with the **Paint Bucket** tool. However, averaged colored pixels will result, which may pose problems later when you want to change colors. This is always the dilemma of anti-aliasing. You can choose to not use the function, but if you do, you must work in high resolutions (such as 300 dpi) so that the hardness of your line's edge doesn't appear obvious to the user's eye.

♦ The **Paint Bucket** tool allows you to quickly fill an area that has a boundary. If there are holes in the outline, the color will bleed; thus you need to ensure that no holes exist.

Speed Line Drawing Option

If you work in high resolution on a white background and draw with the **Line** tool with *Anti-alias* turned off (or the **Pencil** tool), you can quickly draw and erase, using only the **Line** tool (and no **Eraser**). This is achieved by swapping the *foreground* and *background* colors as you draw. Begin drawing, using black as the *foreground* color. Then, when you want to erase, simply press *X* on the keyboard to swap the *foreground* and *background* colors, and with white as the *foreground* color you can draw over the area that you want to remove. Then, press *X* again and swap to black as the *foreground* color and continue drawing with the tool.

 Adding Shadow Colors

If you want to add more depth to your drawings, create and use a deeper shade of a color to fill in the back of collars, necklines, and other parts.

The rearranged garment pieces

The effect of anti-aliasing when filling a garment is shown above. The lines on the left were drawn with Anti-alias turned on, and the line on the right was drawn with anti-alias turned off. Both were filled using the Paint Bucket with Anti-alias turned on.

The SnapFashun library palette

Step-by-Step
Adobe Illustrator: Opening Style Libraries

1. In Illustrator, open the **SnapFashun** library by choosing the *Window>Show SnapFashun Library* menu command. A new palette called *SnapFashun* will appear.

2. To open a SnapFashun library, click on the **Open** button. If you have already opened some libraries, they will be visible in the palette and each will have a tab with the library title. You will then need to click on the SnapFashun tab first, and then click on the **Open** button. A file requestor window will open. You will most likely need to direct the file requestor to the **SnapFashun** folder, which should be located inside your **Illustrator** folder on your hard drive. On the Macintosh, this is generally located in the **Applications** folder. On Windows it is generally located in the **Adobe** folder found in the **Program** *Files* folder. You will need to choose the *Collection Suite* and subsequent folders to get the library of your choice (e.g., *Application>Illustrator>Collection Suite>Women's Library>Items*).

Using the Open dialog to locate the SnapFashun library of your choice

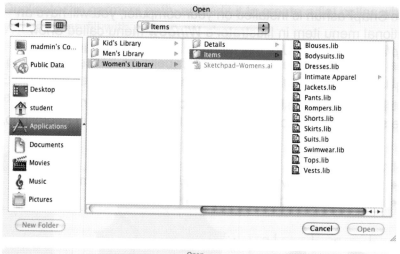

SnapFashun Decisions
SnapFashun offers three fashion libraries (Women, Men, and Kids). Within each library, you can choose to view Items (garments) or Details (specific design details).

SnapFashun in Use
Numerous illustrations in this book were created using SnapFashun garments. The Textile Design Exercises often use SnapFashun flats, as students were focusing on creating the textile, not the garment.

3. Click on the collection suite of your choice (Kid's, Men's, or Women's), then on either *Details* or *Styles,* and finally the library of your choice (e.g., Jackets). A library window will open. **Alternatively**: You may also load a style library by clicking on the arrow to the right of the palette and choosing the **Open** option.

Once libraries are open, they will appear as separate palettes docked to the main *SnapFashun* palette. Each separate library can be torn off to become a separate palette. You may rejoin palettes by dragging them into the palette window of other palettes.

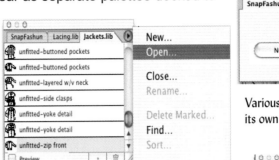

Various palette libraries, each with its own tab

To View and Load Styles

1. Click on a library tab to make the library active (e.g., *Blouses.lib*). A list of styles will appear. You may enlarge the palette to view more styles.

2. Click on the **Preview** check box in the lower-left corner of the window. This will enlarge the window so that you see a drawing of the selected style.

3. View styles by clicking on their names in turn.

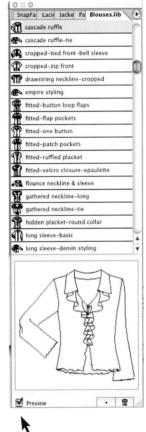

4. When you find a style that you want to retrieve, place your cursor over the image of the style and *click+hold+drag* it over onto your Illustrator document.

5. If you want to resize the drawing while in Illustrator, use the **Scale** tool. Make sure that the image is selected (with the **Selection** tool), then double-click on the tool. When the dialog opens, type in 200%. Click **OK**.

6. Save the file as an AI or EPS file in preparation for taking it to Photoshop.

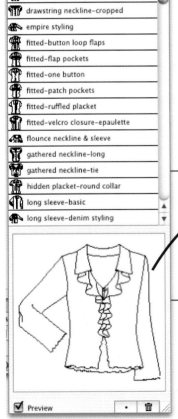

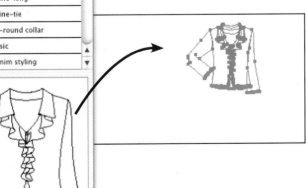

A SnapFashun blouse style

Loading the SnapFashun Image into Photoshop

Since the file we want to use is an Illustrator file, do NOT double-click on the file to open it, as it will open Illustrator. You will place the file into an existing Photoshop document and rasterize it so that you may color it, fill it, and so on.

Step 2: The File>Place command.

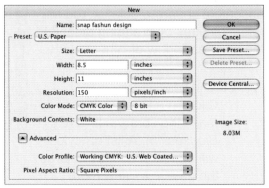

Step 1: Setting up the new file.

1. Choose the *File>New* menu. When the *New* dialog opens, set a custom size of 8.5 × 11 inches, a resolution of 150, and a white background. The color mode can be either CMYK or RGB. In the *Name* field, type **snap fashun design**. Click **OK**. The document will open.

2. Choose the *File>Place* command. Direct the *Place* file requester to the **Garments** folder on the accompanying art DVD. Inside the folder is a file called **snap4.ai**. Choose this file and click **OK**. The image will load into Photoshop as a Smart Object.

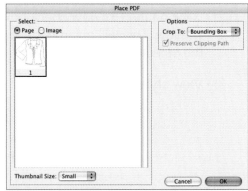

Step 2: Placing the file.

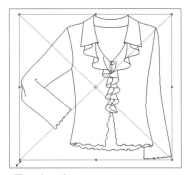

The placed art

3. If you want to resize the image at this point, move your cursor to a corner of the image. When you see the resize cursor, *press+hold* the *Shift* key and then drag the box larger or smaller, as desired. When you are satisfied with the size, double-click inside the box, or click on the **Commit** button in the options bar. If you observe the *Layers* palette you will see the *Background* and a *Smart Object layer*.

4. In order to edit the art in Photoshop, you need to rasterize the drawing. In the ***Layers*** palette, choose the *Layer>Rasterize>Layer* menu command. The image will rasterize.

You are now able to fill, erase, redraw, or perform other art operations on the SnapFashun image.

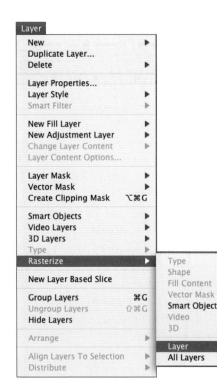

Step 4: Rasterizing the layer.

The garment filled with pattern and solid fill

Exercise #8: Translating a Hand-drawn Fashion Pose to Digital Format

Goal

The goal of this exercise is to walk through the process of translating a hand-drawn line art fashion illustration to a digital form. You may use your own artwork or utilize the art samples provided on the DVD. The original artwork used for this exercise was larger than the scanner bed, so the image was scanned in two parts. You will learn how to combine the parts and prepare the image for use in your computer work.

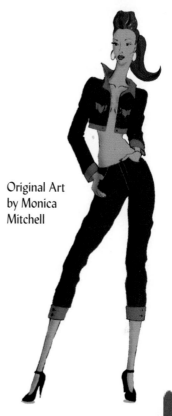

Original Art by Monica Mitchell

Natalie Richardson

Photoshop Tools and Functions

- **Selection** tools
- Cut/Paste (*Edit* menu)
- Layers, adjustment layers, and the Layers panel (CS4)
- Image adjustments
- Touch-up tools such as **Burn**, **Dodge**, etc.
- Filters such as *Noise*, *Blur*, *Sharpen*, etc.

Quick Overview of the Process

In this exercise you will load two images that need to be joined together to form one illustration. You will start by increasing the canvas size of the main drawing so that you have room for the feet of the model. Then, you will bring the feet from the second image over (via the clipboard), pasting them into your main document as a layer. After positioning the feet, you will merge the two layers and perform various image adjustments to improve the quality of the line art image.

The general approach is as follows:

1. Join the two scanned images to create one complete pose.
2. Resize the fashion pose document so it fits on an 8 × 10 page.
3. Perform adjustments or use filters to improve the scanned image.
4. Use the **Magic Wand** tool to clean up final extraneous pixels.
5. Color the image using the **Paint Bucket** tool and the *Edit>Fill* command.

Review the concepts presented in Chapters 4 and 5 and Basic Exercises #2 and #3.

New Concepts

- o   Joining two images
- o   Using adjustment layers and image-editing tools
- o   Using filters

Sources of Imagery

- o   Hand-drawn line art fashion illustrations and flats

Step-by-Step

Loading and Joining the Images

1. On the enclosed DVD, you will find a folder called **Fashion Exercises,** and inside this is a folder called **Scanned Art**. Inside this folder are two files of scanned hand-drawn fashion illustrations and flats. Use Photoshop's *Bridge* or *Browse* feature (*File>Browse*) to locate the **Scanned Art** folder and open the two files, **pose1a.jpg** and **pose1b.jpg**.

Note: Paper Quality and Clean-up Work!

The type of paper you use for your hand-drawn art will affect the quality of the scanned image. Tracing paper and textured papers often scan with "noise" or "dirt," which translates to miscellaneous gray pixels. The original art for this exercise was drawn on paper that resulted in a lot of "noise" once scanned. This image was specifically chosen so that you could learn how to work with this type of art.

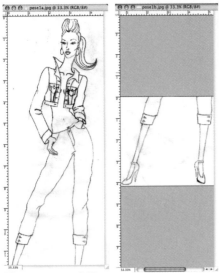

The two original files

Above: Image with additional canvas added to allow for the feet of the model

Use Transparency
Make the Leg layer somewhat transparent to allow you to see through it and thus position the legs.

2. It is always a good idea to look at the image size and resolution of the files you are using. Do this with the *Image>Image Size* menu. Note that these files each use a 200 dpi resolution. Examine the two files and determine how much additional length and width you need to add to the **pose1a.jpg** file in order to create room for the feet from **pose1b.jpg**.

3. Move to the **pose1a.jpg** file (either by using the *Window* menu or by clicking on the document or tab in CS4 to bring it to the front).

4. Click on the default color icon in the Toolbox to set the *foreground* color to black and the *background* color to white.

5. Choose the *Image>Canvas Size* menu command. The *Canvas Size* dialog will open. The current size is 4.645 by 11.665 inches. Change the canvas size to 6 wide by 14 tall and set the anchor point to the upper-right corner of the document (which will cause all new canvas to be added below and to the left of the current image). Ensure that the *Canvas Extension Color* is white. Click **OK**. The canvas will grow to accommodate the new size.

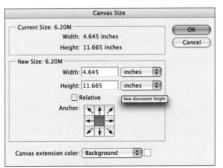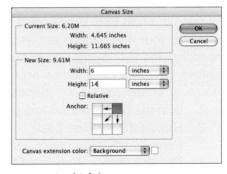

Step 5: The original canvas size (left) and the new canvas size (right).

6. Save the file with a new name such as **posefinal** and change the file format to Photoshop PSD or TIF so that layers will be supported.

7. Move to the **pose1b.jpg** file (the feet). Choose the *Select>All* menu command to select everything in the image. Choose the *Edit>Copy* command to copy the image to the clipboard.

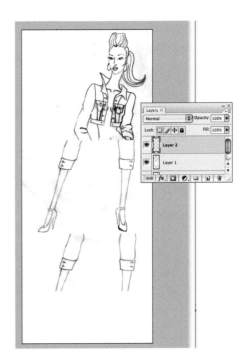

Steps 7–9: The feet of the model are pasted into the main document and then moved to position. The arrow keys on the keyboard are used to fine-tune or "nudge" the feet into position. Then the layers are merged using the Merge down command in the Layers palette menu.

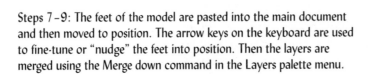

8. Move to **posefinal.psd**. Choose the *Edit>Paste* command. The feet from the second image will now paste into your main image, and a new layer containing the feet will appear in your *Layers* palette.

9. Choose the **Move** tool in the Toolbox. Click on *Layer 1* to make it active, and then move the feet to a position where they align properly with the legs of the main image. (See the *Use Transparency Tip* on the previous page.) Once you have properly positioned the feet, choose the *Merge Down* option from the *Layers* palette menu. Your *Layer 1* will now be merged with the *background*.

10. Choose the *Image>Image Size* menu. The *Image Size* dialog will open. Since you want the pose to easily fit on a standard piece of paper, set the new height to 10 inches tall (make sure that *Constrain Proportions* and *Resample Image* are checked). The width should adjust accordingly. Click on the **OK** button and the document will now resize. Save the file.

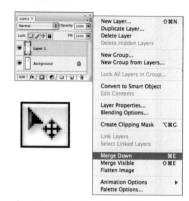

Step 9: Using the Merge Down menu option in the Layers palette to join the feet to the body.

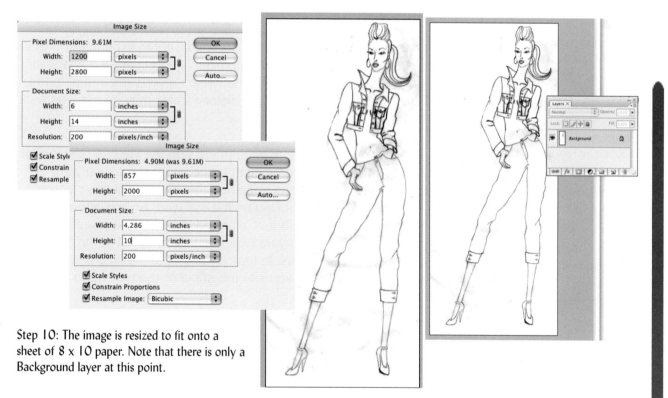

Step 10: The image is resized to fit onto a sheet of 8 x 10 paper. Note that there is only a Background layer at this point.

Adjusting the Artwork: Cleaning Up

Since the original scan of the artwork picked up a lot of texture in the paper, there are darker areas of pixels in the image (known as "noise") that need to be removed. This is necessary to facilitate the process of coloring the image with your chosen colors/fabrics. Although you can eliminate a lot of this cleanup work by drawing on a clean, nontextured paper, it is a good exercise of thought and process to learn how to clean up a "noisy" digital image.

There are various approaches you can take to adjusting the artwork. We will utilize *Adjustment Layers* and various image adjustments such as *Levels*, *Threshold*, and *Contrast/Brightness*. Next we will explore a few

Note: **Practice**
Realize that you may use any combination of the techniques learned in this exercise. We are simply practicing.

Steps 2-3: Loading both files and tiling them so you can see both at once. This allows you to compare results as you work.

Review the following methods of reverting a file to a previous state (pages 22-23):
- File>Revert
- History Palette
- History States
- Snapshots
- Adjustment Layers

CS4 Adjustment Panel

Note:

Photoshop CS4 introduced an Adjustment panel to facilitate the use of adjustment layers.

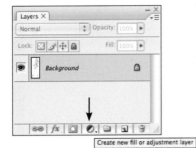

Creating an adjustment layer

touch-up tools and then some *Filters* (Despeckle, Blur, etc.) Since this will be an explorative exercise, it will be helpful to create a second version of the file so that you can compare the changes between the two files.

1. Save the file with a new name (e.g., **finalpose2.psd**). Reload the original file.

2. Resize the two documents so that they both fit on the screen. Position them side by side. You can choose the *Window>Arrange>Tile Vertically* menu command to do this quickly (a handy thing to know).

3. Zoom in to both documents so that you can see the noise that needs to be removed. Use the **Hand** tool to pan to a part of the image that clearly shows the noise problem. Remember that you can pan by pressing and holding the *Spacebar* and dragging your mouse around on the document.

We will be performing our changes on the **finalpose2.psd** file. As we experiment, we will want to return to the original artwork several times. We will use *adjustment layers* to experiment with image adjustments. Before we work with filters we will create a *snapshot* of our image. The *File>Revert* command (which reverts the image to the last saved version) may also be used. History *states* may be used as well.

Using Adjustment Layers

An *adjustment layer* allows you to experiment with the various adjustment options without permanently committing to the change until you want to make it permanent. The changes appear in the adjustment layer, which can be turned on and off by clicking on the *eye* icon. An adjustment layer affects all visible layers beneath it. It is not permanent until you choose it by merging the appropriate layers (whether visible or not at the time). You can *compound* adjustments, in that if you create multiple adjustment layers and they are all visible, you see the effect of them all upon the artwork below.

Each of the following adjustment experiments can be performed on an individual adjustment layer. For each test create a unique adjustment layer and perform the adjustment in the dialog that opens.

To utilize an adjustment layer:

1. Click the **Create new fill or adjustment layer** button at the bottom of the *Layers* palette. A pop-up will open. Slide up to the adjustment you want to try and release the mouse. A dialog will open.

2. Make sure that the *Preview* box is checked to observe the image as you experiment with the settings in the dialog. When you are pleased with the results, click **OK** to finalize the adjustment.

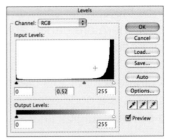

Adjusting the settings in the dialog that opens

For each of the adjustments you experiment with below, create an adjustment layer.

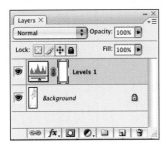

The adjustment layer in the palette. The type of adjustment is indicated in the layer name.

You may turn the adjustment on and off using the *eye* icon. None of the changes will be permanent until you request them to be. As you try each adjustment, turn the eye off on the previously created adjustment layer. This will prevent its effects from displaying. Also, explore combining adjustment layers with the main image by leaving the eye icon displayed on all layers. If and when you are ready to commit to an adjustment, click on the adjustment layer, go to the *Layers* palette menu, and choose the *Merge Down* option (to merge the adjustment with the layer beneath it) or the *Merge Visible* option (to merge the adjustment with all visible layers) in the *Layers* palette.

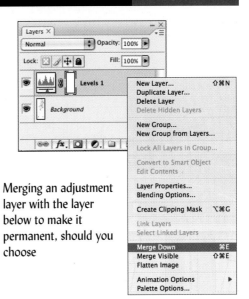

Merging an adjustment layer with the layer below to make it permanent, should you choose

Image Enhancement: Levels

Levels is one of the most used adjustment tools in Photoshop. It allows you to alter a layer's brightness and contrast by adjusting highlights, midtones, and shadows.

1. Create a new adjustment layer, using *Levels* as your option.

2. Move the sliders in the *Levels* dialog. The black slider represents the shadows. The white slider represents the highlights and the center slider represents the midtones. Click **OK** when you are satisfied with the results. The example here used Input Levels of 191–4.89–255.

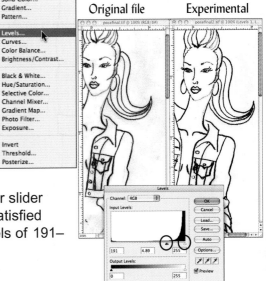

Using a Levels adjustment layer

Image Enhancement: Threshold

The *Threshold* function allows you to make the current layer or background appear with high contrast by converting color or gray pixels to pure black and white pixels.

1. Turn off the view of the *Levels* adjustment layer so that you can see the effect of this next operation. Click once on the eye icon.

2. Create a new adjustment layer, using *Threshold* as your option.

3. Move the sliders and view the effect. Click **OK** when you are through. The example here used a threshold value of 208. If you click on the *Layer thumbnail* of an adjustment layer, you can return to the adjustment dialog and make changes.

Note: View the combination of Levels and Threshold by turning on the view of both adjustment layers (clicking on the eye icon of the Levels adjustment).

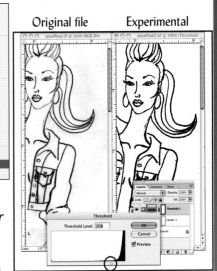

Using a Threshold adjustment layer

Image Enhancement: Brightness/Contrast

The *Brightness/Contrast* command makes simple adjustments to the tonal range of an image. The changes affect all pixels equally.

1. Turn off the *Threshold* and *Levels* adjustment layers by clicking on the eye icon, making sure that the view of the eye is off.

2. Create a new adjustment layer using *Brightness/ Contrast* as your option.

3. Move the sliders and view the effect. Click **OK** when you are through. The sample here used a Brightness setting of −38 and a Contrast setting of +71.

Original file   Experimental

Comparing the results of a
Brightness/Contrast adjustment

At this point you have experimented with various image adjustments. Since you used *adjustment layers*, none of these adjustments are permanent. We will now switch gears and explore a few other options for enhancing scanned imagery. Leave the adjustment layers in place but don't commit to any of them yet. We will take a snapshot of our work, thus creating a point in history that we can easily return to before exploring *Touch-up* tools and *Filters*.

Setting up a Snapshot

Snapshots capture a moment in time and save it so you can return to it later.

1. Turn off all the adjustment layers created in earlier steps of this exercise. Click on the eye icon of each adjustment to make sure it is off. Now you will be able to view the quality of the image in its original state.

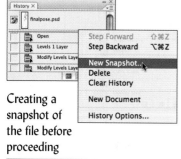

Creating a
snapshot of
the file before
proceeding

2. If the *History* palette is not in view, turn it on now by choosing the *Window>History* menu command.

3. Click on the **arrow** in the upper-right corner of the *History* palette menu and choose *New Snapshot* from the menu that opens. A dialog will open. Type in **prior to filters** and click **OK**. A new line appears in the upper part of the *History* palette indicating the snapshot. You may click on this snapshot at any time to return to the history state/snapshot at the point when it was created.

Creating a snapshot of the file,
using the Create new snapshot
button. You will need to rename
the snapshot once made.

Note: You could have clicked on the **Create new snapshot** button at the bottom of the *History* palette, but then you would have to double-click on the snapshot name to rename it. Using the palette menu opens a dialog that prompts you to name the snapshot at that time.

The History palette with the
snapshot in place

Alternate Image Editing Options

The following are other options you should experiment with when attempting to enhance a scanned line art image.

The Burn, Dodge, and Sponge Tools (O)

 The Burn tool darkens areas of the image.

 The Dodge tool lightens areas of the image.

 The Sponge tool makes color areas more or less saturated.

These tools originated in photography darkrooms. The **Burn** tool allows you to darken pixels while the **Dodge** tool lets you lighten pixels. The **Sponge** tool makes color areas on a layer more or less saturated. The changes you make with these tools affect the image as soon as you use the tool. You may choose to undo the changes or you can return to the *snapshot* state by clicking on the *Prior to Filters* snapshot in the *History* palette. The **Burn** tool seems to be an appropriate choice for darkening the line art drawing in various places.

1. Click on **Finalpose2.tif** to make it your active document (make sure that all adjustment layers are turned off). Select the *Background* to make it active.

2. Zoom into an area of the image that needs to be darkened. Use the **Hand** tool to move around the image (or press and hold the *Spacebar* as you *click+drag* on the document to change to panning mode).

3. Choose the **Burn** tool in the Toolbox (it may be hidden under the **Dodge** tool).

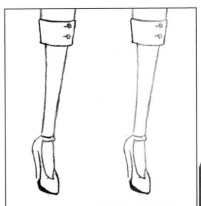

Viewing the effects of the Burn tool. The right image is the original and the left image is the altered art.

4. Adjust the size of the tool tip, as necessary (in the options bar), or press the *left or right square bracket keys*, [or], on the keyboard to increase or decrease the size of the brush tip.

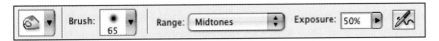

5. Move to areas of your line art image that need to be darkened and *click+drag* the tool back and forth over the drawing. Note how the lines become darker. If you want to lighten the line somewhat, switch to the **Dodge** tool.

6. Experiment with the various tools (**Burn**, **Dodge,** and **Sponge**) and note the effect on the line drawing of the pose.

The Sharpen and Blur Tools

 The Blur tool softens edges.

 The Sharpen tool increases contrast between pixels.

 The Smudge tool makes color areas more or less saturated.

The **Sharpen** tool *increases* the contrast between pixels and is used to more clearly delineate edges between shapes. The **Blur** tool *decreases* the contrast between pixels and therefore softens edges between shapes. The **Smudge** tool allows you to move the mouse over pixels on the document and blend the colors together. In the case of a line art drawing, smudging would blend the black art and white background. For our purposes, sharpening and blurring will most likely be the best options.

1. Click on **Finalpose2.tif** to make it your active document (make sure that all adjustment layers are turned off). Click on the *Prior to Filters* snapshot to return the image to its original form.

2. Zoom into an area of the image that needs to be altered. Use the **Hand** tool to move around the image (or press and hold the *Spacebar* as you *click+drag* on the document to change to Panning mode).

3. Choose the **Sharpen** tool in the Toolbox (it may be hidden under the **Blur** tool).

4. Adjust the *size* of the tool tip and the *Strength* as necessary in the options bar.

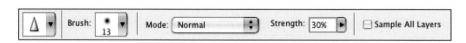

Sharpen vs. Blur
Observe the hair lines in the upper right of each model below. The image on the left used the Sharpen tool and the image on the right used the Blur tool.

5. Move to areas of your line art image that need to be treated and *click+drag* the tool back and forth over the drawing. Note how the lines become darker and more grainy.

6. Experiment with the Blur tool and note how the hairlines soften.

If you like, take another snapshot at this point (using the *History* palette).

Using Filters

Filters allow you to apply a visual effect to your image. We will now be using the *Noise* and *Blur* filters to remove some of the noise from our image. Filters are found in the **Filter** menu and are organized into groups. Some filters will occur immediately upon selection, others will require you to choose settings in a dialog window. If desired, you can apply a filter to a selected area of your drawing only, simply by defining the area with a selection tool and then choosing the filter command.

Using the Noise>Despeckle Filter

Once again, work with both the **posefinal.tif** and **posefinal2.tif** files open so you can see a comparison of the filter you are applying to the original file.

1. Click on **posefinal2.psd** to make this the current document.

2. Click on the *Prior to Filters* snapshot in the *History* palette. This will return you to a point in time prior to the work you performed with the various tools in the previous section.

3. Choose the *Filter>Noise>Despeckle* menu command and observe the changes in the document, comparing it with the original file. Zoom in, as necessary, to see the results.

4. You may choose to run the filter a second time and view changes (if any).

Note: This filter does not produce significant improvement on the current file. However, it may be the best choice with another image, so it is always good to have a knowledge of it tucked away.

Using the Gaussian Blur Filter Followed by a Levels Adjustment Layer

The following technique is one that is commonly used for fixing fax scans, and it works great with line art.

1. Click on **posefinal2.psd** to make this the current document.

2. Click on the *Prior to Filters* snapshot in the *History* palette. This will return you to a point in time prior to the work you performed with the various tools in the previous sections.

The Noise>Despeckle filter is used. The results are not significant with this image, yet may be with another image.

3. Choose the *Filter>Blur>Gaussian Blur* command. A dialog will open. Set the blur to 1.0 and click **OK**. The outlines will soften as will large areas of pixels around the image.

4. Choose *Layer>New Adjustment Layer>Levels.* Note that this is an alternate way to request an adjustment layer. A *New Layer* dialog will open to allow you to type a name for the adjustment layer. Type in *Levels testing with blur* and click **OK**.

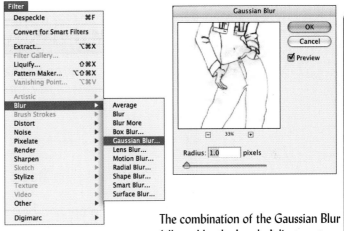

The combination of the Gaussian Blur followed by the Levels Adjustment works well with the image.

5. A *Levels* dialog will open. Move the black slider to the right until the pose/ garment outline becomes as solid as you need it to be. Then, move the white slider to the left until you clean up the noise. Click **OK** to approve and the file will update with the changes.

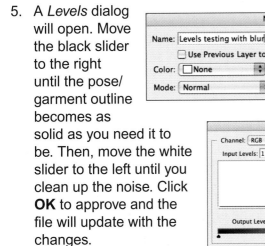

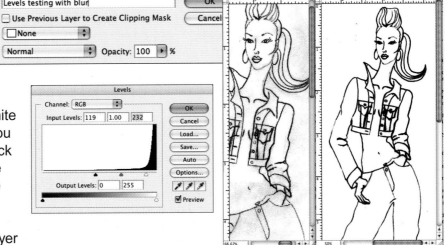

6. Turn the adjustment layer on and off to observe the effect.

At this point you must decide which of the enhancements you want to keep.

The Magic and Quick Selection tools allow you to create selections by color.

Using the Magic Wand or Quick Selection tool to Clean up or Color Noise Areas

The **Magic Wand** may be used at any point in time to select an area of pixels and recolor them. *You may choose to do either or both of the following:*

a. Select the area outside the model and delete all pixels selected, thus turning them to the background color, which ideally is white. If you are on a layer (as opposed to the *Background*), you will delete the colored pixels to a transparent background.

b. Select an area of pixels inside the garment and fill them with color. You may use the **Paint Bucket** or the *Edit>Fill* command to achieve either of these approaches.

Experiment with the *Tolerance* settings in the options bar to find the setting that allows you to select noise pixels without including parts of the garment line drawing.

Cleaning up the Background of the Art using the Magic Wand Tool

Experimenting using the Magic Wand in Contiguous Mode with Anti-aliasing turned on

1. Make sure that the artwork is a *Background*. If it is a layer, choose *Layer>New>Background from Layer*. This will cause the drawing to appear on the background. Thus when you press the *Delete/Backspace* key, the selected area will become the background color of the Toolbox (which will be set to white).

2. Make sure that the *background* color in the Toolbox is white.

3. Choose the **Magic Wand** tool in the Toolbox.

4. In the *options bar*, set the *Tolerance* to 20.

5. Move the **Magic Wand** to your document and click in an area of noise pixels outside of the garment. A selection of pixels will be made.

6. Press the *Delete/Backspace* key on the keyboard and the selected area will change to the background color (white).

Note: The *Delete* key on the Mac is the larger delete key on the keyboard, directly beneath the *F11* key.

At this point in time, you need to determine which of the enhancements work best for your artwork. The results will vary according to the paper you drew on, the quality of your scan or digital image, and the settings you chose to use with each function. Experiment with the adjustment layers to determine which work best. Use your *History* palette and *snapshots* to assist you in this process.

Coloring Your Line Art Drawing

You may select areas inside the garment and color them in one of several ways:

- Using the **Paint Bucket** tool
- Using the *Edit>Fill* command
- Using the *Delete* (Mac) or *Backspace* (Windows) key on the keyboard, which fills to the *background* color in your Toolbox if you are working on a *Background* (as opposed to a layer).

The Paint Bucket tool (above) and the Edit>Fill command and dialog (below)

These options will be covered more fully in Exercise #2.

Color your image and have fun!

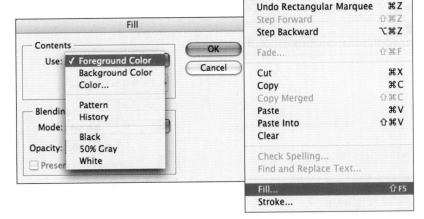

Sandra Gonzales

Rebecca Moman

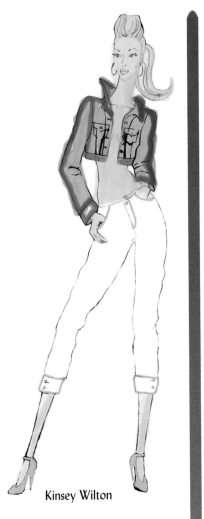

Kinsey Wilton

Student Gallery
Hand-Drawn to Photoshop
Jasha Aitchison

All images were hand-drawn, scanned, and then colored in Photoshop.

Exercise #9: Coloring Line Art Images

Once you have achieved a good line art image you can add color to it by filling the skin, hair, and garment with color. There are various techniques by which you can add color to an image.

These are:

A. Using the **Paint Bucket** tool to fill in areas

B. Using your choice of **Selection** tools to select an area and filling the area with either the *Edit>Fill* menu command or the **Paint Bucket**

C. Using a variety of additional techniques such as painting color in place using the various drawing tools such as **Brush**, **Pencil**, **Eraser**, etc.

Goal of Method A: Using the Paint Bucket Tool

To fill areas of the line art illustration with color using the **Paint Bucket** tool.

Photoshop Tools and Functions

- **Line** tool and **Brush** tools
- *Swatches* and *Color* palettes
- **Paint Bucket** tool
- **Eyedropper** tool

Quick Overview of the Process

In this portion of the exercise you will use the **Paint Bucket** tool to fill in several areas of the drawing. You will begin by conducting a quick examination of your line art to ensure all lines are drawn as needed. Then, you will use colors from the *Swatches* or *Color* palettes with the **Paint Bucket** tool to fill in the areas. Since the Paint Bucket tool will flood the area with color until it hits a boundary, you will learn how to edit your images so that boundaries exist.

Original art by Keith Antonio

New Concepts

- o Working with the *Color* palettes
- o Using the **Eyedropper** tool to select a color from the image
- o Using *Tolerance* on the **Magic Wand** to create a selection that can be filled with the **Paint Bucket**

Sources of Imagery

- o Hand-drawn line art fashion illustrations and flats

General Process

In this exercise we will be performing the following actions:

1. Checking the image for areas that have a break in the line and correcting these so that the **Paint Bucket** flood fill will not leak outside the desired area

2. Using the *Swatches* or *Color* palette to choose a flesh color and fill in selected skin areas of the image

New art by Sandra Gonzales

Line art, scanned from a hand-drawing by Keith Antonio, fashion student, Mesa College

(Left to Right)
The Burn, Brush, and Line tools

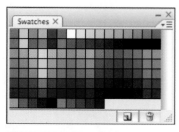

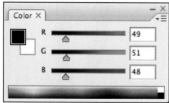

Step 4: Opening the Swatches and Color palettes.

3. Using the **Brush** tool to draw a boundary line that will define or block an area of the lips to be filled

4. Using the **Paint Bucket** tool to fill in the lips

Step-by-Step
Initial Coloring of Flesh Tones

1. Load an image that you want to color. This exercise will use **keithpose.jpg**, a line art illustration of a fashion pose. This file can be found in the **Ex 9** folder which sits inside the **Fashion Exercises** folder on your DVD. Once the image is loaded, save it as **keithfinalcolor** and change the format to a TIF or Photoshop PSD format. Set up your palettes as desired, and make sure that you have the *Layers* and *History* palette at easy access.

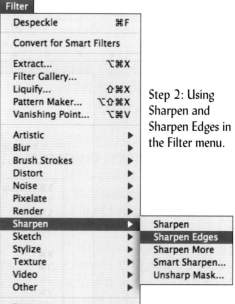

Step 2: Using Sharpen and Sharpen Edges in the Filter menu.

2. Look at the image and determine if the line art is as sharp as you would like. If not, or if you would like to experiment, choose the *Filter>Sharpen>Sharpen* filter or the *Filter>Sharpen>Sharpen Edges* filter. Observe the changes and decide whether to use it.

3. Using magnification and panning, move around the image, checking visually to determine if all lines are drawn as you would want for the image's integrity or to allow you to easily fill areas with color. If you find an area that needs touch-up, use either the **Burn** tool to darken the lines, or the **Brush** or **Line** tool (in *Fill pixels* mode, which is the pixel/raster mode of the tool) to fill in gaps. *Note*: It is not necessary to create line art boundaries everywhere in the image, if the black line does not seem appropriate. Alternate techniques will be discussed. Do not fix the nose and lip area as we will do something with this later.

Choosing the Fill pixels mode of the Line tool

4. Open the *Swatches* and *Color* palettes to view colors.

5. Choose a flesh-tone color in the *Swatches* palette, and click on it to specify it as the *Foreground* color in the Toolbox.

Step 5: Setting a flesh color as the foreground color in the Toolbox.

6. Look for skin areas of the image that need flesh coloring and locate those

that have a complete black outline (e.g., the hand, the various exposures of the arm in the sleeve of the top, etc.).

7. Choose the **Paint Bucket** tool in the Toolbox. This tool fills adjacent pixels that are similar in color value to the pixels you click. Observe the tolerance in the *options bar*. Start with a *tolerance* of approximately 20. Ensure that *Anti-alias* and *Contiguous* are checked. Anti-aliasing will allow the flesh color to meet the line art black and grays in a soft way, mixing the flesh tone with black/gray for the pixels to be used adjacent to the black and gray pixels. The *Contiguous* mode lets you fill only pixels that are adjacent to the one you click on (including adjacent pixels that fall into the tolerance range). Experiment with the tolerance, as necessary.

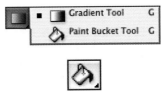

Step 7: Choosing the Paint Bucket tool in the Toolbox and setting its tolerance.

 Tolerance
You may want to experiment with the tolerance as you fill different areas of the arm. Also, try filling an area a second time if you need to expand the fill color slightly to remove a fringe of "whitish" pixels.

8. Zoom in to the model's left hand. Position the **Paint Bucket** icon inside the hand and click. The hand will fill with color. Observe how the flesh color meets with the black outline. If it is OK, continue. If it is not, go back in history, change the Paint Bucket's tolerance, and fill the hand again. You want to find the tolerance level that fills to the black/gray outline pixels without taking them over. There will be a right blend of the flesh meeting the black and gray pixels, whereby new gray-flesh pixels are created and the joining of the flesh tone and the outline is unobtrusive.

Steps 8–9: Using the Paint Bucket tool fill in flesh areas of the arm and hand.

9. Continue to fill in areas of the arm that peep through the cut-out holes of the top.

Coloring of the Lips

1. Select a color for the lips from the *Swatches* or *Color* palette. This will move the color into the *foreground* color of your Toolbox.

2. Magnify the lip area of your image. Note how the lower lip is not completely outlined. This is not a problem, as we will assist the outline by painting one in with our lip color.

3. Choose the **Brush** or **Pencil** tool and a small tip (or the **Line** tool in *Fill pixels* mode). The Brush tool will give you a soft edge and the Pen tool will give a hard edge. The Line tool is best for drawing over large areas of an image.

(Left to Right)
The Brush, Pencil, and Line tools

Tolerance

If the tolerance is set to 20, and you click on a white pixel with your Magic Wand, Photoshop selects that white pixel and includes pixels 20 shades lighter and 20 shades darker in the selection. If you have the Contiguous mode checked, the area of pixels selected will expand until it hits a boundary (as opposed to selecting any pixels on the document with those same colors).

4. Move over to the lower lip and draw in a line to define the edge of the lip color.

5. Change to the **Paint Bucket** tool and fill in the lower lip with color. You may want to experiment with the tolerance to achieve the best fill.

6. Try editing with gray pixels to better define the lip outline. Use the **Eyedropper** tool to pick up a shade of gray (choose the tool, and click on a gray pixel to choose the color). Then, using the **Pencil** tool, draw in the outline with the gray pixels. Repeat with the various shades of gray as necessary to create a good lip outline.

7. Save the image.

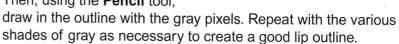

Steps 3–6: Editing the line of the lips and using the Brush, Pencil, or Line tools and the Eyedropper to match colors. Then filling the lips with color using the Paint Bucket tool.

Goal of Method B: Using the Magic Wand and Other Selection Tools in Conjunction with Edit>Fill or the Paint Bucket

To explore techniques of coloring line art drawings using the **Selection** tools in conjunction with either *Edit>Fill* or the **Paint Bucket** tool.

Tools and Functions

♦ **Selection** tools (Magic Wand, Quick Selection, Lasso)
♦ *Swatches* or *Color* palettes
♦ **Paint Bucket** tool
♦ *Edit>Fill* menu command
♦ **Eyedropper** tool

Quick Overview of the Process

In this portion of the exercise you will use various selection tools in conjunction with *Edit>Fill* or the **Paint Bucket** to fill areas of your drawing. The advantage of creating selections is that you can see precisely the area that will be filled with color (as indicated by the marching ants marquee) prior to filling in the color. If you use the **Polygon Selection** tool, you can fill areas that do not necessarily have a black boundary (as can be seen on the face by the nose). Once you have created a selection you can choose to complete the fill with either the **Paint Bucket** or the *Edit>Fill* menu command. The **Paint Bucket** will do a better job of anti-aliasing the joining of the new color to the colors it fills to (according to your *Tolerance* settings and because of the way the tool works). *Edit>Fill* will fill the selected pixels with one color.

Basic Premises for the Following Steps

o   The **Eyedropper** tool allows you to sample or select a color in the image and set it as the current foreground color.

o   The **Magic Wand** tool can be used to create a selection, which can then be filled with the foreground color in the palette.

Step-by-Step

We will continue with the same fashion pose as above.

1.   Choose the **Eyedropper** tool, and click on an area of the flesh on your drawing. This will set the *foreground* color in the Toolbox as the flesh color once again.

2.   Choose the **Magic Wand** tool, set the tolerance (in the *options bar*) to 20, and click on a white area inside the model's torso. Examine the selection made and determine if you should change the tolerance to a higher or lower number. It is best to zoom in and look at how close your selection is coming to the black line edge (or the gray anti-aliased pixels near it). If you want to change the tolerance, deselect it using the *Selection>Deselect* menu command or *Cmd/Ctrl+D* on the keyboard. Then, change the tolerance and check the Magic Wand's selection again.

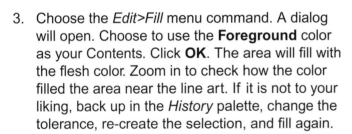

3.   Choose the *Edit>Fill* menu command. A dialog will open. Choose to use the **Foreground** color as your Contents. Click **OK**. The area will fill with the flesh color. Zoom in to check how the color filled the area near the line art. If it is not to your liking, back up in the *History* palette, change the tolerance, re-create the selection, and fill again.

4.   Next, we will fill the face area. Zoom in to the face area of the face and note how the black outline doesn't completely surround the face. Choose the **Magnetic Lasso** marquee tool. Move to the document and outline a small area around the tip of the nose, selecting just enough to include the open area and a small surrounding area. The selection marquee will show you what is actively selected.

5.   Choose *Edit>Fill*. The nose area will fill with the flesh color.

6.   Choose the **Magic Wand** and select the rest of the face. A marquee will show you what is selected.

7.   Choose *Edit>Fill*. The nose area will fill with the flesh color. There is probably a faint line between the two areas of flesh

Step 1: Resetting the foreground color in the Toolbox to the flesh color.

Step 2: Choosing the Magic Wand tool and setting its tolerance level. Observe the selection that is made.

Step 3: Using the Edit>Fill with foreground color to fill the body. Observe the selection.

Edit>Fill menu option and dialog

Steps 4–7: Using the Magnetic Lasso and the Edit>Fill to color the rest of the face.

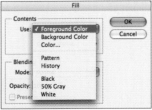

Step 7: Erasing the white line with the Eraser tool, which erases to the background color in the Toolbox.

Hot Tip!
Click on the Switch Foreground and Background Colors icon in the toolbox. This will swap the foreground and background colors. Now, when you have a selection and you are working on a Background (as opposed to a layer) you can simply press the Delete (Mac) or Backspace (Windows) key and the background color in the toolbox will fill into the marquee selection.

that you just filled (the nose area and the balance of the face and neck). Zoom in to inspect the area. You may use a **Brush** tool with the flesh color as the *foreground* color and paint over the white line. Or, you can swap the *foreground/background* colors by pressing **X** on the keyboard and use the **Eraser** tool to *paint erase* over the line. (This will erase to the *Background* color in the Toolbox as you are on a *Background* as opposed to a layer.)

8. Use the **Magic Wand** to select the leg areas and any other areas of the image that need to be filled with the flesh color. Use the *Delete/Backspace* key to fill with color (presuming the flesh color is still your background color). Leave the hose area of the legs until later, as a new skill will be taught at that time.

9. Save the image.

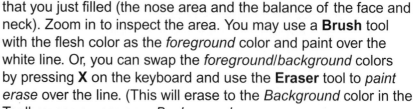

Step 8: Filling other body areas with flesh color.

Method C: Creative Selection
Techniques for Filling Complicated Areas
We are now going to explore more advanced and creative approaches to filling areas of an image that are complex, such as the hose and sweater areas.

Editing the Sweater Ribbings
The ribbings in the sweater will need some help prior to filling the white areas with color. Try filling color in these areas (using the **Paint Bucket**) at this point in time, and you will see the problem... the ribbings need more definition. A greater contrast between the line art and the background is needed.

Ideally the contrast should have been improved prior to filling the skin-tone color into the body. Since we did not do this, you will learn how to work with some advanced-thought selection techniques. We will begin by selecting the skin areas and then reversing the selection so that only the line art and white background areas are affected by changes we make. Work slowly, and try to absorb what the approach is, as it can save you hours of time in the big picture of graphics editing.

Improving the Contrast of the Ribbed Bands
You will be taking a "reverse thought" approach to improving the ribbing lines on the image. Initially, you will select the skin and then inverse the selection so that you have selected everything *but* the skin. Then, you will use the **Lasso** selection tool with the *Intersect* option to select only the area you want to work on to improve the contrast and quality.

1. Using your **Magic Wand** tool and a tolerance of 20, click in the middle of a flesh-colored skin area. A selection will be made.

2. Choose the *Select>Similar* menu command. This will select all the colored skin areas. Choose the *Select>Inverse* menu to reverse the selection so that only nonskin areas are selected.

3. Choose the **Lasso** selection tool. Click on the **Intersect with selection** button in the *options bar.* Take the **Lasso**

Steps 1–2: Inverted selection now selects everything but the flesh color so that you can adjust contrast where needed.

tool and carefully draw a lasso around the top ribbing, the body of the top, and the lower ribbing. Do not include the cut-out sleeve area as we do not want to lose the fine gray scale shadowing in the sleeve area. Once you release the mouse button, the selection will now include only the black and white areas of the ribbings and the main body of the top. No skin is selected.

4. We want to heighten the contrast of the ribbing lines to the background. With the selection still active, choose the *Image>Adjustments>Brightness/ Contrast...* menu. A dialog will open. Move the sliders so that the brightness and contrast improve the ribbing lines and keep a clean background. Our settings were a Brightness of −14 and a Contrast of +70. Click **OK**. You may alternately choose to use an adjustment layer for this operation, which will not be permanent.

Adding Color to the Sweater and Ribbings
1. Double-click on the *background* color icon in the Toolbox with your mouse. A *Color Picker* window will open. Choose the color you want for your sweater. Click **OK**. The color will appear as your *background* color in the Toolbox.

2. Zoom in to the sweater top area of the drawing. Deselect the selection (*Ctrl/Cmd+D* on the keyboard).

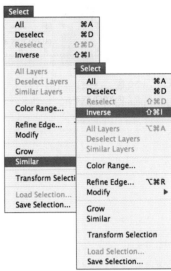

Select>Similar and Select>Inverse are used to select everything but the flesh areas.

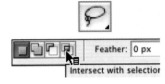

Step 3: Using the Intersect with selection option for the Lasso tool in the options bar.

Step 3: Once complete, you should have a selection of only the black and white areas of the ribbings and main body of the top. No skin should be selected.

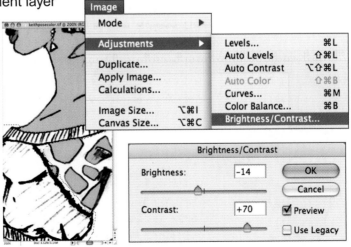

Step 4: Using the Brightness>Contrast adjustment to heighten the contrast between the black and white of the ribbing areas of the top.

Step 1: Setting blue as the background color in the Toolbox.

3. Choose the **Magic Wand** tool. Set the *Tolerance* to 20.

4. Click in the center of the main part of the sweater top. The inner white portion of the sweater will be selected. It will most likely include some of the off-white pixels as well.

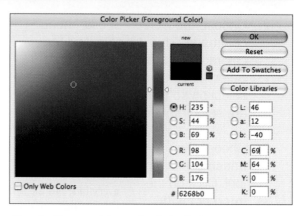

Step 1: Choosing blue in the Color Picker.

5. Choose *Select>Similar* to select all similar white and off-white pixels throughout the entire document. Observe the marching ants.

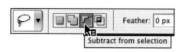

Steps 6–7: Using Intersect and Subtract features of selections to control your selections.

6. Now, switch to the **Lasso Selection** tool. Choose the *Intersect Selection* option in the *options bar*. Using your **Lasso** tool, lasso an area around the sweater. Note that the marquee area outside this disappears, so you have reduced the amount of selected area, but we are not done yet.

7. Switch back to the **Magic Wand** tool. Choose the *Subtract Selection* option in the *options bar*. Click on each of the three selected areas *outside* the figure (to the left, to the right, and inside the arm). What remains is a selection of the white pixels inside the sweater and ribbings. Press the *Delete/Backspace* key on the keyboard and the selection will fill with the background color of blue.

Fantastic! You have just saved a tremendous amount of time, bypassing the need to select and fill each individual area.

The sweater filled with blue

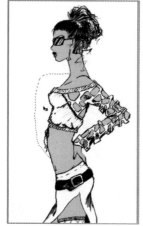

Above: The steps of creating the selection of the knit sweater, using the Intersect and Subtract features of Selections

Coloring the Skirt and Boots

1. Examine the details on the skirt. Note that the top stitching at the waist is not as dark as it might be.

2. Choose the **Burn** tool and *click+drag* the Burn *cursor* back and forth over the top stitching to darken it. Change the brush tip size if you like using the options bar.

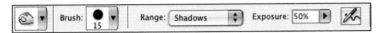

3. Choose the **Magic Wand** tool and set your tolerance so that you can create a clean marquee in the inner buckle. You will need to hold the *Shift* key down as you make multiple selections in order to get a nice oval area around the belt buckle. With white as your background color, press the *Delete/Backspace* key on the keyboard. You may fill the buckle with color or leave it white.

4. Double-click on the background color in the Toolbox to open the *Color Picker*, and choose a color for your skirt. Our choice was brown.

5. Using the **Magic Wand**, experiment with various tolerances until you can create a nice selection of the skirt. Press the *Delete/ Backspace* key and the skirt will fill with color.

Creating Colored Shadows for the Skirt

It is possible to create brown colored shadows for the shaded areas of the skirt. To do this we will create a selection of the shadow and fill it with brown using the *Color Burn Blending* mode.

1. Choose the **Magic Wand** tool. Set your tolerance high (e.g., 50). Click inside the shadow in any of the shaded areas of the skirt. Hold down the *Shift* key and continue to click with the **Magic Wand** until you get a clean selection of the area you are going to recolor.

2. Choose the *Edit>Fill* menu command. The *Fill* dialog will open. Choose the *Background* color, and set the *Blending Mode* to *Color Burn* and the *Opacity* to 50%. Click **OK**. The shaded area will fill

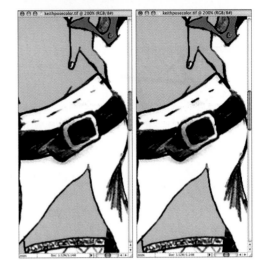

Step 2: Before (left) and after (right), showing the effect of using the Burn tool to darken the top stitching of the skirt.

Left: Step 3: Using the Magic Wand to select the buckle area and fill it with white, the background color.

Steps 4–5: The skirt is filled with brown, the new background color.

Steps 1–3 below: The shadowed areas of the skirt are selected (left) and a Color Burn fill mode is used to fill with color and retain the shadows.

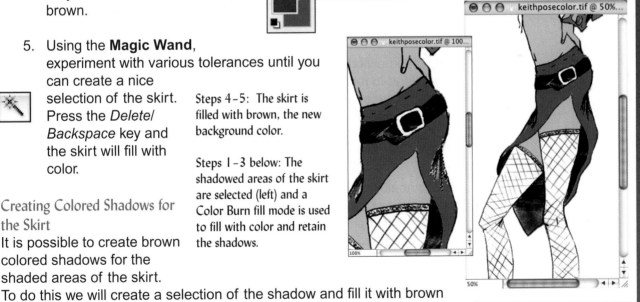

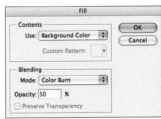

Steps 1–3: Using the Color Burn Blending mode.

with colored pixels, allowing the shadowing to come through in darker values of the original skirt color.

3. Repeat the process for all shaded areas of the skirt.

Enhancing Detail Lines and Coloring the Boots

We want to fill our boots with a medium to dark color. Therefore we need to enhance/lighten the detail lines in the boots so they will stand out against the dark brown background. To do this we will use the *Color Burn* blending mode with the **Brush** tool. You may want to make a snapshot prior to burning your image, just in case you do not like the results.

1. Choose a bright yellow-orange color as your *foreground* color in the Toolbox.

2. Choose the **Brush** tool. In the *options bar*, set the mode to *Color Burn*. Experiment with the brush tip size and opacity as you paint over the lines inside the boot.

3. Use the **Magic Wand** with *Edit>Fill*, or the **Paint Bucket** tool (experimenting with the tolerance) to fill in the remainder of the boot with a darker brown color.

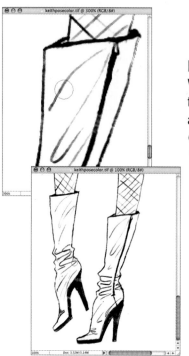

Steps 1–2: Using the Brush tool and Color Burn to enhance the inner lines of the boot.

Step 3: Filling in the body of the boots with brown.

Adding Color to the Hose

Using the knowledge you have gained in this exercise, color the hose area of the legs. You do not need to fill each independent area, one by one. Use the skills you have added to your repertoire.

Touch-ups

Perform touch-ups as necessary in the file. Consider using any combination of the following tools:

    o Brush and Pen tools
    o Eraser
    o Eyedropper
    o Clone Stamp
    o Panning with Hand tool
    o Magnification

Consider setting the *Opacity* of your tools at a level that allows color to paint, but still allows you to see the values of the shadows.

This completes the exercise. You have learned an amazing number of skills. Bank the knowledge.

Student Gallery
Colored Fashion Drawings
Mesa College Fashion Students

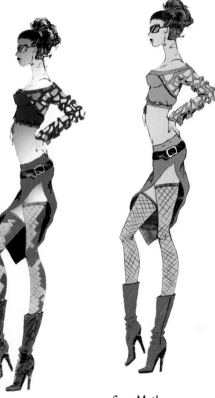

Renee Anderson

Eva Nielson

Sara Mathes

Crystal Ferris

Jessica Coburn

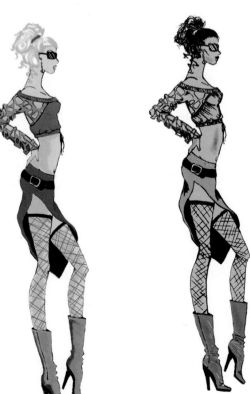

Melissa Luna

Diana Medrano

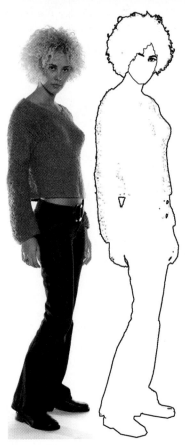

Exercise #10: Extracting a Pose from a Fashion Photo

Goal

In this exercise, we will lift a fashion pose away from its background, copy it to a new layer, and remove the fringed halo of anti-aliased pixels. We will continue to create a quick line art outline of the pose by creating a selection and stroking it. The images available for use in this exercise were created at a fashion shoot where the models were positioned against a neutral and typically contrasting background.

Photoshop Tools and Functions

- ◆ Adding *Canvas* to an image
- ◆ Scale Transformation *(Edit>Transform)*
- ◆ **Magic Wand** and the **Quick Selection** (CS3/CS4) tools
- ◆ Layers and fill layers
- ◆ Defringe function *(Layer>Matting>Defringe)*
- ◆ Stroking a selection *(Edit>Stroke)*

Quick Overview of the Process

In this exercise you will load a fashion pose from the DVD, then increase the canvas size and stretch the legs of the model to assist in creating a taller fashion pose. You will then select the model and copy her pose to a new layer. Using a defringe command you will remove the halo of light colored pixels that surround the pose. A black fill layer will assist you in seeing the halo and results of the defringe command. Once you have separated the pose from the background, you will select it, and then stroke it on a new layer. This will create a quick outline of the image.

The steps are as follows:
1. Load a fashion pose, increase the canvas size (lengthwise), and stretch the model's legs to create a "high fashion" pose.
2. Use the **Magic Wand** or **Quick Selection** tool to select the background, then invert the selection to be that of the model.
3. *Edit>Copy* and *Edit>Paste* the pose of the model to create a new layer with just the pose on it. Name the new layer pose.
4. Create a fill layer using blue as the fill color and position this under the pose layer.
5. Use the *Layer>Matting>Defringe* command to remove some of the halo that exists around the outside of the pose.
6. Save the selection of the model's outline.
7. Stroke the selection on a new layer to create a quick outline of the pose.
8. Fill in any details you want.

New Concepts

- o Using the Defringe command to remove anti-aliased pixels
- o Using *Opt/Alt+drag* to copy an image from one place to another on the same layer

Sources of Imagery

- o Art provided on the DVD

Tracing by Keith Antonio
Model: Paula Tabalipa

Step-by-Step

This exercise will use a photo found in the **Photoshoot** folder of the accompanying DVD. There are various poses for you to choose from. It is best to move or save the photo of your choice to your working folder on your hard drive.

Steps 2–3: Adobe's Bridge allows you to view multiple files in a folder.

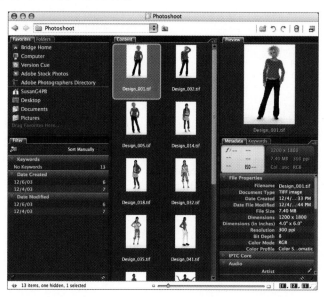

Loading and Prepping the Image

1. Choose the *File>Browse* feature. In Photoshop CS1, a *File Browser* window will open, similar to a file requestor. In Photoshop CS2 and later, the *Adobe Bridge* will open.

2. Using the folders and arrows in the left or upper-left corner of the window, direct the browser to the **Photoshoot** folder on your DVD and double-click on it to open it. Once there, you will see thumbnails of the images in the folder. Scroll down to view all the images. Locate an image with a pose you would like to use. Click on the image to preview it in the *Preview* window. Note that all the files are TIF files. The image used in this exercise is **Design_005.tif**.

3. Double-click on the image in the **Bridge** window to open it in Photoshop. If asked, choose to *Discard the Embedded Color Profile*.

4. Look at the image's file size using the *Image>Image Size* menu. You will see that the image is approximately 4 × 6 inches and uses a resolution of 300. It has a file size of approximately 7 megs. You may opt to reduce the size of your image if file size is a concern, but a resolution of 300 will allow for very smooth lines in the outline you create of the model. If you choose to resize the image using a resolution of 150 pixels, you will find that the file size will be reduced to 1.5 megs. For the purpose of this exercise, we will leave the resolution at 300. Click **Cancel** to close the *Image Size* dialog.

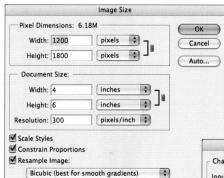

Steps 4–5: Viewing image information and adjusting the levels of the artwork.

5. Using the *Levels* adjustment, (*Image>Adjustment>Levels*) alter the contrast and brightness of your image if necessary. (Review Levels on page 133 and Basic Exercises #3 and #4.)

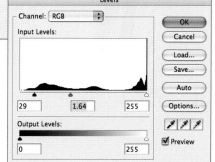

6. Save the file as **masterphoto.tif** in your working folder.

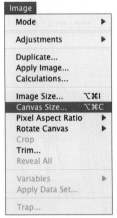

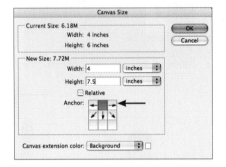

Steps 1–2: The Canvas Size menu command (above) and adjusting the canvas size (below).

The Commit check mark in the option bar finalizes the transform operation.

Stretching the Legs of the Fashion Pose in Photoshop (Optional)

If you want to create a model that has a high fashion build (i.e., a nine- or ten-head tall model), you will need to alter the legs of the model in the fashion pose. Stretching the legs of this model will require two steps: first adding more canvas to the image, and then transforming the legs by selecting them and stretching them.

1. Choose the *Image>Canvas Size...* menu command. A dialog will open.

2. Set the height of the *Canvas* to **7.5** inches, and set the *Anchor* to the upper center by clicking on the upper-center block in the Anchor area. Leave the canvas extension color as *Background*, which in this case is white (the current *background* color in the palette). Click **OK**. The document will enlarge with extra white area added beneath the model as shown below.

3. Choose the **Rectangular Marquee** tool in the Toolbox. Move over to the image and drag a marquee around the legs of the model. When you release the mouse, you will see a rectangular marquee and the "marching ants" surrounding the selected area.

4. Choose the *Edit>Free Transform* menu. Note that the selection box changes and you now have eight anchor squares (center and corner) on the rectangle. Move your cursor to the lower-center square of the rectangle and note how the cursor changes to a double arrowhead when you are over this square. *Click+drag* the square downwards, which will stretch the selected area lengthwise. Stretch the legs until you think they are the correct length. Release the mouse button. To complete the action, double-click inside the transformation or click on the **Commit** check mark, which appears in the options bar at the top of the screen. This finalizes the transformation.

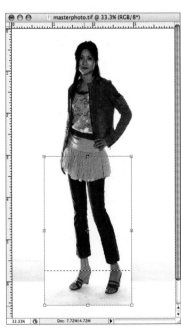

Steps 3–4: Left: The original image   Center: Additional canvas added   Right: The legs of the model are stretched.

5. You will now crop the image to keep only the portions you need to trace. Choose the **Crop** tool in the Toolbox and drag a box around the portions of the image you want to keep (i.e., the fashion model). Once you release the mouse button, the outer nonselected area will turn gray to show you what the cropped image will look like. Double-click inside the cropping box to finalize the operation.

6. Save the file again. The file size will be smaller than it was before cropping.

Step 5: Using the Crop tool to crop the image (left) and the results (right).

Separating the Pose from the Background

1. Zoom out so that you can see the entire pose.

2. Choose the **Magic Wand** tool. In the options bar, ensure that *Contiguous* and *Anti-alias* are checked and set the *Tolerance* to 20 (although you may experiment with this).

The Magic Wand tool and its options

3. Using the **Magic Wand** tool, click in the white area of the background. A selection will occur that encompasses most of the white background, but not the lower part of the image that has more gray in it.

4. Click on the **Add to selection** icon in the option bar. When this is active, you can easily add to the current selection.

5. With the **Magic Wand** tool still active, click in the lower area and observe how the selection (marching ants) grows. Continue to select areas until you have selected all the white background, including the area between the body and the elbow on the right side of the model. Want until you have selected all areas around the shoes.

6. Click on the **Hand** tool in the Toolbox and pan around the image to ensure that you have the selection you want (i.e., all the background of the image). You may also turn on the **Quick Mask** in the Toolbox. If you are not familiar with Quick Mask, see pages 37–39 to review how it works, as this is a fast way to see what is and is not selected.

7. Ensure that white is the *background* color in your Toolbox. Press the *Delete/Backspace* key and the entire selected background will become one color, white.

Steps 3–5: Selecting the background of the image.

Copying the Pose to a New Layer

1. Choose the *Select>Inverse* menu command. This will reverse the selection so that now the pose is the only item selected on the document.

2. Choose the *Edit>Copy* menu to copy the pose to the clipboard.

3. Paste the pose back into Photoshop using the *Edit>Paste* command. It will paste onto a new layer called *Layer 1*. Double-click on this layer name in the *Layers* palette and rename the layer to *Pose*.

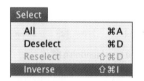

Step 1: Using the Inverse command to invert a selection.

Creating a Fill Layer

In order to see the halo that exists around the pose, you will need to create a *fill* layer of a contrasting color.

1. Click on the *Background* in the *Layers* palette to make it the active layer.

2. Click on the **Create a new fill or adjustment layer** button at the bottom of the *Layers* palette and slide up to the *Solid Color* option. The *Color Picker* will open. Choose blue as the current color (so the black hair will contrast with it) and click **OK**.

A blue fill layer will appear above the background layer and under the pose layer. By clicking on the *Background* prior to creating the fill layer you were able to position this fill exactly where you wanted it.

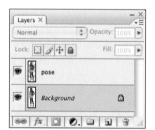

Steps 1–2: Creating a fill layer of blue. Click on the Background layer (above), then choose the Create a new fill or adjustment layer button and select a color from the Color Picker.

Step 2: Creating a fill layer of blue so that you can easily see the halo that surrounds the artwork.

Removing/Improving the Halo

A halo of light pixels often occurs around the edge of an image lifted from a contrasting background. There are two ways to remove this halo. You will want to experiment with both of these techniques as the results will differ from image to image. Make a snapshot of your artwork when you do this so that you can return to this point in time in order to compare the techniques. Do this by clicking on the **Snapshot** button at the bottom of the *History* palette. The snapshot will appear at the top of the palette. Double-click on the snapshot name to edit the name. Change the name to *before halo testing*.

Expanding or Contracting a Selection

1. Click on the *pose* layer to select it.

2. Using the **Magic Wand**, click in the area outside the pose to select the background transparent area of the image.

Creating a snapshot prior to testing the removal of the halo

3. Choose the *Select>Similar* menu to select all the background of the image (including the area between the arm and the body).

4. Zoom in so that you can view the edge of the fashion pose.

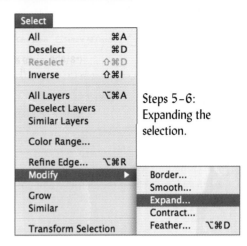

Steps 5–6:
Expanding the
selection.

5. Choose the *Select>Modify>Expand* menu command. A dialog will open. Set the number of pixels to 2 and click **OK**. Look at your results. If you want to experiment a little, undo the operation (*Cmd/Ctrl+Z*) and repeat the operation, but set the number of pixels to 1 and compare the results. Continue to experiment until you find the best result.

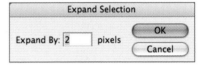

6. When you feel you have expanded the selection to include the proper amount of halo pixels, press the *Delete/Backspace* key on the keyboard to erase the selected pixels (thus changing them to transparent).

7. Make another snapshot at this point of time so that you can compare the results of the next test to those of the current test. Call this snapshot *after expand*.

a   b   c

Removing the Halo
a. A selection is made by selecting the background area of the pose layer.
b. The selection is expanded by 2 pixels using the Select>Modify>Expand menu command.
c. The selection is deleted to transparency, removing most of the anti-aliased pixels.

Using the Defringe Command
This approach doesn't use a selection. Rather, you work with the layer that the artwork sits on.

1. Click on the *before halo testing* snapshot to return to the point in history prior to any halo testing.

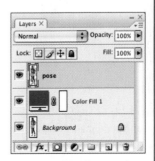

2. Click on the *pose* layer in the *Layers* palette to make it the active layer.

Step 2: Selecting the pose layer.

3. Zoom in so that you can view the edge of the fashion pose.

4. Choose the *Layers>Matting>Defringe* menu command. A defringe dialog will open. Change the setting to *2* and click **OK**. Look at your results. If you want to experiment a little, undo the operation (*Cmd/Ctrl+Z*) and repeat the steps, but set the number of pixels to *1* and compare the results. Continue to experiment until you find the best result.

Step 4: Using the Defringe command in the Layers menu, and setting the Defringe amount to 2 pixels.

Using Defringe: The image on the left shows the artwork prior to using the command, and the image on the right shows the results of the Defringe command. The results are most obvious around the hair.

5. Create a snapshot at this point and name it *After Defringe*.

6. Choose the technique that works best for this image. You can review the results of both techniques by clicking on the snapshots.

7. Save the file.

At this point, you are ready to create the outline of your fashion pose. There are two approaches you may take to do this: using a selection and stroking it, or drawing the outline using paint/draw tools. When you are able to easily create a selection, the former approach works well. When the background of the image is busy, and creating a selection of it is difficult, then simply tracing with a drawing tool is a good approach. Of course, you can always combine the approaches.

Steps 1–4: Changing the fill layer to white and creating a selection of the fashion pose.

Creating a Quick Line Art Outline

At this point, you are ready to create a quick outline of the pose.

1. Change the color of the *fill* layer to white. You can do this by double-clicking on the blue thumbnail in the *fill* layer of the *Layers* palette and changing the color to white in the *Color Picker* that opens.

Step 1: Changing the color of the fill layer by double-clicking on the colored thumbnail and changing the color to white in the Color Picker dialog.

2. Click on the *pose* layer to make it the active layer.

3. Choose the **Magic Wand** tool, and click on the background area to select it.

4. Inverse the selection by choosing the *Select>Inverse* menu command.

Step 5: Saving a selection for future retrieval.

5. Save this selection now in case you want it for future reference. This is achieved by choosing the *Select>Save* menu. When the *Save Selection* dialog opens, name the selection and click on the **OK** button. The selection will save with the file and can be retrieved at any point in time.

6. In the *Layers* palette, create a new layer and name it *outline*. Ensure that this is the active layer. You should still see your live marquee on the document. If you do not, you can load the selection using the *Select>Load Selection* menu command.

Step 6: Creating a new layer for the outline.

The Save Selection menu command

7. Choose the *Edit>Stroke* menu. A dialog will open. Choose a stroke thickness of 2 and choose either center or outside for the location of the stroke. Ensure that you have a black or dark gray color. If you do not, click on the color box in the dialog to open the *Color Picker* and choose a black or gray color. Click **OK**. The selection will be stroked with the color but it will not be easy to see, as the pose is still visible on the document.

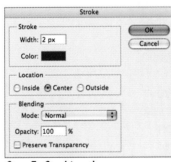

Step 7: Stroking the selection with a black color.

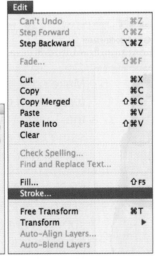

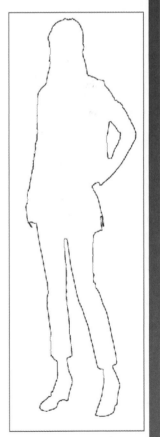

The outline created

8. Hide the view of the *pose* layer and *Background* by clicking on the eye icon of these layers in the *Layers* palette.
You should now see the outline of the fashion pose.

Step 8: Hiding the view of the pose layer and Background.

Note:

Inner Details
You can also use the Selection/Stroke technique to draw some of the inner details if the artwork allows for clean selections. Experimenting with the tolerance settings is suggested for this process.

Using the Line Tool to Outline the Pose or Draw the Inner Details

This approach is easy to learn, as it resembles tracing a pose by hand. You can pick up and move your drawing/painting tool at any point in time, just as you would a pencil. You might choose to use the drawing approach if you have a busy background in your image and you don't want to attempt to remove it. You may choose from an assortment of drawing/painting tools to draw with, such as the **Line**, **Brush**, or **Pencil**, each with a different result.

Since we already have an outline, created by stroking a selection, we will use the **Line** tool to draw in the inner details of the garment.

1. Create a new layer to place the inner details on and name it *details.* This allows flexibility in that you can easily remove the inner details, or edit them, without worrying about changing the outline.

2. Turn the view of the *pose* layer on and change the opacity level to 50%.

Steps 1–2: Creating a details layer and changing the opacity of the pose layer.

3. Choose the **Line** tool. This is most likely buried under the **Rectangle** shape tool in the Toolbox.

4. In the options bar, choose the *Fill pixels* mode, and set the *Weight* to 1 or 2.

Changing the opacity of the pose layer so that you can see the lines as you draw them on the details layer.

5. Make sure that your *foreground* color in the Toolbox is the same color as your outline (i.e., black).

Step 4: Setting the options for the Line tool.

6. Move over to your artwork, and make sure you are on the *details* layer. Draw in the inner details of the garment/pose. It takes a little practice to become good at joining line segments as you draw. You will eventually become quite adept at creating detailed drawings.

Step 6: Drawing in the inner details of the garment on the details layer.

Tips:
- o Turn the pose layer on and off as you work to check your progress.
- o Cross-check your drawing for "holes" that will cause problems later when you go to fill the garments with color.
- o Lock the pose layer so that you don't accidentally draw on it.

Alternate Poses

The accompanying DVD also includes some runway fashion poses for you to use as alternates in this exercise (**Runway Images** folder). The background is busier, and thus you will have more challenges in extracting the pose using the stroking technique. *Consider any of the following:*
- o If there is good contrast between the model and the background, use the **Magnetic Lasso** tool to outline the pose, and then stroke it.
- o Trace the entire pose, using your choice of painting tool (e.g., **Line**, **Pencil**, **Brush**, etc.).
- o Use the **Quick Mask** to assist you in creating a selection so that you can stroke it.
- o Consider creating multiple layers, each for a different garment piece, and use selections and stroking to create the outlines of the different pieces. Erase the portions of a garment on one layer that overlap with the same outline on another layer.

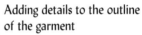

Adding details to the outline of the garment

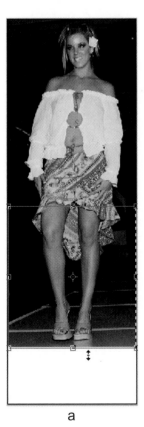

a b c

a. Canvas is added to image.
b. Legs are stretched.
c. Image is recropped to eliminate the excess canvas.

Second pose in the process of being outlined

Student Gallery
Garment Outlines
Mesa College Fashion
Students

Tracing by Rie Sawada
Model: Samantha Song

Tracing by Kathy White
Model: Kinsey Wilton

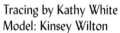

Tracing by Lele Doan
Model: Samantha Song

Tracing by Carol Newland
Model: Paula Tabalipa

Exercise #11: Illustrating Fashion with Art Medium Brushes

Goal

To translate a fashion photograph to art employing artistic brushes and techniques that simulate hand-drawn art mediums such as watercolor, charcoal, and pastels.

Photoshop Tools and Functions

- **Magic Wand** or **Quick Selection** tool
- Quick Mask
- Stroke (*Edit>Stroke*)
- **Brush** tool and options such as *Opacity* and *Flow*
- **Line** tool
- Varying levels of opacity
- *Swatches* or *Color* palette
- **Eyedropper** tool
- Artistic filters
- Layers

Discussion of Art Medium Brushes in Photoshop

Various art medium brushes exist in Photoshop. These allow you to paint in manners that simulate watercolor, charcoal, pastels, and other art mediums. Exploring the **Brush** tool and its options and the *Brushes* palette and all its capabilities will make you aware of the possibilities. In addition, there are various filters that you may employ to create an image that simulates fine art mediums and techniques. Filters can often be used as a finishing technique after your painting is complete to add depth and texture to the art.

Illustration work in this exercise is by Kristin Matoba.

Fashion designer of the original dress: Erika Bueno

This exercise will utilize a photo as an art source. It is best to choose a photo in which the model's pose or clothing contains shadows and highlights that communicate the folds created by the drape of the cloth. Dark colored fabrics are not ideal, as the shadows are more difficult to see.

Your approach to drawing in this exercise is the same as it would be if you were creating a fashion illustration by hand, using the art medium of your choice. *General illustration steps are as follows:*

1. Trace a light outline of the fashion drawing. (See the previous exercise.)
2. Paint a wash of light color over your garment with a large brush tip.
3. Overlay further paint (often using smaller brushes) on the image to indicate the shadows and folds of fabric or shadows in the image.
4. If desired, finish the image by outlining key parts of the garment with a dry, thin outlining brush/color.

Quick Overview of the Process

In this exercise we will be performing the following actions:

1. Load a photo that has shadows and highlights in the garment.
2. Set up layers for tracing and the art mediums.
3. Create/draw a light outline of the figure/garment.
4. Experiment with brush tips, opacity, painting strokes, and so on, on a separate document. Experiment with various brushes, brush tip sizes, and opacity settings to simulate fine art mediums such as watercolors, charcoal, pastels, and others.
5. On a new layer of your fashion pose, create a wash of color in the main areas of the garment (if a wash is appropriate).
6. Using the brushes and knowledge you have learned through experimentation, overlay additional color in the shadow areas of the garment. This can be done on a new layer.
7. If appropriate, re-outline the defining lines of the garment. This can be done on a new layer.
8. Experiment with filters.

New Concepts

o Art Brush tips, accessed through Brush Presets
o Layering of color while painting with Art Brushes
o Artistic filters

Mesa students at the San Diego Museum of Art in Balboa Park

As Prep for This Project

Students at Mesa College are sent to the San Diego Museum of Art to view the art and sketch what they observe. They are given a variety of challenges to complete including the drawing of fabric folds, illustrating sheer fabrics, lace, patterned cloth, and so on. Most have never drawn in this manner, and the end results are not as important as the skill they learn by observation.

Gown Designer: Erika Bueno
Photographer: Jason Christopher
The original photo, reddress.jpg

Step-by-Step

Loading the Photo Files

On the accompanying DVD, there is a folder called **Fashion Exercises**. Inside this folder are exercise folders containing sample files.

1. Choose the *File>Open* menu. Direct the file requestor to the companion DVD or to the location on your hard drive where these files have been moved and stored. Move to the **Fashion Exercises** folder and then the **Ex 11** folder and view the files inside. Select a file to work with. The example used in this exercise is **reddress.jpg.**

2. Choose an image from the samples provided.

3. Rotate the image if necessary, using the *Image>Rotate Canvas* menu.

4. Resize the image so it will fit on an 8.5 × 11 (*Image>Image Size*). Set the height to 10 inches (the width will ajust automatically). Set the resolution to 150 or greater (remembering that the larger the resolution, the larger the file and the smoother the look, but the longer the image will take to print).

5. Save the file with a new name. Save it as a TIF or Photoshop PSD format so that layers can be preserved.

Setting up Layers

We will be using six layers, arranged in the following order, from top to bottom:

o *Details*—where we add back outline detail (if desired)
o *Art medium shadowing*—where we paint with water color, charcoal, etc., brushes
o *Art medium wash*—where we paint with water color, charcoal, etc., brushes
o *Tracing*—for drawing the line art version of the drawing in a gray color
o *Photo*—the original art that we will dim in order to see our work on the upper layers more clearly
o *White fill layer*—so that we can dim the *Photo* layer and not see the checkerboard pattern

The Layers palette with all layers created and ready for use

1. Change the *Background* to a layer so that it can be dimmed. To do this, double-click on the *Background* and when the dialog opens, rename the new layer to *Photo*. Do not dim this layer at this time.

2. Create a *fill layer* by clicking on the **Create new fill or adjustment layer** button at the bottom of the *Layers* palette and sliding up to *Solid Color.* The *Color Picker* will open. Choose white as your color. Click **OK**. Drag this layer to the bottom of the palette, beneath the *Photo* layer

3. Click on the *Photo* layer, and then create a new layer and call this layer *Tracing*. Make sure that this layer is above the *Photo* layer (as it should be, since the *Photo* layer was the active layer prior to making this new layer).

 Levels Tip

If the garment is black, lighten it somewhat using Levels so you can see some of the detail.

4. Create a new layer and call this layer *Art medium wash*. Ensure that this layer is above the *Tracing* layer.

5. Set up the remaining two layers: *Art medium shadowing* and *Details*.

Improving the Quality of the Image and Removing the Background

Before you begin the serious work, it is always a good idea to improve the quality of the artwork. Techniques for this are covered in detail in Basic Exercise #3, Improving the Quality of a Digital Image, pages 184–186.

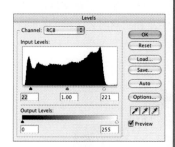

Step 2: Using Levels

Review this information to refresh your skills.

Step 3: Choosing the Sharpen filter.

The image, cropped, and prepped

1. Click on the *Photo* layer to make it the active layer.

2. Since lots of layers are used in this exercise, *Levels* will be employed from the ***Image*** menu, resulting in the adjustment becoming permanent in the artwork. Choose the *Image>Adjustment>Levels* menu command, and when the dialog opens, move the sliders until you feel the lightness/darkness and contrast of the image is good. Click **OK**.

3. Choose the *Filter>Sharpen>Sharpen* or *Filter>Sharpen>Sharpen Edges* menu command. Observe the results and if you are happy with them, continue on. If you do not like the result choose the *Edit>Undo* menu command.

4. Choose the **Crop** tool and crop the image to remove unnecessary background area.

Removing the Background Imagery

The goal now is to remove the busy background from the *Photo* layer. To achieve this, you will create a selection of the background imagery and delete it. The imagery on our example file is busy, and so creating a selection will be a bit more challenging and will entail using **Selection** tools and the **Quick Mask**. You will use skills learned in Basic Exercise #6 (*Creating and Working with Selections*) and Basic Exercise #7 (*Using the Quick Mask to Build or Improve Selections*). Review the techniques at this time if you need a refresher.

Step 2: The initial selection is made.

Edit in Quick Mask Mode

Edit in Standard Mode

1. Click on the *Photo* layer to make it the active layer.

2. Observe the imagery on the art to determine which selection tool will be your best option. Choose the **Selection** tool of choice, and ensure that the **Add to selection** button is active in the options bar. Commence to make a selection of the background art. This doesn't have to be perfect, but the more you select at this point, the less work you will have to perform in the next step. When you are through, you should see the marching ants surrounding the imagery.

3. Double-click on the **Edit in Quick Mask Mode** button in the Toolbox. This opens the *Quick Mask Options* dialog. Choose the color to indicate masked areas (i.e., areas that are protected and therefore not selected). Select a color for the

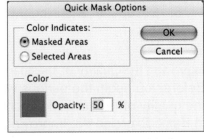

Step 3: Setting Quick Mask Options.

nonmasked areas to be a color significantly different from that of your clothing. We'll use purple, as the default color red is the same as the dress. Click **OK**. You will see that purple is now displayed on the nonmasked areas (i.e., the selection area). You can move in and out of the *Edit in Quick Mask Mode* by clicking on the **Mask** button in the lower Toolbox, which will toggle you between *Edit in Standard Mode* and *Edit in Quick Mask* mode. Notice how the *foreground/background* colors in the Toolbox become black and white when you are *Edit in Quick Mask Mode*.

The Edit in Quick Mask Mode/Edit in Standard Mode button

The Brush tool

4. Choose the **Brush** tool. In the options bar, set the *Mode* to Normal and the *Opacity* and *Flow* to 100%. Choose an appropriate brush tip size from the *Brush Preset* pop-up, keeping it generally relatively small and hard-edged. Use the **Brush** to paint the background and thus improve the masked selection. When you paint with black it will paint with purple and paints the nonmasked areas (i.e., the selected areas). If you want to paint with white (to erase some of the green areas), press the *X* key to exchange the *foreground* and *background* colors. Work with the brush tool, editing the masked and nonmasked areas as necessary. You can increase or decrease the brush tip size by using the square bracket keys, [and], on the keyboard. Move in and out of masking mode to check the selection and thus the progress of your work.

5. When you are happy with the mask, click on the *Edit in Standard Mode* icon and you will see the selection.

6. Press the *Delete/Backspace* key on the keyboard and the busy background will disappear, turning to transparency. Since there is a white fill layer beneath it, you will only see white in the background area of the artwork.

Quick Mask Mode shows the masked areas in purple.

a. The Quick Mask is created.
b. The resultant selection
c. The Background is removed by pressing the Delete/Backspace key.

a   b   c

Creating the Line Art Drawing on the Tracing Layer

1. With the selection active, invert the selection by choosing the *Select>Inverse* menu command. Now the model will be the selected item.

Steps 1–2: Inverting and saving the selection.

2. Save the selection by choosing the *Select>Save* menu command. Type in a name. The selection will be saved as part of the file and can be retrieved at any point in time.

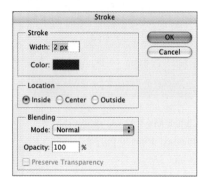

Step 3: Choosing the Edit>Stroke menu command (above) and entering a new setting in the dialog (below).

3. With the selection still active, click on the *Tracing* layer (as this is where we want the line art) and choose the *Edit>Stroke* menu command. A dialog will open. Choose a pixel width of 1 or 2 and a gray color for the stroke color. To change the color to gray, click on the color box and, when the *Color Picker* opens, choose a gray color and click **OK**. Back in the *Stroke* dialog, choose to stroke to the *inside* of the selection (although this is not a critical position). Now, if you hide the *Photo* layer and deselect the selection, you will see an outline of the model.

4. If you want to draw additional detail for your pose, select the **Line** tool, and in the options bar, choose the *Fill pixels* mode and a line weight of 1 or 2 px (make sure it is not inches). Draw in any additional lines or details. Turn the view of the photo on and off as you work to see the details more clearly.

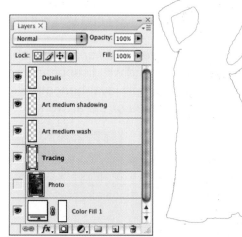

Step 3: Viewing the results of the stroked selection.

Note: You may also add detail by creating further selections and stroking them if this works appropriately. Much will depend on the artwork you chose.

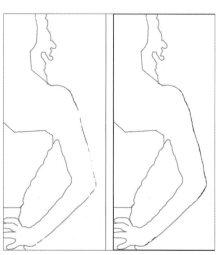

Extra lines added to the artwork

Experimenting with Art Brushes

It is now time to explore using *Art Brushes*. There are a variety of types, which can be accessed through the *Brush Preset pop-up* in the options bar (once a **Brush** tool is selected). If you open the *Brushes* palette you can view the specific settings of brush tips and edit them if you choose. In order to get a sense of how different art brushes work, create a new blank document and experiment with painting on this document.

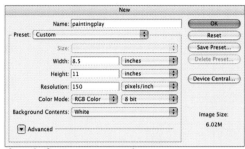

Step 1: Setting up a new document.

1. Choose the *File>New* menu command. Choose a document size of 8.5 × 11 inches, with a white and a resolution of 150. Name the file *paintingplay* and click **OK** and the new document will open.

The Brush tool

2. Click on the **Brush** tool in the Toolbox to make it the active tool. Observe the options bar.

3. Click on the down arrow of the *Brush Preset picker* to open the window. Then click on the arrow in the upper-right corner to open the *Brush Preset Picker menu* and slide down to the *Wet Media Brushes*. Release the mouse and a dialog will open asking if you want to *Replace* or *Append*. Choose *Append*, which will add the new brushes to the existing library, below the current brushes.

Step 3: Loading the Wet Media Brushes into the Preset pop-up and observing the new brush tips.

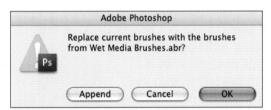

4. Scroll down to the bottom of the presets and hold your mouse over a brush tip. If you wait long enough you will see the name of the tip. This will help you choose brushes for specific end uses. Since we will use watercolor as the medium in this exercise, our experiments will be in this area. You may load a different library of brush tips if you want to work with a dry medium or other type of medium.

5. Open the *Brushes* palette. This will allow you to view additional settings for each brush as you choose it. As you select each

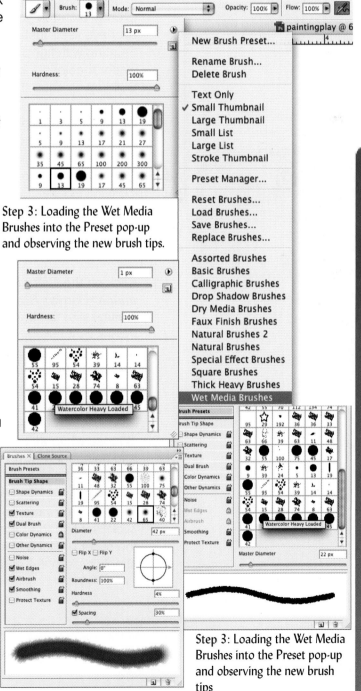

Step 3: Loading the Wet Media Brushes into the Preset pop-up and observing the new brush tips

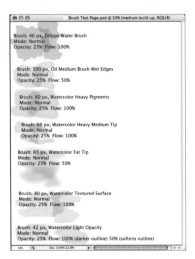

Documenting experiments with
brush tips

brush you can see the various settings that were used to create
it. If you want, you can change or add settings and create a new
Brush Preset. Clicking on the words *Brush Tip Shape* will open a
new window in the palette that shows you more options. There you
have control over the hardness, spacing, and tip shape, among
other things. Read up on the *Brushes* palette on page 171.

6. Move to your document and paint with different brushes. *Explore
   the following:*
   o *Brush diameter* (altered through either the *Preset pop-up* or the
     Brushes palette, or by pressing the [or] keys on the keyboard).
   o *Opacity* and *Flow*, as controlled in the options bar.
   o Various other settings as controlled in the *Brushes* palette.
   o Creating long brush strokes versus short strokes where you
     overlay the area you just painted. You will see that the paint
     overlays itself just as a watercolor would.
   o Painting with light, broad, sweeping strokes, as in laying down a
     wash of color.
   o Building up color through an overlaying process.

7. Create a sample page and use the **Type** tool to label what you did
   as a matter of record.

Adding Canvas and Making the Photo Layer Semitransparent
It will be helpful to view the original photo as you paint, but first we must
make it somewhat transparent. We will also increase the canvas size so
you have some room to test with your brush strokes off to the side of the
artwork.

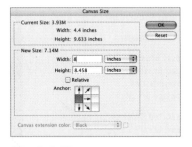

Step 1: Adding canvas.

Steps 1–3: Adding canvas to
the document and changing the
opacity of the photo layer.

1. Click on the *Color Fill 1* layer to make it active. Choose the
   Image>Canvas Size menu. A dialog will open. Increase the
   canvas size to the right of the image by 4
   inches. Set the anchor to the left so that the
   added canvas will appear on the right. Click
   OK and extra canvas will be added. The
   newly added area will have a transparent
   ground.

2. Choose white as the *foreground* color,
   and using the **Paint Bucket** tool, fill the
   transparent area with white.

3. Click on the *Photo* layer to select it. Then
   click+hold on the *Opacity* pop-up and drag
   the slider until the layer opacity is 40% (or
   simply type in the number).

Step 3: Changing the
opacity of the Photo
layer.

Painting a Wash
You are now ready to layer color onto your image.
1. Click on the *Art Medium Wash* layer to make it the active layer.

2. Choose a color for the dress in the *Swatches* or *Color* palette. This will be the *foreground* color in the Toolbox.

3 Choose a brush tip that will allow you to create a wash. The diameter should be rather large and the opacity should be approximately 50%. Test the brush off to the side of your artwork.

4. Paint with broad, sweeping strokes to set down a wash of color. Look through the layers to your photo layer to determine where to paint the wash. You should have learned that holding down the mouse as you sweep with the brush stroke lays the color in a continuous manner without overlay. You do not necessarily need to paint the color to the edge of the outline.

5. Save the file.

The color wash was created using a Watercolor Brush with a tip size of 42 pixels, 25% opacity, and a flow of 50%. Mode was Normal.

Adding Shadows

Now that the wash is complete, you will begin to paint in the overlaying color that defines the shadows in the artwork.

1. Observe the photo image to determine where the shadows exist. If it helps, you can turn the *Art Medium Wash* layer's view off, or change its opacity to a greater transparency so that you can see through it as you lay in the paint for the shadows.

2. Click on the *Art Medium Shadowing* layer to select it.

3. Choose a new brush tip that suits your purpose. Adjust its diameter, opacity, flow, and so on as necessary. Experiment off to the side on the added canvas.

Adding shadows detail using a combination of different brushes, tip sizes, and changing the opacity and flow. This example used Watercolor Heavy Pigment and Light Oil Flat tip brushes.

4. Paint in the shadows, overlaying the paint as you go.

Touching up/Adding Outlining Detail

If appropriate, you can add lines that outline areas that may have become blurred. This is done to accentuate details, to define edges, or for creative effect.

1. Click on the *Details* layer to select it.

2. Choose a color in the *Swatches* or *Color* palette as your outline/detail color (e.g., gray, black, or a deep shade of pink). This will be the *foreground* color in the Toolbox.

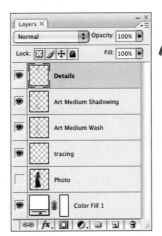

Painting Tip
When painting with the mouse, mimic the movement of the fabric and hair by sweeping and stroking with the mouse.

3. Choose a brush tip that suits your purpose. Typically a dry brush is good for this. Adjust its diameter, opacity, and flow as necessary. Experiment off to the side on the added canvas.

4. Paint in the outlines and detail as necessary.

Adding defining lines on the details layer to accentuate some of the details. The image to the left shows you what was actually drawn on the details layer, and the image on the right shows you the result of all layers.

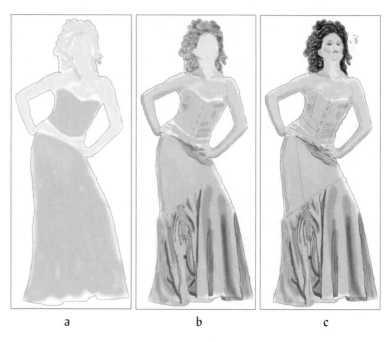

a   b   c

The process of drawing:
a. Creating the wash
b. Adding the shadows
c. Adding the details

You have now finished your drawing simulating a watercolor medium. Explore other paint techniques and mediums.

Using Filters to Add Further Texture to Your Art

Photoshop has various Artistic and Brush Stroke filters that can be added to your drawing, resulting in yet a different look. You can load the *Filter Gallery* to explore these filters. You will need to flatten the artwork so all parts can be affected by the filters.

1. Save your artwork if it is not already saved. It would be wise to save the artwork with a new name so you do not lose the original layered work.

2. Make sure that you are in RGB color mode, as the *Artistic* filters will not work on CMYK artwork. If you need to, choose the *Image>Mode>RGB* menu command to change the color mode to RGB.

3. Choose the *Flatten Image* option in the *Layers* palette menu.

4. Choose the *Filters>Filter Gallery* menu command. The *Filter Gallery* dialog will open.

5. Click on the down arrow of the *Artistic* folder to open it and see all the filter options. Experiment with different filters in both the *Artistic* group and the *Brush Stroke* group. Click **OK** when you are pleased with the artwork, and observe the results.

6. Save the file.

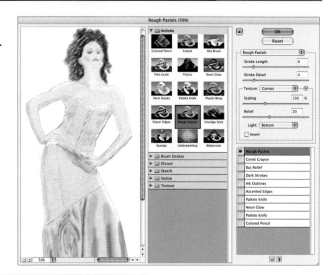

The Rough Pastels filter applied to the artwork

Poster Edges filter

Conte Crayon filter

Angled Strokes filter

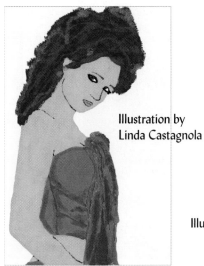

Illustration by
Linda Castagnola

Illustration by
Lele Doan

Wet Art Medium

Dry Media, Oil Pastel

Illustration by Theresa Timony

Model: Kinsey Wilton
Illustration: Renee Anderson

Susan Fefferman

Student Gallery
Art Mediums
Mesa College Fashion Students

Jose Clark

Thais Pacci Barreto

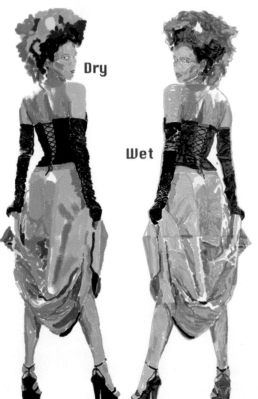

Dry

Wet

Laurel Romeo

Watercolor

Mika Sasaki

Exercise #12: Laying Fabric into Garments

Goal

This exercise will teach you the simple approach to placing fabric into garments and the differences between the *Edit>Paste* and *Edit>Paste Into* commands.

Photoshop Tools and Functions

- ♦ **Selection** tools
- ♦ **Paint Bucket** tool used to fill with pattern
- ♦ *Edit>Fill* with pattern
- ♦ *Edit>Paste* and *Edit>Paste Into*
- ♦ *Edit>Transform*
- ♦ *SnapFashun* garments

Two SnapFashun garments filled with textile prints in this exercise

Quick Overview of the Process

There are several ways in which fabrics can be placed into garments. This exercise will cover the two basic approaches. The first approach uses built-in patterns (in the Pattern Preset library) and the second approach uses scanned fabric or artwork that does not necessarily repeat. Garment flats from SnapFashun will be used as the source of garment art (see Fashion Exercise #7).

In this exercise we will be performing the following actions:

1. Load a drawing of garments.
2. Load a pattern library of textile prints.
3. Use either the **Paint Bucket** tool or a selection and the *Edit>Fill* menu command to fill the inner garment with the pattern.
4. Create a separate document of fabric print.
5. Select a portion of the fabric and copy this to the clipboard.
6. Create a selection of the inside of one of the garments and use the *Edit>Paste Into* menu command to paste the fabric into the selection.
7. Transform the scale and rotation of the print as necessary.

New Concepts

- o Converting an Illustrator AI vector file to a Photoshop raster PSD file
- o Filling selection with pattern
- o Using *Edit>Paste Into*

Sources of Imagery

- o Images on the accompanying DVD
- o Textile print designs created by Mesa College fashion students

Step-by-Step

Loading and Prepping the Garment File

On the accompanying DVD, there is a folder called **Garments**. Inside this folder is a file from Illustrator called **snap1.ai**. This file contains drawings of two garments from the SnapFashun library of flats. We will open this file in Photoshop and convert it to a raster image.

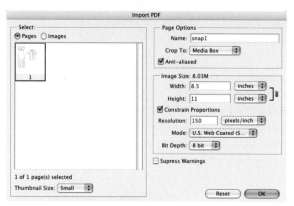

Steps 1–2: Opening an Illustrator file and converting it to raster PSD.

1. Choose the *File>Open* menu. Direct the file requestor to the companion DVD or to the location on your hard drive where these files have been moved and stored. Move to the **Garments** folder and open a file called **snap1.ai**. The Import PDF dialog will open.

2. Click on the *Crop To* pop-up and change it to *Media Box*. This will change the Image Size to 8.5 × 11 inches. Change the *Resolution* to 150 (to reduce the file size) and click **OK**. The image will load into Photoshop. Note that it is on a layer in the *Layers* palette.

3. In the *Layers* palette, choose *Flatten Image* from the palette menu. This will change the layer to a *Background* and flatten the image against a white background so that all parts of the garment are easily read.

4. Double-click on the *Background* and when the dialog opens, rename the new layer *garments*.

5. Save the file as a Photoshop file (e.g., **snap1.psd**).

Step 3: Flattening the image to create a Background.

Flattening the image (left) creates a white background (right).

The Paint Bucket tool

Filling a Garment with Print Using the Paint Bucket Tool

On the accompanying DVD, there is a folder called **Presets**. Inside that folder is a *Pattern Preset* called **textileprints.pat,** which contains textile prints that will be used to fill the garments.

Step 2: Loading a pattern library from the Pattern Preset menu.

1. Choose the **Paint Bucket** tool in the Toolbox.

2. Click on the *Pattern Preset pop-up* and slide

down to the pop-up palette arrow, then *click+hold* and slide over the *Load Patterns* option. When the dialog opens, direct the file requester to the **Presets** folder. Inside this folder you will find a *Pattern* preset file called **textileprints.pat**. Choose this file and click **OK**. When the dialog asks if you want to *Replace* or *Append*, choose the **Replace** option and click **OK**.

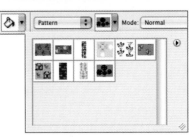

The textilepints pattern library created by Mesa College students

3. Duplicate the garment layer so you have a few garments to play with. In the *Layers* palette menu choose the *Duplicate Layer* option. A new layer called *garments copy* will appear (and you can change the name if you like).

4. Make sure that the *Pattern* option is chosen as the *source for fill area* in the options bar. Choose a pattern from the *Preset Picker*.

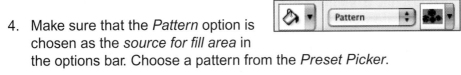

5. Position the **Paint Bucket** tool inside the skirt of the dress and click with the mouse. The dress will fill with pattern. If you do not like your choice of pattern, choose the *Edit>Undo* menu command (or *Cmd/Ctrl+Z* on the keyboard). Select a different pattern and fill the skirt.

6. Choose the **Eyedropper** tool, and click on one of the colors of the print. This will become the *foreground* color in the Toolbox and ultimately, the coordinate solid fabric for the dress.

Step 5: Filling the skirt of the dress with pattern.

7. Choose the **Paint Bucket** tool once again. Change the *source for fill area* to *Foreground* (so that the fill will be with the foreground color in the Toolbox).

Steps 6–8: Filling the bodice and sleeves with a color sampled from the print.

Steps 9–10: Filling the back inner bodice with a deeper value of the bodice color.

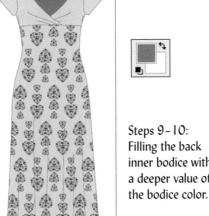

Step 9: Creating a deeper value of the bodice color.

8. Position the cursor inside the bodice of the dress and click. Repeat for the other side of the bodice and then the sleeves.

Step 1: Creating a new document.

9. Double-click on the *foreground* color in the Toolbox to open the *Color Picker*. Lower the value of the current bodice color slightly, and click **OK**.

10. Position your cursor over the inner back of the dress and fill it with a solid color that is slightly darker than the bodice color to indicate the shadow of the back.

Filling a Garment with Print Using the Clipboard and Edit>Paste Into

This technique involves using the **Magic Wand** tool to create selections within the garment and using the clipboard and the *Paste Into* function found in the *Edit* menu to paste fabric into that selection. The extra steps involved are worth the energy as you have the ability to rotate the print in a garment piece. You will fill the shirt with the print you want to utilize.

Step 3: Choosing the Edit>Fill menu command.

1. Create a new document using the *File>New* menu command. Choose a *Resolution* of 150 (the same as the garment document), a *document size* of 8.5 × 11, and white as the *Background Contents*. Name the document **print**. Click **OK** and the document will open.

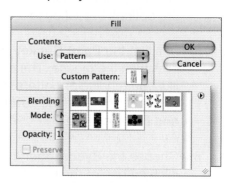

Step 3: Choosing a pattern fill.

2. Choose the **Rectangular Marquee** selection tool and frame off the upper half of the document. You will see marching ants.

3. Choose the *Edit>Fill* menu command. When the dialog opens, click on the *Use* pop-up and choose the *Pattern* option, then click on the down arrow of the *Pattern Picker* and choose a pattern. Leave the Mode as *Normal* and the Opacity set at *100%*. Click **OK** and the selection on your document will fill with pattern.

4. Repeat steps 2 and 3 and fill the lower half of your print document with a second textile pattern.

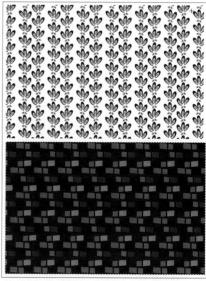

Steps 3–4: Filling the print document with two patterns.

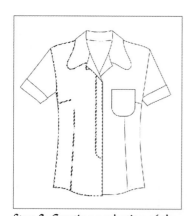

Step 6: Creating a selection of the left front of the shirt.

5. Move to the garment file (**snap1.psd**).

Step 6: Magic Wand settings.

6. Choose the **Magic Wand** tool in the Toolbox. Set the *Tolerance* to a low setting and ensure that *Anti-alias* and *Contiguous* are checked. Click inside one of the shirt fronts and observe the marching ants. Observe also the approximate size of the selection.

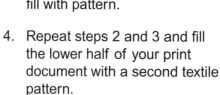

7. Move back to the print image, and using the **Rectangular Marquee**, create a selection of one of the prints that is larger than the shirt front you selected in the garment document. Since the plan is to scale the print down somewhat, choose a fairly large section of the print.

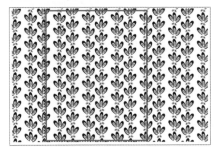

Step 7: Selecting a portion of the print and copying it to the clipboard.

8. Choose the *Edit>Copy* menu command (*Cmd/Ctrl+C*) to copy the print to the clipboard.

9. Move to the garment document. Your selection should still be active. Choose the *Edit>Paste Into* menu command. The print will paste into the selection. The print is a little large for the shirt.

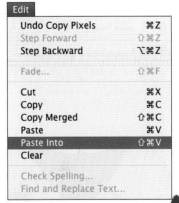

Step 9: Using the Edit>Paste Into menu command.

10. To scale the print, choose the *Edit>Transform* menu command (or *Cmd/Ctrl+T* on the keyboard). You will see a bounding box for the fabric appear on the document. If you move your mouse cursor around the outer edges of the bounding box you will see that it changes according to where you are on the box. If you are at a corner, the double-arrow cursor indicates that you can scale the image. Move the mouse until you see this, then press and hold the *Shift* key on the keyboard while you drag the bounding box smaller. While you are rescaling the image, you may drag it to a new position simply by clicking in the center of the image and moving it. When you are happy with the new scale and with the position of the print, either double-click inside the box, or click on the **Confirm** button in the options bar (the check mark).

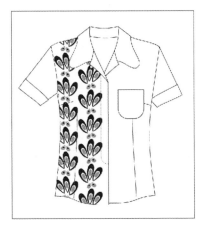

Step 10: The initial pasting in of the print.

Step 10: Rescaling the print using Transformation functions.

Step 10: The resultant scaled print.

Step 11: The layer mask that results once Paste Into is employed.

11. Observe the *Layers* palette at this time and note that you have a new layer. This is a layer mask of the area that you just filled. The fabric can be easily turned "off" by clicking on the eye of the layer to hide its view. Rename this layer to *left shirt print.*

12. Click on the *garments copy* layer to make it the active layer.

13. Repeat the process of steps 6 through 10, this time selecting the left sleeve of the garment, pasting the fabric in, and rotating it to

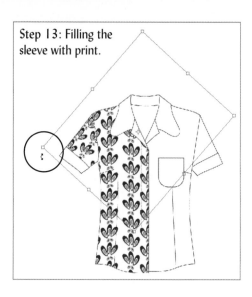

Step 13: Filling the sleeve with print.

match the center grain (the upper fold) of the sleeve. Attempt to match the scale of the print of the front.

14. Rename the layer mask that is created to *left sleeve*. Click on the garment copy layer to make it the active layer.

15. Repeat the steps again to fill the right side of the garment, using a different print. You must always remember to click on the garment layer to make it active, and it is good practice to rename the layer masks as you create them. This time you will try a few new things in an effort to pick up speed, as follows:

o Create the selection with the **Magic Wand** tool.

o Press *Shift+Cmd/Ctrl+V* on the keyboard to use the *Paste Into* command.

o Press *Cmd/Ctrl+T* on the keyboard to start the *Transform* command.

o Use the options bar to scale the print so that you can use the same percentage for the sleeve. Once you have pasted in the print and requested the Transform, click on the **Lock** between the *W* and *H* (width and height) fields in the options bar. Then you only need to type the new percentage in one box. You can also use the options bar to type in the rotation angle when you do the sleeve. You can preview the results as you experiment with different angles.

o Double-click inside the bounding box to complete the transformation.

Step 15: Pasting into and scaling a second print in the right side of the top.

Step 15: Pasting into, scaling, and rotating the second print into the right sleeve.

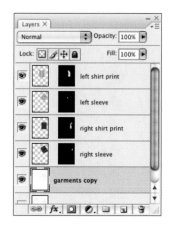

The Layers palette once all the fabrics are pasted in place

Steps 1–2: Filling the collar, cuffs, and pocket with sampled color.

The options bar used in the scaling (above) and rotating (below) operations

Finishing Details

It is now time to fill in the pocket, sleeve cuffs, collar, lapels, and back of the shirt.

1. Choose the **Eyedropper** tool, and sample a color from the print to fill the collar, cuffs, and pocket (using the **Paint Bucket** tool set to *Solid Fill*). Refer to the steps on page 333 of this exercise.

2. Using the **Eyedropper**, choose a different color from each print and fill in the lapels.

3. Use the techniques in the previous section to fill the inner back of the garment with one of the prints. You will need to scale as appropriate. Then, in the *Layers* palette, click on the *Fill interior opacity* pop-up of the new layer and move the slider to approximately 35%, or until the image of the print is quite faint. This represents the back side of the fabric.

Step 3: Using the Layer Fill to create a lighter version of the print in the back inner garment.

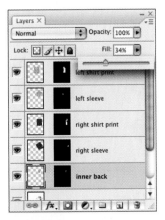

Step 3: Using the Fill interior opacity pop-up to dim the art in the layer.

The final garment showing prints that have been scaled, rotated, and dimmed for various effects

This completes this exercise. You have learned a variety of techniques for creating realistic fabric fills in garments. The next exercise will present yet another technique known as color mapping.

**KING TUT'S
GOLDEN THRONE**
(REPLICA)
PAINTED WOOD WITH GOLD LEAFING
INLAY OF STONE, BONE & IVORY

Student Gallery
Fabric to Garments
Mesa College Fashion Students

Print into furniture by
Susan Fefferman

Greek influenced garments filled with
fabric by Jennifer Norvell

Sugar and Spice

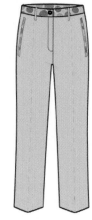

Filling a garment with rendered
and scanned imagery
by Nania Pongpitakkul

Spot print in flats by
Lindsay Hoback

*Print
Design*

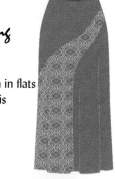

*Texture
Rendering*

Print and denim in flats
by Mary Drobnis

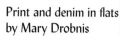

Print and flats by
Paula Tabalipa

Kitty bus by Matt Gilroy

Exercise #13: Laying Fabric into a Fashion Pose Using Color Mapping

Goal
This exercise will teach you a more advanced approach to placing fabric into garments/fashion poses so that a realistic effect can be achieved by having the fabric angle as necessary. A technique called "color mapping" will be used. Essentially, the "grainline" of the fabric is used as a guide.

Photoshop Tools and Functions
- **Selection** tools
- **Line** tool in *Fill pixels* mode
- **Paint Bucket** tool used to fill with solid fill
- **Magic Wand** tool
- *Edit>Paste Into*
- *Edit>Transform*
- Layer masks and layer groups
- **Burn** tool

Artwork and fabrics by Natalie Richardson

Fabric laid into clothing showing proper rotation of the print

Quick Overview of the Process
This exercise builds on Exercise #12 in that you will be using a lot of the same techniques involving *Selections*, *Edit>Paste Into,* and *Rotation* transformations. This time, however, you will be using the clothing on a fashion pose, which requires more angling of the fabric as it is laid into the garment. To understand the process, you will build a color-mapped version of the garment, letting each color represent the angle the fabric will be rotated to when transformed.

In this exercise we will be performing the following actions:
1. Load a line art illustration of a fashion pose and garments.
2. Analyze the garment to determine all the angles that the fabric must be positioned in for a realistic result.
3. Using the **Line** tool and the **Paint Bucket**, create a color map on the garment, in which each color represents the angle of the grain of the textile.
4. Load a document with a textile print. Scale the print to the proper size to relate to the garment document. Use resolution and common sense as your guide.
5. Select a portion of the textile and copy it to the clipboard.
6. On the garment document, use the **Magic Wand** tool to select a colored area of the garment (from the color map).
7. Use *Edit>Paste Into* in conjunction with any additional scaling and rotations necessary to fill the selected area.
8. Repeat for all parts of the garment.

The color map created as a tool for laying in the fabric

New Concepts
- o   Creation of a *color map* to assist in planning rotations of fabric brought into the garment on a fashion illustration
- o   Using *Edit>Paste Into*
- o   Layer masks and layer groups

Nataliepose.tif, the file used in this exercise

Steps 3–6: Creating the angles layer (above) and drawn arrows on the artwork (below), which indicate the angle of the fabric.

Sources of Imagery

o   Fashion illustrations and print designs on the accompanying DVD

Step-by-Step

Loading and Prepping the Fashion Illustration

On the accompanying DVD, there is a folder called **Fashion Exercises**. Inside this folder is a folder called **Ex 13**, and inside this are several files that are used in this exercise.

1. Using the *File>Open* menu command, direct the file requester to **Ex 13** folder inside the **Fashion Exercises** folder and open a file called **nataliepose.tif**. This is a drawing created by student Natalie Richardson.

2. It is always a good idea to look at the image size and resolution of files you are using. Do this with the *Image>Image Size* menu. Note that this file has a resolution of 150 dpi and is approximately 8 × 10 inches in size.

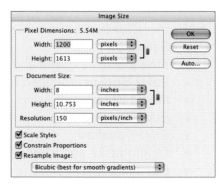

Step 2: Examining image size.

Prior to laying the fabric into the garment, you need to analyze and color block your fashion illustration according to the various "angles" you see within the garment. It is helpful to create a new layer and draw lines on this layer that show the angles of the different areas of the garments, per the grain lines of the garments.

3. In the *Layers* palette, create a new layer and name it *angles*. Make sure that this is placed above the *trace* layer.

4. Choose the **Line** tool. In the options bar, ensure that you are on *Fill pixels* mode. *Click+hold* on the *Geometry options pop-up* and check to add arrowheads to the line. Set the line width at 2 pixels.

5. Choose the color red as your *foreground* color in the Toolbox.

Step 4: Setting up the Line tool to draw with arrowheads.

6. Make sure that you are on the *angles* layer, and draw a series of lines over the garments to indicate the angles that the fabric should be laid in.

Color Blocking the Garments

You will be alternating between the **Line** tool (to assist you in outlining areas in the garment) and the **Paint Bucket** tool (which will allow you to quickly fill in areas that have boundaries) to complete this set of operations. If you want to pick up speed, learn to use the keyboard shortcuts for choosing these tools. *They are:*

Line Tool—U on the keyboard, set as 1 pixel wide, and no anti-aliasing
Paint Bucket Tool—G on the keyboard, set with a *Tolerance* of 15,
and allowed to anti-alias.

The Line tool   Paint Bucket
tool

1. Make a copy of the *trace* layer by choosing *Duplicate Layer* from the *Layers* palette menu. When the dialog opens, name this layer *color blocking*. This is a conservative approach to working with color blocking in that you will always retain the outline layer.

2. Choose the **Line** tool in the Toolbox. *Click+hold* on the *Geometry options* pop-up and *uncheck* the arrowheads. Set the line *Width* to 1 pixel and uncheck *Anti-alias*.

Steps 1–2: Duplicating the outline layer and naming it color blocking.

3. In the *Layers* palette, click on the *color block* layer to make it the active layer.

You are now ready to start color blocking the garments. You will choose unique colors to represent different fabric angles. Anti-aliasing was turned off so that your lines are drawn clearly, and later when you fill the entire area, the amount of anti-aliasing with colors that will not be part of the garment will be reduced.

4. Double-click on the *foreground* color in the Toolbox to open the *Color Picker* and select a unique color, unlike any in your drawing. Click **OK**.

5. With the **Line** tool, draw in a line to define the boundary of one of your color block areas. Zoom in if necessary, and ensure that the line goes all the way to the outline of the garment or some other defining line.

6. Choose the **Paint Bucket** tool. In the options bar, set the *Tolerance* to 15 and leave *Anti-alias* on. (Note: in this case, we want anti-alias to assist us since we want the new fill to meet the outlining color without leaving a halo of old color.)

Step 3: Clicking on the color block layer to make it active.

 Anti-alias?

You do not want the lines you draw to anti-alias so that one color directly meets the next. You do, however, want the fills to anti-alias into the garment outline.

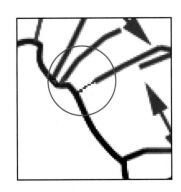

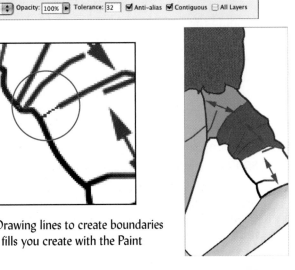

Steps 4–6: Drawing lines to create boundaries for the color fills you create with the Paint Bucket tool.

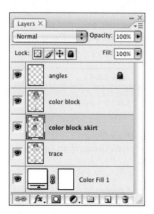

Creating and using a separate layer to build the skirt color blocking

7. Continue to alternate between the **Line** tool and the **Paint Bucket** tool, drawing lines and filling in areas with color. The goal is to color map all areas to define the rotation of the fabric.

Tips:

o Use either the **Line** tool or the **Pencil** tool to touch up spots that don't fill properly.

o If you notice that your outlines are disappearing, you need to lower the *Tolerance* of the **Paint Bucket** tool.

o If two areas of the garment will have fabric on the same angle, you can use the same color to define these areas and then bring the fabric into both of them at the same time. This is not always the best approach, as you may need a large area of fabric.

o Learn to zoom in and out as you work, so you can easily see what you are doing. Use the keyboard shortcuts to do this.

o You can create another copy of the original outline layer for mapping the skirt and keep this separate from the top.

The progression of building the color blocks for the jacket and then the skirt. The arrows on the angles layer are shown and used to assist in planning the color block area.

Loading the Textile Image

We are going to fill the jacket with a herringbone fabric that was rendered using the **Line** tool and grid (see Textile Exercise #9). At this point, you need to set yourself up so that you have the fashion drawing on one page, and your fabric on another page. Ideally, you want to scale the fabric (using the *Image>Image Size* menu command) so that it is already the right scale for your garment, as this will save constant rescaling once you bring the fabric to the garment. This also conserves memory as you send smaller images through the clipboard.

It is helpful to view both the illustration and the fabric at the same zoom level, as you can quickly determine the amount you need to scale the fabric down.

1. Load the file called **herringbone.tif**. This is in the **Ex 13** folder in the **Fashion Exercises** folder.

2. Choose the *Image>Image Size* menu command to observe its size and resolution. You will see that it is at the same resolution as your illustration (i.e., 150 dpi). This is important, as you are now comparing apples to apples between the two images. Click **OK** to close the dialog.

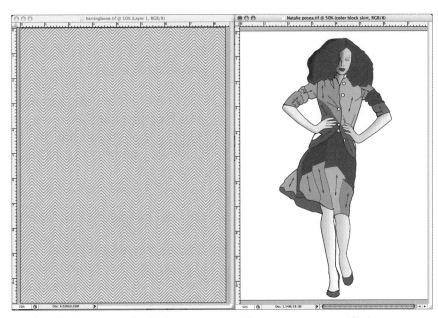

3. Resize your documents and move them side-by-side so you can see both at the same time. Make sure that you are at the same zoom level as well.

Step 3: Comparing the fabric and garment files at the same zoom level.

When you complete this, you will see that the herringbone is a little large in scale for the jacket.

4. Click on the herringbone file to make it the active image. Choose the *Select>Select All* menu command to select the entire image.

5. Choose the *Edit>Transform* menu command, or *press Cmd/Ctrl+T* on the keyboard. A bounding box will surround the fabric.

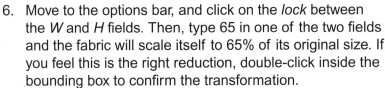

6. Move to the options bar, and click on the *lock* between the *W* and *H* fields. Then, type 65 in one of the two fields and the fabric will scale itself to 65% of its original size. If you feel this is the right reduction, double-click inside the bounding box to confirm the transformation.

The fabric is now ready and in scale to be brought to the garment.

Placing the Fabric in the Color Blocked Garment

In this part of the exercise, you will be moving back and forth between the fabric page and the garment (although you can always use one selection of fabric on the clipboard to be pasted into many different parts of the garment and rotated accordingly). If you leave the two documents side by side you can observe what you are doing, but of course, your monitor resolution has to be high enough to allow you to easily see both documents at one time.

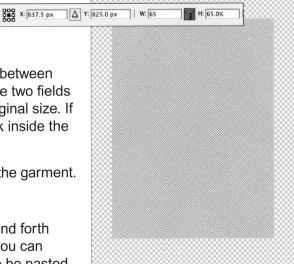

Steps 5–6: Scaling the fabric.

1. Click on the garment document to make it the active file. Since we will be focusing on the jacket, turn off the view of the color blocked skirt in the *Layers* palette.

Note: Additional Shortcuts
You will be using the various tools a lot in this section of the exercise, so learn the keyboard shortcuts that occur in this sequence:
M—Rectangular Marquee
Cmd/Ctrl+C—Copy
W—Magic Wand
Shift+Cmd/Ctrl+V—Paste Into
Cmd/Ctrl+T—Transform

The Rectangular Marquee

The Magic Wand

The next sequence of steps will become a repetitive pattern, so prepare to do these without referring to the text. You may not need to copy the fabric to the clipboard each time, as you may be using the same size of selection for several areas of the color-blocked garment.

2. Determine which part of the jacket you want to place fabric in first, and make a mental note of its size.

3. Click on the fabric page to make it the active document. Choose your **Rectangular Marquee** tool and select an area of fabric that is larger than the area of the garment you want to fill. Using the *Edit>Copy* command (or *Cmd/Ctrl+C*), copy this to the clipboard.

4. Move to the garment page.

5. Click on the *color block* layer to make it the active layer.

6. Choose the **Magic Wand** tool in the Toolbox. Set the *Tolerance* to approximately 12 (but be willing to experiment). Click over the color of the first area of color that you want to fill with fabric. Marching ants will appear around the color. Confirm visually that you got all parts you wanted to select.

7. Choose the *Edit/Paste Into* menu to bring the fabric into the selected area. A new layer and layer mask will appear and you can perform transformations on this layer.

8. If you need to scale or rotate the fabric, choose the *Edit/Transform* menu command (or *Cmd/Ctrl+T* on the keyboard). A bounding box will appear around the fabric.
   o If you need to *scale* the fabric, do so by dragging one of the corners inwards or outwards while holding the *Shift* key.
   o If you need to rotate the fabric, move your cursor over a corner of the bounding box until you see the curved rotation cursor, then *click+hold+drag* diagonally to rotate the fabric. You can match the edge of the fabric to the angle of the arrows that are still showing.
   o Reposition the fabric by *clicking+dragging* inside the bounding bond.
   o Double-click inside the bounding box to confirm the transformation.

Steps 5–8: Using Paste Into to bring fabric to the block and then performing a rotation.

The Move tool

9. Repeat steps 2 through 8 to lay fabric into all the remaining color blocked areas. If you will be using the same image of the fabric on the clipboard, continue to repeat steps 5 through 8. You may want to name the layer masks as you create them to assist in keeping things organized later.

10. Use the **Move** tool to move any of the fabrics (layer mask) around and line it up with an adjacent fabric. This is particularly important with striped and similar linear fabrics. You will have many layers. Each one may be altered independently.

11. Save the file.

The completed jacket, with the arrows of rotation (left) and without the arrows (right)

Managing Layers

Since you have many layers to manage, you can do one of three things:

- ♦ Create a *Layer Group* and place all the layer masks into the layer group.
- ♦ *Merge* all the layer masks into one layer (by selecting all the layers and choosing the *Merge Layers* option in the *Layers* palette menu).
- ♦ *Flatten* the image (by choosing *Flatten Image* in the *Layers* palette menu).

We will create a Layer Group.

To create a Layer Group:

1. Extend the *Layers* palette so you can see all the layers.

2. Click on the first layer mask of fabric (Layer 1).

3. Hold the *Shift* key on the keyboard and click on the last layer mask (Layer 10). All the layer masks should now be highlighted.

4. Choose *New Group from Layers* in the *Layers* palette menu. A dialog will open. Name the group and assign a color if you like. Click **OK**.

The various operations of creating a Layer Group

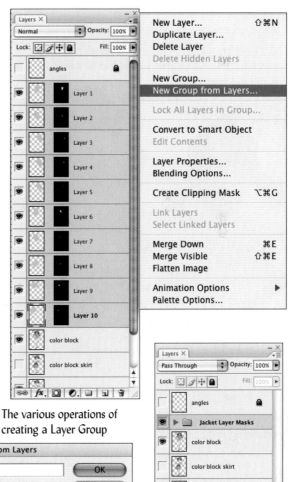

Placing the Fabric in the Color Blocked Garment

You can now repeat the same process for placing fabric in the skirt. This time we will use a different fabric file, one that will coordinate with the herringbone fabric.

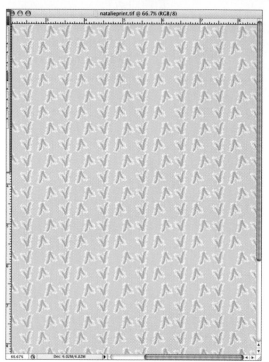

The print file called natalieprint.tif, used to fill the skirt in this exercise

1. Load the file called **natalieprint.tif**. This is in the **Ex 13** folder in the **Fashion Exercises** folder.

2. Choose the *Image>Image Size* menu command to observe its size and resolution. You will see that it is at the same resolution as your illustration (i.e., 150 dpi).

3. Resize your documents and move them side-by-side so you can see both at the same time. You will see that the print is a good scale to work with the skirt.

4. Click on the print file to make it the active image.

5. Choose your **Rectangular Marquee** tool and select an area of fabric that is larger than the area of the garment you want to fill. Using the *Edit>Copy* command (or *Cmd/Ctrl+C*), copy this to the clipboard.

6. Move to the garment page. Turn on the view of the *color block skirt* layer and click on it to make it the active layer. Turn off the view of the *color block* layer associated with the jacket. Ensure that the *angles* layer is in view, as the arrows help you with the rotations.

7. Repeat steps 6 through 10 on page 344, filling the skirt with the print and rotating as necessary to create a realistic result. When you get to the section that is the back inner skirt (at the hem), you can lower the *Fill interior opacity* for the layer so it is somewhat transparent.

The process of bringing the print fabric into the skirt and performing rotations on it

8. Create a layer group for the skirt layer masks and call it *Skirt Layer Masks*. Assign a color if you like to the layer group (in the dialog), and click **OK**.

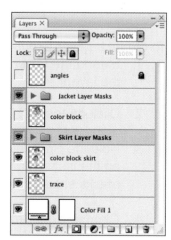

Step 8: Creating a new layer group for the skirt layer masks.

9. In the *Layers* palette, turn off the view of the layer mask groups. You now have your finished garment.

![Tip icon] **Conserve Memory**
Exercise caution when selecting the fabric to copy to the clipboard, and try to select just enough, and not extra, as you will increase file size with large sections of fabric in the many layer masks.

Final Touches

There are a few things that you can do to add some pizazz to the image. You will need to flatten the image first so you can easily paint and adjust it.

1. Save the file with a new name so that you don't lose the original with all the color blocking. Save the file as **natalieposeflat.tif.**

2. Flatten the image by choosing the *Flatten Image* option in the *Layers* palette menu. All layers will flatten to a *Background*.

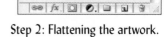

Step 2: Flattening the artwork.

3. Choose the **Burn** tool in the Toolbox and paint over the areas where shadowing should occur. You will be guided by the defining lines that were drawn and by the areas where the fabric changes angles.

4. Using the **Eyedropper** tool, select a color from the herringbone print (which will become the *foreground* color in the Toolbox). Then, using the **Paint Bucket** tool, you can fill in the pockets, collar, and buttons. You can draw the missing collar (on the left side) and fill this in with color as well.

5. Save the file again.

The final artwork with shadowing and final fills

Eva Neilson

Student Gallery
Fabric Insertions
Mesa College Fashion Students

Printed Trendy

Lakiesha Bell

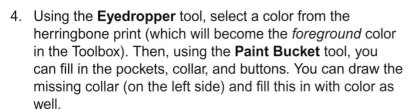

Mildred Carney

Susan Fefferman

Monica Mitchell

swamp eyelash–mesh shrug

pinstripe cowl tank

Keith Antonio

Leticia Leon

Misty Frank

Student Gallery
Fabric Insertions
Mesa College Fashion Students

Kanae Otaka

Exercise #14: Working with Clipping Paths

Goal
This exercise will teach you how to use a *clipping path* to define transparent areas in fashion photos to facilitate layout in published documents.

Photoshop Tools and Functions
- **Selection** tools
- **Line** tool in *Fill pixels* mode
- **Paint Bucket** tool used to fill with solid fill
- **Magic Wand** tool
- *Edit>Paste Into*
- *Edit>Transform*
- Layer masks and layer groups
- **Burn** tool

Photo styling and photo
by Petra Ostermuencher

Quick Overview of the Process
Clipping paths are used to isolate imagery from its background and create a background that is transparent once exported to a publishing package. This can facilitate printing only the foreground and placing Photoshop images in other applications where you want the background to be transparent.

In fashion, clipping paths are used in prepping garments for catalogue layouts. You can easily stack garments in a desktop publishing package for creative layout.

In this exercise we will be performing the following actions:
1. Load a photo of a garment that has been styled and photographed.
2. Using **Selection** tools, create a quick selection of the background area around the garment. This does not have to be perfect.
3. Inverse the selection so that the garment is now the active selection. Save the selection.
4. Convert the selection to a work path.
5. Using vector-based tools, edit the clipping path to best outline the garment.
6. Create a clipping path from the work path.
7. Use *Edit>Paste Into* in conjunction with any additional scaling and rotations necessary to fill the selected area.
8. Repeat for all parts of the garment.

Note: **Vector Editing**
The processes and tools used in this exercise involve the vector-based tools in Photoshop. You can use these tools as an alternate approach to creating a selection and will do so if you are comfortable working with vector tools.

New Concepts
- o   Work paths
- o   Vector tools (Pen, Path Selection, Direct Selection, Add Anchor Point, etc.)
- o   Clipping paths
- o   Using *Edit>Paste Into*
- o   Layer masks and layer groups

Step-by-Step
Loading and Prepping the Image

On the accompanying DVD, there is a folder called **Photo Styling**. Inside this folder are several images that can be used for this exercise. These garments were prepped and photographed as part of a fashion photo styling class at Mesa College.

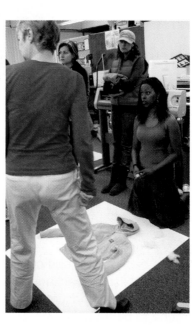

Note: Photo Styling Images

The photos provided in the Styled Garment folder on the accompanying DVD were taken in the Photo Fashion Styling class at Mesa College. Students in this course learn how to prep and style a garment for catalogue and other end uses. The instructor, Susan Linnet Cox, has authored a book called "Photo Styling. How to Build Your Career and Succeed," published by Allworth Press. ISBN: 1-58115-452-6

1. Using the *File>Open* menu command, direct the file requester to the **Photo Styling** folder on the companion DVD. Open the file called **Petrajacket.jpg**. This image was posed and photographed by Petra Ostrameuncher, fashion student.

2. Choose the *Image>Image Size* menu command to learn about the image. You will see that the image has a resolution of 150 and it measures approximately 7 inches wide by 5 inches tall. (Note that the original image was shot at 300 dpi, but was reduced to 150 to keep the file size manageable for this exercise.)

Steps 2–4: The original image of the styled jacket (lower left) and the image with adjustments and cropping (below).

3. Use *Levels* to improve the contrast and brightness of your image, if necessary (*Image>Adjustments>Levels*). Use the *Sharpen* filters to sharpen the art if necessary (*Filter>Sharpen*). See Basic Exercise #3 to review these techniques.

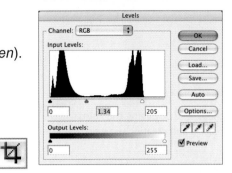

4. Choose the **Crop** tool and drag a box around your garment to crop away the area you don't want. Once you have created the cropping box, you can adjust its width and height by clicking on the drag boxes on each side and moving them. Double-click inside the box when you are through.

Step 3: Using Levels to improve the image.

Creating a Selection of the Garment

You will select the background of the image and then invert it to select the garment.

1. Choose the **Magic Wand** tool, and set the *Tolerance* to 32. Click in the background area of the image to select the background. Observe the selection. You may perform any of the following to get a good selection of the nongarment area of the image.

   o Use the *Select>Grow* menu to enlarge the selection slightly.

   o Use the *Select>Similar* menu to select other areas of white (e.g., the area between a bent sleeve and the body).

   o Use the **Add to Selection** button in the options bar and the **Rectangular Marquee** tool to select and add areas of the background image that were not included in the original selection.

   o Use the **Magic Wand** tool and press and hold the *Shift* tool to add to the selection.

Step 1: Creating a selection with the Magic Wand tool.

Note: The most difficult part of the jacket image is the area between the right arm and the body of the garment. Do not worry about getting a perfect selection as you can use the clipping path to assist you later.

Note: You may also use the **Quick Selection** tool for this selection task if you have CS3 or CS4.

2. When you feel you have a good selection of the nongarment area, reverse the selection by choosing the *Select>Inverse* menu command.

3. Save the selection by choosing the *Select>Save Selection* menu command. Name the selection and click **OK**.

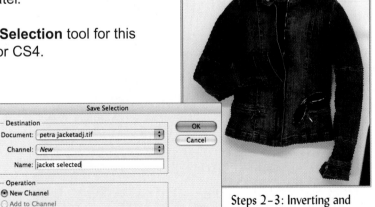

Steps 2-3: Inverting and saving the selection.

The Work Path

Step 3: Converting the Background to a layer and dimming it using an Opacity setting of 80%.

The various vector drawing and editing tools

 Vector Editing Tip
When using the Add Anchor Point tool, the cursor changes to the Direct Selection tool when you are directly above an existing anchor point. This allows you to easily edit the points, moving them where you need them.

Step 5: Using the Direct Selection tool to select points and using the various editing tools to adjust the path around the garment.

Creating and Editing a Clipping Path

You will turn the selection into a *work path* and then edit the path using an assortment of vector-based tools.

1. Open the *Paths* palette by choosing the *Window>Path* menu or opening it in the palette dock.

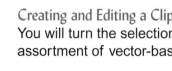

2. With the selection still active, click on the **Make work path from selection** button at the bottom of the *Paths* palette. The marching ants marquee will disappear and be replaced by a black outline, which is actually a vector path. If you observe the *Paths* palette, you will see the *Work Path* of the garment there. Remember that a work path is not an actual drawn image, it is simply a memory of the path. You will need to proceed in order to turn this into something you can use.

3. In order to see the black outline more clearly (since you are working on a dark garment), we will change the *Background* to a layer, and then dim the layer using the *Opacity* setting. Double-click on the *Background* in the *Layers* palette, and then rename it *Photo*. Then, move the opacity setting of the layer to 80%.

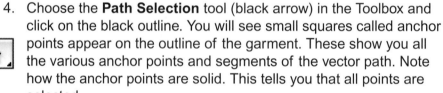

4. Choose the **Path Selection** tool (black arrow) in the Toolbox and click on the black outline. You will see small squares called anchor points appear on the outline of the garment. These show you all the various anchor points and segments of the vector path. Note how the anchor points are solid. This tells you that all points are selected.

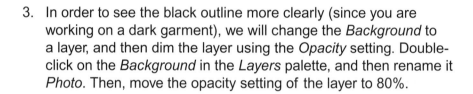

5. Choose the **Direct Selection** tool (white arrow, stacked beneath the Path Selection tool). Use this tool to click on an anchor point. Note how the selected point is solid and the other points are hollow. The **Direct Selection** tool allows you to edit individual points. When you click on a point attached to a curved segment, you will see direction lines extend from the point. You may click on the little square at the end of a direction line and use this to edit the arc of the curve. The goal is to adjust all the anchor points, and segments to better fit the outline of the garment. *Editing procedures include:*

   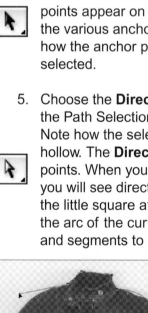

   o *Click+hold* on an anchor point and drag it to move it to a new position.
   o Click on an anchor point attached to a curve, view the direction line, and then *click+hold+drag* on the square to readjust the arc of the curve.
   o Use the **Add Anchor Point** tool to add anchor points where you need them in order to better adjust the work path to fit the edge of the garment.
   o Use the **Delete Anchor Point** tool to remove unnecessary points.

o   Use the **Convert Point** tool to change an anchor point from a corner point (connecting a straight segment to a straight or curved segment) to a smooth point (connecting curves).

o   Edit the work path/points as necessary with the goal of having the work path surround the outside of the jacket as closely as possible. *The following tips may help you:*

o   Learn to use the *Cmd/Ctrl* key as an aid to toggle between the **Direct Selection** tool and the **Add Anchor Point** tool.

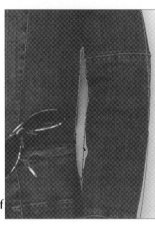

Editing in process: The goal is to move and adjust the anchor points of the path so that it tightly surrounds the image.

o   Learn how to press and hold the *Spacebar* on the keyboard in order to *click+drag* pan around the image as you work.

o   Zoom in and out of your work to assist you in tough areas. Sometimes it is easier to see things when zoomed in, and at other times it is necessary to zoom out.

o   Don't be afraid to drag/extend the direction lines of curves in order to arc a curve more.

o   Sometimes you need to add two points close together in order to move gracefully around a strong elbow bend (or a similar shape).

o   Don't add tons of anchor points; learn how to use the Bezier curves to achieve the same result but with fewer points to manage.

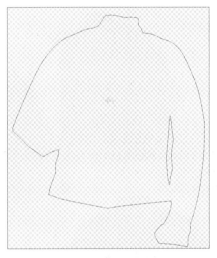

The final path (with the image of the jacket turned off temporarily)

At this point in time, you have two options: you can either continue and make the clipping path (which is the focus of this exercise), or you can create a selection (using *Make Selection* in the *Paths* palette) and invert it to remove the background. We will continue with the clipping path route, but do understand that you can use the vector tools as an aid to creating or improving a selection.

To Save the Path as an Image Clipping Path

You are now ready to convert the work path to a *Clipping Path*.

1. Using the *Paths* palette menu, save the work path as a path.

2. Choose *Clipping Path* from the *Paths* palette menu, set the following options, and click **OK**.

o   For *Path*, choose the work path you want to save. Since you only have one in this document you can choose the one that is selected by default (in the pop-up menu).

Saving the path (above and above right) and creating a clipping path (right and below)

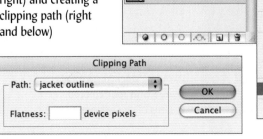

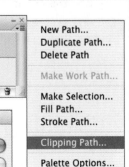

o   For *Flatness*, leave the flatness value blank to print the image using the printer's default value. If you experience printing errors, enter a flatness value to determine how the PostScript interpreter approximates the curve. See Adobe's Help files for further info.

3.   If you plan to print the file using process colors, convert the file to CMYK mode (using *Image>Mode*).

4.   Save the file by doing one of the following:

o   To print the file using a PostScript printer, save in Photoshop EPS, DCS, or PDF format.

o   To print the file using a non-PostScript printer, save in TIFF format and export to Adobe InDesign, or some other publishing package. In Photoshop, you will not see the background disappear, but when you take the image into InDesign (or some other publishing package), the background will not exist.

prepped denim jacket for garment catalogue layout

Garments stacked in Photoshop (left) and in InDesign (right). The background of the image is clipped from view in publishing packages.

Changing Colors of the Garment

You can use color adjustments to change the colors of the garment and still retain the texture and tones of the fabric. In the example below the color of the jackets was changed using the *Image>Adjustment>Hue/Saturation* menu command and checking *colorize.* Each version was saved and placed into InDesign.

Layout of stacked garments created with four colored versions of the original file

This completes the fashion exercises.

Textile Design

In this chapter, you will learn how to create textile prints and rendered fabrics. Print design involves the use of motifs and repeat networks. Textile rendering is a process whereby you learn how to paint or create a fabric that looks like the source textile.

Motif and Textile Print development by Julie Velasquez

The first exercise introduces you to a filter in Photoshop called *Pattern Maker*. This filter allows you to build quick patterns by randomly slicing your original art and putting it in repeat. The second exercise teaches you how to extract a motif from an existing piece of fabric and then build a repeating pattern of the motif using the *Define Pattern* command. In the third exercise you learn how to develop and create motifs using transformations and other design approaches. Exercise #4 will teach you how to build more complicated repeats of a motif through the use of block, brick, and half-drop networks. Exercise #5 will show you how to use Photoshop's *Offset* filter to build repeats and Exercise #6 will introduce some creative approaches to developing more interesting repeat patterns. In Exercise #7 you will learn how to plan for and set up to create multiple colorways of one print. You will develop a custom color palette and save this for future use. You will then learn how to build the multiple colorways in Exercise #8. In Exercise #9 you will learn how to use various Photoshop tools and filters to render fabrics such as corduroy, denim, and tweed, and in Exercise # 11 you will learn how to build a plaid using a layer mask. At times, it may be necessary to build or render fabrics in actual scale, so Exercise #10 will teach you how to use a "pixel ruler" to measure an existing fabric and replicate it in scale. The last exercise, Exercise #12, will teach you how to render knits and how to use the Pattern Fill and Pattern Stamp tool as aids.

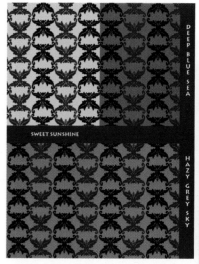

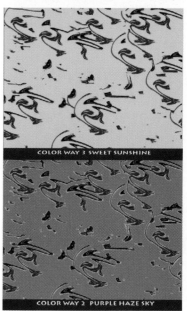

Exercises include:

Exercise #1	Using the Pattern Maker Filter (CS3)
Exercise #2	Extracting a Motif to Create a New Pattern Design
Exercise #3	Motif Development
Exercise #4	Creating Repeat Patterns Using the Block, Brick, and Half-Drop Repeat Networks
Exercise #5	Using the Offset Filter to Create Repeats
Exercise #6	Creative Techniques for Pattern Repeat
Exercise #7	Planning Multiple Colorways for Textile Prints and Creating a Custom Palette
Exercise #8	Building Multiple Colorways for Textile Prints
Exercise #9	Rendering Fabrics
Exercise #10	Rendering Fabrics to Scale
Exercise #11	Rendering Plaids in Photoshop
Exercise #12	Rendering Knits

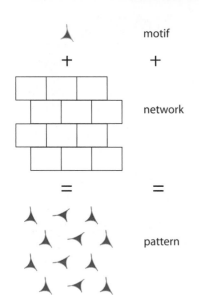

motif

+

network

=

pattern

The evolution of pattern

Variation of half-drop repeat by
Bianca Berry

Block repeat by Sarah Mathes

General Textile Terminology

Motif—An element (or elements) of design, developed to become the basic unit that is typically repeated in textile patterns.

Network— The systematic manner in which motifs are repeated to create a pattern. Examples include block, brick, and half-drop.

Pattern—The resulting imagery created when a motif repeats in a regular design network.

motif + network = pattern

Photoshop Fill Pattern Terminology

Pattern —The result of motifs repeated in a systematic manner. Photoshop offers several methods by which to achieve pattern. You may use the *Edit>Define Pattern* menu command to create and add a pattern to the pattern library. These patterns may be applied using the *Fill* command, the **Paint Bucket**, or the **Pattern Stamp** tool. The *Pattern Maker* filter allows you to slice an image and create random patterns.

Pattern Preset—The way a pattern is stored for future retrieval. It becomes part of the *Pattern library* and is accessed through the *Pattern Picker*.

Tiling—The method Photoshop uses to create a fill pattern. Patterns begin tiling from the upper-left corner of the document and repeat in a left-to-right and top-to-bottom sequence until the selection is filled.

Pattern Tile—An area defined either by a selection made with the **Rectangular Marquee** tool. The tile **must** be rectangular or square and it becomes the basic unit of design that repeats.

Rendering—An art technique or method by which fabrics are created/ drawn to look like the original fabric. This technique is used for nonmotif types of fabrications such as corduroy, plaids, and twills.

Things to Note When Working with Fill Patterns

Patterns use an incredible amount of memory. As you start to use them, you may find the following:

- File size increases.
- Printing slows down and can occasionally refuse to work.
- Screen refreshing takes longer.

5.

Exercise #1: Using the Pattern Maker Filter (CS3)

Goal

This exercise teaches you how to use Photoshop's Pattern Maker filter to create quick seamless patterns. You may use your own images or utilize the art samples provided on the DVD.

Photoshop Tools and Functions

The fc
repeai

Ge

♦ **Selection** tool
♦ Layers
♦ *Pattern Maker* filter
♦ *Fill* layers

Quick Overview of the Process

Til
Us

The *Pattern Maker* filter allows you to quickly generate multiple patterns from artwork on a layer or artwork placed on the clipboard. The source image is not used in its exact form; rather, it is sliced and reassembled, so don't be surprised by the results.

In this exercise we will be performing the following actions:

Us

1. For the first approach, load a digital image of a small art image to be used as a motif and copy this image to the clipboard.
2. Create a new document and set up a layer for your pattern.
3. Use the *Pattern Maker* filter to generate several patterns and then choose your favorite.
4. Create a *fill* layer placed under the pattern layer and experiment with background colors.
5. For the second approach, load an image with art, and duplicate the layer that contains the art.
6. Use the *Pattern Maker* filter to generate several patterns and then choose your favorite.

Wi

Of

Am

New Concepts

Sm

o *Pattern Maker* filter
o Using a *fill layer* as a colored background for textiles

Sources of Imagery

Sa

o Digital images of artwork that are motif-oriented

Step-by-Step

Pre
Sh

Load the Initial Art Image and Copying It to the Clipboard

On the accompanying DVD (or location on your hard drive you moved the files to), you will find a folder called **Textile Design Exercises.** Inside this folder is a folder called **TD Exercise 1**, and inside this folder are several motif-type images.

Tile

1. Using the *File>Open* menu, direct the file requestor to the **TD Exercise 1** folder and load an image from the folder. There are four flower images and one of a door knob. The example used in this exercise is **flower2.psd**. Note that all the images load as a single layer and the motif sits against a transparent background. These files have been prepped in this manner.

Tile
Up

Patterns generated using the Pattern Maker filter in Photoshop

Note: Pattern Maker
Imagery
Imagery created with the Pattern Maker filter typically does not strongly resemble the original artwork, yet is interesting and can be easily used as backgrounds for art, Web pages, and other applications.

flower2.psd

Smudge

Brush

Eyedropper

♦ **Clone Stamp**—to "borrow" imagery from neighboring areas to paint over another area. Press the *Opt/Alt* key while you "sample" an area (the clone stamp turns white and "rises" while you pick up a color) and then release the *Opt/Alt* key when you paint with a color (the clone stamp turns black and lowers).

♦ **Smudge**—allows you to drag one color onto another to blend them together.

♦ **Brush**—to paint in new parts.

♦ **Eyedropper**—to locate/sample colors and make them become the current color.

Magic Wand

In our example:

1. Choose the **Magic Wand** tool. In the options bar, set the *Tolerance* to approximately 20. Click in the background area of the fabric.

Add to selection

2. Click on the **Add to selection** icon in the options bar. Continue to click with the **Magic Wand** to select more of the image.

3. Grow the selection if necessary by choosing the *Select>Grow* menu. Continue this process until you have the background selected.

The Layer palette showing the original art and the motif layers

4. Choose the *Select>Inverse* menu to invert the selection.

5. Choose the *Edit>Copy* menu to copy the motif to the clipboard.

6. Choose the *Edit>Paste* menu to paste the motif back it. It will paste onto its own transparent layer. Rename this layer *Motif*.

a

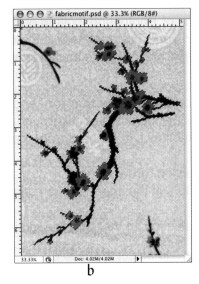

b

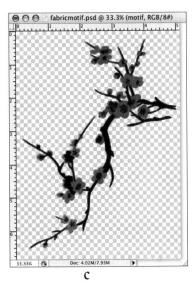

c

Isolating the motif:
a. Selecting the background/nonmotif area
b. Inverting the selection, then copying the image to the clipboard
c. Pasting the image back in from the clipboard, which places it on its own layer, then turning the view of the original artwork off

7. Hide the original layer and observe the edges of the motif. Perform any cleanup work necessary on create a nice edge on the motif.

To Build the Repeat Fabric

1. Keep the image of the original fabric hidden.

2. Select the motif (using the *Select>All* menu command).

Step 3: Naming the pattern.

3. Choose the *Edit>Define Pattern* menu. A dialog will open. Name the motif. The name **motif 1** was used for our example. Click **OK**.

4. Create a new file, making it approximately 8 × 10 inches large. Choose a *Resolution* of 200 (the same as your motif resolutions), a *Color Mode* of RGB, and a Transparent *Background Content*. Name the document *Fabric 1* and click **OK**. A document will open with one layer that is transparent. Rename *Layer 1* layer to *Pattern*.

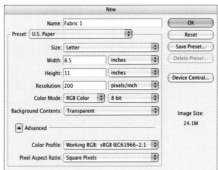

Step 4: Creating a new document for the pattern.

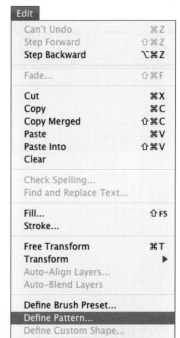

Step 3: Using the Edit>Define Pattern menu command.

5. In the *Layers* palette, click on the *Pattern* layer to make it active.

6. Choose the *Select>All* menu. This selects the entire document so that you may fill the selection in the next step.

7. Choose the *Edit>Fill* menu command. When the dialog opens, choose the *Pattern* option from the *Use* pop-up in the dialog. In the custom *Pattern* pop-up, click and slide over to the *Motif 1* pattern. Click **OK**. The document will fill with the **motif 1** artwork in a simple block repeat. You will see the repeated motifs on a transparent ground.

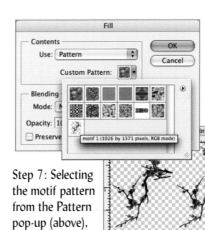

Step 5: Making the Pattern layer active.

Step 7: Selecting the motif pattern from the Pattern pop-up (above), and the resulting pattern (right).

Creating a Fill Layer for the Background Color of the Pattern

Your pattern exists on a transparent ground. Building a *fill* layer under the pattern layer allows you to complete your pattern image and easily experiment with different background colors.

1. If you want to use the approximate same background color as your original fabric, use the **Eyedropper**

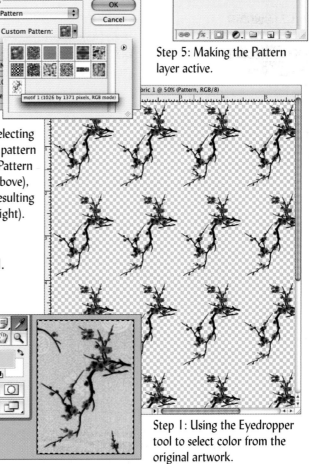

Step 1: Using the Eyedropper tool to select color from the original artwork.

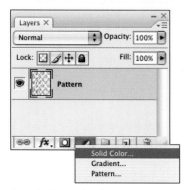

Step 3: Using the Create new fill or adjustment layer button to create a fill layer.

Step 4: Repositioning the layers so the fill layer is beneath the Pattern layer.

Step 1: Double-clicking on the fill layer thumbnail to change the fill color.

tool to select a color from your **fabricmotif.psd** file. This color will become the *foreground* color in the Toolbox.

2. Move to the **Fabric 1** file, using the *Window* menu or by clicking on the document to make it active. Deselect all layers by clicking away from the *Pattern* layer.

3. Click on the **Create new fill or adjustment layer** button at the bottom of the *Layers* palette and slide up to the *Solid Color* option. Release the mouse and the *Color Picker* will open. Since the current color is the color you want, simply click on the **OK** button to accept the color. You will now see a *Color Fill* layer of the light green color.

   Right: The fill layer creates the background color of the fabric.

4. Click on the *Pattern* layer and drag it above the *fill* layer.

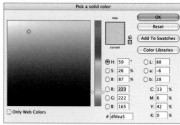

Step 3: Changing the fill layer color in the Color Picker.

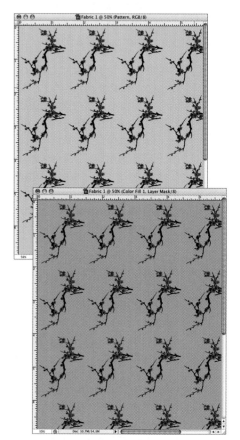

The new colorway created by changing the fill layer color

Quick Color Changes of the Color Fill Layer

Using a *Solid Color Fill layer* allows you to quickly experiment with different background colors for your pattern.
To change the background colors:

1. Double-click on the *Color thumbnail* in the *Color Fill* layer. This will open the *Color Picker*.

2. Choose a new color from the *Color Picker*, and click **OK**. You will now see the results.

3. Continue to experiment with new colors for your fill until you find the one you want to use.

Experiment with different motifs and color fills.

Exercise #3: Motif Development

Goal

The goal of this exercise is to introduce methods by which motifs may be developed to create more interesting imagery for fabric design.

Original motif

Photoshop Tools and Functions

- Transformations such as *Scale*, *Rotate*, *Flip*, *Distort*, etc.
- **Selection** tools
- **Drawing/Painting** tools

Variations of the original

Comments on Motif Development

To begin a pattern design, you will need to find or develop a motif. This is a single unit or element of design. One can find motifs everywhere: in design books, on napkins, on matchbox covers, in magazines. If you are afraid to create your own motif, begin by using one that is easy to draw such as a stick person, a simple geometric shape.

There are certain characteristics that are common to all motifs. *These are:*

Central Point—Each motif tends to have a central focus point. Generally, this is in the center of the motif. Noncentered focal points typically go hand in hand with asymmetrical motifs, and these offer different looks when rotated and flipped.

Symmetrical or Asymmetrical—Motifs may be symmetrical or asymmetrical. Asymmetrical motifs lend themselves to a greater variety of repeat systems and they produce a different feel in the pattern. Symmetrical motifs may not noticeably be flipped and rotated as much as asymmetrical motifs, therefore the number of variations is reduced.

Amount of Positive and Negative Space—Included in a unit of repeat is the motif itself, and the amount of space around it. This is called positive and negative space. The amount of open space (or negative space included around the image) will cause a repeat pattern to be "open" or "tight" in its layout once patterning begins.

The motif to the right is a simple cactus motif. It is slightly asymmetrical and the focal point of the motif is more or less in the center. This motif will be used as an example throughout this chapter. You may use this motif (supplied on the Art DVD) or you may create one of your own.

The cactus motif

Quick Overview of the Process

In this exercise we will be performing the following actions:

1. Choose or design a motif.

2. Perform a series of operations to create variations of the original motif image, each one utilizing a different approach to motif development.

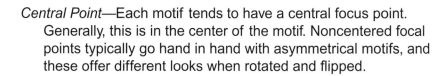

New Concepts

- o Textile motif manipulation techniques
- o Filter Gallery

Step-by-Step

The following instructions walk you through various approaches to motif development. Choose one motif as your starting point, and walk it through the various operations to create multiple variations on a theme.

Prepping the Motif

There are two operations that assist in motif development. The first is reducing the number of colors in the artwork. Techniques for this type of work are discussed in Basic Exercise #8 beginning on page 213. The second operation involves separating the motif from its background. *This can be achieved by performing the following steps:*

1. If the imagery is on the *Background*, change the background to a layer by double-clicking on it and renaming the layer to *motif*.

2. Choose the **Magic Wand** or other selection tool to select the background and remove it by pressing the *Delete/Backspace* key on the keyboard.

Step 2: Using the Magic Wand tool to remove the background.

Step 1: Setting up the layer so that a transparent background can be used.

The original motif called cactus.tif, found in the Textile Design Exercise 3 folder on the DVD.

Simplification

In this method of motif development, you simplify or reduce the amount of detail of your original design.
This can be achieved in the following ways:

- ♦ Remove some of the elements of the motif.
  Tools/Functions:
  - o **Eraser** tool
  - o Create a *selection* and press the *Delete/Backspace* key.

- ♦ Reduce the number of colors in the motif by melding two colors into one.
  Tools/Functions:
  - o Use a Selection tool to select one color and fill it with another color.

Simplification techniques to modify the original artwork

Extraction

The extraction technique involves choosing a portion or "extraction" of the original motif and either developing that into a separate motif, or using it to build further on the original motif.

This can be achieved in the following ways:
- ♦ Use a portion of the original motif as your basis for development.
  Tools/Functions:
  - o Create a *selection* around a portion of the original motif to isolate it and use this as the basis for a new motif.

- ♦ Develop a portion of the original motif into a new motif.
  Tools/Functions:
  - o Create a *selection* around a portion of the original motif and use this as the basis for a new motif.

Transformation

In this method, you manipulate or transform the motif to create a new version of it. Transformations include flipping, rotating, scaling/stretching, and distorting. In design, motifs may be rotated in four different positions. *These are known as:*

Position 1–the normal position of the motif
Position 2–a 90 degree turn of position 1
Position 3–a 180 degree turn of position 1
Position 4–a 270 degree turn of position 1

All operations below begin with creating a selection of the motif, and then:

Extractions and modifications applied to the original artwork

Position 1   Position 2   Position 3   Position 4

- ♦ **Flip/reflect** the motif left to right (on the horizontal X plane) or upside down (on the vertical Y plane).
  Tools/Functions:
  - o *Edit>Transform>Flip Horizontal* or *Edit>Transform>Flip Vertical*

- ♦ **Rotate** the motif in 90 or 180 degree turns, or some other angle of rotation. You can use the options bar and type in the amount if you like.
  Tools/Functions:
  - o Use *Edit>Transform>Rotate 90 CW/Rotate 180/90 CCW* to rotate 90 or 180 degree angles (or use the options bar).
  - o Use *Edit>Transform>Free Transform* to rotate any angle, using the bounding box (or the options bar).

- ♦ **Scale** the motif left to right (on the horizontal X plane) or upside down (on the vertical Y plane).
  Tools/Functions:
  - o Use *Edit>Transform>Scale* to change the scale of the motif. You can lengthen it, widen it, or rescale in proportion using the *Shift* key as you drag the bounding box that appears around the image.

Flipping the original motif (left) horizontally (right)

Rotating the original motif (left) 80 degrees (right)

Scaling the original motif (left) in different ways

Transformation

You can perform transformations as you paste motifs in place from the clipboard while building a repeat pattern to give more interest to your work. Experiment with pasting a motif, manipulating the next motif, and then pasting it in place.

♦ You can use **skew/distort/perspective/warp** functions to alter the motif left to right (on the horizontal X plane) or upside down (on the vertical Y plane).
Tools/Functions:
o Use *Edit>Transform>Skew/Distort/Perspective/Warp* to alter the motif. You can move individual anchor points or bounding lines. Experiment.

Skewing the original motif (left) to create a new version

Distorting the original motif (left) to create a new version

Using Perspective to alter the original motif (left) to create a new version

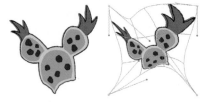

Using Warp to alter the original motif (left) to create a new version. You can see the anchor points and lines as the alterations are being performed.

Using Photoshop Filters

There are various filters in Photoshop that can be used in motif development. Using the *Filter Gallery* simplifies the process. The examples below illustrate how the master motif changed as different filters were applied to it.

You may apply multiple filters to a motif for added interest. The above image was created by combining the Glowing Edges and Stained Glass filters.

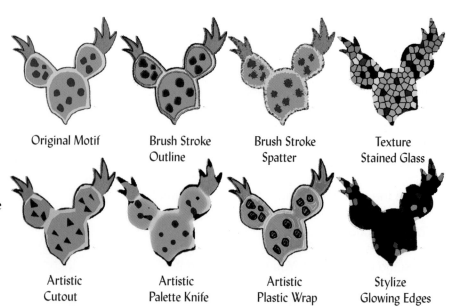

Original Motif

Brush Stroke
Outline

Brush Stroke
Spatter

Texture
Stained Glass

Artistic
Cutout

Artistic
Palette Knife

Artistic
Plastic Wrap

Stylize
Glowing Edges

Building on a Motif: Compound Motifs

Compound motifs are created by combining one motif with another motif, or by adding additional elements to an existing motif. There are many ways to build a compound unit. *The following are some suggestions:*

1. Multiples of One Motif

The simplest way to create a compound unit is to use the clipboard and paste in the multiples of the same motif. Use various *transformations* (scale, flip, rotate, etc.) and the **Move** tool to build a new motif.

Above: Building a motif by combining multiples of the same original. In this example, the motif on the left was repeated three times and rotations were performed on each element.

2. Combining Different Motifs

You may create a compound unit by *combining* two or more different images to create a larger, more intricate motif. Consider placement and the use of space, positive and negative, when you do this.

Left: Combining different motif elements to create a new motif

3. Extracting from a Motif to Add Additional Elements

An easy way of creating more interesting patterns is to *extract* a portion of the master motif to add to the compound unit you are building. The example to the right shows you the original motif and then the new motif built by adding the dots and medallion components of the original (left) to new areas in the new motif (right)

Original motif: Alana Rillo

Example of extracting elements from a motif to build a more intricate version

4. Creating Bridges between Motifs

Once you have created a basic repeat pattern, you may create *Bridges* or *Joins* between the images on all or part of the image. This can help you create a flow for the eye to follow. The single unit itself becomes harder to identify and the pattern begins to look more complex than it really is.

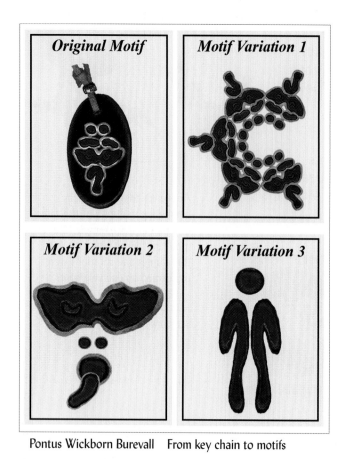

Pontus Wickborn Burevall   From key chain to motifs

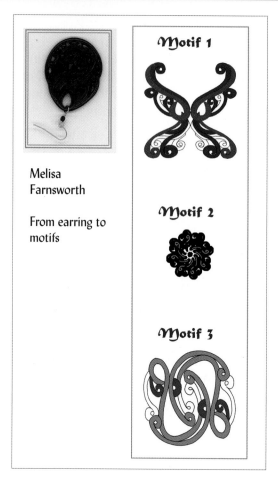

Melisa Farnsworth

From earring to motifs

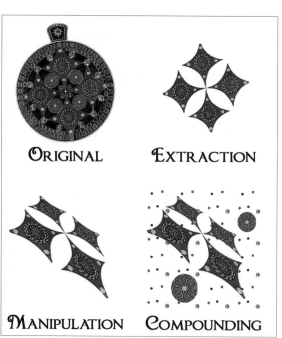

Alana Rillo
From pendant to motifs

Student Gallery
Motif Development from Found Objects
Mesa College Fashion Students

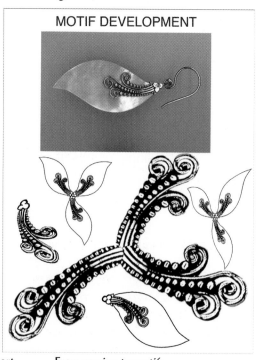

MOTIF DEVELOPMENT

Jodi Smart   From earring to motifs

Exercise #4: Creating Repeat Patterns Using the Block, Brick, and Half-Drop Repeat Networks

Goal
The goal of this exercise is to develop a simple motif and repeat it in three different repeat networks: block, brick, and half-drop. A grid and grid snap will be utilized to facilitate the design process.

Photoshop Tools and Functions
- ◆ View grid
- ◆ Snap to grid
- ◆ *Edit>Define Pattern*
- ◆ *Edit>Pattern Fill*

Quick Overview of the Process
In this exercise, you will develop a simple small motif (no larger than one square inch) as your starting point in design. A small motif will allow you to view and understand the repeat networks more fully as you view the multiple motifs on one page. You will use Photoshop's *Edit>Define Pattern* function to place a tile in the *Pattern Preset* library. As you work. you will use one document as your "development" page, and create three additional documents, one for each repeat network. You will use the development page to build the different repeats by the placement of your motifs. You will use the *Grid* and *Snap to Grid* functions to assist in accurately positioning the motifs so that your repeat will be accurate. The snap to grid function will assist you in positioning and selecting motifs.

In this exercise we will be performing the following actions:
1. Design a motif and scale it to no larger than one square inch.
2. Utilizing *Grid Snap*, select the motif and define the pattern (using *Edit>Define Pattern*).
3. Create a new document and use a *Fill Pattern* to fill the document with the block repeat. Remember to choose the new tile in the *Pattern Picker*.
4. On the original motif page, duplicate the motif using snap to grid, and position the duplicates to build the foundation of a brick and half-drop repeat system.
5. In turn, define the pattern for the brick and half-drop patterns, and then, on new documents, fill each page with pattern.

New Concepts
- o Use of a grid to visually and physically assist in the development of repeats.
- o Defining a tile or unit of repeat by creating a rectangular selection and using *Edit>Define Pattern*. This works through multiple layers. Make sure feathering is not turned on.
- o Using *Edit>Pattern Fill* to fill an area with a repeating tile.
- o *Opt/Ctrl+drag* to duplicate a selection, which allows you to copy a motif on the same layer.

Repeats:
- o Block (yellow)
- o Brick (red)
- o Half-drop (purple)

Note: Grid Snap
A Grid Snap causes a selection to jump or snap to the increments of the grid.

Tip: Feathering off & Marquee Tool
If feathering is on when a selection is made, the Define Pattern option will be unavailable. Selections need to be made with the Rectangular Marquee tool.

Note: Layers and Define Pattern
The Define Pattern function captures the imagery through all layers, not just the active layer.

View the Grid Shortcut

Use the Cmd/Ctrl+H keyboard shortcut to hide/view the grid.

Fill Layer

A fill layer will be used beneath the motif layer so that you can easily see what you are doing. The checkerboard display of a transparent layer "busies" the image and makes it hard to read.

Step 2: Creating a fill layer of white.

The Layers palette setup

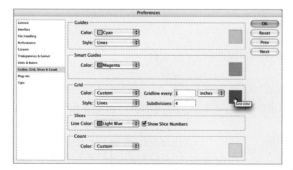

Step 5: Setting up the grid in Preferences.

Sources of Imagery

- Original drawn art
- Clip art
- Photographs

Terminology Refresher

Motif—An element (or elements) of design, developed to become the basic unit, which is typically repeated in textile patterns.

Network—The systematic manner in which motifs are repeated to create a pattern. Examples include block, brick, and half-drop.

Pattern—The resulting imagery created when a motif repeats in a regular design network.

motif + network = pattern

Step-by-Step

Setting up the Document and Grid

1. Choose the *File>New* menu command and set up a document that measures 8.5 × 11 inches. Set the *Resolution* to 150 and choose transparent background. Click **OK**. A layer will appear in the *Layers* palette. Rename this layer to *Motif Development*. **Click away to deselect the layer.**

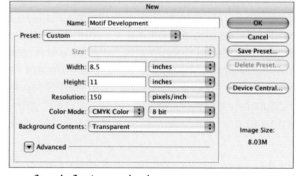

Step 1: Setting up the document.

2. Click on the **Create new fill or adjustment layer** button at the bottom of the *Layers* palette and slide to the *Solid Color* option. Release the mouse and the *Color Picker* will open. Choose white as the fill color and click on **OK**. You will now see a *Color Fill* layer of white.

3. In the *Layers* palette, click on the *Motif Development* layer and drag it above the *fill* layer.

4. Turn on the view of the *Info* palette by accessing it in the palette dock, or by choosing the *Window>Info* menu command.

5. Set up the grid by choosing the *Photoshop> Preferences>Guides, Grid, Slices & Count* (Mac CS3/CS4) or *Edit>Preferences>Guides, Grid, Slices & Count* (Windows CS3/CS4). Select a new grid color (e.g., red) by clicking on the grid color box in the dialog and choosing a new color from the *Color Picker* that opens.

If you are using a transparent layer with no *fill* layer beneath, you will want to choose a grid color other than gray, as this will not be easy to see on the checkered background. Set the *Gridline every* to 1, the *Style* to Lines, and the *Subdivisions* to 4. Click **OK**. The grid will not yet appear on the screen.

6. Choose the *View>Show>Grid* menu command to view the grid. You will see solid red lines every inch and dotted red lines every quarter inch.

Develop a Motif

1. Click on the *Motif Development* layer to make it the active layer. Make sure that the *Snap* function is off or unchecked (*View>Snap*).

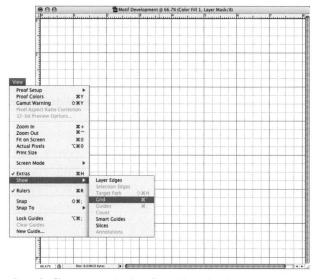

Step 6: Choosing to display the grid on the document.

2. Using the various art tools, draw or doodle a motif on the *Motif Development* layer. It is best to make the motif asymmetrical as this will allow you to build repeat patterns that have more rhythm and greater interest. (See Textile Exercise #3 for a discussion on motif development.)

3. If you draw your motif larger than one inch, use the *Edit>Transform>Scale* menu command to resize the motif down to a size that is one inch or less in size.
Note: It is best to limit the number of colors you use in the motif, as it will be easier to create new colorways if you work with fewer colors. Practically speaking, most textile prints have six or fewer colors in them, in order to be cost effective to print in the traditional screen printing method.

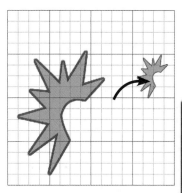

Step 3: Drawing the motif and resizing it to fit into a square inch.

4. Save the file.

Building a Block Repeat

The block repeat is a network whereby motifs are placed directly beside, and directly above and below each other. To create this simple repeat pattern you will utilize the *Define Pattern* function found in the **Edit** menu.

The block repeat network

1. Ensure that your motif is less than one inch in size. You should be working on the *Motif Development* layer.

2. Using the **Rectangular Marquee** selection tool (if necessary to select the motif) and the **Move** tool, reposition the motif so that it appears inside the lines of one square inch.

3. Turn on the *Snap* function by choosing the *View>Snap* menu command. Check to make sure that the Grid is one of the chosen options for "snap" using the *View>Snap To>Grid* menu command.

Step 3: Turning on the Snap function.

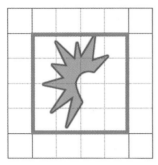

Step 4: Selecting one motif using grid snap to assist in the process.

4. Using the **Rectangular Marquee** selection tool again, frame off the motif. Notice how the marquee snaps to the grid lines. Make sure that you are capturing one square inch by observing the *Info* palette as you perform the operation.

5. Choose the *Edit>Define Pattern* menu command. A dialog will open. Name the pattern *block repeat* and click on **OK**. One tile of repeat will be placed in the *Pattern Preset* library.

Step 5: Defining and naming the pattern tile that will be saved in the Pattern Preset library.

The Layer palette setup

Creating a New Document and Filling with Pattern

1. Choose the *File>New* menu command and set up a document that measures 8.5 × 11 inches. Set the resolution to 150, choose transparent background, and name the file **Block Repeat**. Click **OK**. A layer will appear in the *Layers* palette. Rename the layer *Motifs*. Click away to deselect the layer.

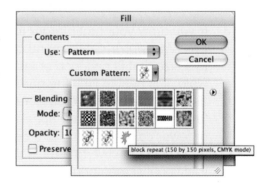

2. Create a *Solid Color fill* layer of white and *position* this under the *Motifs* layer. Click on the *Motifs* layer to make it the active layer.

Step 3: Defining and naming the pattern tile that will be saved in the Pattern Preset library.

The block repeat pattern

3. Choose the *Edit>Fill* menu command. A dialog will open. Choose the *Pattern* option in the *Use* pop-up and then *click+hold* on the *Custom Pattern* down arrow to open the Preset library of patterns. Slide over to your block repeat pattern and release the mouse. This will select the motif as your tiling image. Make sure that the Fill Mode is set to *Normal*. Click **OK** to close the dialog and your file will fill with a block repeat of the pattern.

4. Save the file.

Think in Terms of Units for Brick

If you consider the base motif to be one unit, then a brick base unit becomes a 1 × 2 unit (one wide by two tall).

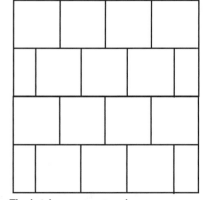

The brick repeat network

Building a Brick Repeat

The *Brick repeat* is a network in which every other row of motifs is shifted to the right a half step, resembling the standard pattern found in a brick wall. The repeat for the design requires two rows. To create this repeat pattern, you will copy and drag the master motif to multiple positions until you have enough in place to select a perfect repeat and use the *Define Pattern* function to define the new repeat.

Selection tool

Move tool

1. Return to the *Motifs Development* file. Make sure that *Grid Snap* is on. You should be working on the *Motifs* layer.

2. Using the **Rectangular Marquee** tool, select the original scaled motif. The active snap should cause the selection to "snap" to the grid lines. Marching ants should be dancing around the motif.

3. Select the **Move** tool. Press and hold the *Opt/Alt* key on the keyboard and drag the selected motif to a new empty area of the document. This will copy the motif from the original and create a second motif on the same layer. This is called *copy+drag* (or *Opt/Drag* or *Alt/Drag*).

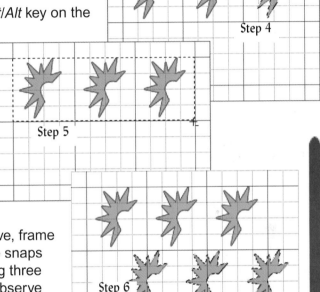

4. Repeat the *copy/drag* process, aligning three motifs in a horizontal row. Ensure that each motif is placed in *precisely* the same place within each inch square.

5. With the **Rectangular Marquee** tool still active, frame off the three motifs. Notice how the marquee snaps to the grid lines. You should now be capturing three grid squares (3 inches wide by 1 inch tall). Observe the *Info* palette for verification.

6. Select the **Move** tool and *Opt/Alt+drag* the three motifs down 1 inch and over 1/2 inch.

7. Turn the view of the *fill* layer off by clicking on the eye icon in the *Layers* palette. You do not want this to be on when you perform the next step; if it is, the white background of the *fill* layer will be captured as well.

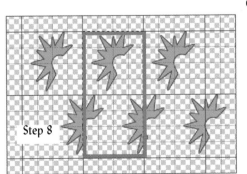

8. Select an area of the motifs that measures 1 inch wide by 2 inches tall and contains motifs.

9. Choose the *Edit>Define Pattern* menu command. A dialog will open. Name the pattern *brick repeat* and click on **OK**. One tile of repeat will be placed in the *Pattern Preset* library.

The brick repeat pattern

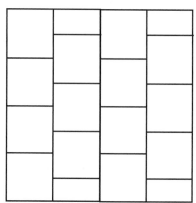

Half-drop Network

Think in Terms of Units for Half-Drop

If you consider the base motif to be one unit, then a half-drop base unit becomes a 2 × 1 unit (two wide by one tall).

10. To create a document for the pattern, repeat the operation of creating a new document and filling it with pattern (as discussed on page 371). This time, however, choose the *Brick repeat* motif in the *Pattern Preset* library Name and save the file as **Brick Repeat**.

Building a Half-Drop Repeat

The half-drop repeat is a network in which every other *column* of motifs is shifted down a half step. The repeat for the design thus requires two columns. To create this repeat pattern, you will copy and drag the master motif to multiple positions until you have enough in place to select a perfect repeat and use the *Define Pattern* function to define the new repeat.

1. Return to the *Motifs Development* file. Ensure that *Grid Snap* is on. You should be working on the *Motifs* layer. Turn on the view of the *fill* layer by clicking on the eye icon on the layer.

2. Using the **Rectangular Marquee** tool, select the original scaled motif. The active snap should cause the selection to "snap" to the grid lines. Marching ants should be dancing around the motif.

3. Select the **Move** tool. Press and hold the *Opt/Alt* key on the keyboard and drag the selected motif to a new empty area of the document. This will copy the motif from the original and create another motif on the same layer.

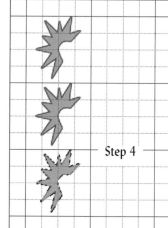

Step 4

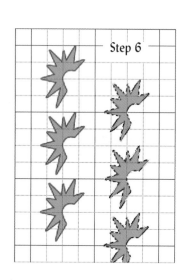

Step 6

4. Repeat the *copy/drag* process, aligning three motifs in a vertical column. Make sure that each motif is placed in *precisely* the same place within each inch square.

5. With the **Rectangular Marquee** tool still active, frame off the three motifs. Notice how the marquee snaps to the grid lines. You should now be capturing three grid squares (1 inch wide by 3 inches tall). Observe the *Info* palette for verification.

6. *Opt/Alt+drag* the three motifs over 1 inch and down 1/2 inch.

Step 8

7. Turn the view of the *fill* layer *off* by clicking on the eye icon in the *Layers* palette. You do not want this to be on when you perform the next step; if it is, the white background of the *fill* layer will be captured as well.

8. Select an area of the motifs that measures 2 inches wide by 1 inch tall and contains motifs.

9. Choose the *Edit>Define Pattern* menu command. A dialog will open. Name the pattern *Half-drop* and click on **OK**. One tile of repeat will be placed in the *Pattern Preset* library.

Creating a New Document and Filling with Pattern Using the Paint Bucket

This time you will use the **Paint Bucket** tool to fill the document.

1. Choose the *File>New* menu command and set up a document that measures 8.5 × 11 inches. Set the *Resolution* to 150, choose transparent background, and name the file **Half-Drop Repeat**. Click **OK**. A layer will appear in the *Layers* palette. Rename the layer *Motifs*.

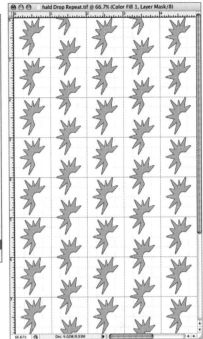

The half-drop repeat pattern

2. Create a *Solid Color* fill layer of white (using the **Create new fill or adjustment layer** button in the *Layers* palette) and *position* this under the *Motifs* layer. Click on the *Motifs* layer to make it active.

Step 4: Choosing the Pattern option in the Fill Source (below) and choosing the Half-drop pattern in the Pattern Picker (right).

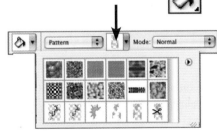

Note: Two Methods to Fill with Pattern
Pattern fills may also be achieved with either the Paint Bucket tool or the Edit>Fill menu command.

3. Choose the **Paint Bucket** tool in the Toolbox.

4. Click on the *Fill Source* pop-up and choose the *Pattern* option. Then click on the *Pattern Picker*, and choose the *Half-drop* pattern. Ensure that the fill *Mode* is set to *Normal*.

5. Move the *Paint Bucket* icon over your document and click. The *Motifs* layer will fill with pattern.

6. Save the file.

Tip
Two-Way Prints
Create a two-way print by flipping motifs vertically in your textile pattern. This allows for greater economy of fabric in manufacturing as clothing patterns can be laid on the fabric in both a top-to-bottom or bottom-to-top manner.

Quick Color Changes of the Color Fill Layer

Using a *Color Fill* layer allows you to quickly experiment with different background colors for your patterns.

1. Double-click on the *Color thumbnail* in the *Color Fill* layer. This will open the *Color Picker*.

2. Choose a new color from the *Color Picker*, and click **OK**. You will now see the results.

3. Continue to experiment with new colors for your *fill* layer until you find the one you want to use for each repeat.

Exploring colored fills

Tips

♦ Turn the Grid on and off at the appropriate times.
♦ Use fill layers, which allow you greater flexibility in filling in the background color of a print.
♦ Make sure feathering is not turned on when you select an image to define a pattern.
♦ Make sure you understand the difference between a *Background* and a *layer*.
♦ Fill Mode should be set to *Normal*.

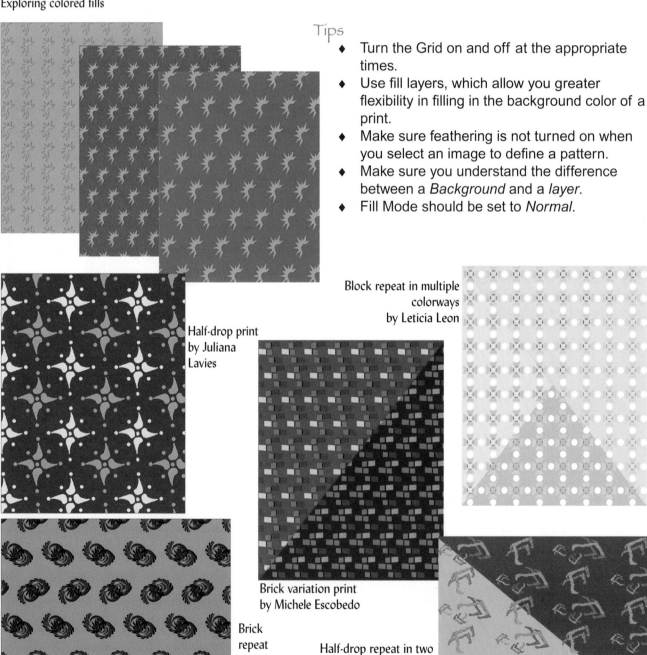

Block repeat in multiple colorways by Leticia Leon

Half-drop print by Juliana Lavies

Brick variation print by Michele Escobedo

Brick repeat print by Michele Jensen

Half-drop repeat in two colorways by Emeline Niyomwungere

Exercise #5: Using the Offset Filter to Create Repeats

Goal

In this exercise, Photoshop's *Offset* filter will be used to build a brick and a half-drop repeat pattern. This is an alternative to techniques covered in Exercise #4.

Photoshop Tools and Functions

- ◆ Selection tool
- ◆ Offset filter (*Filters>Other>Offset*)
- ◆ Canvas size
- ◆ *Edit>Define Pattern*
- ◆ *Edit>Pattern Fill*

Examples of brick (left) and half-drop (right) repeats created using the Offset filter

Quick Overview of the Process

This exercise introduces you to an alternate approach to creating repeating patterns using Photoshop's Offset filter. You will begin with a single motif on a colored ground. You will copy this to the clipboard to hold in memory. Then, you will use the Offset filter to offset the artwork, using the wrap option. Once this is complete you will increase the canvas size (by doubling its *height* for the brick repeat, and by doubling its *width* for the half-drop repeat). You will then paste in the original image and position it under (brick) or beside (half-drop) the original. This will give you the basic unit of repeat, which you may use to define the pattern and fill a new document.

In this exercise we will be performing the following actions:

1. Design or load a motif and, using the *Image>Image Adjustment* menu, note its size in pixels.
2. Select and copy the motif to the clipboard.
3. Use the *Offset* filter to perform an offset to the artwork.
4. Increase the *Canvas size* to allow for a second motif (the original version sitting on the clipboard).
5. Paste in the original image from the clipboard and position it.
6. Select the entire image and define the pattern (*Edit>Define Pattern*).
7. Create a new document and fill this with the new pattern.

New Concepts

- o Using the *Offset* filter to splice and offset a motif to assist in the process of building a brick or half-drop repeat pattern
- o Using the *Define Pattern* function to capture a motif/unit of repeat that sits on two layers, and defining a pattern with this repeat
- o *Image>Duplicate* command

Sources of Imagery

- • Original drawn art
- • Clip art
- • Photographs

Note: **Two Techniques** Two techniques of pasting in the second part of the motif are discussed in this exercise. The second technique, used in the half-drop example (using a simple Edit>Paste command), was the preferred method of students in class.

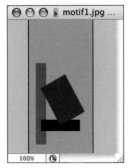

The master motif

Step-by-Step

Loading the Initial Motif and Copying It to the Clipboard

On the accompanying Art DVD or the location on your hard drive you moved the files to, locate the folder called **Textile Design Exercises.** Inside this folder is a folder called **TD Exercise 5**, and inside this folder are several motif images.

1. Using the *File>Open* menu, direct the file requestor to the **TD Exercise 5** folder and load an image from the folder. This exercise uses **Motif1.jpg**. If you are using original artwork, make sure that it uses a RGB or CMYK color mode so that you can use filters.

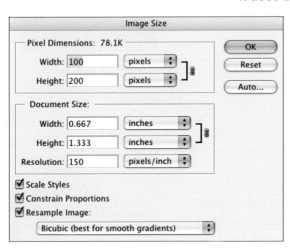

Step 2: Observing the image size.

2. Choose the *Image>Image Size* menu to observe the resolution and image size of the artwork. You will see that the image measures 100 pixels wide and 200 pixels tall, and has a resolution of 150 dpi.

3. Choose the *Select>All* menu command to select the entire image.

4. Choose the *Edit>Copy* menu command to copy the image to the clipboard.

5. Create a second and a third document for the brick and half-drop patterns. Do this by choosing the *Image>Duplicate* menu command twice. Save one of the new files as **halfdrop.psd** and save the second as **brick.psd.** This allows you to retain the original file.

Building the Unit of Repeat for a Brick Repeat

1. Make sure that the **brick.psd** file is active. You will see the single motif. Choose the *Filter>Other>Offset* menu command. The *Offset* dialog will open.

2. Click on the *Wrap Around* radio button in the *Undefined Areas* section of the dialog. Click on the *Preview* check box so that you can see a preview of what you are creating.

3. For a brick repeat, set the *Horizontal* offset to 50 pixels, which is half the width of your original image (100 pixels by 200 pixels). It is not critical that you use exactly half, but this is the most typical for brick repeats. Click **OK** and the motif will offset by 50%.

Step 1: Choosing the Offset filter command.

Steps 2–3: Setting the options in the Offset dialog.

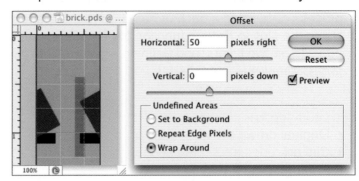

4. Choose the *Image>Canvas Size* menu command. When the dialog opens, set the new height of the image to be 400, double that of the original. Set the anchor to be at the top of the image, and click **OK**. More canvas will be added to the art, directly below the original motif.

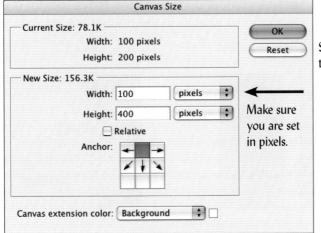

Step 4: Adjusting the canvas size.

Make sure you are set in pixels.

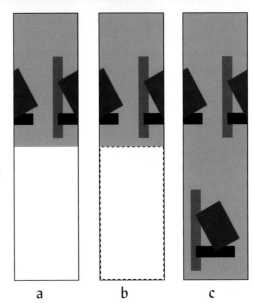

a   b   c

Steps 4–6: Creating the new motif unit.
a. Step 4: Adding canvas
b. Step 5: Selecting the nonmotif area
c. Step 6: Using the Paste Into command

5. Choose the **Rectangular Marquee** tool, and carefully frame off the lower portion (nonmotif) of the document. Ensure that you have the exact nonmotif area selected.

6. Choose the ***Edit>Paste Into*** command, and the original motif on the clipboard will paste into the white space. Make sure that the new motif is positioned correctly; if it is not, then use the **Move** tool to reposition it. You will now see a second layer, which contains the motif just pasted in from the clipboard.

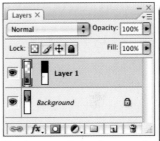

The Layers palette after step 6 has been performed

7. Save the file.

Building the Unit of Repeat for a Half-Drop Repeat

1. Ensure that the **halfdrop.psd** file is active (Choose the *Window>halfdrop.psd* menu command).

2. Choose the *Filter>Other>Offset* menu command. The *Offset* dialog will open. The setting for the last setup will still be active.

3. For a half-drop repeat, set the *Horizontal* offset to 0 pixels, and the *Vertical* offset to 100, which is half the height of your original image (100 pixels by 200 pixels). It is not critical that you use exactly half, but this is typical for half-drop repeats. Click **OK** and the motif will offset by 50%.

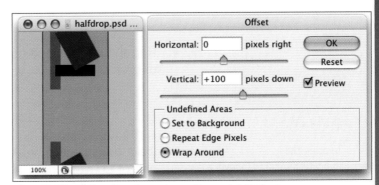

Step 3: The Offset filter is used to splice and shift the image.

4. Choose the *Image>Canvas Size* menu command. When the dialog opens, set the new width of the image to be 200, double that of the original. Set the anchor to be at the left side of the

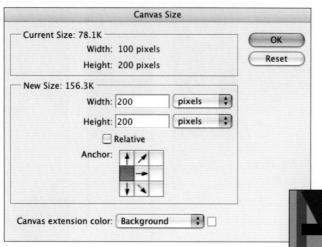

Step 4: Adjusting the canvas size.

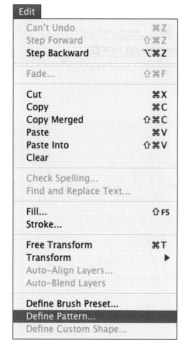

Step 3: Choosing the Edit>Define Pattern command.

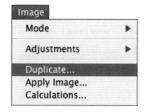

Step 7: Choosing the Image>Duplicate command (above) and typing the name of the new image (below).

image, and click **OK**. More canvas will be added to the art, directly to the right of the original motif.

5. As an alternate method to steps 5 and 6 of the Brick repeat procedure, simply paste the image from the clipboard into the document (without a selection), and then use the **Move** tool to reposition it directly to the right of the original.

6. Save the file.

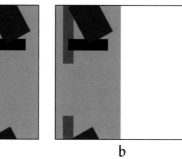

Steps 4–6: Creating the new motif unit.
a. The original offset motif
b. Step 4: Canvas is added.
c. Step 5: Using the Edit>Paste command to bring in the original image to complete the new motif unit

Setting up New Documents and Creating the Pattern Repeats

1. Move to the **brick.psd** file (*Window>brick.psd*).

2. Choose the *Select>All* menu command. The entire document will be selected.

3. Choose the *Edit>Define Pattern* menu command. A dialog will open. Name the repeat and click **OK**.

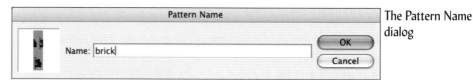

The Pattern Name dialog

4. Repeat the previous three steps for the **halfdrop.pds** image and pattern.

5. Choose the *File>New* menu, and create a document that is 8.5 × 11 inches in size with a resolution of 150. If you use the same resolution as your motif, you will have a sense of how big the motif will be. This, however, is not a necessary step, just one of convenience. Choose the RGB *Color Mode* and set the *Background Contents* to White.

6. Save the file as **brickpattern.psd.**

7. Duplicate the file (*Image>Duplicate*) and when the *Duplicate* dialog opens, type in the name *halfdrop pattern*. Click **OK** and save the file, making sure that it saves as a PSD file (although the file format is not critical).

8. In turn, fill each of the new documents with the correct pattern. Use the *Edit>Fill* menu command, and choose a *Pattern* fill and the corresponding pattern from the pattern preset library.

9. Save each file to update it.

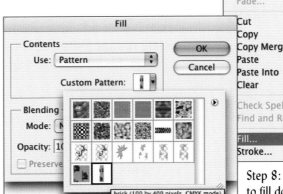

Step 8: Using a pattern fill to fill documents with final pattern.

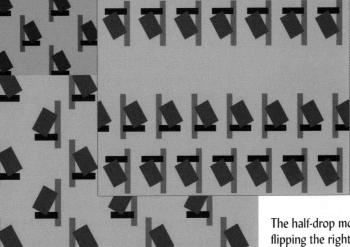

The brick motif is built by flipping the lower half of the motif horizontally and vertically.

The final patterns:
brick (above) and half-drop (right)

Variations ...
To add some interest to your patterns you can flip the second motif of the pattern after you paste it in using *Edit>Transform>Flip Horizontal*. The examples here show you a brick (upper example) and a half-drop (lower sample) repeat motif that were created with the right side of the motif flipped horizontally. The resulting pattern appears to the right of the motif.

The half-drop motif is built by flipping the right side of the motif horizontally.

Exercise #6: Creative Techniques for Pattern Repeat

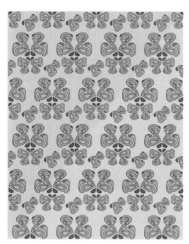

Print design using extraction and scale techniques
Thais Pacci Barreto

Goal

This exercise introduces concepts that will assist you in creating more interesting repeat patterns. A series of design techniques and Photoshop functions will be introduced and explained.

Photoshop Tools and Functions

- ♦ Transformations (*Flip*, *Rotate*, *Scale*) accessed through the *Edit* menu
- ♦ Grid and snap to grid
- ♦ Layers used to build more complex motifs
- ♦ *Edit>Define Pattern*
- ♦ *Edit>Pattern Fill*

Quick Overview of the Process

Each technique covered in this exercise will commence with a quick overview of the approach to be taken and the tools to be used. You can simply read the exercise to understand the techniques used, or you can load a motif and practice the steps discussed.

Design Concepts

- o Using positive and negative space to create more interesting patterns.
- o Using motif rotations and flipping to introduce more interesting patterns.
- o Building more complex motifs through the use of *Layers* in Photoshop.

New Concepts

- o Using *Edit>Pattern Fill* to create a tile of the imagery as exists in all layers under the selection
- o *Opt/Ctrl+drag* to duplicate a selection, which allows you to copy a motif on the same layer.

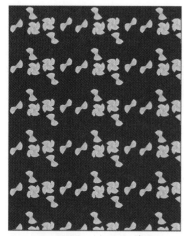

Print design using compounding and extraction
Annette Camarena

Pasta motif

Use of Reflection (Flipping)

In textile design, motifs are often reflected (flipped) to create more interest in the print. You can flip the motif left to right (on the horizontal X plane) or flip it upside down (on the vertical Y plane). Motifs reflected vertically allow you to create a two-way print that has no apparent up or down and thus allows clothing patterns to be laid on the fabric in either direction. This cuts costs in clothing manufacturing.

To reflect/flip a motif (or group of motifs):

1. Select the motif you want to reflect (the **Rectangular Marquee** selection tool is the best tool to use for the selection).

2. Choose the *Edit>Transform>Flip Horizontal* or *Edit>Transform>Flip Vertical* menu command and the motif will reflect. You can flip individual motifs while building a pattern unit, or an entire row or column.

3. Once you have performed the reflection operation, identify the new base unit of repeat. Then use the **Rectangular Marquee** tool, select the unit, and choose the *Edit>Define Pattern* menu command to create the new pattern tile. Name the tile in the dialog and click **OK**.

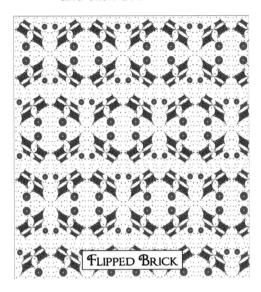

The motif (above) was flipped horizontally and vertically to create the brick pattern (left).

Design by Alana Rillo

The Flip commands

Use of Rotation

Motifs are often rotated in the process of design. In textile design, there are four standard rotations called position 1, position 2, position 3, and position 4. Position 1 is the motif in its original form, and each position after that rotates the motif a quarter turn or 90 degrees clockwise. Of course, you can use any angle of rotation to create interest. As with reflection, rotations allow you to create interest in the pattern.

To rotate a motif:

1. Select the motif you want to rotate (the **Rectangular Marquee** selection tool is the best tool to use for the selection).

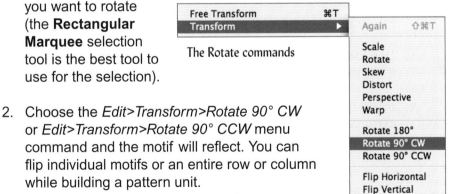

The Rotate commands

2. Choose the *Edit>Transform>Rotate 90° CW* or *Edit>Transform>Rotate 90° CCW* menu command and the motif will reflect. You can flip individual motifs or an entire row or column while building a pattern unit.

3. Once you have performed the reflection operation, identify the new base unit of repeat. Then use the **Rectangular Marquee** tool to select the unit, and choose the *Edit>Define Pattern* menu command to create the new pattern tile. Name the tile in the dialog and click **OK**.

Note: Rotations
In the Rotation menu commands, CW means clockwise and CCW means counterclockwise.

Note: Rotations
In design, motifs may be rotated in four different positions. These are known as:
Position 1 - the normal position of the motif
Position 2 - a 90 degree turn of position 1
Position 3 - a 180 degree turn of position 1
Position 4 - a 270 degree turn of position 1

It is important to understand that rotation differs from flipping horizontally and vertically. Compare the motifs on this page and on the preceding page for clarification.

The motif above was rotated and compounded to create a second motif and then laid in a repeating pattern.

Osbaldo Ahumada

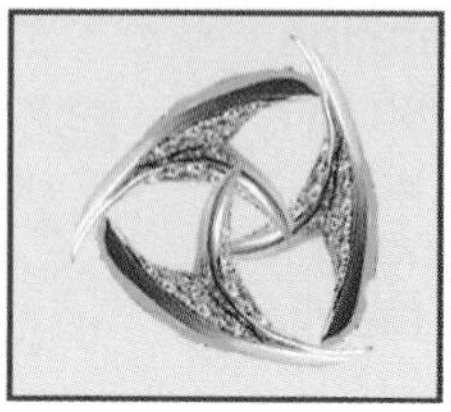

PASSION MIX
(PANTONE 182C)
osbaldo Ahumada

Note:

Transformations

The Free Transform menu (Cmd/Ctrl+T) and settings in the options bar may also be used to rotate motifs.

Use of Overlap

Motifs may be overlapped to create interest in a design. This is most easily achieved through the use of a grid and the *Snap To* grid function. Essentially, the selected motif is one size, and the measurement of the unit of repeat is smaller. This results in an overlapping motif. Using the clipboard to paste in copies of the original motif (each onto its own layer) will allow you some flexibility in design in that you can move things around a bit as you create the overlapping pattern.

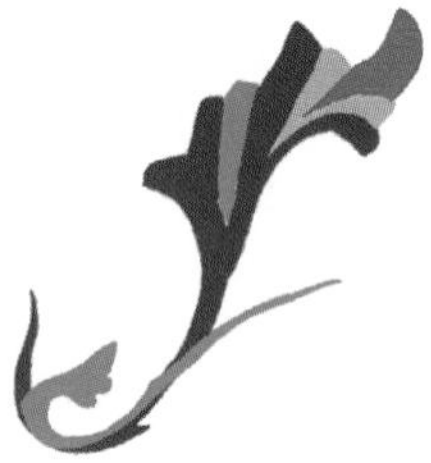

Original motif by Kari Pacheco

To create an overlapping motif:

1. Set up the grid and snap to grid functions per Textile Design Exercise #4 beginning on page 375. Temporarily turn the *Snap* function off (make sure that *View>Snap* has no check mark).
2. On a transparent layer, create a motif of a specific size (e.g., 2 inches square). It is best to design a motif that is somewhat open so that the overlap has a chance to be seen easily. Now, turn the *Snap* function on (using *View>Snap*).
3. Use the **Rectangular Marquee** tool to select the motif, then copy it to the clipboard using the *Edit>Copy* menu command.
4. Paste the motif back in from the clipboard using the *Edit>Paste* command. Each paste command will paste a motif onto its own layer.
5. Choose the **Move** tool, reposition the pasted-in motif(s) until you create an overlap that you like. As an example, if the motif is 2" square, consider moving one of the new motifs over 1-1/2". You will most likely want to do this on both sides of the motif to create a consistent repeat pattern.
6. Once you have established a row or column of the overlapped motifs, you will want to perform a similar action to build the overlap in the opposite direction.

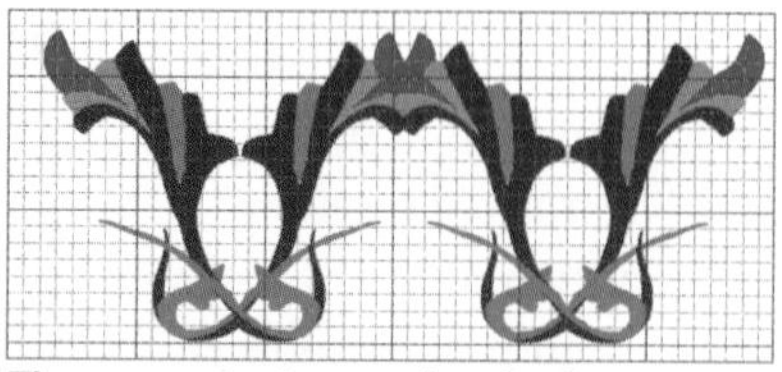

The examples here utilize both overlap and reflection in both directions.

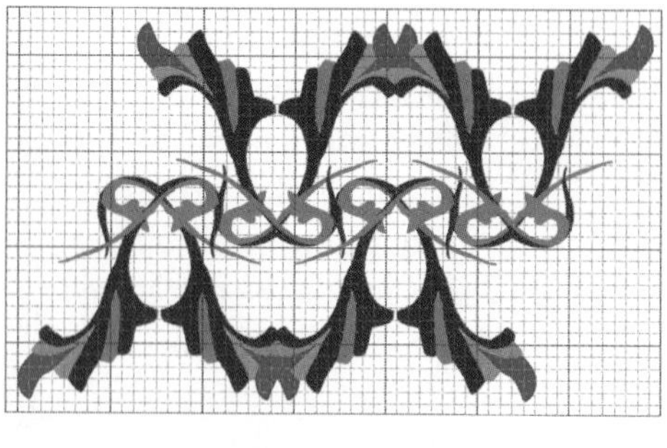

7. Identify the new unit of repeat, which in a simple design approach would be 1-1/2" square (if you moved the motif 1-1/2" each time in your overlapping operations).

8. Choose the **Rectangular Marquee** tool, select the new unit, and then choose the *Edit>Define Pattern* menu command to create the new pattern tile. Name the tile in the dialog and click **OK**.

Once the overlap pattern is created, you need to identify and define one unit of repeat, as shown above.

Transformations
You do not need to merge layers when you are performing the Define Pattern process, as imagery from all layers will be included. However, you might want to turn off the background or any fill layers you have created so you can retain the transparent background under the motifs.

The original motif (above) and the resulting pattern (right), which utilizes overlap in both directions

Use of Open Space

Balancing the use of positive and negative space in a design is an art unto itself. The use of open space prevents a design from becoming too busy and allows the motif to stand out. The use of *Opt/Alt+drag* to copy motifs on the same layer suits this technique as you are allowing space between them. You can also use the clipboard to bring multiple motifs to the document.

The original motif (right) and the process of building a repeating pattern that incorporates open space. The result is on the next page. Motif designed by Theresa Mays.

To build a repeat unit with open space:

1. Set up the grid and snap to grid functions per Exercise #4. Temporarily turn the *Snap* function off (make sure that *View>Snap* has no check mark).

2. On a transparent layer, create a motif of a specific size (e.g., 1" square). Now, turn the *Snap* function on (using *View>Snap*).

3. Use the **Rectangular Marquee** tool to select the motif. Then use the *Opt/Alt+drag* copy function and grid snap to create additional motifs on the same layer. Use the *Snap to Grid* function to space the motifs in an area greater than 2 inches square. You may do this in one or both directions.

   Note: If you prefer, use the clipboard as in the *Overlap* instructions and then use the **Move** tool to reposition the motifs as you work.

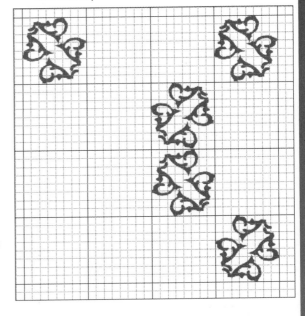

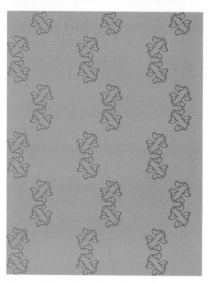

The motif, designed by Theresa Mays, was laid into a repeating pattern using open space.

4. Once you have established a row or column of motifs with open space, you will most likely want to perform a similar action to build the openness in the opposite direction. Pay attention to the size of your motif and the amount of open space you are using as this will help in the next step.

5. Identify the new unit of repeat, which includes the motif and the open space allowed in either or both the horizontal and vertical directions.

6. Choose the **Rectangular Marquee** tool, select the new unit, and then choose the *Edit>Define Pattern* menu command to create the new pattern tile. Name the tile in the dialog and click **OK**. Remember, you do not need to merge layers when you are performing the *Define Pattern* process, as imagery from all layers will be included. However, you might want to turn off the background or any *fill* layers you have created so you can retain the transparent background under the motifs.

Use of Scale

You may work with "scale" as a tool to create more interest in your designs. As you build the motif or motif group, alter the scale of the motifs.

The motif was laid into a repeating pattern using scale as a design tool to create interest in the pattern.

Motif and pattern designed by Mariel Diaz-Medoza

Building Compound Motifs and Patterns Using Multiple Layers

In this technique, you will use layers to build a pattern stack of motifs and then define a pattern through the stack. This technique allows you great flexibility in arranging the placement of each element of the final motif while observing how its position (in repeat) works with the rest of the design. You will end up with what is known as a *compound motif* (i.e., a motif built of several parts or components). You will build a repeating pattern of each component, each on its own layer, and as long as there is a relationship shared in the repeat size of the pattern, you can build one final pattern that incorporates all components. The grid is an aid, as it aids visualization and assists with the mental math of creating a repeating pattern. The key to this approach of design is that each repeat used must be a factor or multiple of the others.

Building an advanced pattern using layers

Example

Layer 4	Medallions	Repeat of 3" × 4"
Layer 3	Scroll Pattern	Repeat of 3" × 4"
Layer 2	Stripe Pattern	Repeat of 1-1/2" × 2"
Fill Layer	Fill Layer of Solid Color	
Final Repeat Size		**3" × 4"**

The Various Layers of the Textile Print

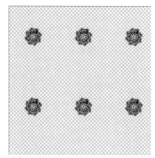

Medallions

The basic steps are as follows:

1. Build each of the motif components on a transparent ground.

2. Define the pattern for each component, making sure that you have all solid layers turned off so the repeating pattern sits on a transparent ground. Make sure that the sizes of all your tiles work as factors or multiples of each other.

3. Create multiple layers and fill each layer with the appropriate pattern.

4. Use the **Move** tool to move the motifs around on a layer and see how changing the placement affects the overall look of your design.

Scroll Pattern

5. When you are satisfied with the final placement, redefine a pattern using the largest repeat as your tile size.

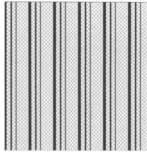

Stripe

Advantages

The advantages of using this approach to building textile patterns are as follows:

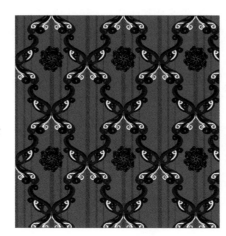

Resulting pattern from all layers

- You can easily remove a layer from the pattern.
- You can shift the position of one design element by moving the layer.
- You can add new design elements easily as long as you keep to a multiple or factor of the original motif size.

Solid Fill

Variations on a theme: Additional options are created by duplicating a layer, repositioning layers, and so on.

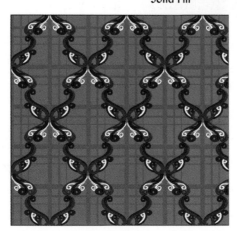

Flora Luna

Flora Twilight

Student Gallery
Fabric Designs
Mesa College Fashion Students

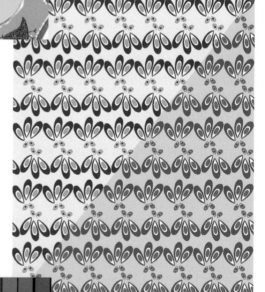

Three motifs create this print by Kristin Matoba.

Layering two motifs by Pinar Aslan

Creative play with repeat and nonrepeat by Nania Pongpitakkul

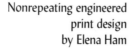

Milky-run-way

Scanned imagery was the source of this print by Mariel Diaz-Mendoza.

Compound motifs built using scale by Rebecca Moman

Nonrepeating engineered print design by Elena Ham

Exercise #7: Planning Multiple Colorways for Textile Prints and Creating a Custom Palette

Goal
To plan for multiple colorways of a textile print and build and save a custom palette.

Color inspiration from nature

Photoshop Tools and Functions
- ◆ *Swatches* palette and its various functions
- ◆ **Eyedropper** tool
- ◆ Loading and saving custom palettes
- ◆ *Color Picker* and the *Add to Swatches* function
- ◆ Use of Color Libraries (such as Pantone)
- ◆ Color fills

Quick Overview of the Process
A colorway is a term used in the textile industry to denote color combinations used in fabrics. You will build and save a custom palette that will contain only the colors used in the three textile prints.

The steps are as follows:
1. Load the original textile print.
2. Analyze the print for the colors used and build a chart documenting these. Plan two additional colorways retaining the color values for each color in the pattern.
3. Load a blank custom palette for use.
4. Use the **Eyedropper** tool to select the colors from the original print and place these in the *Swatches* palette.
5. Use the *Color Picker* to choose the new colors for the additional two colorways and place these in the custom palette. Save the palette.
6. Explore additional methods of developing colorways.

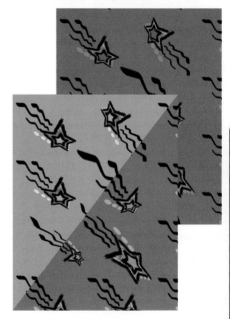
Print design by
Cynthia Martinez

Thoughts on Planning New Colorways
As a general rule of thumb, when you build colorways of the same print, you tend to keep the values of the various objects similar. Therefore, it is a good exercise to stop and analyze the original colorway to determine which color is the prominent color, which is subordinate, which is a "zinger" color, and so on. The intensity and value of the colors are often used to direct the eye and control how the user sees an image, so consider the values of various objects as you look at the image.

New Concepts
- o Loading and saving custom palettes
- o *Color Picker* and the *Add to Swatches* function (CS3/CS4)

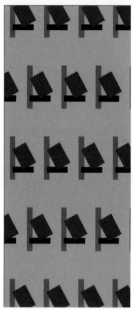

A brick pattern repeat of the original motif

o   Use of Color Libraries (such as Pantone)

Sources of Imagery

o   Digital images of motif artwork and photographs

Step-by-Step

Identify the Colors Used in a Fabric and Plan Additional Colorways

The fabric used in this exercise will be the artwork utilized in Textile Design Exercise #5.

1. Using the *File>Open* menu, direct the file requestor to the **TD Exercise 5** folder and load an image from the folder. This exercise uses **Motif1.jpg**. Load this motif, or you may load a document that contains a repeating pattern of the motif. **Halfdrop.psd** and **Brick.psd** are the two files created in the Exercise.

The master motif

2. Examine the original fabric design and determine how many colors are used in it. If you look closely, you will see that some anti-aliasing occurs; but primarily, there are four unique colors in the motif: Medium Gold, Light Olive, Black, and Rust.

3. On a piece of paper, create a chart listing the colors used. Label these as Background, Foreground #1, Foreground #2, and Foreground #3.

4. Plan two additional colorways, bearing in mind the values of each of the colors. Try to keep the value of each color the same so the print will retain its integrity. Thus the elements you see when you look at the design won't change. The chart to the left shows you two new colorways. Note how the general values of the colors were retained. The background is a medium value, two of the foreground colors are dark, and the other is light.

Location	Original	Colorway 2	Colorway 3
Background	Medium Gold	Medium Purple	MediumTan
Foreground #1	Light Olive	Light Blue	Light Orange
Foreground #2	Black	Dark Gray	Dark Brown
Foreground #3	Rust	Deep Pink	Deep Teal

Step 4: Planning a color chart of the original and new colors.

Creating and Saving a Custom Swatches Palette

The default palette has multiple colors in it. You can either remove the unused colors, or begin with a blank palette that you have already created and saved. There is a blank palette on the accompanying DVD, **Empty Swatches.aco**.

The Empty Swatches palette contains only black and white.

Step 1: Loading a new Swatch library using the Replace Swatches command.

⚡ Removing Colors from the Palette

To remove unwanted colors from the Swatches palette, press and hold the Opt/Alt key on the keyboard. The cursor will change to a pair of scissors as you move it over a color in the Swatches palette. If you click on a color, it will be "cut" or removed from the palette.

1. In the *Swatches* palette menu, choose the *Replace Swatches* menu command. You will be asked if you want to save the current swatches. Choose the *Don't Save* option. Direct the *Load* file requestor to the **Palettes** folder on the accompanying DVD. Inside this folder you will find a file called **Empty Swatches.aco**. Choose

this file and click **Load**. The current swatches will be replaced with a palette that contains only a black and white swatch.

Choosing colors and adding them to the Swatches palette.

2. Choose the **Eyedropper** tool, and click on the background Gold of the original design. This will move the color to the *foreground* box in the Toolbox.

3. Move your cursor over to the *Swatches* palette, and note how it changes to a *Paint Bucket*. Position the cursor over an empty palette swatch and click. A dialog will open. Type in a name for the color and click **OK**. This will move the color into the *Swatches* palette.

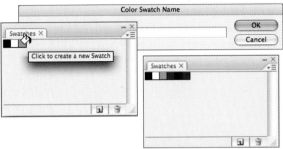

Steps 3–4: Adding swatches to the palette (left) and the final palette with the four original colors (right).

4. Repeat the process with the other colors in the artwork. When you are done, you should have four colors in the *Swatches* palette (beyond the standard black and white).

5. Now, refer to your color chart, and then use the *Color Picker* to choose the colors you want and add these to the palette. Double-click on the *foreground* color in the palette to open the *Color Picker*. Find a color you want to use as the background color in Colorway #2 (e.g., Purple). In CS3 or CS4 click on the **Add To Swatches** button. This will open the *Color Swatch Name* dialog. Name the color and click **OK**. In earlier versions of Photoshop, click **OK** to close the *Color Picker*, and observe the new color in your *foreground* in the Toolbox. Move your cursor over an empty palette position in the *Swatches* palette and click with the mouse. This will open the *Color Swatch Name* dialog. Name the color and click **OK**.

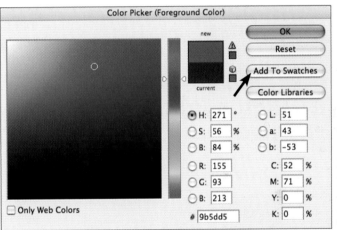

Step 5: Using the Color Picker to build new colorways.

6. Continue adding colors to the *Swatches* palette until you have all the colors from the original and two new colorways in the palette.

Step 7: Saving the custom Swatches palette.

7. Save the palette using the *Save Swatches* command in the *Swatches* palette menu. Name the palette. **GeoFabrics** was the name used in our example. An ".aco" extension is added to a custom palette.

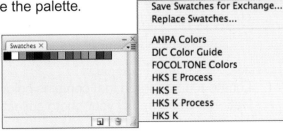

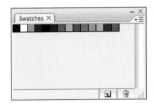

The final palette with three colorways

Step 1: Setting the first color as the foreground color in the Toolbox.

Developing New Colorways: Options

There are various ways of coming up with additional colorways for fabrics as well as other types of artwork. Some ideas are presented below.

Selecting Colors from the Color Picker

A simple approach to creating new colorways is to choose new colors from the *Color Picker*. Our approach will be to ensure that your colors are more or less in the same value scale. *Use the following steps:*

1. Choose the **Eyedropper** tool and click on the first color of the main image (gold in our example). This will place the color in the *foreground* color of the Toolbox.

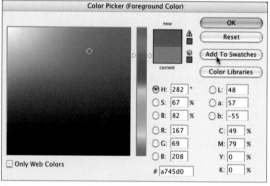

Step 2: Opening the Color Picker.

Step 3: Choosing a new color with the same value as the original Gold color.

Note: Moving the white arrowheads allows you to move up and down the hue spectrum within a specific value setting.

2. Now, double-click on the *Foreground* icon in the Toolbox to open the *Color Picker* dialog. Notice that a black circle appears in the main color box of the dialog. This is showing you the **value** position of the gold. There is a vertical color strip to the right of this that has two arrowheads on either side of it. These point to the current hue that is selected (in this case, gold).

3. Now, take your cursor and move the white arrows on the color strip up and down to select a *different hue* with the *same value* as the gold. Medium purple was the selected hue in the example here. Note how it has the same value as the original green, and how the *saturation* and *brightness* levels do not change. Note also how you can see the original gold color and the new purple color above it in the color indicator section of the dialog. This shows you the original and new colors. In CS3/CS4 click on the **Add To Swatches** button and a dialog will open allowing you to name the color and then move it to the *Swatches* palette. Click **OK** to close the dialog. In earlier versions of Photoshop, click **OK** to close the *Color Picker*, and observe the new color in your *foreground* in the Toolbox. Move your cursor over an empty palette position in the *Swatches* palette and click with the mouse. This will open the *Color Swatch Name* dialog. Name the color and click **OK**. The purple color will now be the *foreground* color in your Toolbox.

4. Repeat the process with each of the colors from the original textile print. Using this approach ensures that you have chosen the same values for each of the colors in your design, and the resulting colorways/patterns you create will maintain the same look and feel.

Borrowing Colors from a Photograph

1. Locate a photograph that contains colors you like. Consider National Geographic, your photo collection, art books, and other sources.

2. If the image is on paper, you can simply look at it and use the *Color Picker* to choose colors. Or, you may scan it or take a shot of it with a digital camera. Once the image is in a digital format, you may load it into Photoshop and use the **Eyedropper** tool to select a color from it and place it in the *foreground* color of the Toolbox. Then move the chosen colors into the *Swatches* palette using any of the techniques discussed earlier in this exercise.

Using the Pantone Color Library

If you own a Pantone Color book, locate colors that you want to use for the various colorways. Follow the principles of keeping tones and values in line with your original swatch. *To insert the chosen colors into your Swatches palette:*

The Eyedropper was used to sample colors from the flower image to build the palette on the right side of the image.

1. Click on the *Swatches* palette menu to open the options and choose the Pantone library of your choice. Once a library is chosen, a dialog will open asking you if you want to **OK** the new palette (which means to replace the old one) or if you want to **Append** the existing palette (which means you will add to the existing palette). Click **OK** to open a Pantone palette only. A new palette window will appear.

ANPA Colors
DIC Color Guide
FOCOLTONE Colors
HKS E Process
HKS E
HKS K Process
HKS K
HKS N Process
HKS N
HKS Z Process
HKS Z
Mac OS
PANTONE color bridge CMYK EC
PANTONE color bridge CMYK PC
PANTONE color bridge CMYK UP
PANTONE metallic coated
PANTONE pastel coated
PANTONE pastel uncoated
PANTONE process coated
PANTONE process uncoated
PANTONE solid coated
PANTONE solid matte
PANTONE solid to process EURO
PANTONE solid to process
PANTONE solid uncoated
Photo Filter Colors
TOYO 94 COLOR FINDER
TOYO COLOR FINDER
TRUMATCH Colors
VisiBone
VisiBone2
Web Hues
Web Safe Colors
Web Spectrum
Windows
Empty Palette

Choosing a Pantone library from the Swatches palette menu

Adobe Photoshop

Replace current color swatches with the swatches from PANTONE process coated.aco?

Append   Cancel   OK

2. Experiment with different views and options of the *Pantone Swatches* palette. *These include:*
   o Choose to see a thumbnail view of the colors by choosing *Small* or *Large Thumbnail* view from the palette menu.
   o Choose to see a list view of the colors by choosing *Small* or *Large List* view from the palette menu.
   o Move your cursor and hold it over any color and wait to view the Pantone color number of the swatch.

✓ Small Thumbnail
Large Thumbnail
Small List
Large List

Swatch views: Thumbnail (below left) and List (below right)

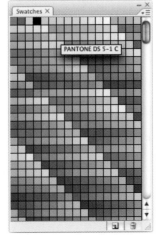

PANTONE DS 5-1 C

PANTONE DS Process Cyan C
PANTONE DS Process Magenta C
PANTONE DS Process Yellow C
PANTONE DS Process Black C
PANTONE DS 1-1 C
PANTONE DS 1-2 C
PANTONE DS 1-3 C
PANTONE DS 1-4 C
PANTONE DS 1-5 C
PANTONE DS 1-6 C
PANTONE DS 1-7 C
PANTONE DS 1-8 C
PANTONE DS 1-9 C
PANTONE DS 2-1 C
PANTONE DS 2-2 C

3. Once you have located the color you want, click and hold on this color, and drag it into the *Swatches* palette.

4. Repeat the process for the next color you need in the colorway, following the same sequence you used in the original swatch above (i.e., background, primary foreground, etc.).

Regardless of which method you use to locate the colors you want for the additional colorways of your textile, you will need to move the new colors into the *Swatches* palette.

Saving a Swatch Library

Once you have created your custom swatch library, you can save this as a swatch library. This allows you to retrieve it at any point in time, or open it in any document. *To save a swatch library:*

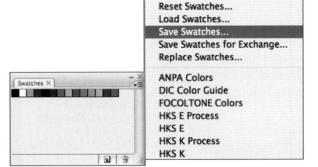

Steps 2–3: Choosing to save a Swatches library.

Step 4: Saving the Swatches library.

1. Ensure that you have the colorways palette created in this exercise open. If you haven't already, name each color in the palette for reference at a future date. Double-click on the color in the *Swatches* palette and when a dialog opens, name the color and click on **OK**.

2. *Click+hold* on the arrowhead in the upper-right corner of the *Swatches* palette to access the palette menu.

3. Slide down/up to the *Save Swatches...* option and release the mouse. A dialog will open.

4. Type in a name that you want to identify the swatch library with and direct the library to a location you will remember. A good location would be Photoshop's own *Color Swatches* folder found in the **Presets** folder, which is located in the *Photoshop* **application** folder. Palettes save with an ".aco" extension.

Exercise #8: Building Multiple Colorways for Textile Prints

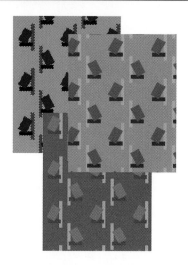

Goal
This exercise will teach you how to build multiple colorways of one textile print and to create a split-colorway image. Additional coloring techniques will be introduced.

Photoshop Tools and Functions
- **Selection** tools and *Selection* menu commands
- *File>Duplicate* menu command
- *Edit>Fill* menu command
- *Edit>Paste Into* menu command
- Changing the color of a fill layer
- Image adjustments (*Hue/Saturation* and *Replace Color*)

Multiple colorways as planned in Exercise #7 of the geo print fabric created in Exercise #5

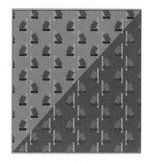

Quick Overview of the Process
This exercise will introduce you to the process of creating multiple colorways. You will use the colorways planned in Textile Design Exercise #7 and create three unique fabrics.
You will be performing the following steps:
1. Load the **halfdrop.psd** file created in Textile Design Exercise #5, or load **halfdropvar.psd**.
2. Refer to the chart of planned colorways created in Exercise #7.
3. Create two duplicates of the fabric file using the *File>Duplicate* menu command and rename the two duplicate documents.
4. Using various selection tools and recoloring techniques, change the colors of the two new files.
5. Duplicate the third colorway image and rename it with "split" as part of the name.
6. Copy the image of the second colorway image to the clipboard.
7. On the "split" image document, select half of the image and use the *Edit>Paste Into* command to paste the colors of the second colorway into the selection on the document. This creates a split coloration on one page.
8. Explore additional textile coloring techniques.

A split-screen display of two colorways

New Concepts
- o Recoloring functions
- o Using *Edit>Paste Into* to bring one print into a selected area of another print

Sources of Imagery
- o Textile print images

Review Basic Exercise #8 (Techniques for Reducing the Number of Colors in an Image) and Basic Exercise #9 (Recoloring Images).

Step-by-Step

The fabric design used in this exercise will be the artwork created in Textile Design Exercise #5, **halfdrop.psd**. If you did not complete this exercise, a file is provided on the DVD for your use.

The Halfdrop variation document

Loading and Prepping the Multiple Documents

1. Using the *File>Open* menu, direct the file requestor either to the fabric you created in Exercise #5 or to the **TD Exercise 8** folder on the Art DVD, and load the **Halfdropvariation.psd** image.

2. Choose the *Image>Duplicate* menu. A dialog will open. Name the document **Halfdropvariation col2.psd** and click **OK**. Now save the file using *File>Save*.

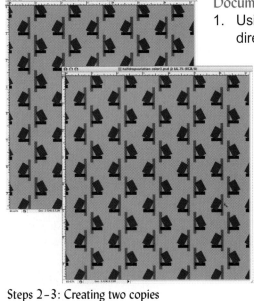

Steps 2-3: Creating two copies of the original print and renaming them.

3. Repeat the process to create a third file called **Halfdropvariation col3.psd**. Save the file. You now have three files, one of the original design and two waiting to have new colorways.

Location	Original	Colorway 2	Colorway 3
Background	Medium Gold	Medium Purple	MediumTan
Foreground #1	Light Olive	Light Blue	Light Orange
Foreground #2	Black	Dark Gray	Dark Brown
Foreground #3	Rust	Deep Pink	Deep Teal

Step 4: The color plan from Exercise #7.

4. Refresh your memory on the color plan created in Exercise #7.

5. Using the *Swatches* palette menu, load the custom palette created in the last exercise; this is **GeoFabrics.aco**. This may already be open if you just finished Exercise #7. Use the *Replace Swatches* command in the *Swatches* palette menu and choose not to save the current swatches when the dialog warning opens.

Step 5: Load the custom palette created in Exercise #7.

Creating the Colorways

The pattern that you will be recoloring contains relatively solid colors with minor anti-aliasing. This will make color selection and recoloring relatively simple and the **Magic Wand** will be the tool of choice. We will change the colors in the order presented in the chart, beginning with the Background and moving to Foreground #1, Foreground #2, and Foreground #3.

1. Choose **Halfdropvariation col2.psd** as the active document (*Window> Halfdropvariation col2.psd*).

Steps 2: Setting purple as the foreground color.

2. Click on the *Medium Purple* color in the *Swatches* palette to make it the current foreground color in the Toolbox.

Step 3: Choosing and setting options for the Magic Wand tool.

3. Choose the **Magic Wand** tool in the Toolbox. In the options bar, set the *Tolerance* to 10 and ensure that *Contiguous* and *Anti-alias* are checked. Set the selection mode to *New Selection*.

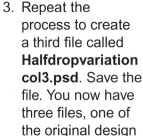

4. Click on the gold background of the fabric. Most of the gold will be selected, except those areas between the geometric shapes. Choose the *Select>Similar* menu command and observe that the remaining gold areas become selected.

5. Choose the *Edit>Fill* menu command and when the dialog opens, ensure that the *Contents* uses the *Foreground* color and that the *Opacity* setting is 100%. The gold will be replaced with purple. Deselect the selection (*Cmd/Ctrl+D*).

Step 5: Choosing options in the Fill dialog.

6. Click on the light blue in the *Swatches* palette to move it into the *foreground* color in the Toolbox.

Steps 3–5: Creating a selection of the original gold (upper left) and filling it with purple (lower right).

7. Using the **Magic Wand**, click on one of the light olive color rectangles on the fabric. Most of the gold will be selected, except those areas between the geometric shapes.

8. Choose the *Select>Similar* menu command and observe that the remaining olive shapes become selected.

9. Choose the *Edit>Fill* menu command and when the dialog opens, the Foreground color set at 100% will still be active. Click **OK** and the olive will be replaced with light blue. Deselect the selection.

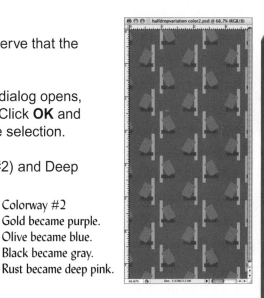

10. Repeat the process for the Dark Gray (Foreground #2) and Deep Pink (Foreground #3) colors. Use the chart plan as your guide.

11. Save the file.

Colorway #2
Gold became purple.
Olive became blue.
Black became gray.
Rust became deep pink.

Creating the Second Colorway

1. Choose **Halfdropvariation col3.psd** as the active document (*Window> Halfdropvariation col3.psd*).

2. Repeat the process of steps 2 through 10, substituting the colors from Colorway #3.

3. Save the file.

Creating a Split Color Presentation

This technique allows you to show two colorways of one fabric within one document. You need to have two colorways as separate documents. Make sure that both images are set to the same resolution and thus are the same size in scale.

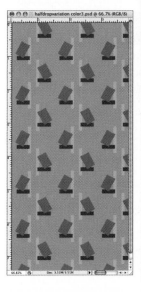

Colorway #3
Gold became tan.
Olive became orange.
Black became brown.
Rust became teal.

1. Open both images, each in its own document. You will be using **Halfdropvariation col2.psd** and **Halfdropvariation col3.psd**

Steps 2–6: Selecting a diagonal half of the first fabric (above) and using Edit>Paste Into to bring in a second fabric (below).

2. In the **Halfdropvariation col2.psd** file, choose the *Select>All* menu and then choose *Edit>Copy*. This copies the design onto the clipboard.

3. Move to the **Halfdropvariation col3.psd** image.

4. Choose the **Polygon Lasso** tool in the Toolbox.

5. Click in the lower-left corner to start the selection. Move to the upper-right corner and click. Move to the lower-right corner and click, and then double-click to complete the selection. You should have half the document, split diagonally, selected.

6. Now, choose the *Edit>Paste Into* menu command and the fabric from the first image will paste into your selection. Save the image.

Additional Thoughts on Building New Colorways

The approach you choose to changing colors in a fabric will vary according to the number of colors in the artwork. The steps followed for the geometric fabric earlier in this exercise were relatively simple, as the number of colors (including shading and anti-aliasing) were relatively limited. The key factors in fabric recoloring come down to how easy a color (or color range) can be selected and whether you are changing the selection to a single solid color or allowing the shading to remain. *Your approach will depend on the following:*

o   If the image has been reduced to a limited number of solid colors to begin with (e.g., five)

o   If the image has lots of tonal differences and you want to keep these tonal changes in the design

o   The ease with which you can select a given color using **Magic Wand** or **Quick Selection** tools, color masking, or other selection tools

o   Whether you are changing the background only, or the foreground imagery as well

Step-by-Step

The following techniques cover a range of scenarios that can exist with fabric that needs to be recolored. Review Basic Exercise #8 (Techniques for Reducing the Number of Colors in an Image) and Basic Exercise #9 (Recoloring Imagery).

Step 1: Loading Butterfly.tif designed by Angel Beckworth-Malone.

The Layers palette of Butterfly.tif showing a motif layer and a color fill layer

Changing the Background Color of the Textile Print Using Fill Layers

If you designed a pattern and kept the motif on a layer (which has a transparent background), it is simple to experiment with different background colors for the fabric. This is most easily achieved using *color fill layers.*

1. Load a file called **butterfly.tif**. This is located in the **TD Exercise 9** folder, which sits inside the **Textile Design** folder on the Art DVD. Observe the layers of this image. The motif pattern is on a transparent layer, and a pink *Solid Fill layer* is used for the background color. The process of creating prints like these was covered in Textile Design Exercise #4.

2. To change the color of the background, double-click on the *fill*

layer thumbnail and the *Color Picker* will open. Choose a new color and click **OK** and the fill layer color will now become the new color.

Changing Colors of Fabrics with Simple Coloring

This process is what was covered with the **Halfdropvariation.psd** file. It works well in instances where the textile design has a limited number of colors that contrast with each other somewhat so that selections are easily made. *The steps in summary are:*

1. Use the **Magic Wand** tool to select a portion of the first color.

2. Use the *Select>Similar* menu command to select all other instances of the color.

3. Set the color you want as the new color as the *foreground* color in the Toolbox.

4. Choose the *Edit>Fill* menu command and ensure that the *Foreground* color is the chosen fill option and that you are filling with 100% *opacity*.

Step 2: Double-clicking on the fill layer thumbnail and changing the color in the Color Picker.

Changing Colors of Fabrics with Complex Coloring

If your fabric has complex coloring that involves tonal subtleties or similar shade colors, your task for recoloring becomes more complex. In the end, it comes down to how accurately you can make a selection of the color you want to change. Once a selection is made, you can choose to fill the selection with a solid color (using the *Edit>Fill* menu command), or you can retain the tonal differences using color adjustments such as *Hue/Saturation* or *Replace Color*. Review Basic Exercises #8 and #9 for discussion on these. In the example below, the fabric is a mono-colored print with many shades of similar color.

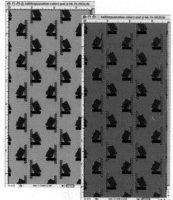

Creating a selection and changing the selected color

Loading the Fabric and Creating a Selection

1. Load the fabric called **fabric3.jpg**. This is located in the **Fabrics** folder, which is on the Art DVD. Zoom in to observe the fabric. You will see lots of different unique colors, which together make up each of the components of the print (i.e., the background, the flower stems, and the flower heads). Simplified, the print could be narrowed down to three or four distinct colors.

2. Choose the **Magic Wand** tool in the Toolbox. In the options bar, set the *Tolerance* to a number that represents your educated guess as to how broad you want to make the selection. A tolerance setting of 20 was initially used for this fabric. Make sure that *Contiguous* and *Anti-alias* are checked and choose the **Add to selection** option.

Step 1: Loading fabric3.jpg.

3. On your artwork, click on an area of the background pink. Determine if your selection of colored pixels is good and expands consistently in the area, including

Step 2: Setting up the Magic Wand tool.

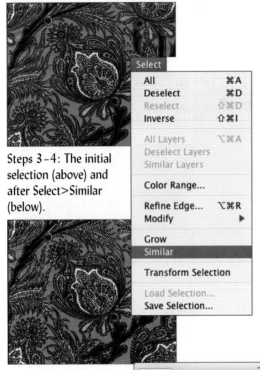

Steps 3–4: The initial selection (above) and after Select>Similar (below).

all pixels. If necessary, choose the **Add to selection** button (or the **Subtract from selection** button), as appropriate. You may also adjust your *Tolerance* setting.

4. Once you are happy with the contiguous nature of the pixels selected in the area you are working on, choose the *Select>Similar* menu command to select all pixels of the same color on your artwork.

5. Since we are going to compare changing colors in a couple of ways, save the selection using the *Select>Save Selection* menu command. Name the selection in the dialog that opens and click on **OK**.

6. If you like, create a snapshot in the *History* palette and name it *prior to color change.*

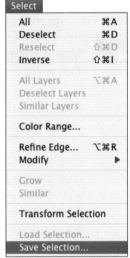

Step 5: Saving the Selection using the Select>Save Selection menu command and dialog.

Step 6: Creating a snapshot with the selection active.

To Retain the Shading Using a Hue/Saturation Layer Adjustment

1. With the selection active, move to the *Layers* palette and click on the **Create new fill or adjustment layer** button at the bottom of the palette. Slide up to the *Hue/Saturation* option and release the mouse. A dialog will open. Adjust the *Hue*, *Saturation*, and *Lightness* sliders until you create the color you want. Click **OK** and the color of the fabric background will now change. Deselect the selection (using *Cmd/Ctrl+D*).

Let's experiment...

2. Turn off the view of the new adjustment layer and click on the *Background* layer to make it active.

3. With no selection active, move to the *Layers* palette and click on the **Create new fill or adjustment layer** button at the bottom of the palette. Slide up to the *Hue/Saturation* option and release the mouse. A dialog will open. Adjust the *Hue*, *Saturation*, and *Lightness* sliders until you create the color you

Step 1: Changing the color of the selection only.

The Layers palette showing both adjustment layers

Step 3: Changing the color of the entire image with an adjustment layer.

want. Click **OK** and the color of the entire piece of fabric will now change.

To Create a Single-Color Background

There are two ways to execute changing the selection of background to a solid color. You will want to click on the snapshot to return to the moment when the background of the fabric was selected and ready for coloring.

Using Edit>Fill

1. Choose a color that you want to have as the new color and move it into the *foreground* or *background* color of the Toolbox.

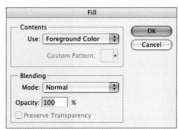

2. With the selection active, choose the *Edit>Fill* menu command. A dialog will open. Make sure that the opacity setting is 100%. Set the *Use* pop-up to either *Foreground Color* or *Background Color* to match the location in the Toolbox of the desired color. Click **OK**. A solid single color will now replace the tonal background.

3. Deselect the selection (using *Cmd/Ctrl+D*).

Using the Erase to Background Technique on a Background

This technique will work only if you are working with a *Background* in the *Layers* palette.

1. Choose a color that you want to have as the new color and move it into the *background* color of the Toolbox.

2. With the selection active, press the *Delete/Backspace* key on the keyboard and the selection will "erase" to the current background color in the Toolbox. A solid single color will not replace the tonal background.

3. Deselect the selection (using *Cmd/Ctrl+D*).

Repeat the color selection and fill techniques of your choice for other colors in the fabric. The key to success is the quality of your selection, so take the time necessary to create an accurate selection.

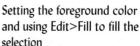

Setting the foreground color and using Edit>Fill to fill the selection

Setting the foreground color and using Edit>Fill to fill the selection

Brick repeat print with split
colorways by Lindsay Palmer

Motif was extraced from a scallend
fabric and put into a block repeat.

Scanned fabric, reduced to three
colors by Melisa Molina

Student Gallery
Fabrics
Mesa College Fashion Students

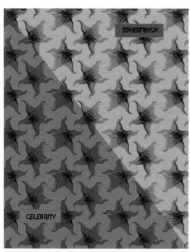

Half-drop repeat in two colorways
by Denita Mora

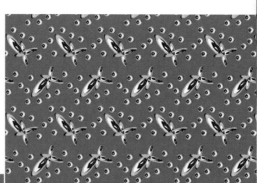

Print from a found object
by Paula Tabalipa

Paisley Print using scale
by Mildred Carney

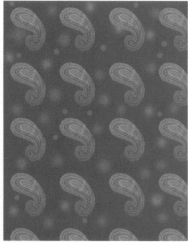

Paisley Print
by Kinsey Wilton

Mermaid Print
by Nadia Lopez

Exercise #9: Rendering Fabrics

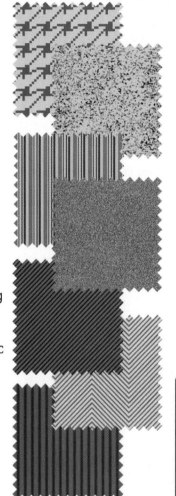

Goal
In this exercise you will use various Photoshop tools to render fabrics such as tweed, corduroy, plaids, and fake fur.

Photoshop Tools and Functions
- **Selection** tools
- Filters (such as *Sharpen*, *Blur*)
- Various painting tools (**Line**, **Brush**, **Pencil**)
- *Fill* layers

Rendering Discussion
Fabric *rendering* is the process of sketching or illustrating textiles to appear on paper as they would in real life. Most often, these fabrics have special characteristics that must be considered when drawn. These illustrations require special art techniques to be employed in the sketching stage. If you are rendering a specific fabric, you need to go through a few steps of analysis before drawing in Photoshop. *These are:*
  o Determine what the basic elements of the fabric are. Look at the fabric and squint. What do you see? Try to break the fabric down to its basic elements. For example, if you squint while looking at corduroy, you will see vertical lines running at a certain parallel distance. You will also notice the highlights, shadows, and other features.
  o Determine if there is a repeat to what you see, as you will then need to draw only one unit of this repeat.
  o Determine the scale of what you see; is it large, small, and so on.
  o Determine what tools and functions you will use in the paint program to draw the elements you defined.

A collection of rendered fabrics created in this exercise

Quick Overview of the Process
In this exercise we will be performing the following actions for each of several fabrics:
  1. Observe the fabric and analyze it per the list discussed above,
  2. Choose the painting tools and functions that allow you to build a rendering of the textile.
  3. Build a basic unit of the fabric. This may be one repeat, or a section of the fabric.
  4. If applicable, using the *Rectangular Marquee* selection tool, select one unit of repeat and define this as the pattern.
  5. Fill a larger selected area of the document with the fabric or create a new document and fill it with the fabric. *Note*: There will be some fabrics that will not work using the pattern fill.

New Concepts
  o Pattern fills
  o Pattern Stamp tool
  o Custom brushes
  o Photoshop filters

Sources of Inspiration
  o Fabric swatches of textiles to be rendered

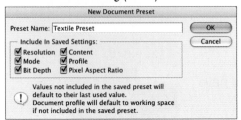

Steps 1–2: Creating a Preset file.
The File>New dialog (above) and the New
Document Preset dialog (below)

Steps 3–4: Creating a fill layer.

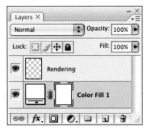

The Layers setup that
results in the Basic Setup

The Swatch template to be built

Step-by-Step

The following discussion will guide you through the process of building a document *Preset*, creating a swatch template and the rendering of several fabrics.

Creating a Textile Preset

A document *Preset* is a document whose settings are predetermined. The Preset you are about to build will be utilized in several of the rendering techniques.

1. Using the *File>New* menu command, create a new document that is 8.5" × 11" with a transparent background. Choose the RGB mode and a resolution of 150.

2. Click on the **Save Preset** button. A dialog will open. Type in *Textile Preset* and click **OK**. Click **OK** again to exit the *File>New* dialog. This will create a document preset that you can use every time you want to create a textile with the same basic settings.

Basic Setup (to be used in various renderings in this exercise)

The following four steps will be repeated through this exercise as the starting point for various textile renderings.

1. Create a new document, choosing the *Textile Preset* in the *File* dialog. Type in a name for the file that is appropriate to your textile. Click **OK**.

2. Rename the layer *Rendering* (or some other more specific name, according to the fabrics being rendered). Click "away" from the layer to deselect it (i.e., click elsewhere in the *Layers* palette).

3. Click on the **Create a new fill or adjustment layer** button at the bottom of the *Layers* palette and choose the *Solid Fill* option. When the *Color Picker* opens, choose a white or light color as the fill color. Click **OK**.

4. *Click+hold* on the *fill* layer and drag it beneath the *Rendering* layer. Click on the *Rendering* layer to make it the active layer.

Creating a Swatch Template

The following steps show you how to build a template to use in displaying your swatches. Experiment with this and other techniques to create swatch templates.

1. Create a new file and choose the *Textile Preset*. Use the name *Swatch Template* for your regular layer.

2. Set up the grid by choosing the *Photoshop>Preferences>Guides, Grid, Slices and Count* (Mac) or *Edit>Preferences>Guides, Grid, Slices and Count* (Windows). Use the default gray grid color or select a new grid color by clicking on the grid color box in the dialog and choosing a new color from the *Color Picker* that opens. Set the *Gridline every* to 1, the *Style* to Lines, and the *Subdivisions* to 8. Click **OK**. The grid will not yet appear on the screen.

3. Choose the *View>Show>Grid* menu command to view the grid. You will see solid gray lines every inch and dotted gray lines every eighth inch.

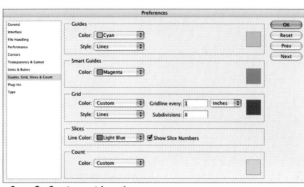

Step 2: Setting grid preferences.

4. Turn on the *Snap to Grid* function by choosing the *View>Snap* menu command.

5. Choose the **Line** shape tool in the Toolbox. In the options bar, choose the *Fill pixels* drawing mode and set the line *Weight* of 3 pixels. Uncheck the *Anti-alias* option. Set the *foreground* color in the Toolbox to a color of your choice. A medium blue was used in this exercise.

The Line tool (above) and line options (below)

6. On the document, begin drawing with the **Line** tool, drawing zigs and zags as you click and release the mouse across the drawing. The snap function will make this drawing easy as you snap to the grid. Build the first line of zig and zags (approximately 3 inches long).

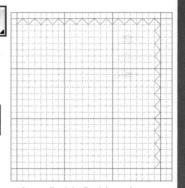

Step 6: Building the first zig-zag line of the swatch.

7. Choose the **Rectangular Marquee** selection tool, and select the zig-zag line. Copy this to the clipboard using the *Edit>Copy* command.

8. Paste in the zig-zag strip (*Edit>Paste*), and then choose the *Edit>Transform>Rotate 90 CW* menu command to rotate the new strip a quarter turn.

9. Use the **Move** tool to position the second leg of the swatch.

10. Choose *Edit>Paste* and then the *Edit>Transform>Rotate 180* menu command, and then position the third leg of the swatch.

Steps 7–11: Building the swatch edges (above and below).

11. Choose *Edit>Paste* and then the *Edit>Transform>Rotate 90 CCW* menu command, and then position the last leg of the swatch.

12. You are now ready to merge the four layers used to build the swatch. In the *Layers* palette, turn off the view of the *fill* layer by clicking on the eye icon. Now, click on the *Swatch Template* layer to make it your active layer.

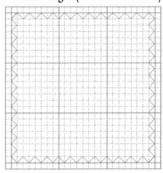

Steps 12–13: Merging layers.

13. In the *Layers* palette menu, choose the *Merge*

The final swatch, filled with color

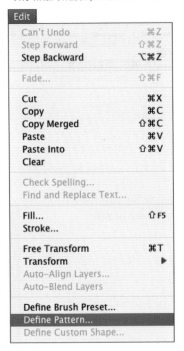

The Define Pattern menu command

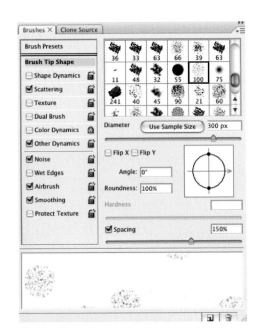

The Brushes palette

Visible option, and all visible layers will merge to become one with the *Swatch Template* layer. The four sides of the swatch will now be joined.

14. Choose the **Paint Bucket** tool. Click inside the swatch and it will fill with color to create a solid zig-zag swatch.

15. Save the file as **SwatchTemplate.psd**.

General Approach to Renderings

As you build each fabric rendering, the goal will be to either:

Create a Pattern Tile—Develop a repeat of the rendering that will appear seamless (or close to it). Select this unit and use the *Edit>Define Pattern* menu command to create a pattern.

Render the textile over a large area—Paint the textile over a larger area of the document and then select and copy the image to the clipboard. Paste the artwork into whatever selection you choose, whether it be a garment, a swatch, or other.

Once you have created a rendering, you can fill a swatch template with the rendering. If you defined a pattern, you will fill the selection or drawing with pattern. If you used the second approach and placed your rendering on the clipboard, you will use the *Edit>Paste>Into* command to bring the rendering to the swatch. This will allow you to use the *Transformation* commands to adjust the scale of the rendered fabric in the swatch.

Tweed 1: Using the Brush Tool

Tweeds are fabrics created by blending multiple colors of fiber together. Small flecks of color are often visible on the surface. You will render this fabric by stamping little dots of color on the document. The key will be to create multiple dots of color in a manner that doesn't appear to have a repeat or heavy and light areas.

1. Perform the *Basic Setup* (see page 402) but use the name *Tweed* for the regular layer.

2. Double-click on the *Layer thumbnail* on the *fill* layer and choose a light color in the *Color Picker.* Click **OK**.

Steps 1–2: Setting up the layers.

3. Open the *Brushes* palette (*Window>Brushes*) and choose the **Brush** tool in the toolbox. Choose the *Rough Round Bristle Brush* (or one similar to it) in the *Brushes* palette. In CS3/CS4 this is Brush 100. Increase the brush diameter to 300, and the spacing to 150. Turn *Color Dynamics* off, and ensure that *Scattering* is on.

4. Decide what two or three colors you will use for your tweed fleck colors. Choose the first of these as your current *foreground* color in the palette.

5. Make sure that you are on the *Tweed* layer. Using the **Brush** tool, stamp the colored *flecks* on the page over a large area. Attempt to stamp the image down in a manner such that the flecks appear evenly. Leave plenty of negative space, as there will be additional colors. Experiment with the various settings in the *Brushes* palette, as there may be other brush tips and/or settings that work well for you.

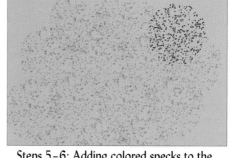

Steps 5-6: Adding colored specks to the art.

6. Change the *foreground color* in the Toolbox to a different color. If you want, you can make a new layer in the *Layers* palette for each *fleck* color, or you may stamp all colors on the same layer. The choice is yours. Stamp the second contrast color on the document, attempting to keep an even spattering of the design. Repeat with the third *fleck* color.

7. Save the file as **Tweed1.psd**.

8. Using the **Rectangular Marquee** tool, select an area to either define as a pattern (*Edit>Define Pattern*), or to be moved via the clipboard into a garment/swatch.
   Tweed Tips:

   o If you are defining a pattern tile, it may take several attempts to find a portion of the image that doesn't show a repeating pattern.

   o If you are using the clipboard to transfer the image, you may need to merge layers or flatten the image to have all parts of the image copy via the clipboard.

The final tweed swatch

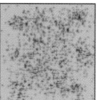

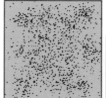

Splattered colors

with Blur...

with Gaussian Blur...

Tweed 2: Using the Noise Filter to Create a Monochromatic Splatter

This technique requires a solid color background, either on the *Background* or on a layer.

1. Create a new document named **Tweed2** that is 5 inches wide by 5 inches tall, uses a resolution of 150, and has a white background. If you want to work with a colored background, use the **Paint Bucket** tool to fill the image with color.

2. Select the *Filter/Noise/Add Noise* filter. A dialog window will open.

3. Click on the *Monochromatic* check box and choose *Uniform* Distribution option.

4. Experiment with the *Amount* slider to achieve the effect you are after.

5. Click **OK** when you are through, and you will now have a monochromatic splattering of colors.

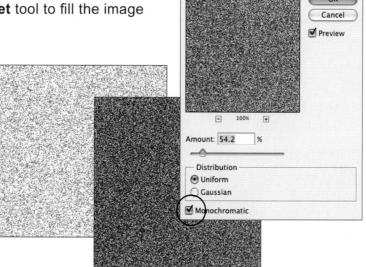

Steps 2-5: Using the Noise filter to create a tweed.

6. Save the file as **Tweed2.psd**.

7. Using the **Rectangular Marquee** tool, select an area to either define as a pattern (*Edit>Define Pattern*), or to be moved via the clipboard into a garment/swatch.

The final tweed swatch created with the Noise filter

Using a transparent fill on a tweed-like design

To change the color of an existing monochromatic, you can apply a transparent color fill over the spattered texture.

1. Choose a new color as your foreground color in the palette.

2. Choose the *Edit>Fill* menu. A dialog will open.

3. Choose *Foreground Color* in the *Use* pop-up and change the *Opacity* level to approximately 30. Click **OK** and this will overlay a transparent film of color

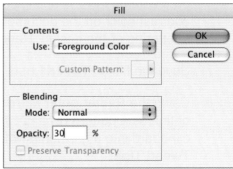

Step 3: Using a transparent fill.

on top of the spatter. If you do not like the look, undo and repeat steps 2 and 3, trying new opacity levels each time.

Stripes

Examine your fabric and determine the width and color of each stripe in the pattern. If your textile is a two-color print, then determine the width of the stripe and the distance between. Record this information on a piece of paper.

1. Perform the *Basic Setup* (see page 402) but use the name *Stripe* for the regular layer.

2. If there is an apparent background color on your textile, double-click on the *Layer thumbnail* on the *fill* layer and choose a color in the *Color Picker* that represents this color. Click **OK**.

3. Choose one of the stripe colors as your *foreground* color in the Toolbox.

4. Choose the **Rectangle** shape tool and make sure that you are in *Fill pixels* mode in the options bar. Turn the *Anti-alias* option off by unchecking it.

Step 4: Setting Line tool options.

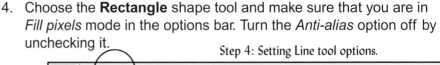

5. Draw the stripe with this new color on your fabric. Press and hold the *Shift* key as you draw to constrain the line.

6. Continue changing foreground colors and using the Rectangle tool to draw additional stripes. The stripes do not need to be long.

Stripe pattern

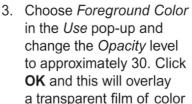

The Layers palette

Steps 5–6: Building the stripe pattern.

7. Choose the **Rectangular Marquee** selection tool and select one repeat of the stripe pattern.

8. Choose the *Edit>Define Pattern* menu item. When the dialog opens, save the pattern with a name. Click **OK**.

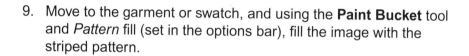

Step 9: Using the Paint Bucket tool set to Pattern fill.

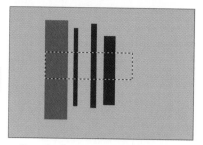

Step 7: Capturing a repeat.

9. Move to the garment or swatch, and using the **Paint Bucket** tool and *Pattern* fill (set in the options bar), fill the image with the striped pattern.

Note: You may also fill an image or selection by using the *Edit>Fill* menu command and choosing the pattern option.

Final stripe

Corduroy

Corduroy is a fabric that has a raised pile, which appears as a rib. When you examine it you will note that different values of the same color exist within the cloth. Squint to assist your comprehension. You will build corduroy in the same manner as you built the striped fabric, except that you will vary the *value* of the color used for the stripes in an effort to show depth and shadows versus highlights. The wale will be drawn in a lighter shade of the color you use to create the background of the fabric.

1. Examine your fabric and determine the width of each stripe value and the distance between.

2. Create a new document (*File>New Document*) using a resolution of 150 and a white background. Click **OK**.

3. Set the *foreground* color of the Toolbox to become the color of the background of the corduroy. This tends to be the darkest shade of the colors you will use.

Corduroy

4. Using the **Paint Bucket** tool (in the *Solid* fill mode), fill the document with the color you want to use as the base color of the fabric (e.g., dark green).

5. Change the *foreground* color to a lighter shade that will be used to draw the wale of the corduroy. This is easily achieved by double-clicking on the *foreground* color in the Toolbox, and choosing a lighter value of the color in the *Color Picker*. Click **OK**.

6. Choose the **Line** tool. In the options bar, make sure you have selected the *Fill pixels* mode. Set the line *Weight* to be a number that will allow you to draw a wale of corduroy in the correct width. The sample here used a pixel width of 15. Draw a short, straight line on the fabric, using the *Shift* key to ensure that the line is straight.

Step 6: Setting the Line tool options and drawing the first line of the wale of corduroy.

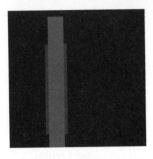

Step 7: Adding the medium value stripe.

Step 8: Capturing one repeat of the wale.

The final swatch

7. Change the value of your *foreground* color to be slightly darker than the wale color yet lighter than the background color. Change the width of your **Line** tool to be narrower than the width of your wale (e.g., 3 pixels). Draw a stripe of the new shade on either side of the wale of the corduroy. Simulate the wales of the corduroy as closely as possible.

8. Choose the **Rectangular Marquee** selection tool and select one repeat of the stripe pattern. This will include the wale and some space to one side of it.

9. Choose the *Edit>Define Pattern* menu item. When the dialog opens, save the pattern with a name (e.g., corduroy). Click **OK**.

10. Move to the garment or swatch, and using the **Paint Bucket** tool and pattern fill (set in the options bar), fill the image with the corduroy pattern.

Corduroy Tip: It is a good idea to experiment with the amount of wale versus background when defining the pattern repeat.

Alternate Approach: Instead of using different values, experiment with the *Opacity* level of one color as you lay the stripes (in the options bar).

Note: You may also fill an image or selection by using the *Edit>Fill* menu command and choosing the pattern option.

Herringbone
This is a fabric characterized by diagonal lines that reverse direction as you move across the fabric. It is most easily rendered by utilizing the *Grid* and *Grid Snap*.

Herringbone rendering

1. Perform the *Basic Setup* (see page 402) but use the name *Herringbone* for the regular layer.

2. Set up the grid by choosing the *Photoshop>Preferences>Guides, Grid, Slices and Count* (Mac) or *Edit>Preferences>Guides, Grid, Slices and Count* (Windows). Use the default gray grid color or select a new grid color by clicking on the grid color box in the dialog and choosing a new color from the *Color Picker* that opens. Set the *Gridline every* to 1, the *Style* to Lines, and the *Subdivisions* to 8. Click **OK**. The grid will not yet appear on the screen.

3. Choose the *View>Show>Grid* menu command to view the grid. You will see solid gray lines every inch and dotted gray lines every eighth inch.

4. Turn on the *Snap to Grid* function by choosing the *View>Snap* menu command.

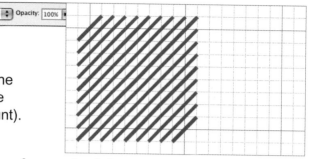

Step 5: Setting the line tool options.

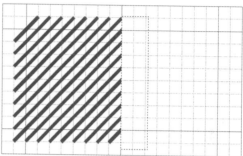

Step 7: Drawing the initial diagonal lines.

5. Choose the **Line** shape tool in the Toolbox. In the options bar, choose the *Fill pixels* drawing mode and set the line width to 5 pixels (or other amount). Uncheck the *Anti-alias* option.

6. Set the *foreground* color in the Toolbox to a color of your choice.

7. Zoom into the artwork, and draw diagonal lines per the illustration to the right until you complete a one-inch square. Extend beyond the one-inch square 1/8 inch on each side, and be careful to draw perfectly diagonally. If you press and hold the *Shift* key as you draw you can constrain your actions to a perfect 45 degree angle.

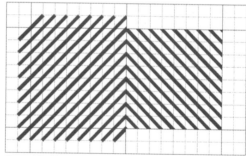

Step 8: Erasing unwanted lines on the right side.

8. Choose the **Rectangular Marquee** tool and select the diagonal lines that extend beyond the right side of the one-inch square. Press the *Delete/Backspace* key on the keyboard to erase these pixels.

9. Using the **Rectangular Marquee**, select all artwork in the one-inch square. Choose the *Edit>Copy* menu command to copy the imagery to the clipboard.

10. Choose the *Edit>Paste* command to paste a copy of the diagonal lines into a new layer. Choose the *Edit>Transform>Flip Horizontal* command to flip the artwork, and then use the **Move** tool to carefully position the artwork so that it is reversed from and perfectly aligned with the original square.

Step 10: Flipping the diagonal lines.

11. Change the *fill* layer color if you want. Click back on the *Herringbone* layer to make it active.

12. Choose the **Rectangular Marquee** selection tool and select a 2 inch wide by 1 inch tall section of the drawing.

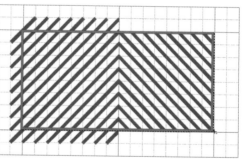

Steps 12–13: Defining the pattern.

13. Choose the *Edit>Define Pattern* menu command. When the dialog opens, name the pattern *herringbone*. Click **OK**.

Note: If the *fill* layer display is turned off, you will not include the solid background in the pattern.

14. Fill a swatch of fabric or a garment with the pattern.

From this point forward, the detailed instructions will become shorter, as you should be understanding the basic concepts of building a base for a fabric and creating and building a design layer.

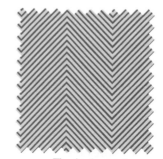

The final swatch

Twill rendering

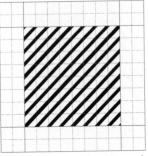

Step 1: Creating the diagonal line structure.

Houndstooth rendering

Denim or Twills

Denim and twill fabrics are characterized by diagonal lines that become visually prominent at some level in the structure. The process of building a twill fabric is very similar to the initial drawing of the Herringbone fabric.

1. Perform steps 1 through 7 of the *Herringbone* instructions but name your working layer as *Twill*. If you want a finer twill line, you may want to use 16 squares per inch for the grid setup and use a finer line to draw with.

2. Change the *fill layer* color if you want. Click back on the *Twill* layer to make it active.

3. Using the **Rectangular Marquee**, select all artwork in the one-inch square.

4. Choose the *Edit>Define Pattern* menu command. When the dialog opens, name the pattern *Twill*. Click **OK**.

Steps 2–3: Creating the fill layer and defining the area to repeat.

Note: If the *fill* layer display is turned off, you will not include the solid background in the pattern.

5. Fill a swatch of fabric or a garment with the pattern. Experiment with the relationship of values.

Houndstooth Checks

1. Perform the *Basic Setup* (see page 402) but use the name *Houndstooth* for the regular layer.

2. Look at a piece of fabric with a houndstooth check to determine its basic shape.

3. Using the **Line** or **Pencil** tool, draw one motif of the check in the proper scale. You may use the grid to assist you in the process, as shown to the right. The trick is to see how the diagonal lines form a continuous bridge between the body of the motif.

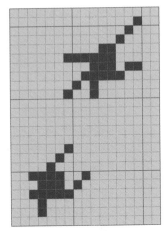

Step 3: Drawing the houndstooth pattern with the Line or Pencil tool.

4. Using the **Rectangular Marquee**, select all artwork in the one-inch square.

5. Choose the *Edit>Define Pattern* menu command. When the dialog opens, name the pattern *herringbone*. Click **OK**.

Note: If the *fill layer* display is turned off, you will not include the solid background in the pattern.

6. Fill a swatch of fabric or a garment with the pattern.

Spacing the Lines
You will need to experiment with the spacing between your diagonal lines so that the pattern can actually be seen on the printout. The higher the resolution, the more you need to pay attention to this.

Houndstooth
There are many variations to the houndstooth motif. The fabric is based on a twill weave design, so all houndstooth fabric will have a strong diagonal line statement.

Fake Fur

You can use a custom brush tip to create the hair effect of fake fur.

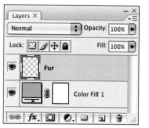

Initial Layer setup for the Fur rendering

Fur rendering

1. Perform the *Basic Setup* (see page 402) but use the name *Fur* for the regular layer.

2. Double-click on the *Layer thumbnail* on the *Fill layer* and choose a light color in the *Color Picker*. Click **OK**.

3. Open the *Brushes* palette (*Window>Brushes*) and choose the **Brush** tool in the Toolbox. Choose the *Dune Grass* brush (or one similar to it) in the *Brushes* palette. In CS3/CS4 this is Brush 112. Click on the words *Brush Tip Shape* in the upper-left corner of the window. This will open further options. Set the *Master Diameter* to approximately 112, and the *Spacing* to approximately 50%. Turn *Shape Dynamics*, *Other Dynamics,* and *Smoothing* on and the other options off. Experiment with other settings.

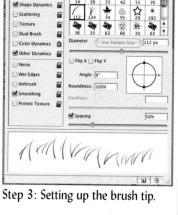

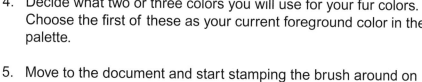

Step 3: Setting up the brush tip.

4. Decide what two or three colors you will use for your fur colors. Choose the first of these as your current foreground color in the palette.

5. Move to the document and start stamping the brush around on an area of the document. You can *click+drag* the brush around to place fur in place. Experiment.

Steps 5–7: Stamping the fur in place and creating a selection to define as the repeat.

6. Change the *foreground* color in the Toolbox to a different color and stamp/paint this on your sample. Repeat for the third color.

7. If you want to build a repeating tile of your fur, use the **Rectangular Marquee** to select a portion of the fur and create a tile repeat of it using the *Edit>Define Pattern* menu command. Then fill a swatch or other with the pattern. If you see somewhat of a repeat, do not worry, as you will correct it in the next step.

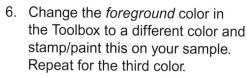

Before (above) and after step 8 (below)

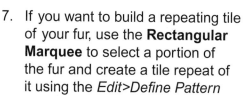

8. Use the **Brush** tool and stamp more of the hair on your swatch to cover the obvious tiling lines. You can also extend the "fur" over the edges to create a more realistic swatch.

Fur Tips

o Use the *Flip* and *Angle* options in the *Brushes* palette to rotate/flip the brush tip as you stamp/paint the fur on your image.

o Load a swatch template, and select the inside of it. Then, stamp your fur brush on the selected area only. Deselect and stamp over the edges slightly for a more realistic look.

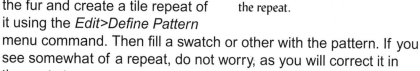

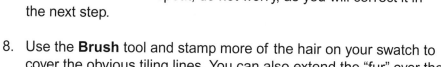

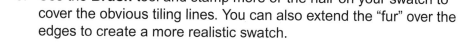

To increase the realism of fur, use the Flip and Angle options in the Brushes palette.

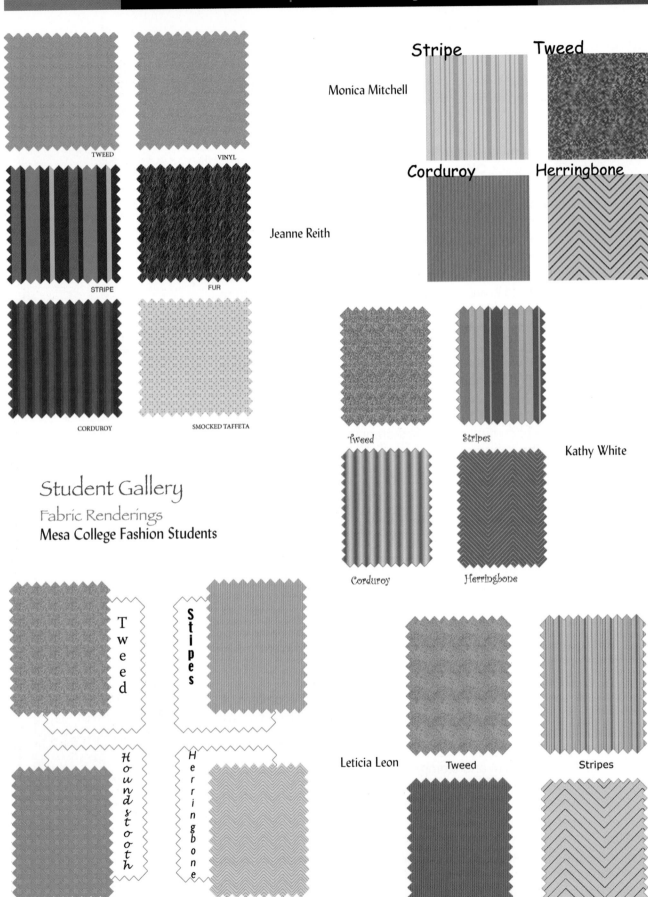

TWEED

VINYL

STRIPE

FUR

CORDUROY

SMOCKED TAFFETA

Stripe

Tweed

Monica Mitchell

Corduroy

Herringbone

Jeanne Reith

Tweed

Stripes

Kathy White

Corduroy

Herringbone

Student Gallery
Fabric Renderings
Mesa College Fashion Students

Tweed

Stipes

Houndstooth

Herringbone

Leticia Leon

Tweed

Stripes

Corduroy

Herringbone

Natalie Richardson

Exercise #10: Rendering Fabrics to Scale

Goal
In this exercise you will learn how to render a stripe fabric to scale using a "pixel ruler" as an aid.

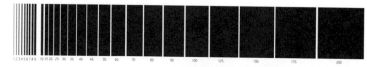

200 resolution Pixel Ruler

Photoshop Tools and Functions
- ♦ **Pencil** tool
- ♦ **Rectangular Marquee** selection tool
- ♦ *Edit>Define Pattern*

Quick Overview of the Process
You will begin by printing out a prepared graphic of a "pixel ruler." You will lay this on top of the striped fabric you are rendering. You will use the ruler to measure how many pixels wide each stripe in the fabric is. Document the stripe color and width (in pixels). In Photoshop you will paint the stripes in scale using the same colors as in the stripe.

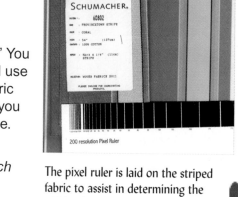

The pixel ruler is laid on the striped fabric to assist in determining the width of each colored strip.

In this exercise we will be performing the following actions for each of several fabrics:

1. Print out a *Pixel Ruler* (found on the accompanying DVD).
2. Lay the ruler on a piece of striped fabric and measure the width of each color of the stripe. Record this information.
3. Create a new document using the same resolution as the pixel ruler.
4. Using the **Pencil** tool and colors matching the stripes of the fabric, build a strip of the striped pattern in scale to the fabric.
5. Use the **Rectangular Marquee** to select one repeat of the stripe and define this as a pattern (*Edit>Define Pattern*).
6. Fill a larger document or a fabric swatch with the plaid.

New Concepts
- o Pixel ruler

Step-by-Step
Load and Print the Pixel Ruler
On the accompanying DVD or the location on your hard drive you moved the files from the DVD to, you will find a folder called **Textile Design Exercises.** Inside this folder is a folder called **TD Exercise 10,** and inside this folder are two pixel ruler files you can use to assist in rendering fabrics to scale.

200 resolution Pixel Ruler

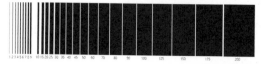

300 resolution Pixel Ruler

1. Using the *File>Open* menu, direct the file requestor to the **TD Exercise 10** folder and load one of the pixel ruler images (**pixel ruler 200.jpg** and **pixel ruler 300.jpg**).

Two pixel rulers available for your use; one is created at a resolution of 200 dpi and the other uses a resolution of 300 dpi.

2. Choose the *Image>Image Size* menu to observe the resolution of the ruler. This is critical knowledge, as you must use the same resolution in your file as the ruler you are measuring with.

3. Print the pixel ruler.

Using the Ruler to Measure the Width of Stripes on Your Fabric

1. Fold the printout so that the edge of the ruler is on the fold of the paper. This will make measuring your stripes easier.

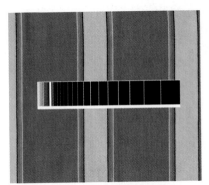

Step 3: Laying the pixel ruler on the fabric to determine the width of each stripe.

2. On a piece of paper, write down the color of each stripe as you work your way across one repeat of the striped pattern. In our example, the colors are Black, Green1, Green2, White, Rust, White, Green2, Green1, Black, and Yellow.

3. Lay the ruler on your striped fabric, and determine the number of pixels in each stripe, working your way across the fabric. Record this information on the paper where you wrote down the colors of each stripe. Since this stripe has large, wide areas of rust and yellow, you can easily measure these widths in inches and multiply each by 200 (i.e., 200 pixels per inch) to determine the number of pixels.

Black	6 pixels	
Green1	24 pixels	
Green2	20 pixels	
White	10 pixels	
Rust	500 pixels	2-1/2 inches
White	10 pixels	
Green2	20 pixels	
Green1	24 pixels	
Black	6 pixels	
Yellow	240 pixels	2-1/4 inches (slightly less)

The total width of the repeat is just slightly greater than 4-1/4 inches, and this would be 860 pixels, so you can cross-check your stripe breakdown in pixels with the total width of a repeat.

Drawing the Stripes in Photoshop

1. Create a new document (*File>New*) using the same resolution as the pixel ruler. Choose a transparent *Background Content*. Name the file *Stripe* and click **OK**. Rename the layer *Stripe*. Click away from this layer to deselect it.

2. In the *Layers* palette, create a *fill* layer by clicking on the **Create a new fill or adjustment layer** button at the bottom of the palette and sliding up to the *Solid* fill option. When the *Color Picker* opens, choose a light color and click **OK**. You do not want to choose a white ground, as white is one of the colors of the stripe.

3. Choose the *Line* tool in the Toolbox. In the options bar, choose the *Fill pixels* mode, and turn *Anti-aliasing* off.

Matching Color

Color Matching is not an easy task. Software exists for calibrating monitors to printers, but there is a learning curve. You can print out test swatches of the various colors and check these against your original fabric. Cochenille Design Studio creates an inexpensive tool that you can use to assist in color matching. It is called the Color Aid RGB disk. Read about it at http://www.cochenille.com/product.html/prodclipart.html/

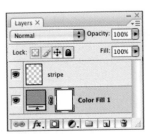

Step 2: Setting up the layers.

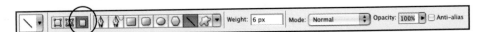

4. Set the foreground color to that of your first stripe. Set the *Line Weight* in the options bar to be that of your first stripe.

5. Draw the first stripe by clicking and then pressing the *Shift* key (to constrain the stripe so that it is straight), and dragging vertically. You do not need to draw an extremely long line, just an inch or so in height.

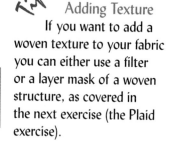

Adding Texture
If you want to add a woven texture to your fabric you can either use a filter or a layer mask of a woven structure, as covered in the next exercise (the Plaid exercise).

6. Change the color to that of your second stripe, and change the line width to match the width of the second stripe. Draw the new

Steps 5–7: Drawing the stripe pattern.

stripe line beside the first, being careful not to overlap. Sometimes it is easier to draw the stripe elsewhere on the document and then use the **Rectangular Marquee** and **Move** tools to align the stripe in the strip that you are building.

7. Repeat the color and line weight changes as you progress across the striped pattern, until you have one repeat of the stripe.

Step 8: Capturing one repeat of the stripe.

8. Using the **Rectangular Marquee** tool, select one repeat of the stripe pattern and then choose the *Edit>Define Pattern* menu. Name the pattern in the dialog that opens, and click **OK**.

The final rendered stripe, which matches the actual fabric it was drawn from

9. Fill a larger portion of the image with the repeating pattern, or fill a new document.

10. Print the new image, and lay the printout against your fabric to determine if you were accurate in your measuring. Perform any corrections as necessary, and recapture a new repeat.

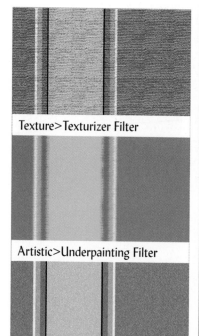

Texture>Texturizer Filter

Artistic>Underpainting Filter

Texture>Grain Filter

Using Filters to Add Fabric Texture

You can add some texture to your fabric using some of the filters found in the ***Filter*** menu.

1. Make sure that your file is in RGB mode if you want access to all filters.

2. Select the area of the fabric if you want to apply texture to only a portion of the document, or if you do not make a selection, then the entire document will have the texture added to it.

3. Choose the *Filter>Filter Gallery* menu command and experiment with the filters.

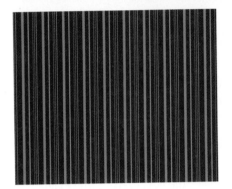

Sara Mathes

Sahara Stripe Rendering

Student Gallery
Fabrics Rendered to
Scale from Actual
Samples
**Mesa College Fashion
Students**

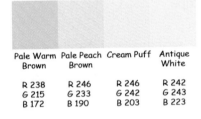

Pale Warm Brown	Pale Peach Brown	Cream Puff	Antique White
R 238	R 246	R 246	R 242
G 215	G 233	G 242	G 243
B 172	B 190	B 203	B 223

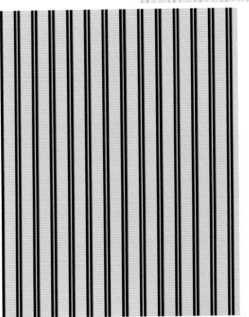

Sahara Stripe

Carol Newland

Renee Anderson

Paula Tabalipa

Sequins by Kathy White

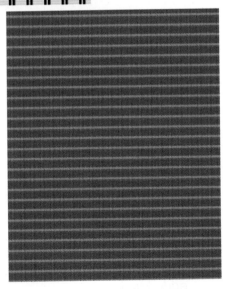

Michele Escobedo

Exercise #11: Rendering Plaids in Photoshop

Goal

To create a plaid fabric through the construction of a warp, a weft, and a twill structure, and the combination of these three elements.

A plain weave plaid

Photoshop Tools and Functions

- ♦ **Selection** tools
- ♦ **Pencil** tool
- ♦ *Edit>Define>Pattern*
- ♦ Layer mask
- ♦ Adjusting image size using *Nearest Neighbor*
- ♦ Replace Color function (*Image>Adjustment>Replace Color*)

Quick Overview of the Process

A *layer mask* will be employed in this exercise. A mask allows you to peep through one layer (in our case, the weft) and see what is beneath (in our case, the warp). The mask is set by using the color black as the "see-through" color.

In this exercise we will be performing the following actions for each of several fabrics:

1. Build a vertical stripe pattern to represent the warp threads of a plaid.
2. Duplicate the *Warp* layer and rename it *Weft*, and then rotate the artwork in the document so that the stripe pattern is horizontal.
3. Build a fabric structure on a separate document, and select and define the structure as a pattern.
4. Create a layer mask on the *Weft* layer of the plaid document.
5. Fill the layer mask thumbnail with the structure.
6. Resize the image (if necessary) to create a larger version of the plaid.
7. Select the plaid and define it as a pattern.
8. Fill a larger document or a fabric swatch with the plaid.

A twill weave plaid

Note: Sample Note
If you are copying a plaid, use the Pixel Ruler technique in the previous exercise to accurately measure and re-create the plaid.

New Concepts

- o Layer mask
- o Nearest Neighbor in *Adjust>Image Size*
- o Replace Color (Image Adjustment)

Step-by-Step
Create the Warp

1. Open a new document, using a resolution of 72, and making it 24 pixels wide by 24 pixels tall. Name it *Plaid*. Click **OK**. The document will open.

2. Zoom in so you can see the document (using the magnification mode of your choice).

3. Open the *Color* palette (*Window>Color*). You will select your colors from here.

4. In the *Layers* palette, rename the *Background* to *Warp*.

Step 1: Creating a new document.

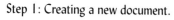
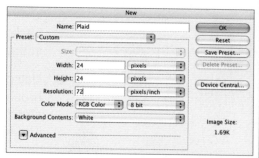

Step 2: Zooming in.

Step 3: Opening the Color palette.

The Warp layer

5. Choose the **Pencil** tool and a single pixel brush tip, and paint a stripe pattern across the first row or two of the document, using two to four colors. This will be the basis of your fabric warp.

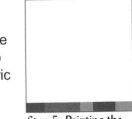

Step 5: Painting the first stripe pattern.

6. Using the **Rectangular Marquee** tool, select the "striped row" and then define a pattern (*Edit>Define Pattern*). When the *Pattern* dialog opens, name the pattern warp and click **OK**.

7. Create a selection of the entire document (*Select>All*) and fill this with the pattern (*Edit>Fill*, set to the Warp pattern).

Create the Weft

1. Now duplicate the layer by choosing the *Duplicate Layer* option from the *Layers* palette menu. Rename this new layer *Weft*.

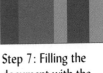

Step 7: Filling the document with the striped pattern.

2. Make this the active layer by clicking on it in the *Layers* palette (if it is not already selected).

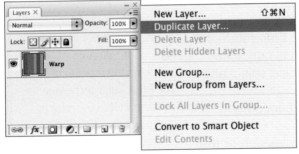

Steps 1–2: Duplicating the Warp layer (above) and renaming it (below).

3. In your document, use the *Select>All* menu command to select the entire image and then choose the *Edit/Transform/Rotate 90 degrees CW* menu to rotate this layer 90 degrees clockwise.

Now you should have two layers: one that is the warp, one that is the weft.

The results of the transformation

Create the Structure

1. Using *File>New*, create a new document that is 4 pixels wide by 4 pixels tall. Set a resolution of 72 and a white background. Name the file *Structure*. Click **OK**. Zoom in to see the image.

2. Using the default black color, the **Pencil** tool, and a single pixel brush tip, paint in a plain weave structure (checkerboard) or a twill structure (a diagonal line). See the illustrations of each to the left. The twill pattern there is a 3 × 1 twill.

A Plain weave structure (left) and a twill weave structure (right)

To Build the Plaid

1. In the **Structure** document, select all (*Select>All*), and define this as a pattern (*Edit>Define Pattern*). Name the pattern *structure*.

2. Move to the **Plaid** document (*Window/Plaid*).

3. Click on the *Weft* layer to make it the active layer (in the *Layers* palette).

4. Create a *Layer Mask* by clicking on the *Add layer mask* button in the lower bar of the *Layers* palette. A white box appears on the *Weft* layer. It is now active. It is important to understand that you can click on the white thumbnail or the weft thumbnail to set either as the active entity. You want the layer mask (the white box) to be active. Click on this.

Step 4: Adding a layer mask.

5. Fill the *Layer Mask thumbnail* with the structure pattern using the *Edit>Fill* menu command, choosing the structure pattern as your fill. You will now see a plaid fabric in your document. Essentially, you are looking through the black pixels of the layer mask to see the warp stripes beneath.

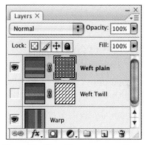

Step 5: Click on the layer mask thumbnail to make it active.

A twill weave plaid (above) and a plain weave plaid (below)

6. If you want to experiment with both the twill and the plain weave structures, duplicate the weft layer (using the *Duplicate Layer* command in the *Layers* palette menu), then click on the layer mask thumbnail of the new layer, press the *Delete/Backspace* key to remove the mask that exists, and fill the mask with the alternate structure pattern. Rename the layers *Weft Twill* and *Weft Plain*. You will need to hide the view of one weft layer or the other to properly view the fabric.

7. Save the file (**plaid.psd**).

To Create a Fabric

You will now want to define this plaid as a pattern, thus creating a pattern tile. If you want the plaid to be magnified somewhat (as it is very fine in detail), you can resize it and then define the new pattern.

Step 6: Creating a second layer mask layer with the alternate structure pattern.

1. Make sure that the layer thumbnail of your weft layer is selected (as opposed to a layer mask thumbnail).

2. Select the entire image using the *Select>All* menu command.

3. Define this image as a pattern (*Edit/Define Pattern*). Name the pattern and click **OK**.

Step 1: Selecting the layer thumbnail of the layer.

4. To save a larger version of the pattern tile of your plaid, resize the **Plaid** document. Choose the *Image>Image Size* menu command. When the dialog opens, set the new size to be a multiple of 24

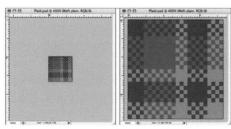

Step 4: Using the Image Size menu command to enlarge the plaid.

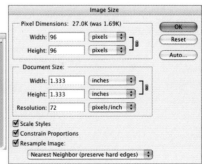

Step 4: The Image Size dialog and settings.

pixels (e.g., 48, 72, or 96). Choose the *Nearest Neighbor* setting in the pop-up menu at the bottom of the dialog. Click **OK**. The image will enlarge and keep its sharp clarity. The *Nearest Neighbor* function allows you to rescale and keep the details without anti-aliasing.

5. Select the entire document and redefine the pattern (*Edit>Define Pattern*), and give the pattern a slightly different name (e.g., plaid enlarged).

Step 5: Naming the enlarged plaid pattern.

6. Create a new larger document (8.5 × 11 inches), or load the swatches template image created in the last exercise. The resolution of this document will dictate the scale of the plaid. The higher the resolution, the finer the plaid.

7. Fill the new document or swatch with the plaid pattern using the *Edit>Fill* menu command. Save the new document with a different name (e.g., **plaidfabric1.psd**).

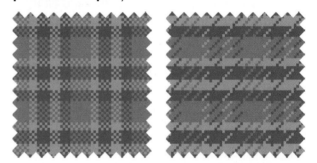

Two finished plaids: a plain weave version (left) and a twill weave version (right)

To Create a New Colorway

There are many approaches to changing colors of an existing plaid. The instructions below show you how to use the *Replace Color* command, which is found in the *Image>Adjustment* menu.

It is best to change the colors in the original *Plaid* document, as this is where the colors are pure and true, and no anti-aliasing has occurred.

1. Move to the **Plaid** document and save this as a new file (e.g., **PlaidCol2.psd**).

2. Flatten the layers using the *Flatten Layers* menu command in the *Layers* palette menu.

3. Choose the *Image>Adjustments>Replace Color* menu command. A dialog will open.

Step 2: Flattening all layers (above) to create a single background (below).

Step 3: Choosing the Replace Color command.

4. Use the **Eyedropper** tool in the dialog and click on one of the colors. Move the sliders back and forth in the lower portion of the dialog to change the color. Click **OK** when you are through to change this single color.

5. Repeat steps 3 and 4 for each color in the plaid.

6. Once all colors are changed, define a pattern with the new colorways so you may fill a larger area with the plaid.

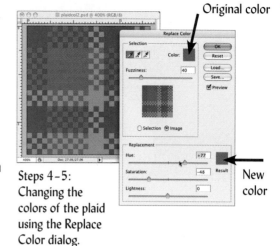

Original color

New color

Steps 4–5: Changing the colors of the plaid using the Replace Color dialog.

The final plaid

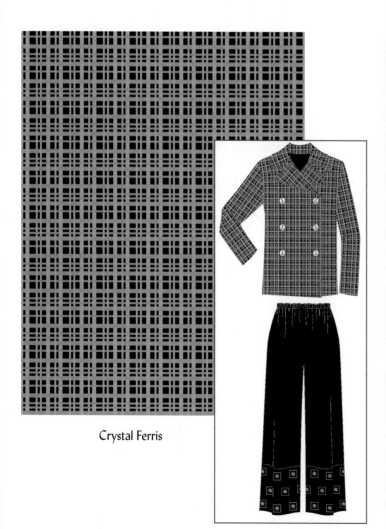

Crystal Ferris

June Triolo

Exercise #12: Rendering Knits

Goal
To draw and use knit stitch patterns to render knitwear.

Photoshop Tools and Functions
- Various drawing/painting tools (**Line**, **Brush**, **Pencil**)
- **Selection** tools
- Creating patterns (*Edit>Define Pattern*) and Brush Presets (*Edit Define Brush*)
- **Pattern Stamp** tool
- *Brush* palette and **Brush** tool

Quick Overview of the Process
Renderings of knit textures will be created using various drawing/painting tools. These will be selected and defined as a pattern so that they may be used to fill a swatch or knit garment. You can begin the process by examining a knit fabric or garment and breaking down the stitch pattern into simple elements. For example, a knit stitch generally appears as a little "V." Purl stitches appear as horizontal bars. Cables appear as intertwining curves.

In this exercise we will be performing the following actions for each of several fabrics:

1. Analyze sweaters and knits to determine how to illustrate stitch patterns. You can scan a knit and use this as a basis for drawing if you like.
2. Draw a knit stitch using basic painting/drawing tools or selection stroke operations.
3. Select one unit of repeat of the knit stitch (either from the scanned image of from your drawing) and define it as a pattern (*Edit>Define Pattern*). At the same time, define it as a Brush Preset (*Edit>Define Brush Preset*).
4. Fill a garment or selected area with the stitch pattern (*Edit>Pattern Fill* or using the **Paint Bucket** tool set to Pattern fill with the correct pattern).
5. Experiment with using the **Pattern Stamp** tool to paint stitches in a garment.
6. Experiment with the **Brush** tool and a custom knit brush tip.

New Concepts
- Custom **Brushes** and the *Brushes* palette
- **Pattern Stamp** tool
- Using filters

Sources of Imagery
- Digital images of artwork and custom Presets on the DVD

Step-by-Step

Analyze Knit Scans and Prepping for Drawing Stitches
On the accompanying DVD or the location on your hard drive you moved the files to, you will find a folder called **Textile Design Exercises.** Inside

this folder is a folder called **TD Exercise 12**, and inside this folder is folder called **Knit Scans**. You will examine these files to see how knits are structures.

1. Using the *File>Open* menu, direct the file requestor to the **Knit Scans** folder and load one or more of the files. Look at the knits and analyze them. Think about how you would draw or render the individual stitches in the design. The file called **knitpresetsamples.tif** in the **Presets** folder shows you some examples of stitches that have been drawn.

2. Create a new document, choosing the *Basic Preset* in the *File* dialog (as created on page 410) but using the name *Knit Drawing* for the regular layer. Name the file **Knit Sample.** Click **OK**.

3. If you need to refer to an image of a knit, move to a scanned image of knit stitches and using the **Rectangular Marquee** tool, frame off a small area of the knit and then use the *Edit>Copy* to copy this to the clipboard. Move to the **Knit Sample** file and use *Edit>Paste* to paste in the sample. It will paste onto a separate layer. Click on the *Knit Drawing layer* to make it active. You will use the scanned image as a reference only. OR, you can define a stitch unit of the scanned image as a pattern. We will be using the drawing approach in this exercise.

Drawing a Knit Stitch Unit and Defining It as a Pattern or Brush

You are now ready to draw a stitch unit. Observe the shape of a knit stitch. It is composed of two ovals paired in a "V" format. You will now build one knit stitch unit.

1. Choose the **Elliptical Marquee** tool in the Toolbox. Choose a gray color as the foreground color in the Toolbox.

2. On the *Knit Drawing* layer, *click+hold+drag* to create an oval-shaped selection. When you release the mouse you will see the marching ants.

3. Choose the *Edit>Stroke* palette. When the dialog opens, set the pixel *Weight* to 2 and the stroke *Location* to the inside of the selection. Click **OK**. The ellipse will now be stroked with a gray outline. Do not deselect.

4. While the selection is still active, choose the *Edit>Transform* command, or press *Cmd/Ctrl+T* on the keyboard. Move the options bar and type **-30** in the *angle* field and press the *Return/Enter* key. The oval stitch will rotate. Click on the **Commit Transform** button in the options bar (the check box) or press the *Return/Enter* key on the keyboard. Do not deselect.

Note:

Textile Preset
See page 410 for information on how the Basic Preset was created.

Step 3: Viewing the scanned knit and observing how stitches are formed.

The Layers palette after a reference knit is moved into the document

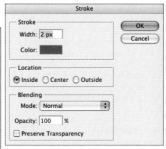

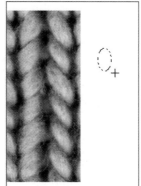

Steps 1–3: Creating an elliptical selection and stroking it with a light gray color.

Options set for the Transformation

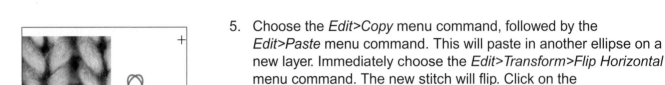

Steps 5–6: Copying and pasting in a second ellipse (above) and moving it in position (below).

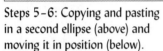

Step 7: Using the Merge Down command in the Layers palette to merge the stitches on two layers.

5. Choose the *Edit>Copy* menu command, followed by the *Edit>Paste* menu command. This will paste in another ellipse on a new layer. Immediately choose the *Edit>Transform>Flip Horizontal* menu command. The new stitch will flip. Click on the **Commit Transform** button in the options bar (the check box) or press the *Return/Enter* key on the keyboard. Do not deselect.

6. Choose the **Move** tool in the Toolbox, and move the new stitch over to the right, separating the stitches. Be sure to keep them on the same level. You can do this by holding the *Shift* key as you move the stitches. You may also use the arrows on the keyboard to nudge the stitches gently.

7. In the *Layers* palette menu, choose the *Merge Down* command. This will merge the right side of the stitch onto the same layer as the left side of the stitch. Turn the display of the *Fill Layer* off. This will allow you to fill solid colored areas with stitch patterns later.

8. Using the **Rectangular Marquee** tool, select the two stitches, copy them to the clipboard (*Edit>Copy*), and then paste them into the document using *Edit>Paste*. Move this new stitch unit down beneath the first stitch unit. You can experiment with the offset between the first two stitch units, but the simplest approach is to move the second unit just under the first (with no overlap). This step helps you set the offset space between the two vertical stitches. If you are using some overlap you will need to build one additional stitch so that you can capture an accurate unit for repeat.

9. Using the **Rectangular Marquee** tool, select one pair of stitches, leaving a little space to the right of the unit (which will allow you to see columns of stitches more easily). Choose the *Edit>Define Pattern* menu command. Name the pattern in the dialog that

Step 9: Defining the pattern or the Brush preset using the Edit menu.

Steps 8–9: Creating a second stitch unit and then selecting one unit to define as the repeating tile and also as a Brush preset.

opens and click **OK**. At the same time, choose the *Edit>Define Brush Preset...* and name the preset in the dialog that opens. Click **OK**. We will use the *Brush* preset later in the exercise.

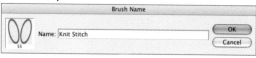

Step 9: The Pattern Name (above) and Brush Name (below) dialogs used to name the pattern fill and the Brush preset.

10. Test your stitch pattern by creating a selection off to one side of your document and filling it with the pattern of the stitch. If you need to correct your defining selection, do so and repeat the process again.

11. Save the file in case you want to alter it, or change the scale of your knit stitch pattern. If you do, select one stitch unit and use the *Transform* commands to scale it down, then redefine the pattern or brush.

Step 10: Testing a stitch pattern in repeat.

Note: **Scaling Pattern Fills**
When using pattern fills, it is always easier to make the unit of repeat in the largest size you might want, as it is easier and cleaner to scale artwork down. If you need to scale up a small repeating tile, the image often becomes fuzzy. Sometimes you might prefer to make tiles and define patterns of different sizes.

Filling a Garment with the Knit Pattern

You will need to create a full page of the knit stitch pattern. You will then load a drawing of a garment (or draw your own) and fill this garment with the knit pattern. Instead of using the simple fill approach (i.e., filling an area with a pattern), you will learn how to copy a pattern to the clipboard and then create a selection and *"paste into"* the selection. This allows you to transform and scale the artwork.

1. Create a new document, choosing the *Textile Preset*. Fill this document with the knit stitch pattern using the *Edit>Fill* command or the **Paint Bucket** tool set to a pattern fill. The pattern of stitches will appear on a transparent ground and this is what we want. Save this image as **stitch pattern fill.tif**.

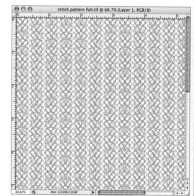

Step 1: Filling a document with the stitch pattern.

2. Load a drawing of a garment. There is a sample top in the **Garments** folder on your Art DVD. Using the *File>Open* command, load an image called **Top1.tif**. This is a T-shirt type top that is colored. The top came from the SnapFashun collection of images. Observe the size of the top.

3. Move back to the knit pattern document. Choose the *Select>All* menu to select the entire image and then copy it to the clipboard (*Edit>Copy*).

4. Return to the garment document. Choose the **Magic Wand** tool and use a low *Tolerance* setting (e.g., 1–5). Make sure that the *Contiguous* and *Anti-alias* options are checked. Click inside the body of the top to select all the orange color.

Step 4: Using the Magic Wand to select the inner T-shirt (selecting by color).

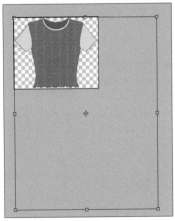

Steps 5–6: Using Paste Into to bring the stitches into the garment and then starting the transformation process.

The Layers palette showing the layer masks created for the body of the garment

5. Choose the *Edit>Paste Into* menu command. The knit stitches will paste into the selected area only. They will appear large.

6. Choose the *Edit>Transform* menu command, or press *Cmd/Ctrl+T* on the keyboard. You will see a bounding box appear around the knit stitch pattern that sits inside the garment. It may be helpful to zoom out so you can see more of the bounding box.

7. Adjust the size of the knit stitches by resizing the bounding box or by typing in the new scale in the options bar. The latter approach is recommended if you will be filling in multiple areas so that you can keep the scale of the adjusted knit consistent. Adjust the placement of newly adjusted knit within the body of the garment by moving the box around. Experiment with finding the right size of stitch pattern to top. It is often helpful to allow the stitch patterns to be slightly larger so they can be seen. When you are happy with the transformation, click on the **Commit** button in the options bar or press the *Return/Enter* key on the keyboard. Note that a layer mask now exists above the garment layer. Rename this layer *Body*.

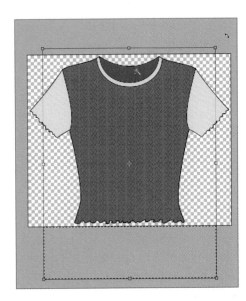

Step 7: Adjusting the scale of the knit stitches within the body of the garment. Pay attention to the scale for future reference if you choose to place knit stitches in the sleeve.

8. If you want to place stitches in the sleeves, repeat steps 4 through 7 above, and add a rotation to the transformation. It would be best to fill one sleeve at a time, and pay attention to the degree of rotation so you can match the angle on both sleeves (although one sleeve will be the negative angle of the other). To conserve memory and facilitate the process, use a smaller piece of the knit stitches on the clipboard prior to the *Paste Into* step. Rename the new mask layers *Left Sleeve* and *Right Sleeve*.

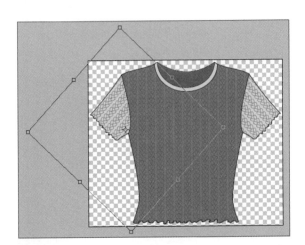

Step 8: Using the Paste Into command and transformations to place the knit stitches in each sleeve.

The Layers palette showing the layer masks that have been created

9. If you want to change the color of the gray stitches, click on the any of the layer masks and then choose the *Image>Adjustments>Hue/Saturation* menu command. A dialog will open. Click on the *Colorize* check box and adjust the sliders. You will be able to change the color and saturation of the stitch pattern. It is ideal to turn the stitches to a deeper value of the garment color in that area. You will need to adjust each layer mask separately. Record the formula you use on the first sleeve so you can adjust to the same color on the second sleeve.

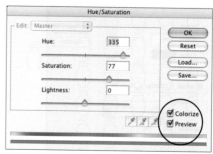

Step 9: Adjusting the color of the knit stitches in the layer mask. Make sure that the Colorize option is checked.

 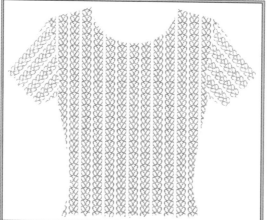

The final sweater with stitches in place and recolored (left). The illustration on the right shows you what exists on the three layer masks.

Developing a Knit Cable Using Paths and the Brush Tool

A knit cable will be developed using **Shape** and **Pen** tools and the *Path* palette.

1. Create a new document using the *Textile Preset*. Create a new layer and call it *Stitches*. Open the *Paths* palette (*Window>Paths*).

Step 1: Opening the Paths palette.

2. Choose the **Ellipse** shape tool in the Toolbox. In the options bar, choose the *Paths* option (the center icon in the drawing mode group).

Step 2: Choosing and setting up the Ellipse tool.

3. Draw an ellipse on your document in the scale you want it. You will see a *Work Path* appear in the *Paths* palette. This path is just a guide. It is not a physical object until you make it so.

Step 3: Drawing the ellipse.

4. In the *Paths* palette, click on the **Load path as a selection** button (in the center of the strip of icons at the bottom of the *Paths* palette). The drawing will now turn into a selection.

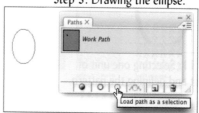

5. Make sure that gray is the current *foreground* color in the Toolbox.

Step 4: Creating a selection from the path.

Step 2: Creating a selection of the inner sweater.

Using the Pattern Stamp Tool

This tool allows you to choose an existing pattern and then paint with it in a brushlike manner. You do not need the grid to use this tool; however, you need to make sure you draw with enough strokes on the screen to fully paint the image in place. You will load a drawing of a sweater and paint knit stitches within it. By making a selection of the inside of the sweater, you can easily control where you paint the knit stitches.

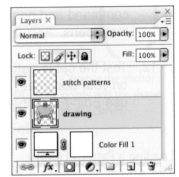

1. Using the *File>Open* command, load a file called **sweater1.tif.** This is located in the **Garments** folder on the Art DVD.

2. Choose the **Magic Wand** tool. Set the *Tolerance* to 32. Click inside the sweater body to select the main body and sleeves. Save this selection in case you want it for later using the *Select>Save Selection* menu command.

3. Create a new layer in the *Layers* palette and name this *stitch patterns*. Make sure that this is the active layer.

Step 5: Painting inside the selected area.

4. Choose the **Pattern Stamp** tool in the Toolbox (or press *S* or *Shift+S* on the keyboard). It is located beneath the **Clone Stamp** tool. Choose a knit pattern using the *Pattern picker* pop-up. In the options bar choose a brush tip of about *60* pixels, set the *Opacity* and flow to 100%, and make sure that the *Aligned* box is checked. Aligned ensures that the pattern stamps in a perfect block repeat manner, regardless of how you move your brush on the screen.

Example of using a contracted selection and painting inside of that

Example of using a soft-edged brush and painting in a portion of the garment

5. Move your cursor over the selection on the document. Begin to paint by stamping and dragging the cursor over the selection. You will see that your stitch pattern paints in repeat inside the body of the sweater and on its own layer.

The result will be a painted repeat of your motif in a "block" grid design approach.

The Brush tool

Tips and Creative Suggestions
♦ If you choose a soft-edge brush, the edges will be soft when you paint with the brush.
♦ Do not paint the entire area of the body of the garment; rather, just paint in selected areas.
♦ Create a selection inside the image of your garment, then reduce the selection. (Use *Select>Modify>Contract* and choose the number of pixels to contract the selection (e.g., 25).)
♦ Experiment with adjusting the *Opacity* and *Flow* settings.
♦ To quickly increase or decrease the Brush diameter as you paint, use the [and] keys on the keyboard.

Using the Brush Tool and a Custom Brush Tip

This last example shows you how to paint with a custom knit brush tip. You will use the Brush you defined and saved on page 433 (called Knit Stitch). Painting with a custom brush tip is different from working with the **Pattern Stamp** tool in that you can overlap and layer stitches as you paint. You also have a lot of control over the size and spacing of the brush tip.

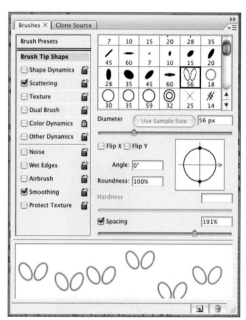

Setting options in the Brush palette for the knit stitch brush tip

1. Using the *File>Open* command, load a file called **sweater2.tif.** This is located in the **Garments** folder on the Art DVD.

2. Choose the **Magic Wand** tool. Set the *Tolerance* at the default 32. Click inside the sweater body to select the main body and sleeves.

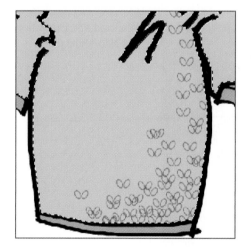

Example of painted stitches, created using the Brush tool and a custom tip

3. Create a new layer in the *Layers* palette and name it *stitch patterns*. Make sure that this is the active layer.

4. Choose the **Brush** tool in the Toolbox (or press *B* or *Shift+B* on the keyboard).

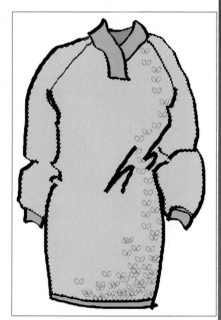

5. Open the *Brushes* palette (*Window>Brushes*). Choose the knit stitch brush tip you created earlier in the exercise. Click on the word *Brush Tip* in the upper-left corner of the palette. This will open new options in the display. Adjust the *Spacing* (e.g., to 191%) and the *Diameter* (e.g., to 56) of the brush. Experiment with different options. Our example will use *Scattering* and *Smoothing*, but there are lots of fun

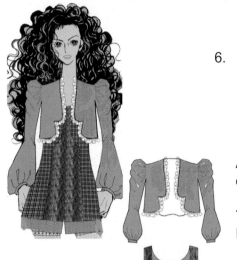

combinations. Observe the preview area as you experiment with settings.

6. Move over to your drawing where the selection is active on the stitch patterns layer. Paint stitches on the sweater. Note how you can overlap them if you lift and repaint in the same area. Have fun painting in a knit texture.

As you can see, using a custom brush tip simply provides another option for rendering.

This completes the Textile Design Exercise portion of the book.

Rendered Knit illustration and flats by Nania Pongpitakkul

Student Gallery
Rendered Knits
Mesa College Fashion Students

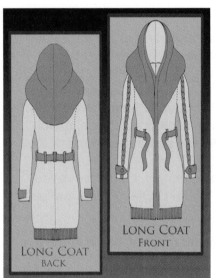
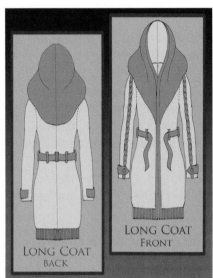

Rendered Knit illustration by Osbaldo Ahumada

Rendered Knit illustration by Mariel Diaz-Mendoza

Rendered Knit Flats by Amber Lake

Presentation Exercises

This chapter includes a series of exercises that focus on various presentation techniques.

The exercises are divided into groups. The first two exercises focus on working with type and effects. The second set focuses on layout and methods of presenting your work. The third set of exercises teaches you how to prep files for presentations (to reduce file size), how to use Photoshop's Actions palette to automate processes, and how to build an electronic portfolio of your Photoshop images in Adobe Acrobat.

Exercises include:

Adding Pizazz to Your Art

Exercise #1   Creative Techniques with Type
Exercise #2   Using Layer Styles

Creative Layout

Exercise #3   Creating Interest in Layouts
Exercise #4   Merchandising with Snapshots

Prepping Files for Presentations

Exercise #5   Prepping Graphics for Presentations
Exercise #6   Using Actions to Facilitate the Design or Graphic Preparation Process
Exercise #7   Building an Electronic Portfolio Using Adobe Acrobat

Trend Knitwear Presentation and flats for Fall/Winter 08/09 by Osbaldo Ahumada

Note: Instructions
The detail of the instructions will be somewhat simplified at this point.

Composite
and Garment
Design by
Pontus Wickbom
Burevall

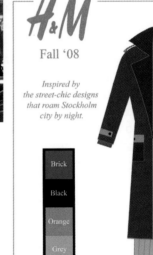

H&M

Fall '08

*Inspired by
the street-chic designs
that roam Stockholm
city by night.*

| Brick |
| Black |
| Orange |
| Grey |
| Brown |

Creative Color Trend
Presentation by Mariel
Diaz-Mendoza

Kristine Delosreyes:
Effects on fashion illustration

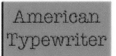

Curlz MT

Font: Drop Shadow
　　　Bevel/Emboss
　　　Satin
　　　Color overlay
Box: Drop Shadow
　　　Inner glow
　　　Gradient Overlay

HERCULANUM

Font: Drop shadow
　　　Outer Glow
　　　Inner Glow
　　　Bevel/Emboss
　　　Gradient overlay
　　　Pattern overlay
Box: Drop Shadow
　　　Bevel/Emboss
　　　pattern overlay

American
Typewriter

Font: Drop Shadow
　　　Inner shadow
　　　Outer glow
　　　Bevel/emboss
　　　Stroke
Box:Drop Shadow
　　　Bevel/Emboss
　　　Satin

Font: Drop Shadow
　　　Outer/Inner Glow
　　　Satin
　　　Pattern Overlay
Box: Drop shadow
　　　Inner/outer glow
　　　Inner shadow
　　　Bevel/emboss
　　　Gradient/Pattern
　　　　　Overlays

Nadia Lopez: Creative play with fonts

Planning Layouts

When you begin a project, or when it becomes time to lay out various images for a presentation, you must consider how you will combine the use of imagery, space planning, type and text effects, and more to achieve the desired results.

Planning up Front

If you are going to be building art on multiple documents that will later be combined for a presentation, it is wise to think ahead before you paint, design, or create. *The following is a list of tips to consider:*

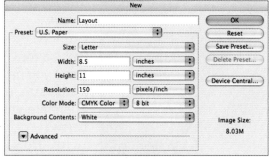

New Document (File>New)

o   Determine what the generic print *resolution* for the documents will be and set up all documents with the same resolution. If you don't do this up front, you can later scale some of the images to match; but when you do this some pixel distortion may occur.

o   Determine if you are going to build your layout in *Landscape* or *Portrait* mode and set the document up accordingly.

o   If you are working with *scanned art*, attempt to scan images at a resolution that matches, or is close to the resolution you want in the image.

o   Determine the approximate size of each element/ garment to be placed in the layout and attempt to draw/ design in that size. One way to do this is to mock up a paper sketch showing placement and size of the various elements to be included in the layout. If you are going to use text for titles or labeling, include this in your layout too.

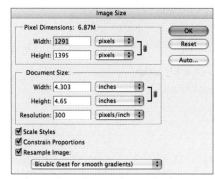

Image Size (Image>Image Size)

o   Once you have brought a scanned image in, crop it to remove all unnecessary art, then modify its resolution and image size to the predetermined desired size. Use the *Image>Image Size* menu command.

Combining Multiple Images into a Layout

If you are working with multiple images generated in separate documents, you will need to bring them together.
Consider the following:

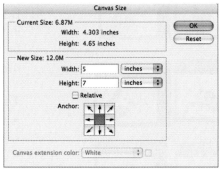

Canvas Size (Image>Canvas Size)

o   Although it is not critical, it is helpful to have your images in scale with each other. You can check this by confirming that the resolution of the various documents are the same. Then, zoom the scales of the images so that they are the same (e.g., 100%). Compare the arts. If they are close, you can safely transport one document to the other and perform any minor scale operations in the layout document.

o   Decide which image will become the master layout image. If it is not the desired size, increase its canvas to the size you want. Choose the position of your artwork as you set the canvas size (using the anchor point), or select and move the image to its final location in the layout.

o The artwork in one document can be moved to another document by using the clipboard (select, copy and paste) or by using *drag and drop*.

General Work Flow in Creating a Layout

The following is the typical sequence of steps performed when creating layouts:

Mariel Diaz-Mendoza:
Creative Layout

Position the Graphics

Once you have worked out the details of your graphics (i.e., resolution, image size, etc.), you are ready to begin the layout for your presentation. There are various things that need to be considered. *Review the list below:*

o How large does the entire document need to be in order to accommodate all the graphics that must be combined? Use *Image>Canvas Size* to assist you here.
o Use *Drag and Drop* to bring images from different documents together so that layers will be preserved with proper names.
o Are layers set up properly (i.e., the stacking order)? If not, move them by dragging them to the proper position in the *Layers* palette.
o Once all graphics are brought into the document, are they positioned where you want them? If not, use the **Move** tool to arrange them.
o Do any transformations need to occur (i.e., to resize graphics, rotate them, etc.)?

Add the Descriptive Text

Adding type to a document is simple. *The steps are as follows:*

1. Click on the **Type** tool (Horizontal or Vertical).
2. Choose the desired settings in the options bar. These include the font, font size, style, color, and so on.
3. Place your cursor on the screen and click where you want to place the text. Alternatively, drag a text box using *click+hold+drag*.
4. Begin to type. When you are done, click on the **Commit** button in the options bar to confirm the text and finish the process (or press the *Cmd/Ctrl+Return/Enter* keys on the keyboard). The text appears on its own *Type* layer.

June Triolo :
Creative Color Story

The following is true of text:

• It sits on its own layer. Multiple layers of text can be linked so that they act as one layer.
• It can be edited by choosing the **Type** tool again, clicking on the text layer, positioning the cursor, and changing the text. You can highlight the text and edit it, just as in a word processor.
• It can be moved (using the **Move** tool).

Adding Pizazz

To add the final pizazz to your artwork, you can use *Filters* and *Layer Styles*. The use of drop shadows, bevel and emboss, outline boxes (stroking a selection), and other features all assist in creating a polished look to your art.

Exercise #1: Creative Techniques with Type

Text with a pattern and clipping mask

Goal

To experiment with type and techniques to use it creatively. This exercise will use *Clipping Masks, Typing on a Path,* and *Text Warping* techniques.

Photoshop Tools and Functions

- ◆ **Horizontal Type** tool
- ◆ Type layers
- ◆ *Clipping Mask*
- ◆ *Character* and *Paths* palettes
- ◆ **Pen** tool and placing type on a path
- ◆ *Text Warping* (**Create Warped Text** button in the options bar)

Type placed on a path

Quick Overview of the Process

There are various techniques you can use to liven up your type in Photoshop. This exercise will explore three techniques.
The general process, however, is as follows:

Text with a Clipping Mask
1. Load artwork you want to place inside the type.
2. Create type on the document and position the layers properly.
3. Choose the *Create Clipping Mask* function from the Layers palette.

Typing on a Work Path
1. Using the **Pen** tool, create a work path of a curved line.
2. Choose the **Horizontal Type** tool, and type on the path.

Warping Text
1. Using the **Horizontal Type** tool, type something on the document.
2. Duplicate the type layer several times.
3. Click on the **Create Warped Text** button in the options bar and experiment with settings.

Text Warping examples

New Concepts

- o Clipping masks with type
- o Typing on a work path
- o Text Warping

Step-by-Step

The following discussion will teach you a variety of techniques you can use with type to add interest to your presentations.

Using a Clipping Mask with Type

In this first technique, you will load a photograph and then use a clipping mask to position imagery from the photo inside the type. Consider the font style and size and the imagery from the photo that you want to place inside the text. If necessary adjust the size of the artwork.

A clipping mask is used to bring the fabric into the type.

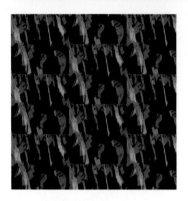

Fabric design created by Jeanne Reith in Textile Design Exercise #1

The Horizontal Type tool

After the type is created it appears as its own layer in the Layers palette.

Step 9: Repositioning the layers so that the fabric layer is above the type layer.

Step 1: The Layers palette upon opening the image.

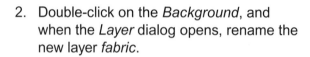

The Character palette

After the type has been committed and before the repositioning of layers

1. Load a photograph or artwork that you want to place inside the type. The example here uses a file called **jeannefabric.jpg** found on the Art DVD in the **Ex 1** folder located in the **Presentations** folder. This is an image created in Textile Design Exercise #1. The image will be a *Background* in the *Layers* palette.

2. Double-click on the *Background*, and when the *Layer* dialog opens, rename the new layer *fabric*.

3. If necessary, use transformations to resize the artwork (or portion of the artwork) that you want to be positioned in the type (*Edit>Transform*).

4. Open the *Character* palette (*Window>Characte*r) or click on the character thumbnail in the palette dock.

5. Choose the **Horizontal Type** tool in the Toolbox. Use the *Character* palette to select a font and set the size to approximately 100.

6. Choose a bright color as your *foreground* color in the Toolbox or in the *Character* palette.

7. Position your text cursor on the document where you want to begin typing and click. Type the word *textile*. If you want to reposition the type as you are typing, *press+hold* the *Cmd/Ctrl* key on the keyboard and drag the type to a new position. You can work with the type as if you were in a word processor program, highlighting letters, changing the font or font size, and so on.

8. When you are happy with the type, press and hold the *Cmd/Ctrl* key and then the *Return/Enter* key. Or you can click on the **Commit** button in the options bar. Note how there is now a new type layer and its name is the text you entered.

9. Reposition the layers so that the *fabric* layer is **above** the *Type* layer. Make sure that the *fabric* layer is the active layer.

10. In the *Layers* palette menu, choose the *Create Clipping Mask* command. A clipping mask will remove all the area outside the text from view.

11. You can reposition the imagery in the text by choosing the **Move** tool in the Toolbox and dragging the fabric around. Observe the *Layers* palette.

12. If you want to reduce the file size, you can combine the fabric and type layers (using the *Merge Visible* option in the *Layers* palette menu). You will no longer have the flexibility to reposition the imagery, but the file size will be greatly reduced.

13. Save the file.

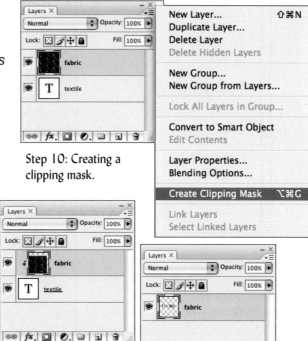

Step 10: Creating a clipping mask.

Step 12: Merging the layers (before above, and after to the right).

The various stages of creating a clipping mask. To the left you have the type above the print (prior to repositioning the layers). Below you have two views of the masked type, showing two different positions of the print inside the type.

Typing on a Work Path

If you want to have type positioned along a curved line, the easiest way to do this is to create a work path and then place the type along the path.

1. Open the *Character* and *Paths* palettes.

2. Choose the **Pen** tool and make sure that the *Paths* option is active in the options bar.

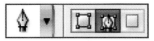

The Pen tool in Path mode

3. Click with the **Pen** to place the first anchor point. Move to the position of the second anchor point, and *click+drag* with the mouse to set the next point and create a curved segment. Continue to draw with the **Pen** until you have a curved segment you like. End the work path by pressing the *Cmd/Ctrl* key and clicking away. Observe the work path in the *Paths* palette.

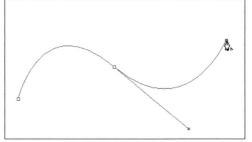

Step 3: Creating the curved path.

4. Choose the **Horizontal Type** tool in the Toolbox.

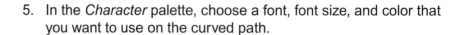

The Character palette

5. In the *Character* palette, choose a font, font size, and color that you want to use on the curved path.

6. Position your type cursor at the beginning of the work path and click. You should see a vertical line that is perpendicular to the path. Commence your typing and watch the words flow along the curved path. While typing, you can perform various word processing operations such as repositioning the cursor within the text, highlighting text to edit, change fonts, and so on. When you have completed typing, press the *Cmd/Ctrl+Return/Enter* keys on the keyboard (or click on the **Commit** button in the options bar).

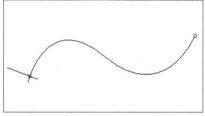 

Step 6: The process of adding type. Left: Positioning the cursor; Center: Typing the text; Right: The final text.

7. Observe the *Paths* palette. You will see the work path and a type path.

8. Save the file.

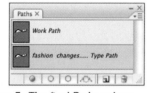

Step 7: The final Paths palette.

Warping Text

You can create interesting text by using the various *Create Warped Text* options. These are accessed either by clicking on the **Create Warped Text** button in the options bar or by choosing the *Layer>Type>Warp Text* menu command.

1. Open the *Character* palette.

2. Choose the **Horizontal Type** tool in the Toolbox.

3. In the *Character* palette, choose the desired font, font size, and color. Use a rather large font size (e.g., 100) so you can easily see the results of the warping.

The Horizontal Type tool

4. Type the word *Couture* on your document. Press the *Cmd/Ctrl* key and the *Enter/Return* key to finalize the text, or click on the **Commit** button in the options bar.

Step 4: The word Couture typed.

5. If you want to experiment, duplicate the type layer two or three times so that you can try a different warp on each layer.

Step 3: Choosing the font, font size, style, and color in the Character palette.

6. Select one of the copied layers in the *Layers* palette and make sure that the **Horizontal Type** tool is active in the Toolbox.

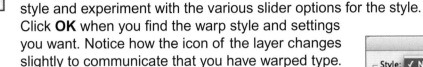

Step 7: Clicking on the Create warped text button in the options bar.

7. Click on the **Create warped text** button in the options bar. This will open a dialog. The *Warp Text* dialog will open. Choose a new style and experiment with the various slider options for the style. Click **OK** when you find the warp style and settings you want. Notice how the icon of the layer changes slightly to communicate that you have warped type.

8. Repeat steps 6 and 7 for the other type layers, and experiment with the warp options. *Arc Upper*, *Bulge*, and *Wave* were utilized in the examples below.

9. Save the file.

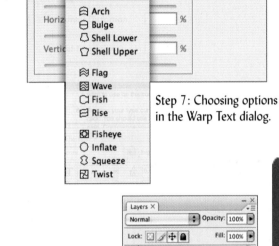

Step 7: Choosing options in the Warp Text dialog.

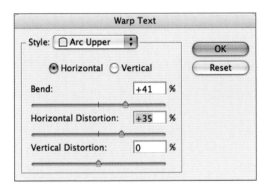

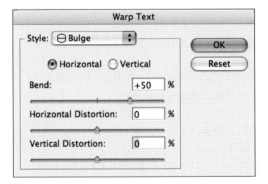

The Layers palette showing the various type layers

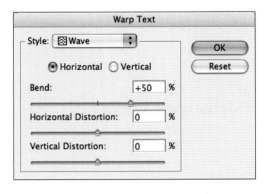

Examples of warped text. The original text appears at the bottom and the dialog to the left shows you the settings for each of the three warps created.

Exercise #2: Using Layer Styles

Goal
In this exercise you will use various *Layer Styles* (or *Effects*) to enhance your artwork.

Photoshop Tools and Functions
- *Layer>Layer Style* menu
- **Add a layer style** button (*Layers* palette)
- *Shape* layer
- *Linking* layers
- *Type* layer
- *Stroking* a selection

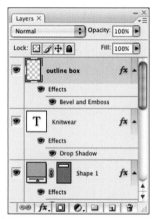

The Layer Styles shown in the Layers palette

Preparatory Thoughts
Styles can be applied to artwork on layers and are accessed through the **Layer** menu or the **Add a layer style** button in the *Layers* palette.
Styles include the following:
- o   Drop or Inner Shadow
- o   Inner or Outer Glow
- o   Bevel or Emboss
- o   Satin
- o   Various Overlays

Quick Overview of the Process
You will add layer styles or effects to artwork in a variety of ways.
The general process will be as follows:
1. Load or create artwork or type.
2. Choose the layer that has the artwork or type you want to add a style to.
3. Add a layer style using the *Layer>Layer Style* menu command or the **Add a layer style** button in the *Layers* palette.
4. Experiment with the settings in the *Layer Style* dialog.
5. Create a *Shape* layer and add a style to it.
6. Create a *Type* layer and add a style to it.
7. Select the outer edge of the document and *stroke* it to create a border. Then add a layer style.

New Concepts
- o   Layer styles
- o   Shape layer
- o   Type layer
- o   Linking layers
- o   Creating a border using *Edit>Stroke* and layer styles

Sources of Imagery
- o   Artwork provided on the DVD

Step-by-Step

Load or Create Artwork

On the accompanying DVD are some sample garments. We will use one of these for our artwork.

1. Using the *File>Open* menu command, direct the file requestor to the **Garments** folder on the DVD and open a file called **sweater1.tif**. If you examine the *Layers* palette, you will see that the sweater appears on its own layer and sits above a *Solid Fill* layer.

Step 2: Duplicating the drawing2 layer.

sweater1.tif

2. Duplicate the layer twice so that you can apply various styles and see the results of each.

Experimenting with Styles on the Sweater

Drop Shadow

1. In the *Layers* palette, click on the *drawing2* layer to make it the active layer. Hide the view of the other layers by turning the eye off on them.

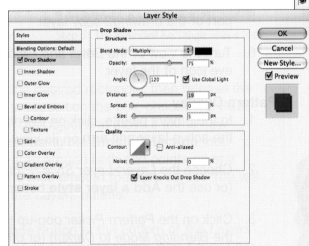

2. *Click+hold* on the **Add a layer style** button at the bottom of the *Layers* palette, slide to the *Drop Shadow* menu option, and release the mouse. A dialog will open.

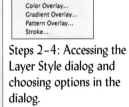

Steps 2–4: Accessing the Layer Style dialog and choosing options in the dialog.

3. Make sure the *Preview* check box is checked.

4. Experiment with the various options in the dialog and when you are happy, click **OK**. In the example to the right, the distance that the shadow extends from the garment was increased.

5. Observe the *Layers* palette and you will now see a layer effect as part of the *drawing2* layer. To edit the style, simply double-click on the *Drop Shadow* style submenu and the dialog will re-open. If you want to remove the style, open the dialog and uncheck the *Drop Shadow* option.

Step 5: Observing the Layers palette to view the effects added.

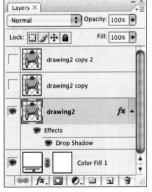

sweater1.tif with a drop shadow applied

6. Turn the view of the *Drop Shadow* example off by clicking on the *eye* icon on the layer.

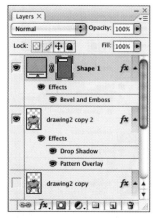

Layers palette with Bevel and Emboss effect

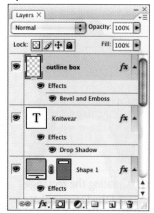

Layers palette with the type and Drop Shadow added

Step 11: Linking the Type and Shape layers.

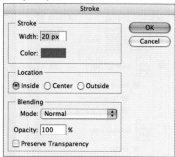

Step 12: Stroking a new layer and adding a Bevel and Emboss effect.

that you can turn the effect off and on by clicking on the *Eye* icon.

Before Bevel and Emboss

After Bevel and Emboss

6. Change your foreground color to the color you would like your type to become.

7. Click on the **Horizontal Type** tool in the Toolbox. In the options bar, choose a font that you want to use and set the font size.

8. Place your cursor above the rectangular box on the document and click. Type the word *Knitwear*. When you are happy with the text, press the *Cmd/Ctrl* keys and *Enter/Return* on the keyboard to finalize the text. You will now have a *Type* layer in the *Layers* palette.

9. Choose the **Move** tool in the Toolbox and reposition the text so that it is over the rectangle. If you need to edit (resize or move) the rectangle, use the **Selection** tools (**Path Selection** and **Direction Selection**). If you need to move the type, use the **Move** tool.

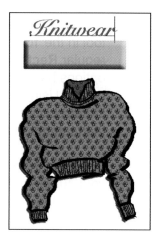

Step 8: Adding type above the box.

10. Add a drop shadow to the text using a layer style on the *Type* layer. You can choose whichever approach you desire to open the *Layer Style* dialog.

11. Link the *Type* and the *Shape* layers by holding the *Shift* key as you select each of the two layers in the *Layers* palette, then choose the *Link Layers* option in the *Layers* palette menu. Doing this will allow you to move both items together with the **Move** tool.

12. To finish the image, create a new layer (call it *outline box*) and then choose the *Select>All* menu to select the entire area. Choose a color for outlining the box as your *foreground* color. Choose the *Edit>Stroke* menu command and when the dialog opens, set the stroke to 20 pixels and use the *Inner* option. Click **OK**. Add a *Bevel and Emboss* layer effect. This completes the exercise.

Steps 9–12: Repositioning the text and creating the box that surrounds the image.

Exercise #3: Creating Interest in Layouts

Goal
To build a layout with the fabric in the background and the fabric swatches and illustration in the foreground.

Photoshop Tools and Functions
- Layer *Transparency*
- *Drag and Drop* of layers between documents
- *Transformations* and moving images
- Type
- Layer *Styles*

The layout with fabric swatches and fashion illustration created in this exercise. Textile and Fashion Illustration by Monica Mitchell

Quick Overview of the Process
You will work with three images: a full page rendering of a plaid, an image of swatches, and an illustration. These images will be combined and presented in one document. *Drag and Drop* (between documents) will be used to combine the images. *The general approach is as follows:*
1. Load the three images and observe image information.
2. Arrange the images so that you can view them all at one time.
3. Drag the layers of the swatch and illustration files into the plaid file. This is called "drag and drop" and the layers will be intact in the plaid document.
4. Use transformations and repositioning as necessary to arrange the images for your layout.
5. Add a title to your image.
6. Apply layer effects as desired.

New Concepts
- o   Drag and drop

Sources of Imagery
- o   Images on the Art DVD or other appropriate artwork

Step-by-Step

Open the Art Files and Observe Image Information
On the accompanying DVD, there are three files that will be used in this exercise: **plaid.tif, swatches.tif,** and **illustration.tif**.
1. Using the *File>Open* menu command, direct the file requester to the **Ex 3** folder inside the **Presentations** folder on the DVD and open all three files at once. You can do this once you are in the *Open* dialog. After you have located the files, press the *Shift* key on the keyboard and click on all three files to select them. Then when you click on **Open**, all three files will open.

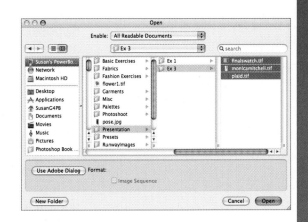

Step 1: Opening the files to be used in this exercise.

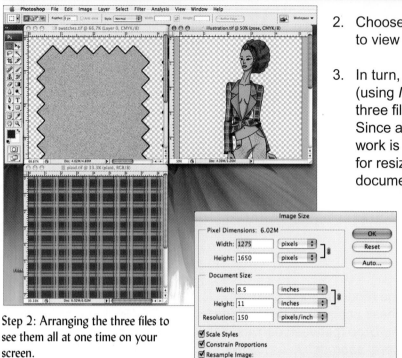

Step 2: Arranging the three files to see them all at one time on your screen.

Step 3: Viewing image size information.

2. Choose the *Window>Arrange>Tile Vertically* to view all three files on your monitor.

3. In turn, examine the image size of each file (using *Image>Image Size*). You will see that all three files were created at a resolution of 150. Since all files share the same resolution, our work is simplified somewhat in that the need for resizing imagery is reduced. The largest document size occurs with the **plaid.tif** image, which is 8.5 × 11 inches. This is good, as this will be the background image upon which we will arrange the other two images.

4. Observe also that all three files are layers. This is good as this will facilitate laying one image on top of another and it allows for the use of transparency.

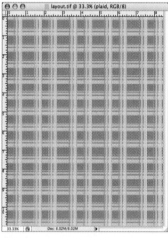

Steps 2–3: The result of changing the Opacity level on the plaid layer and adding a solid fill layer of white beneath the Plaid layer.

Commencing the Layout and Merging Images into One File

The plan will be to bring the swatches and illustration images into the plaid document and create a layout there. We will need to dim the plaid so that the swatches and illustration can be easily seen.

1. Click on the plaid document to make it the active file. Save this with a new name (using *File>Save As*). Name this file **layout** and save it as either a TIF or PSD file.

2. In the *Layers* palette, change the *Opacity* level to 50%. You will be able to see through this to the transparent checked background.

3. In the *Layers* palette, click on the **Create new fill or adjustment layer** button and create a solid fill layer of white. Reposition this beneath the *Plaid* layer so that you can better see the opacity change. You can change the opacity of the plaid at any time.

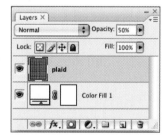

The Layers palette after the opacity is changed and a solid fill layer is added and arranged under the plaid

4. Click on the *Illustration* image to make it the active window. Make sure that you can see all three files at the same time on the screen.

5. *Click+hold* on the *pose* layer in the *Layers* palette and drag it over on top of the *layout* document. Release the mouse button. This operation is called *"drag and drop."* If you now look at the *Layers* palette, you will see the *pose* layer now exists in the layout file, as does the artwork.

6. Repeat the process for the *swatches* file by moving the swatches layer over to the *Layout* document. Do not worry if the swatch image is larger than you want; you will adjust this in the next section.

Step 5: Dragging the pose layer of the pose image into the Plaid document.

7. Save the file.

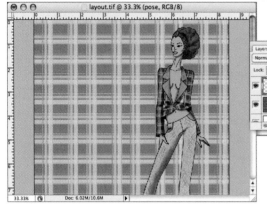

Observe the Layers palette of the layout image after dragging the pose layer into the document.

Developing the Layout

The swatches are too large, so the first change will be to scale these. Then, type will be added and layer styles will be added.

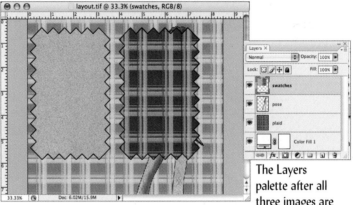

The Layers palette after all three images are combined

1. Click on the *swatches* layer to make it the active layer. Press the *Cmd/Ctrl+T* keys on the keyboard as a shortcut to the *Transform* menu command (**Edit** menu). A bounding box will appear around the swatches. Move to the options bar, click on the link between the *Width* and *Height* fields and experiment with numbers for scaling. Since you clicked on the link, both the width and height will change together. At the same time, if you want to rotate the swatches, type a number in the rotations field. Our example uses a -90 degree rotation. You can move the artwork while still experimenting simply by *clicking+holding* inside the bounding box and dragging the art to the new location. When you are pleased with the transformations, either click on the **Commit** button in the options bar, or press the *Cmd/Ctrl + Enter/Return* keys on the keyboard.

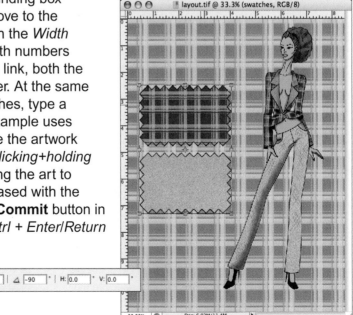

Using the options bar to perform transformations

Step 1: Performing transformations on the swatches.

2   Add a title to the layout. Click on the **Horizontal Type** tool in the Toolbox. In the options bar or *Character* palette, choose the *font*,

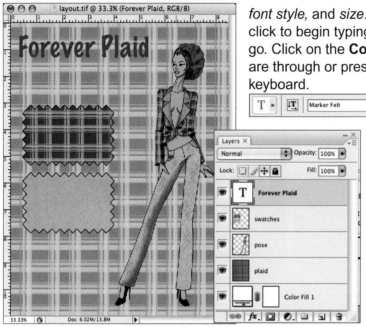

A type layer is created.

font style, and *size.* Place the cursor on your illustration and click to begin typing. Add your title, editing as necessary as you go. Click on the **Commit** button in the options bar when you are through or press the *Cmd/Ctrl +Return/Enter* keys on the keyboard.

Step 2: Adding type to the layout.

3. Reposition the various components, as necessary, using the **Move** tool and clicking on the appropriate layer.

4. Examine the artwork and determine which elements of the layout could utilize layer styles of some sort. Add these to the appropriate layer first by clicking on the layer, then choosing the **Add a layer style** button and sliding to the appropriate layer style. When the *Layer Style* dialog opens, adjust the settings as necessary.

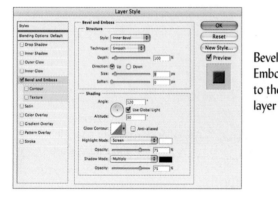

Bevel and Emboss added to the type layer

5. Use the **Type** tool to add fabric numbers to the swatches.

6. Create a new layer and stroke the outer edge of it. See page 444, step 12 for information on how to do this.

7. Save the file.

Black Drop Shadow added to the swatches layer

Colored Drop Shadow added to the illustration layer

The final layout with labeling and effects in place

Exercise #4: Merchandising with Snapshots

The merchandise presentation with snapshots created in this exercise

Goal

To build a merchandising layout incorporating one garment and three snapshots of the same garment showing different colorways.

Photoshop Tools and Functions

- ♦ Layers
- ♦ *Recoloring* techniques
- ♦ *Transformations* and moving images
- ♦ Type
- ♦ Layer *Styles*

Quick Overview of the Process

In this exercise you will take one garment and prepare a merchandising layout through the creation of recolored snapshots of the garment. *The general approach is as follows:*

1. Load the original garment and position it on your document.
2. Using the **Rectangular Marquee** tool, create a selection of a portion of the garment, copy it to the clipboard, and paste it in three times (creating separate layers). Position these three snapshots on the document.
3. Recolor the snapshots.
4. Using the **Horizontal Type** tool, add descriptive text (i.e., a title, style, and colorway numbers).
5. Create a company logo.
6. Apply layer effects as desired.

Note: Snapshots
The term "snapshot" used in this lesson refers to a cropped portion of an entire garment, not to Snapshots as used in the History palette.

New Concepts

o   Creation of snapshots

Sources of Imagery

o   Images on the Art DVD or other appropriate artwork

Step-by-Step

Setting up

1. Using the *File>New* menu command, create a new document that measures 11 inches wide by 8 inches tall. Use a *Resolution* of 150, *Color Mode* of CMYK, and *Background Contents* of White. Name the file **Merchandise Layout** and click **OK**.

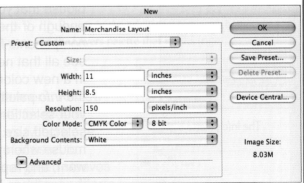

Step 1: Setting up the new document.

2. Place the blouse image by choosing the *File>Place* menu command and directing the file requester to the **Ex 4** folder inside the **Presentations** folder on the DVD. Choose the **Blouse.tif** file and click on **Place**.

Step 2: Choosing new colors for the additional colorways.

2. Using techniques learned in Textile Design Exercise #7, use the **Eyedropper** tool to sample and move the current garment background color and the lighter version of it used in the inside of the garment into the *Swatches* palette. Also sample the two shades of green and move these into the custom palette.

3. Using the *Color Picker*, create three new colors and lighter shades of these and move them into the *Swatches* palette. CS3/CS4 users may use the **Add to Swatches** button to make this process simple.

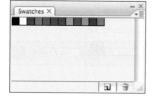

The palette of colors built with the existing and new colors

4. Save the palette using the *Save Swatches* command in the *Swatches* palette menu.

Recoloring the Garment Snapshots
You are now ready to exchange the background fabric color in each of the snapshots. This will involve turning off and on the snapshot layers, each in turn, as you work.

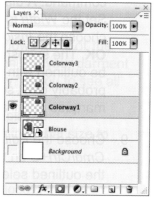

1. Rename each of the snapshot layers at this time. Call them *Colorway1*, *Colorway2*, and *Colorway3*.

Step 1: Renaming the layers.

Step 3: Using the Magic Wand to select the dark purple color.

2. Turn off the view of all layers except *Colorway1* (using the *eye* icon).

3. Choose the **Magic Wand** tool in the Toolbox and choose the **New selection** button in the options bar. Set the *Tolerance* to approximately 20. Click on the dark purple background color of the blouse. You will see marching ants around some of the purple background of the blouse. Choose the *Select>Similar* menu command and the rest of the purple in the blouse will become selected.

Magic Wand settings in the options bar

4. Set the first new color (dark blue) as the foreground color in the Toolbox.

5. Choose the *Edit>Fill* menu command and when the dialog opens, choose the *Foreground* option, and click **OK**. The dark purple of the blouse will change to blue.

Step 5: Filling the selection with teal (left) and deselecting the marquee (right).

6. Repeat the process with the lighter version of blue, placing it in the inner back of the blouse.

7. Turn off the view of *Colorway1* and turn on the view of *Colorway2* in the *Layers* palette. Make sure that the *Colorway2* layer is the active layer. Repeat the color exchanges per steps 3–6.

8. Repeat the same process for *Colorway3*.

Each of the snapshots is recolored to show the different colorways of the garment. Dark and light versions of the colors are exchanged to show the main fabric and the wrong side of the fabric as viewed through the neck opening.

Adding Manufacturer and Style Information

You are now ready to add text to your layout. This would include the manufacturer's name, style name and number, and colorway numbers. Consider where you want this information to appear on the layout.

1. Choose the **Horizontal Type** tool. In the options bar, choose a font, font size (e.g., 42), font style, and color. You can borrow a color from one of the blouses if you like.

2. Position the type cursor on your document and type the manufacturer's name. Press *Cmd/ Ctrl+Return/Enter* on the keyboard to finalize the type. Reposition it if necessary.

3. Continue adding type for the style name and number and the colorways. Use various options in the options bar to assist you. *Examples include:*

   o Change the font color using the **Set the text color** button in the options bar.

   o Change the font orientation by clicking on the **Change the**

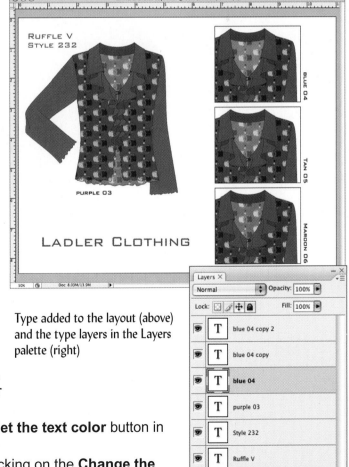

Type added to the layout (above) and the type layers in the Layers palette (right)

text orientation button in the options bar.

o   Fonts may also be changed using standard transformation procedures on the layer.

o   You can select type and *opt/alt+drag* it to a new location (as in the case of the colorway numbers), and then edit the text.

Adding Layer Styles

You can add some pizazz to your layout using *Layer Styles* as discussed in the previous exercise. *The general procedure is as follows:*

1.   In the *Layers* palette, click on the layer you want to add a style to.

2.   Choose the **Add a layer style** button at the bottom of the *Layers* palette and slide up to the style of your choice. A dialog will open.

3.   Experiment with the various style settings. Click **OK**. You will now observe the style in the *Layers* palette.

The example below uses primarily *Drop Shadows* and *Bevel and Emboss* layer effects. A logo was created using type that was rasterized into a graphic so it could be offset as shown below.

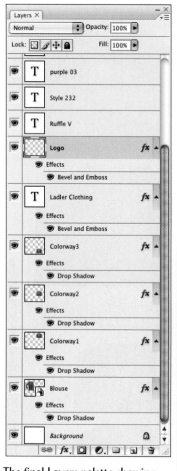

The final Layers palette showing layers, effects, type, etc.

Exercise #5: Prepping Graphics for Presentations

Goal
To prepare graphics for presentations including Microsoft PowerPoint, Adobe Acrobat, or Web use, focusing on keeping the file size small yet maintaining quality in image.

Photoshop Tools and Functions
- ◆ **Selection** tools
- ◆ **Crop** tool
- ◆ Image size and resolution (*Image>Image Size*)
- ◆ Flattening layers in an image
- ◆ Save for Web option (JPG)
- ◆ Save PDF

Preparatory Thoughts
When preparing files for presentations, it is generally wise to reduce the file size so that the presentation tool (i.e., PowerPoint, Acrobat, or the Internet) can load and display the file quickly. As a general rule, it is wise to work with a copy of the original art, so you don't accidentally make changes that cannot be undone (e.g., the flattening of layers).

- o If you are saving the file for a PowerPoint presentation, or for the Internet, you should use a JPG or GIF format, which will reduce the image in an efficient manner. The best method for saving JPG images in Photoshop is through the use of the *File>Save for Web* menu command.

- o If you are prepping artwork for Adobe Acrobat, save the files as PDF files. This is achieved by choosing the PDF format in the pop-up menu of the *Save* dialog. Make sure the option to save with layers is not checked as layers will increase your file size.

Quick Overview of the Process
The steps you take will differ slightly, depending on which file format you are moving to (i.e., JPG versus PDF). *The general process, however, is as follows:*

1. Load your Photoshop image. Either load a copy of the original, or immediately resave the file with a different name. You may also save the file in a different folder so that it now exists in two different places.
2. Prepare the image, as necessary, cropping, adding type, cleaning up details, and so on.
3. Observe the information about the file size and other characteristics (*Image>Image Size* menu command).
4. Reduce the resolution or image size as necessary.
5. Save the file in the desired file format.

New Concepts
- o Flattening layers
- o Saving for Web (JPG)
- o Saving as a PDF image

The Evolution of File Size Reduction as Covered in This Exercise

Original File Size
            115.2 megabytes
Flattening Layers
            13.7 megabytes
Reduce Resolution
            1.23 megabytes
Image Size Change in Pixels
            726 kilobytes
Save for Web, quality 60, JPG
            13.73 kilobytes

The multilayered file reduced from 115.2 megs to 13.73 kB in this exercise

Step-by-Step

The order in which you perform some of the steps below will depend on where you will use the file when all tasks (i.e., Web publishing, Acrobat booklet, Powerpoint presentation, press printing, etc.) are complete.

Cleaning up Your Artwork

As you prep images for presentations you should examine each carefully to determine if the art is a good representation of what you want to show. *Consider the following:*

Move tool

Crop tool

- o Is the art positioned in the document the way you want it? If not, move it (**Move** tool) or crop it (**Crop** tool).
- o Is any clean-up work necessary (such as removing unwanted pixels, touching up areas of the imagery, etc.)? If so, perform the operation.
- o Would the use of *Type* enhance the image in any way, or allow the viewer to have a greater understanding of the art (without compromising the artwork itself)? This will vary according to the kind of presentation you are creating, and whether type will be added outside the art.
- o Can the layout be improved in any way? If so, perform the operation.

If you perform any of the steps above and want the resulting changes to be part of the master file, save the file before moving on to other operations.

The context menu on the Macintosh, accessed by Ctrl+clicking on the file on the desktop. Windows users will right mouse click on the file to open the context menu.

Creating a Copy of Your File

Before working on an image (with techniques that you do not want to permanently alter the artwork) or preparing to perform file reduction techniques on a file, you should create a copy of the original art. *You can create a copy of a file in several ways:*

- o *Opt/Alt+drag* the file from one folder to another on your desktop
- o Use the *Save As...* menu command to save a copy of the file in the format that best serves your purposes.
- o Use the *Context* menu (*Ctrl/Right Mouse button+click* on the file on the desktop) to open the context menu and then choose the *Duplicate* command. The file will duplicate with the word "copy" in front of the name. Rename the file if you want.
- o Copy the images you plan to work on into a separate folder, thus creating a backup.

Reducing File Size

There are many reasons to reduce the file size of an image. The primary motivation is to create files that load and transmit quickly.

- o You have the ability to efficiently transmit a file or presentation (Acrobat or PowerPoint) via the Internet or e-mail.
- o Smaller files reduce download time.
- o PowerPoint presentations or Acrobat booklets will display quickly as you move from page to page and the file (and presentation) won't "choke."

The following are methods or techniques that can be used to reduce file size:
Cropping the Image

Crop tool

1. Choose the **Crop** tool in the toolbox.

The Process of Cropping:

Left: Original image   Center: Cropping in action   Right: The cropped image

2. On your artwork, *click+hold+drag* to select the portion of the image you want to keep. When you release the mouse, the outer area of the artwork (i.e., the nonselected area) will become darker.

3. Double-click inside the cropping box to finalize the operation and crop the image.

Flattening Your Artwork

If your artwork has multiple layers, you can greatly reduce the file size by flattening the art into one layer (i.e., the *Background*). Make sure that you are working on a copy of the artwork, as once this operation is performed, and the file is saved, you can no longer retrieve the original art with all your layers. Many a tear has been shed over the accidental save without a backup. You can observe the flattened versus nonflattened file size in the *Status Bar,* which is located in the lower-left corner of the document window.

1. Make sure you are working on a copy of the image; or, if you are a risk-taker, work on the original and REMEMBER to save the file with a new name, once it is flattened.

2. In the *Layers* palette, choose the *Flatten Image* menu command. If there are hidden layers, you will be asked if it is OK to discard them. Click **OK**. If you change your mind (or realize that you didn't save a version with layers), you can undo the flattening step, or you can go back in *History* if you did not save a version of the file that retains the layers.

Status Bar and File Size
You can view the file size of your image in the Status Bar in the lower-left corner of the document window. The first number is the size of the file if it were flattened. The second number shows you the file size with all the layers.

Status Bar info

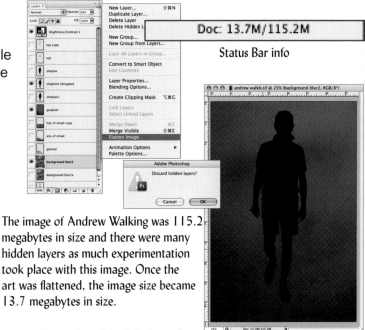

The image of Andrew Walking was 115.2 megabytes in size and there were many hidden layers as much experimentation took place with this image. Once the art was flattened, the image size became 13.7 megabytes in size.

Lowering File Resolution

In most presentation modes, people will view your graphics on their monitors, which are very low resolution (72 dpi). Therefore, when you are building graphics or resizing graphics, you can move to 72 dpi in the image size, depending on the artwork, although this is not always necessary or recommended. The higher an image's resolution, the larger the file will be. Thus, one way to reduce the file size is to lower the image's resolution. Always keep an eye on the visual clarity of the image, and attempt to keep the image's integrity.

1. Choose the *Image>Image Size* menu. A dialog will open. This will show you the file's resolution.

2. Change the resolution or the image size, as desired.

3. Click **OK** and the file will adjust in resolution. Look at it (and zoom in, if necessary) to ensure that the visual quality of the image is retained.

Sharpen Filter

When you reduce a file size by resolution, pixel size, or dimension size, you may want to use the Sharpen filter to "crisp" it up a bit again. There are several options in the Filter>Sharpen menu area.

Reducing the Image Size (in Pixels or Dimensions)

Resizing artwork to reduce its size in pixels or dimensions is another way one can reduce the file size. Here again, you must consider what the end-use of the artwork will be, and how large (in size) the file should be for best display. Part of the consideration in this approach is the pixel display setting used by the majority of your viewers. Web images have more restrictions than most other graphics. In times past, a screen resolution of 800 × 600 was the standard and the norm. This has moved up to 1024 × 768, and for many people, even higher. If you anticipate that your viewer will be using a 1024 × 768 display, you will likely want to keep your artwork smaller than this. In Web page design, you must allow for browser menus, top of page titles, and other elements. If you are prepping images for PowerPoint, you may want to reduce the size of the image like you would for the Web, as you are still dealing with a viewer who will only see the image on-screen. If you are prepping files for an Acrobat booklet presentation, you may want your image sizes to be 8.5 × 11, or you can reduce them as you deem appropriate.

The image size before changing the resolution (left) and after changing the resolution (right). The file size was reduced from 13.7 megabytes to 1.23 megabytes when the resolution was lowered from 240 to 72 dpi.

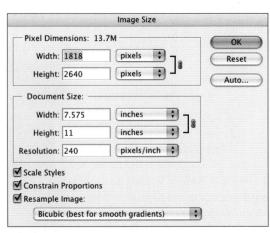
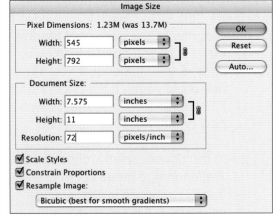

To reduce the image size:

1. Choose the *Image>Image Size* menu command. A dialog will open. This will show you the file size in pixels and dimensions (as well as resolution, as discussed above).

2. Make sure that the *Constrain Proportions* and *Resample Image* options are checked. If *Styles* have been used in the artwork, make sure *Scale Styles* is checked as well.

3. Change the image size, as desired (either Pixel Dimensions or Document Size).

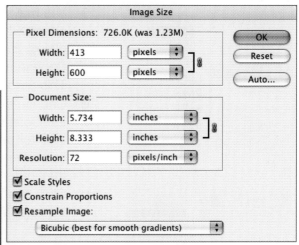

4. Click **OK** and the file will resize. Look at it (and zoom in, if necessary) to ensure that the visual quality of the image is retained.

The image size of the Andrew Walking art is changed to 600 pixels high. The Width automatically adjusts. The file size was reduced from 1.23 megabytes to 726 kilobytes.

As you can see from the various operations performed on the *Andrew Walking* image, file size has been reduced from 1.23 megabytes to 726 kilobytes. This is substantial, to say the least.

Saving Files for the Web or PowerPoint

Photoshop provides a special menu command that allows you to save files in a very efficient way for the Web. Not only will the saved art load quickly on the Internet, but it is also good for PowerPoint presentations in that the graphics do not take much space within PowerPoint. Thus page display is improved as you move through a presentation.

Perform the necessary operations (as discussed above) to each file before using the Save for Web command. As was demonstrated, the file size will change dramatically in just these steps alone.

When you use the *Save for Web* command in Photoshop's File menu, you will have the option to save the file in one of several formats. The type of image you are working with will dictate which format you choose. For example, photo-type images are generally saved in **JPG** formats. Line art and drawn artwork are generally saved in **GIF** format. If you want to have a transparent background around your image on the Web, you will need to save the file as a GIF and define the transparent color.

The Save for Web & Devices menu command

To save the file:

1. Choose the *File>Save for Web…* (CS1 or CS2) or *File>Save for Web & Devices…* (CS3 or CS4) command. A dialog will open.

2. Choose the 4-up or 2-up option by clicking on the appropriate tab at the top of the window. This allows you to view four options of the file, one of which is the original image (the left image).

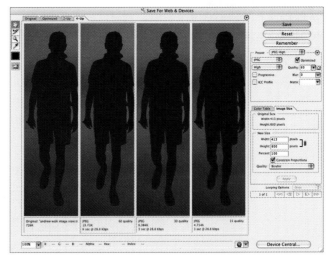

The 4-up display option of the Save for Web dialog

Choosing a Preset (left) or File format (above)

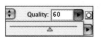

Choosing the Quality of an image using the slider or the Quality pop-up

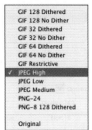

The various tools in the Save for Web dialog: Hand, Slice, Magnifier, and Eyedropper

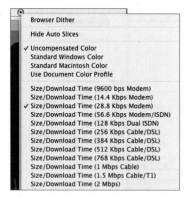

Viewing the various download times as dictated by the speed of the Internet connection

3. You may click on any of the images, and change the settings on the right side of the dialog. *Experiment with the following:*

o Choose a *Preset* from the Preset pop-up. This automatically sets the other options.

o Choose the *File Format* of your choice from the *Optimized File Format* pop-up. Choose JPG for photo-type images and GIF for line art images or when you want to define transparency.

o Click on the *Quality* pop-up to determine the level of quality you want for the chosen image.

o Choose the level of *Compression Quality* from this pop-up.

o Choose between the *Color Table* and the *Image Size* tabs to see information on the art. You can change the image size within this dialog by typing in new numbers. The *Color Table* will show you information only if you have a GIF file format chosen.

o Use the tools on the left side of the dialog to move the image (the **Hand**), to zoom (**Magnifier** tool), and to sample colors (**Eyedropper** tool), among other operations.

o Click on the *Preview Menu* arrowhead (at the top of the dialog, near the **Save** button) to view or change the speed of the Internet connection. This allows you to see how long it will take to download the image from the Web.

As you make changes to the above, you can view your selected image to see how big the file size is and how long a download on the Web will take.

4. Conduct experiments on each of the three new images if you like and compare the results.

5. Click on the image you want to keep, then click on the **Save** button and name your file.

6. If you are not building a thumbnail, close the original document without saving it. This way if you made changes along the way, you won't alter the original image.

In continuing with the experiments with the Andrew Walking image, the resulting JPG file saved with a quality of 60 was 13.73 kB. You have now seen this file journey from 115.2 MB to 13.73 kB. Amazing!

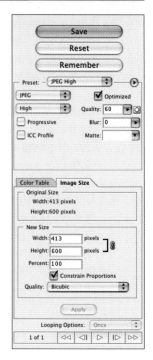

Save for Web options

View of the file size of each option in the dialog in the lower area of the display

Review of File Reduction

Original file size	115.2	megabytes
Flattening layers	13.7	megabytes
Resolution change from 240 to 72	1.23	megabytes
Image size change in pixels	726	kilobytes
Save for Web, quality 60, JPG	13.73	kilobytes

Building a Thumbnail for the Web

A *thumbnail* is a small version of your image. It is used on a Web page to show the user a small version of the graphic, and typically the thumbnail is linked to the larger version of the file.

1. Open your large file (or work with the file that remains open from the above series of steps). Determine whether you want to shrink the entire image, or simply crop a portion of the image for the thumbnail.

2. If you want to shrink the entire image, choose the *Image>Image Size* menu command.

3. Make sure the *Constrain Proportions* and *Resample Image (Bicubic)* options are selected. Type in the new width or height. A height of 150 is generally good for use on the Web. Click **OK**. The file will resize.

The thumbnail built by resizing the image to become 150 pixels wide

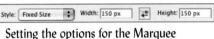

Setting the options for the Marquee

Alternatively:

If you want to crop the image, you can choose the **Rectangular Marquee** tool, set the *Style* pop-up in the options bar to *Fixed Size*, and then enter 150 px × 150 px as your fixed size. When you select a portion of the image, the marquee will become the fixed size you set and you can move it over the image until you find the area you want. Then choose the *Image>Crop* menu command.

Above: The thumbnail created by using a Fixed Size marquee of 150 pixels wide and tall

Right: You can position the marquee where you want it.

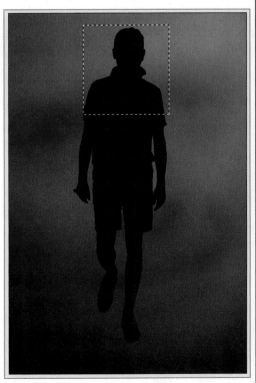

4. Sharpen the image with the *Sharpen* filter and prepare to undo if you think the result is not good. (*Filter>Sharpen>Sharpen*).

5. Choose the *File>Save for Web…* command. A dialog will open.

6. Repeat the tests discussed above, and save the file with the same name + "sm" after it. For example if your larger version of the file is **andrew.jpg,** then save the thumbnail version as **andrewsm.jpg.**

7. Close the original document **without** saving it. This way you won't alter the original image. Be sure to do this, especially if you do not have a backup of the file somewhere.

A setting of "3" for feathering
(above) and the results (below)

Feathering
    In CS3 and CS4 you
may add feathering after a
selection is made by clicking on
the Refine Edge button in the
options bar and adjusting the
feathering slider by moving it
to the right. Remember to turn
the feather option off when you
are through with it.

Creative Effects for Graphics: Softening the Edge
If you want to have a softened halo around your Web graphic, then you
need to add a couple of extra steps to your process.

1. Choose the **Rectangular** or **Elliptical Marquee** tool in the
   Toolbox.

2. Set *Feather* in the options bar to 2 or 3 (the larger the number, the
   softer the feathering).

3. Using the tool, select a portion of your image.

4. Choose the *Edit>Copy* menu.

5. Choose the *File>New* menu. A dialog will open. It will be the size
   of your image on the clipboard, so do not change anything with
   the size. Click **OK**. A blank document will open.

6. Choose the *Edit>Paste* menu command. Your image will paste
   into the new document with a softened edge. This is caused by
   turning feathering on prior to making the selection.

7. Save the file for the Web as above.

Creative Effects for Graphics: Defining Transparent Colors
If you want to have certain colors of your graphic appear transparent on
Web pages, you must use the **GIF** file format.

1. Prepare your file by controlling its size, image contrast, and other
   characteristics (as previously discussed). Ideally, you will want
   to put a solid color in the area you want to be transparent. The
   fastest way to achieve this is to select all pixels in the area you
   want transparent, and then press the *Delete/Backspace* key to
   make all pixels in this area either transparent (if you are working
   on a layer) or the current *background* color in the palette (if you
   are working on the background).

If you prepped your art so that it is on a layer and transparency already
exists, then you do not need to do anything further when you save
for Web (short of using the GIF format). If your artwork exists on the
background and you have a solid color area, then you can use the *Save
for Web* dialog to assist.

2. Choose the *File/Save for Web…* menu command.

3. When the window opens, click on the tab for a 2-up or a 4-up
   display to view multiple copies of the image.

4. Click on one of the images and choose the GIF file format from
   the file format list.

5. Click on the **Eyedropper** tool on the left side of the window.

6. Click on the color you want to be transparent (in the case of the
   example here, white).

The original image with a white
background

7. Click on the *Map Selected Colors to Transparent* button on the lower-right side of the window (see the arrows in the illustration to the right). The white will become transparent, and when you save the file as a GIF file, the transparent color will not appear in the image.

Note: You may have multiple transparent colors.

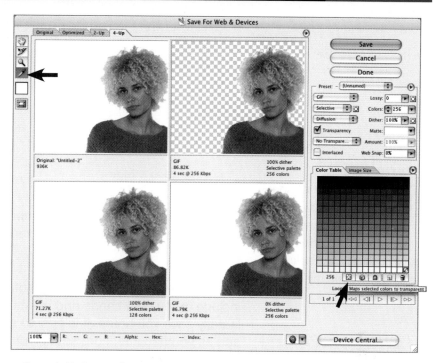

Steps 4–7: Setting the transparent colors in a GIF image as it is prepped for the Web.

Color Considerations

There are 216 colors used by browsers that are Web-safe regardless of the platform (Windows or Macintosh). The browser your audience chooses will change all the colors in your image to Web-safe colors when it displays them on an 8-bit screen. When you use safe colors, the colors you use in your images will not "dither" or speckle, which ensures a display with a look close to the original.

You can choose to work with a Web-safe swatches palette. This is accessed by viewing the *Swatches* palette (*Windows>Swatches),* clicking on the arrowhead of the *Swatches* palette menu, and choosing the *Web Safe Colors* palette from the list. When asked if you want to replace the current *Swatches* palette with the *Web Safe* palette (as opposed to appending the current palette), choose to *replace,* as this will keep things simpler.

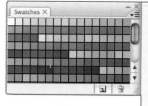

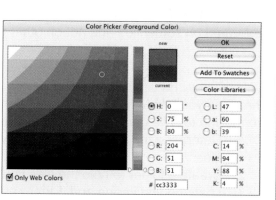

Choosing to use Web-safe colors by loading the palette (far right), or selecting this option in the Color Picker (above)

If you double-click on the *foreground* color in the Toolbox, you will open the *Color Picker* window and view the color formulas for the colors you are using. In HTML coding, colors are expressed either as hexadecimal values (e.g., #FF0000) or as color names. Depending on your Web development software you may want to write down the hexadecimal value and use it elsewhere in the software to build color-coordinated layouts.

Exercise #6: Using Actions to Facilitate the Design or Graphic Preparation Process

Goal

To use Photoshop's *Action* palette and functions to record a sequence of steps, thus automating multiple operations and facilitating the work flow.

Photoshop Tools and Functions

- ◆ *Action* palette
- ◆ Various operations used in prepping files for presentation (as covered in Presentation Exercise #5).

Preparatory Thoughts

An action is a recorded sequence of Photoshop operations. These include menu commands and palette operations. Creating an action can literally save you hours. It is best to start with a short sequence of steps, and as you become more savvy, you can create more involved action sets. The *Action* palette is used to record, save, play back, load, delete, and edit actions. You can view your named action as a button or as a list item. In this exercise, you will create an action to facilitate file prep for building a portfolio of images in Adobe Acrobat. Many of the steps have already been discussed in Exercise #5, as files need to be prepped for presentation (either visually or size-wise). The process of creating an action begins by evaluating the operations that need to be performed on a group of images. Identify the operations you will need to perform on each and every file, as these will be candidates for an action. You may indeed build more than one action, as you discover things that need to be performed on some files and not on others.

Note: Photoshop Actions

Photoshop has many prebuilt actions available for use. These are divided into groups by function. Explore the Action palette and the Action palette menu.

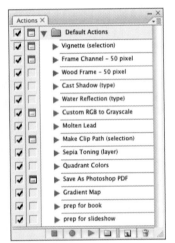

Photoshop actions in List view (above) and Button view (below)

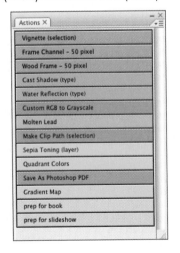

Quick Overview of the Process

The steps you take will differ slightly depending on which file format you are moving to. *The general process, however, is as follows:*

1. Determine the various operations you want to perform to multiple files.
2. Create a folder to hold the files you run the action on.
3. Load the first image and if there are any unique steps that must be performed on it, do so before recording the action (i.e., cropping, adding type, cleaning up details, etc.)
4. Commence a recording. Record the following steps: flattening the image, reducing the resolution to 72 dpi, and saving the image as a PDF file in the new folder. Then close the image. End the recording.
5. Load the next image and run the action.
6. Repeat for all files that suit the action.

New Concepts

- o Creating an action using the *Actions* palette.
- o Running an action on multiple files.

Step-by-Step
Planning and Prepping

1. Load and examine some of the files you want to process through a series of actions. Determine what the specific actions will be, and write down a list of these on a piece of paper. If you are preparing files for a multipage Acrobat file, you could consider flattening a multilayered image, reducing the resolution, or saving as a PDF file.

2. Create a new folder on your computer where you will place the files once the action set has been run on them.

3. Ensure that the *Actions* palette is open and available (*Window>Actions*).

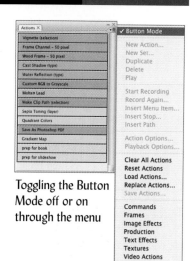

Toggling the Button Mode off or on through the menu

Creating an Action

You are now ready to build an action.

1. Load the first image. If there are any unique steps (i.e., those not to be included in the action set), perform these steps now.

2. Make sure you are in *List* view. If you are in Button mode, click on the *Actions* palette menu arrow and highlight the *Button* option. This will "uncheck" the option and move you to *List* view.

3. Choose the *New Action* menu command from the Actions palette menu. A *New Action* dialog will open.

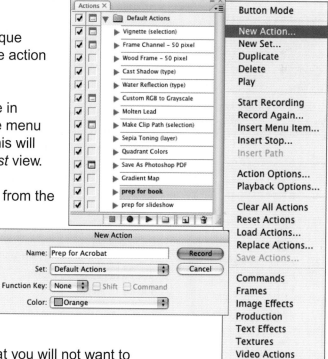

4. Type in a name for the action and then, if you want, choose a color for the action in the *Color* pop-up. You may also choose a keyboard shortcut for the action, but be careful with this, as there are many standard shortcuts that you will not want to interfere with. Click on the **Record** button. As soon as you do this you are beginning the recording sequence and every operation you perform will be recorded.

Commencing to build an action by choosing the menu command and naming the action in the New Action dialog

5. Perform the sequence of steps you want to be part of the action. *For this exercise, these include:*
   o Flattening the image (*Flatten Image* in the *Layers* palette menu)
   o Changing the resolution to 72 dpi (*Image>Image Size* menu)
   o Saving the image as a PDF file using the *File>Save As* menu, moving to the folder you created, and choosing the PDF file format in the *File Format* pop-up (you might have to choose various options in the PDF save).
   o Closing the image without saving it.

6. End the recording by clicking on the **Stop Playing/ Recording** button at the bottom of the *Action* palette.

The Stop Playing/Recording button

Flatten the image

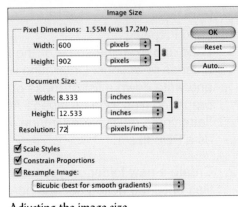

Adjusting the image size

The various operations performed on the file as part of the action being created

Save as PDF

The Actions palette showing the list of steps

The new action in List view (above) and Button view (below)

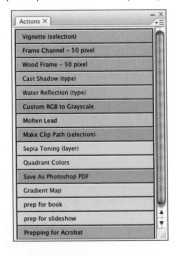

Playing Back an Action

1. Load a new image that you want to process with your recorded action.

2. Perform any operations that are not part of the action.

3. Run the action by clicking on the *Action name* in the *Actions* palette to select it, and then clicking on the **Play Selection** button at the bottom of the palette.

If you want to view and use actions in *Button* mode (which is easier to see and use), choose *Button Mode* from the *Action* palette menu. Then when you want to run an action, click on the button and the action will run.

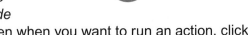

Other Action Ideas

There are many operations that would be facilitated by creating an action. *Consider:*

Image rotations, Saving for Web, stroking a selection.

Exercise #7: Building an Electronic Portfolio Using Adobe Acrobat

Goal

To build an Acrobat portfolio with PDF images created in Photoshop
Note: This lesson requires that you have Adobe Acrobat Professional.

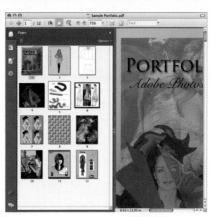

Building an electronic portfolio with Adobe Acrobat

Acrobat Tools and Functions

♦ *Document* menu and functions
♦ *Pages* and *Bookmarks* tab and functions

Planning a Portfolio

When planning a portfolio of your artwork, there are numerous things to consider and evaluate. *Some of these are:*

o What images to place in the portfolio
o How to group the images into themes in a way that makes the greatest sense to the person viewing the portfolio
o What order to show them in
o What information would help the viewer understand the portfolio with nobody present to explain things. This generally amounts to adding some type/text to your portfolio pages.
o What transition/title pages could assist the viewer in understanding the portfolio.

Prep Work

You will need to prep your files in three ways:

1. Examine and improve the layout (if necessary) of the images on the page.
2. Reduce the file size (see Presentation Exercise #5).
3. Save each image as a PDF file.

Quick Overview of the Process

It is presumed that your artwork has been prepped, optimized (file size), and saved as PDF files.
The general process of building a portfolio in Acrobat is as follows:

1. Load the first image into Acrobat and then save the project as an Acrobat file.
2. Import the remaining images into the project file using the *Document>Insert Pages* menu command.
3. Click on the *Pages* tab and organize the sequence of the pages (if necessary).
4. Click on the *Bookmarks* tab and create book marks for the project.
5. Save the file.

New Concepts

o Using Adobe Acrobat as a tool for building an electronic book or portfolio and saving the PDF document
o Creating bookmarks

Step 1: Using the File>Open menu command to open the cover document.

Step 2: Saving the file.

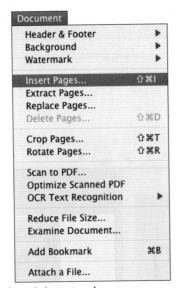

Step 4: Inserting the pages.

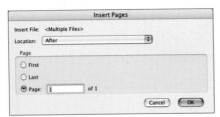

The Insert Pages dialog

Step-by-Step

This exercise assumes that you have prepared and saved all the files you want to use in the portfolio in one folder. It also assumes that you have Adobe Acrobat Professional (not simply Acrobat Reader). You will need the full program in order to build a portfolio. A folder of prepared PDF files exists in your Art DVD. The instructions given here are basic. There is much more to be learned about Adobe Acrobat, but that is not the primary focus of this book. Consult Acrobat's Help files for further information.

Loading the Images into Acrobat

The first step involves loading your prepared images into Adobe Acrobat.

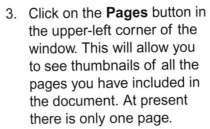

1. In Adobe Acrobat, choose the *File>Open* menu command and direct the file requestor to the Art DVD (or wherever you have placed the files on the DVD). Open the **Presentations** folder and locate the **Ex 7** folder. Once inside that folder, choose the file called **cover.pdf** and click on **Open**. The image will load into Acrobat.

2. Choose the *File>Save As* menu command and save the file as **My Portfolio.pdf.** You can save this in the same folder as the files or elsewhere (but you cannot save to the DVD).

3. Click on the **Pages** button in the upper-left corner of the window. This will allow you to see thumbnails of all the pages you have included in the document. At present there is only one page.

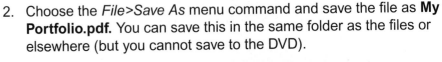

Step 3: Choosing to view the pages.

4. Choose the *Document>Insert Pages* menu command. When the dialog opens you will see all the files in your **Ex 7** folder (unless you redirected the file requestor when you saved the portfolio file, in which case, direct the requestor back to the **Ex 7** folder). *Press+hold* the *Cmd/Ctrl* key on the keyboard and click on all the files except for the **Cover.pdf** and **My Portfolio. pdf** images, and then click on **Select**. The *Insert Pages* dialog will open asking you if you want to insert the images after the current image. You may change this, but we do not want to for our purposes, so click **OK**.

Step 4: Selecting multiple files.

Organizing the Images

You now have all the images loaded into the file and are ready to organize them.

1. Widen the *Pages* panel, which displays the thumbnails of the images, by positioning your cursor to the right of the panel, between the thumbnail panel and the main display panel. Move your cursor until you see the resizing icon, then *click+hold+drag* the cursor to the right. This will widen the thumbnail panel so you can see all the images.

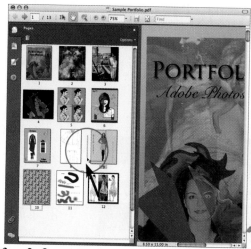

Step 1: Widening the Pages panel.

2. Organize the images by clicking on one and dragging it to a new position among the thumbnails. Since this is a small and simple portfolio, no divider pages were created to divide the topics of the imagery. Our goal here is to learn how to insert and organize images and then how to bookmark them. *In this set of images there are:*
   - o Three collage images
   - o Three self-portrait images
   - o Two garment flat images
   - o One fashion illustration
   - o One textile design
   - o Two paint medium images, one showing brush strokes and the other showing mediums in use in an illustration

   Organize these as you see appropriate.

As you drag images from place to place a vertical blue bar will appear when you are between images. This marker assists you in seeing precisely where you are.

Step 2: Organizing the images.

Creating Bookmarks

Bookmarks allow the user to jump to a page in the portfolio quickly. You can create bookmarks for the various sections of a document, and then, when users turn the view of *Bookmarks* on, they can maneuver quickly to the sections of your document that they are interested in. When you build bookmarks, the key is to first move to the page where you want a bookmark, and then create the bookmark.

The steps are as follows:

1. In the *Pages* panel, click to the first page where you want to place a bookmark (e.g., the **Intro Page**). When you click on the page it will appear in the main window of the document.

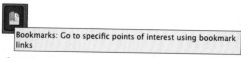

Step 2: Clicking on the Bookmarks button to open the panel.

2. Click on the **Bookmarks** button in the upper-left side of the window. This will move you out of the *Pages* panel and into the *Bookmarks* panel. You will see a blank area where the pages once were.

Step 3: Clicking on the New bookmark button to create a bookmark.

3. Click on the **New bookmark** button at the top of the Bookmarks area. A bookmark called *Untitled* will appear below, waiting for you to edit the name. Type in the new name and press *Return/Enter* on the keyboard.

The first bookmark

4. Click on the **Pages** button to move back to the *Pages* view, and click on the next key image (e.g., the first composite image).

5. Click on the **Bookmarks** button to move to the *Bookmarks* view.

6. Click on the **New bookmark** button, type in the name of the bookmark when the field appears, and press the *Return/Enter* key on the keyboard.

7. Repeat the process of moving back and forth until you have bookmarked all the pages you want to.

8. Save the file.

Bookmark Tips
The following are a few tips for creating bookmarks. Consult Adobe Acrobat's Help feature for more information and a greater wealth of assistance with Acrobat.

Note:

Bookmark Overkill
The example here goes to the extreme of creating bookmarks to show you the process. Generally one does not create a bookmark for every image in a book.

To position a bookmark in a specific spot on the list:
1. Once you have entered the *Bookmark* mode, click on the bookmark you want to position the new one under. Then click on the **New bookmark** button. If you do not do things in this order, the new bookmark will go to the end of the list.
Note: Positioning works with the hierarchy if you have one (see below).

To create a bookmark hierarchy:
1. Create the new bookmark.

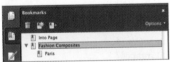

Creating a hierarchy of bookmarks

The final book/portfolio

2. *Click+hold+drag* the bookmark under and to the right of the bookmark you want it to be a sub of. Observe the arrowhead marker as you do this, as it assists you in knowing where the new position will be.

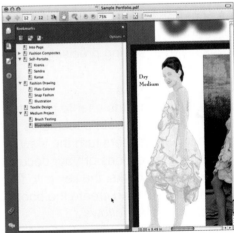

All bookmarks in place (more than typically suggested were made for this exercise)

Displaying the Book
1. Save the file.

2. Close all panels on the left (Bookmark, Pages).

3. Explore settings in the *View* menu to customize the view.

4. Click on the arrows in the *Navigation* panel at the top of the document to move through the book. Use the bookmarks if you need them.

This completes all the exercises in this book.

Index